Sword found in the tomb of Sancho IV, King of Castile 1284–95, in the Capilla Mayor in Toledo Cathedral. *Frontispiece*

THE ARCHAEOLOGY
OF WEAPONS

ARMS AND ARMOUR FROM PREHISTORY TO
THE AGE OF CHIVALRY

R. EWART OAKESHOTT

Illustrated by the Author

DOVER PUBLICATIONS, INC.
MINEOLA, NEW YORK

Bibliographical Note

This Dover edition, first published in 1996, is an unabridged republication of the work originally published by Lutterworth Press, London, in 1960. The map originally found on the endpapers has been moved to pages 4–5 in the present edition.

Library of Congress Cataloging-in-Publication Data

Oakeshott, R. Ewart.
   The archaeology of weapons : arms and armour from prehistory to the age of chivalry / R. Ewart Oakeshott ; illustrated by the author.
       p.   cm.
   Originally published: London : Lutterworth Press, 1960.
   Includes bibliographical references and index.
   ISBN 0-486-29288-6 (pbk.)
       1. Military weapons—History.   2. Armor—History.   3. Military history, Medieval.   4. Armor, Medieval—History.   I. Title.
   U800.03   1996
   623.4'41'09—dc20   96-8921
                                                                            CIP

Manufactured in the United States of America
Dover Publications, Inc., 31 East 2nd Street, Mineola, N.Y. 11501

For

NICK

who said, " Why not write a book?"

The GREAT MIGRATIONS

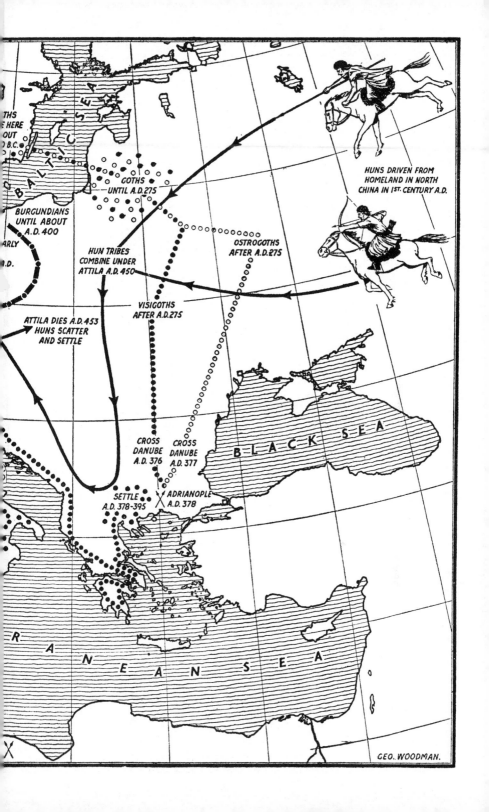

THS
E HERE
OUT
O B.C.

BALTIC SEA

GOTHS
UNTIL A.D. 275

BURGUNDIANS
UNTIL ABOUT
A.D. 400

ARLY

D.

HUN TRIBES
COMBINE UNDER
ATTILA A.D. 450

OSTROGOTHS
AFTER A.D. 275

HUNS DRIVEN FROM
HOMELAND IN NORTH
CHINA IN 1ST. CENTURY A.D.

ATTILA DIES A.D. 453
HUNS SCATTER
AND SETTLE

VISIGOTHS
AFTER A.D. 275

CROSS
DANUBE
A.D. 376

CROSS
DANUBE
A.D. 377

BLACK SEA

SETTLE
A.D. 378-395

ADRIANOPLE
A.D. 378

R

A   N   E   A   N   S   E   A

X

GEO. WOODMAN.

ACKNOWLEDGEMENT

"THE DWARF," says Coleridge, "sees farther than the giant, when he has the giant's shoulder to mount on." Any book of this kind must be based upon the work of previous scholars, and I owe much to many giants, whose names will be found in the bibliography. For the mediaeval section, one is outstanding: Henry Hewitt, whose *Antient Armour*, published in 1860, has perhaps more of real value to offer the student of mediaeval arms than any other book. This exhaustive study is based upon contemporary documents, and contains none of the theories which have so bedevilled later research. In my study of the mediaeval sword I have followed his example, for my sources too have been original. As anyone who is interested in mediaeval life must, I owe a great deal to the countless painters and sculptors who have left so rich, detailed and accurate an account of the costume and arms of their contemporaries. My work is based upon theirs; here and there I have illustrated my text with copies of pieces of it, and though these lack the character of the originals, they are accurate copies. I have taken great care not to "improve" on the original, the better to show detail. Everything is as it was put on to the vellum or carved in the stone.

Having expressed my gratitude to these giants of the past, I find I have scarcely room to name all the living people to whom I owe so much. Sir James Mann, K.C.V.O., F.B.A., Hon. Vice-President Soc. Antiquaries, Master of the Armouries of the Tower of London, whose encouragement and interest have always sustained me; Mr. R. L. S. Bruce Mitford, B.A., F.S.A., of the British Museum, and Mr. Martin Holmes, F.S.A., of the London Museum, who have firmly steered me into the correct paths of research; my friends Dr. Hilda Ellis Davidson, M.A., F.S.A., to whom I owe almost everything I know about the Migration and Viking periods,

Mr. Claude Blair, F.S.A., and Mr. J. F. Hayward, of the Victoria and Albert Museum, whose scholarship and immense knowledge of armour have been so generously at my disposal, and Mr. John Wallace, whose enthusiastic interest and wise criticism have often made the crooked ways straight and the rough places plain. Both Mr. Blair and Mr. Wallace read my book in typescript, an irksome chore which has added greatly to its value; and my friends at the Armouries in the Tower of London.

I must also thank those who have allowed me to illustrate objects from their collections, and in many cases have supplied photographs: Mr. R. T. Gwynn, Mr. C. O. v. Kienbusch, Mr. E. A. Christensen, Mr. John Wallace, Mr. M. Dineley, Mr. Harold Petersen, Mr. David Drey, and Mrs. G. E. P. How.

Five short passages from *Beowulf* are in the translation by Charles W. Kennedy, copyright 1940 by Oxford University Press, Inc., New York, and are reprinted by permission of the publishers. I am also indebted to Constable and Co. Ltd. for permission to include four stanzas from *MSS. of Salzburg, Canterbury and Limoges*, translated by Helen Waddell in her *Mediaeval Latin Lyrics*.

I cannot cut this list short without expressing my thanks to two secretaries, Mrs. Barbara Escott and Mrs. Anne Motion, who each enthusiastically typed thousands of words before Matrimony snatched them away from *The Archaeology of Weapons*. My most sincere thanks go also to Mrs. Alma Molseed, who typed the last part in her spare time and had the kindness to say when it was all over that she had not been bored by it, and to my friend Mr. Patrick J. Jones for his patient skill in taking endless photographs of things in my own collection; and I cannot forget the helpfulness of my publishers during the two years the book has been in preparation.

And, of course, my wife. She has had to put up with a houseful of weapons for nearly twenty years, as well as a husband who has frequently been a domestic menace by occasional absences of person in search of material, and permanent absence of mind by reason of brooding upon it. Her patience and encouragement and tolerant acceptance of these things has made everything possible which without them would have come to nothing.

R. EWART OAKESHOTT

CONTENTS

Part Four

THE AGE OF CHIVALRY

LIST OF PLATES

The sword of Sancho IV, King of Castile, 1284–95. From his tomb in the Capilla Mayor in Toledo Cathedral   *frontispiece*

(*Between pages 184 and 185*)

12   Monument above the tomb of Can Grande Della Scala (+1329), Verona.

13   Sword-hanger from a late fourteenth-century hip belt of copper-gilt (*coll. J. Wallace, Esq., ex. coll. author*); pair of spurs of gilt bronze, with their original cloth-of-gold straps (*ex coll. Sir G. F. Laking*).

14   Bascinet, *c.* 1390, with snouted visor (*Wallace Collection no.* 74); armet, probably Italian, *c.* 1470 (*Wallace Collection no.* 85); barbute, Italian, *c.* 1440 (*coll. R. T. Gwynn, Esq.*); sallet, German, *c.* 1450 (*coll. R. T. Gwynn, Esq*).

15   Complete armour made between 1497 and 1503 in Nürnburg for Kunz Schott von Hellingen (*coll. R. T. Gwynn, Esq., ex coll. W. R. Hearst, ex coll. Count Erbach zu Erbach*).

16   Sword, blade with inscription inlaid in yellow metal (*National Museum, Copenhagen*); sword found in London, *c.* 1320–50 (*British Museum*); sword found in the River Cam, *c.* 1375–1410 (*Fitzwilliam Museum, Cambridge*); sword, *c.* 1360–1400 (*coll. A. E. Christensen, ex coll. author*); sword, probably part of the funeral furniture of Henry V (*Muniment Room, Westminster Abbey*).

17   Sword of doubtful ownership in Toledo Cathedral, *c.* 1310–30; sword of Can Grande Della Scala (*Archaeological Museum, Verona*).

18   Scottish sword, early fifteenth century (*coll. Mr. C. O. v. Kienbusch, New York*); incised slab in the churchyard at Kinkell, Aberdeenshire; sword, *c.* 1300, found in the River Trent (*in a private collection*).

19   Sword, Italian, *c.* 1460–80 (*coll. author*); sword, Italian, *c.* 1485–1500 (*coll. David Drey, Esq., ex coll. author, Douglas Ash, Esq., and the late Baron de Cosson*); sword, perhaps Flemish, *c.* 1450–75 (*coll. author*); sword, Italian, *c.* 1450–1500 (*coll. C. O. v. Kienbusch, ex Londesborough and Bernal collections*).

20   Sword with blackened hilt and finger-ring, 1432 (*Armouries, Tower of London, ex coll. W. R. Hearst, Baron de Cosson*); sword with side ring, *c.* 1420–50 (*coll. author, ex coll. E. J. Sullivan*); sword with blackened hilt, "Pas d'Ane" and ring. Spanish, *c.* 1480 (*coll. author*); "Landsknecht" sword, *c.* 1520 (*coll. author*).

21   Short sword, Italian, *c.* 1470–90; dagger and sheath, *c.* 1450–80 (*both coll. author*).

22   Cinquedea, *c.* 1490 (*coll. C. O. v. Kienbusch, ex coll. author*); cinquedea, with blade etched in the manner of Ercole de Fideli (*Wallace Collection, no.* 100).

INTRODUCTION

AMONG the most plentiful objects surviving from Man's remote past in Europe are his weapons. The dead generally had arms laid in the grave with them, and great hoards of armour and arms and all the miscellaneous hardware of war were sacrificially deposited in hallowed spots. This is rich material for study, so rich that such prehistoric militaria are usually dealt with as isolated groups of region or period within the framework of the larger science of archaeology. Rarely are they treated in continuity from the Bronze Age to the time of the triumph of gunpowder. The archaeology of weapons and of war is a study of arms tied down to no particular time or place, followed throughout history as one might follow a dark thread running through a tapestry. In the sketch (which is all that a single book can be, even of this bulk, of so vast a subject) I have tried to follow the development of European arms in logical sequence, showing how changes were wrought by the use of new materials or by the ever-shifting demands of war and fashion, yet how at the same time there is unbroken progression from age to age.

The Art of War is a fascinating subject, but the study of armour and arms is even more so, for we are dealing with objects of great human interest, often of great beauty, which we know to have been invested with many high and solemn significances. From the ages of prehistory plenty of actual weapons survive, largely owing to the pagan practice of putting them into the grave or dumping them in sacrifice, but as the Middle Ages advance there is less and less to be found. The tombs of princes may contain swords and spurs—several have been found to do so, and many more await investigation—but most of the objects from the times after the end of pagandom in North-West Europe are only casual finds dug from river beds or ploughed up in fields or recovered from the ground in digging foundations; but though this earth-yielded raw material is scanty (and so exceedingly dead) the art in which its common usage is enshrined, whether poem or picture, is plentiful and most vigorously alive.

Until quite recently much of the vital literary material—the Old Testament, the works of Homer and the "folk-tales" of the Celts and the northern races—was regarded as legendary stuff with little historical foundation or value, while the "Rigveda", a great corpus of epic poems, religious texts, stories and popular songs produced by the Aryans during the second millennium B.C., the foundation upon which all the thought of Buddhism and Hinduism is based, was little known and equally dismissed as romantic and mystical, the stuff of dreams.

Now all is changed. The events recorded in the Bible are known to be based solidly upon facts, often narrated with great accuracy; Homer's heroes and the stage on which they played their tremendous parts are legendary no longer; the stories of Ossian and Grania, Finn and the Fianna bring much dead archaeological material in the museums of Ireland to life; while the Eddas of the north and the epic of "Beowulf" are no more regarded as mythical. The Norse Sagas, which have always been accepted as partly true because of their curt, hard-boiled realism, are explained and fixed firmly into their historical setting by much fascinating material got out of the ground. And the Rigveda, once only dimly understood as historical narrative, is explained by, and in its turn throws light upon, the discovery of the great, ancient civilization of the Indus valley, over-thrown in about 1900 B.C. by the Aryans, an Indo-European people whose "Bible" it was.

The object of this book is to put before the reader a sketch of part of a colossal subject, to follow this thread of man's invincible penchant for fighting, to trace the development of the instruments he devised to do it with, and to hear what he has to say about how he did it. And how he loved it. "Of arms, and of the man I sing," says Virgil, and he puts arms first. From the very beginning arms have been sacred, invested with a sort of divine potency; a vestige of this could still be found among Occidental people less than a century ago in the West of America, for even such an unromantic-seeming piece of black machinery as the "six-gun" retained a little of the ancient glamour.

14

In any attempt to write historically there must be a starting point. In dealing with the development of arms and the art of war, it seems to be customary to begin at the period when the break-up of the Roman Empire was almost completed. I propose to go to the other extreme and start at a point of time long before Rome itself began. At some time about 1900 B.C. certain events completely changed the warlike outlook of all the peoples of the ancient East and destroyed those who (like the peaceable people of the Indus civilization of Mohenjo Daro) had none. With these events this study will begin, though its main concern is with the Middle Ages.

From somewhere in Western Asia people of a fighting race began to move southward and eastward about 1900 B.C. In the following two centuries the southbound arm of this great prehistoric pincer movement founded the nations of Hatti (known to us as the Hittites) and Mittanni, and imposed upon the indigenous people of the Aegean an aristocracy which Homer called the "brown-haired Achaeans", and which we refer to as the Myceneans, while part of it pressed on to overthrow the weak and divided government of the 14th Dynasty of Egypt, occupying that land for 200 years. The eastbound arm moved upon North-West India, crushing the militarily helpless but otherwise magnificent and powerful people of the Indus.

Modern ethnography has dubbed this race "Indo-European", and they are in every sense the founders of the modern world. From them the Greeks and Romans are sprung, and most of the races of India as well as the Celts and the Teutonic peoples of the North; they are the ancestors of India and of every Western civilization. The reason for their success was their power in war, power based on a concept of fighting which in the second millennium B.C. was entirely new.

This was the use of horses, not as cavalry in the accepted sense but drawing light chariots each carrying one or two armed men, a highly mobile armoured fighting vehicle. When these chariots were deployed in squadrons, acting together as disciplined corps, then the ancient formations of pedestrian spearmen were doomed. The power of Egypt, still mighty in spite of ineffectual government, went down before the chariots of the Hyksos, the hated Sand-Ramblers or

Shepherds, who ruled them until the Princes of Thebes took a leaf out of their oppressors' book and turned their own weapon against them, driving them out of Egypt and far up into Canaan with armies of Egyptian charioteers in about 1580 B.C.

The records of Egypt tell us much of the Indo-Europeans of the Middle East, but the best account they give of themselves in their primitive state before their settling-down, and the liveliest, is left to us by the Aryans, the Indian branch of the family, in the Rigveda. In many of the epic chants and narrative poems in this great literary omnibus we get convincing portraits of their war leaders and the bands who followed them; we can trace the same characteristics as in the much later tales of old Ireland, which were told in very similar language.

About a quarter of the prayers are addressed to Indra, the greatest of the Gods:

> Strong-armed, colossal, tawny-bearded, and pot-bellied from drinking, he wields the thunderbolt in his more god-like moments, but fights like a hero with bow and arrows from his chariot. He is a cattle-raider, and above all he is the destroyer of the strongholds of the enemy, and victorious leader of the Aryans in their conquest of the hated ancient empire of the Punjab. With him fight the young warrior-band, the Maruts, who seem to be commanded by Rudra, rival to Indra and yet in some ways his counterpart, "Unassailable, rapid, young, unaging, ruler of the world..."

The atmosphere is that of the Irish tales that reflect the conditions of the Celtic Iron Age of the first century B.C. in Ulster and North Britain; Indra is often reminiscent of the grotesque Dagda with his insatiable appetite, Rudra and the Maruts make one think of Finn and the Fianna, the young band of heroes, and the cattle-raiding is similar.

> The warrior's look is like a thunderous rain-cloud,
> When armed with mail he seeks the lap of battle.
> Be thou victorious with unwounded body; so let
> The thickness of thy mail protect thee...
> Whoso would kill us, whether he be a strange foe or one of us,
> May all the Gods discomfit him; my nearest, closest
> Mail is prayer.

That is part of an epic chant composed in the plains of the Punjab

3,000 years ago, yet it would not have been out of place in thirteenth-century France. And this:

> With Bow let us win Kine, with Bow in battle, with
> Bow be victory in our hot encounters,
> The Bow brings grief and sorrow to the foeman; armed
> With Bow may we subdue all regions.
> Close to his ear, as fain to speak, she presses, holding
> Her well-loved friend in her embraces;
> Strained on the bow, she whispers like a woman—this
> Bow-string that preserves us in the Combat.

Here the loved weapon is the bow, with the bow-string sounding in the warrior's ear like a woman's endearments, but the sentiment is the same as in the romances of chivalry.

Then, 800 years later, came the tremendous stories of Homer (whoever he may have been, he lived and wrote about 850 B.C.). The material he used had existed for many hundreds of years, passed on orally. In the most vivid and lively language he gives a clear picture of men's minds as well as their actions. These tales were accepted as a true record of events in Homer's own time and in classical Greece as well as during the whole of the Roman period and throughout the Middle Ages; it was the scepticism of eighteenth- and nineteenth-century scholarship which damned them as being mere fairy-tales. Then, during the last years of the nineteenth century, the discoveries of Heinrich Schliemann and Sir Arthur Evans transmuted what was thought to be the base metal of unfounded legend into the pure gold of ascertained fact. They uncovered Troy itself and Golden Mycenae, and the palaces of Minos in Crete. Schliemann even believed he had found the body of Agamemnon, King of Men, in one of the shaft graves at Mycenae, but the personages he dug up had lived some 300 years earlier than the Homeric hero.

Wonderful as these material discoveries were, perhaps their greatest value was the proof that the story of Troy was no legend, but an historical event. This makes sense of the vivid realism of Homer's characters, his attention to small details of behaviour—how clearly we see the sleeping Diomedes:

> They went next to Diomedes son of Tydeus, and found him lying in the open outside his hut, with his armour. His men were sleeping round

him with their shields for pillows. Their spears were stuck on end with the sharpened butts in the ground, and the bronze points flashed in the distance like lightning from Father Zeus. The Prince was asleep, with the hide of a farmyard ox behind him, and a glossy rug drawn under his head. Nestor the Gerenian charioteer went up to him, woke him with a touch of his foot, and flung a taunt at him to rouse him further. "Wake up, Tydeides," he said, "why should you sleep in comfort all night long? Has it escaped your notice that the Trojans are sitting in the plain above us, barely a stone's throw from the ships?"

Diomedes, who had woken and leapt up in a trice, replied with some feeling. "You are a hard old man, sir, and you never take a moment's rest. Are there not younger men in the army to go the rounds and wake up all the kings? There is no holding you down, my venerable lord."

Here indeed is flesh to cover the archaeological bones.

So we come to a point where we can compare actual armour and arms found in the earth with the things a poet says about them; though in Homer's case this is surprisingly little, it is probably because the Mediterranean peoples have never had that extraordinary romantic veneration for their arms so characteristic of Teuton, Celt and Indian—and on the other side of the earth, the Japanese. The Minoans, Egyptians and Sumerians, like the Chinese, disliked war and alternately derided and reviled the soldier. The Myceneans and classical Greeks were Indo-Europeans, and tremendous warriors, like the Romans after them, but they considered that arms were for use in war only and tended to take an entirely unromantic and matter-of-fact view of them. The ancient Greeks certainly considered their arms a worthy vehicle for applied art—the only time Homer really lets himself go over armour is when he describes the shield which Hephaestos made for Achilles, though even then he only describes the scenes with which the god embellished it.

The Roman attitude to arms was perhaps even more matter-of-fact—actually very modern; the civilian fears and shuns them, the soldier has them issued to him, cares for them and keeps them clean and in working order because he will get into trouble if he does not, and has no love for them at all. Tacitus, writing of a particularly warlike German tribe allied to Rome which was given preferential treatment because of its value as a weapon, says:

The Batavi . . . are not insulted by tribute or ground down by the tax gatherer. Free from imposts and special levies, and reserved for battle, they are like weapons and armour, "only to be used in war".

Which very neatly sums up the Roman's view of weapons. How different are the Germans he writes of!

No business, public or private, [he says] is transacted except in arms. But it is the rule that no one shall take up his arms until the State has attested that he is likely to make good. When that time comes, one of the chiefs, or the father or a kinsman equips the young warrior with a spear and shield in the public council.

and again, speaking of council meetings:

. . . if they approve, they clash their spears. No form of approval can carry more honour than praise expressed by arms.

Here indeed we can see the germs of the mediaeval idea of the making of a knight, as well as the great importance of arms to all men, in peace not war; and then we read:

On the field of battle it is a disgrace to the chief to be surpassed in valour by his companions (companions here being used in the sense of personal following) or to the companions not to come up in valour to their chief. As for leaving the battle alive after your chief has fallen, *that* means lifelong infamy and shame. To defend and protect him, to put down one's own acts of heroism to his credit, that is what they really mean by allegiance. The chiefs fight for victory, the companions for their chief. Many noble youths, if the land of their birth is stagnating in a protracted peace, deliberately seek out other tribes where some war is afoot. The Germans have no taste for peace; renown is easier won among perils, and you cannot maintain a large body of companions except by violence and war. The companions are prodigal in their demands on the generosity of their chiefs; it is always "give me that warhorse" or "give me that bloody and victorious spear". As for meals with their plentiful, if homely, fare, they count simply as pay. Such open-handedness must have war and plunder to feed it. You will find it harder to persuade a German to plough the land and await its annual produce with patience than to challenge a foe and earn the prize of wounds. He thinks it spiritless and slack to gain by sweat what he can buy with blood.

A Roman historian writing in the time of Trajan? It reads more like a twelfth-century description of European knighthood. Which, in a sense, it is; for here is the basic stuff of chivalry, though lacking the nobler virtues of courtesy, humility, gallantry and, of course, religion which we may be justified in believing were latent in the Celtic peoples of Gaul and Britain. It was the fusion of these virtues with the harsher Teutonic ones which eventually produced the whole flowering of the chivalric ideal.

Part 1

THE PREHISTORIC PERIOD

Chapter One

"THE PITILESS BRONZE"

WHEN IN THE beginning of the second millennium B.C. the Indo-European people moved into the ancient world, they brought a new concept of war. This was based on the use of swift horse-drawn chariots each carrying a warrior armed with a bow and driven by a charioteer, a fact of great archaeological importance. Not that they invented the chariot—the Sumerians must have the credit for that, for painted on some Sumerian scarlet ware vessels of Early Dynastic I date (c. 3500 B.C.) we find pictures of light two-wheeled cars with high fronts carrying one or two people and drawn by asses or oxen, and there are others in some slightly later Early Dynastic reliefs from Ur and Kafajah, and on the famous "Standard" of Ur from the Royal Tombs (in the British Museum) similar ass-drawn chariots are shown in great detail, with solid wheels made of two half-discs dowelled together against the hub. Slow and clumsy these probably were, but even so must have been a terror to the foes of Sumer.

Early in the second millennium, chariots were in use in Asia Minor, but with very important modifications. They had light, spoked wheels and were drawn by a pair of horses. Such chariots

Fig. 1. Chariot from a Mycenean tombstone

made their appearance in the Aegean countries, significantly associated with Indo-European speakers, soon after this time, in mainland Greece before 1500 B.C. and in Crete about 1450 B.C. A century or so later there is some evidence to suggest that young Achaean noblemen were sent to the Hittite capital to be trained in chariotry.

The chariot was unknown to the ancient Egyptians of the Old and Middle Kingdoms, but Egypt was overrun and occupied by the "Hyksos" Asiatics for a couple of hundred years or so, between about 1750 and 1580 B.C. These invaders were Indo-Europeans, using chariots. Soon after the vigorous rulers of Thebes had thrown the Hyksos out of the Delta in about 1580 B.C. we find the Egyptian armies well equipped with chariots themselves, for the first Pharaoh to press far up into Palestine, Amenhotep I (c. 1550 B.C.), used well-trained squadrons of chariots as the spearhead of his victorious host. After this, for another 150 years, the arms of Egypt were carried by Pharaoh after Pharaoh northwards into Syria, until by 1400 B.C. all the lands as far as the Euphrates acknowledged Egypt's sovereignty. Then the inevitable decline set in and Egypt had to contend with the great Indo-European power of the Hittites, who by about 1270 B.C. had become a mighty nation. In the great clashes of these two powers in the thirteenth century B.C. the issues of battle were decided by charging chariots, just as in the thirteenth century A.D. they were decided by charges of mounted knights.

Everyone is familiar with the Egyptian chariot, which appears so prominently and so often in the reliefs on the walls of temples and tombs; the Cretan and Mycenean chariots are less well known, though there are plenty of representations of them in Minoan-Mycenean art (fig. 1). A few actual chariots still survive in Egypt, and there is the magnificent bronze-covered Etruscan one from Monteleone in Italy (preserved in the Metropolitan Museum in New York)—though this was probably a ceremonial chariot, not for use in war, for by the seventh century B.C. the civilized peoples of the Mediterranean used chariots only for sport and ceremony. It was left to the barbarians to continue the old tradition, in the case of the Celtic West up to the time of the campaigns of Agricola in Britain. There is plenty of literary evidence for the construction of the Celtic chariots, amply supported by archaeological finds of many examples in the tombs of chieftains.

So for more than 1,000 years the aristocratic charioteer was the arbiter of battle all over the world. Then, during the fourth century B.C., army formations similar to the ancient style of Egypt appeared in an infinitely more formidable guise—the legions of Rome. It was not long before the pendulum had swung and the legions swept everything before them, and for the next 600 years the Roman infantry was almost the only military force to be reckoned with in the civilized world. Even so, behind her northern and eastern frontiers were many nations of unsubdued barbarians. Ammianus Marcellinus, writing in about A.D. 400, says:

> At this time, just as though the trumpets were sounding a challenge throughout the Roman world, fierce nations were stirred up and began to burst forth from their territories.

These nations were the force which eventually swung the pendulum back; they flooded into the Empire, not with chariots as of old, but as heavy cavalry. The weapon of impact had come into its own again, and would be the dominant force in the world until the English cloth-yard arrow began to weaken it during the fourteenth century; it finally gave way when the perfection of gunpowder in the fifteenth century brought in its turn another concept of war.

The foregoing paragraphs contain a number of generalizations; my apology for them is that I must at least mention the tremendous events in which the roots of the Middle Ages are planted. I have another reason, too, for going back as far as this. From the Neolithic Age to the present, there have been only two periods when nearly all the personal armaments of war, provided they were of good quality, seem to have been beautiful. One of these periods comes within the Middle Ages, though right at their end; for during the second half of the fifteenth century nearly every weapon and piece of armour of good quality was beautiful—with beauty of form, not of ornament. This we shall see later; but the other is prehistoric. In the period which can be vaguely described as the Celtic Iron Age (more precisely as the time of the La Tène cultures) weapons and

23

armour—far more rare then than in the fifteenth century—show a perfection of form allied to the most superb and masterly decoration. I should hate to have to omit illustrating and trying to describe some of these things, even though description is futile. They are great works of art, and in their presence words are an impertinence.

Underlying all or any tactics of battle is one basic art which for nearly 3,000 years remained unchanged, in spite of chariot or war-horse, long-bow or cannon or musket—the art of hand-to-hand combat with sword and shield. The people of the late Bronze Age had large round shields and beautiful cut-and-thrust swords; how they fought with them the vase-painters of classical Greece show us —and in the same way the clansmen of the Scottish Highlands fought, right up to the '45, with broadsword and targe.

The shield is the most obvious, the simplest and therefore the most primitive item of defensive armour. It does not take much imagination to picture some Palaeolithic hunter grabbing up the first object that came to his hand to ward off the flint spear of an irritated fellow cave-dweller. From this to the fashioning of a wickerwork frame covered with hide is an easy and logical step. A shield is about the most effective piece of defensive equipment one can have, too—hence its early appearance, its universal usage and its survival in the Highlands until the eighteenth century; survival, too, until the present time in such parts of the world where men dwell sufficiently remote from the ballistic blessings of modern civilization.

The round shields of the Western Bronze Age are generally flat, with a diameter of about 2 ft.; they have a small central hollow boss across the inside of which is riveted a short bar for a hand grip. They are of fine workmanship, the most common type being embossed with concentric circular ridges, interspersed with small bosses. The metal is thin, and it would have been backed with layers of leather, put on wet, and pressed into the hollows of the embossed ridges. When dry and hard this would provide an excellent backing for the bronze. Such shields were probably only borne by chiefs and noblemen, but then we may assume that at this time all warriors who bore a sword and shield *were* noblemen.

The Stone Age men fought with axe and spear, for the sword was never a primitive weapon; its earliest forms were as sophisticated and as elegant as its latest—the middle Bronze Age joins hands across thirty centuries with the court of Louis XV. Axe and knife were the first metal implements, and both were domestic—in intention anyway. Their forms passed in easy stages from stone to metal, and the knife became a spear simply by mounting it on a long shaft, and a slashing weapon by fixing it axe-like on a short one. The sword seems to have developed naturally from the knife in Minoan Crete and Celtic Britain at about the same time, between 1500 and 1100 B.C. Both Mediterranean and Western types were thrusting weapons, rapiers, but the Western type shows more clearly how it evolved from the knife. Continual sharpening of these bronze knives—daggers if you like—resulted in a change in the shape of the blade. In a barrow at Helperthorpe in Yorkshire a bronze knife was found which had been ground to a narrow, acutely tapering spike (fig. 2a). Its original form would have been like the blade shown beside it. We may asume that, seeing how effective such a knife would be if used offensively, some weapon-smith hit on the idea of actually casting a longer and better one in the same form. Whether this was the way of it or not, the earliest swords in Western Europe were of this shape. Magnificent weapons they were, too, in their rather limited way. No other country has produced a sword comparable to one found at Lissane in Ireland (fig. 10b). It is over 30 in. long, no broader than $\frac{5}{8}$ in. at the middle of the blade, and has a beautifully formed section of a complex lozenge shape. Although finds of these rapiers are not confined to the British Isles, their home was here, probably in Ireland, for more and finer ones have been found there than anywhere else.

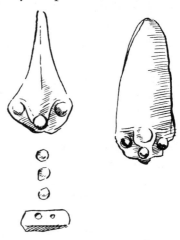

Several of these rapiers are in English collections. The one in fig. 3 was found at

a *Fig. 2.* b

a. *Bronze knife from Helperthorpe, Yorks., showing how it was sharpened to a spike.*
b. *A blade of a similar knife, not sharpened.*

25

Fig. 3. *Early Bronze sword from Pens Pits, Somerset (Blackmore collection, Wilts. County Museum, Salisbury).*

Pens Pits in Somerset, and is in the Blackmore Museum in Salisbury. It is short, really more like a big dagger, and very finely formed, the curves of each edge being most symmetrical; two well-defined ridges run the length of the blade, flattening in a curve into the fan-shaped shoulder on to which the hilt was fixed with two rivets. A similar though slightly larger rapier found on Shapwick Down is in the British Museum. A still larger one, 27 in. long, was found in the Thames near Kew and is in the Brentford Museum (where there is an extremely fine collection of bronze weapons), but none of these can compare with the Lissane sword. The only one which can do so is Cretan. Found in a tomb of the period late Minoan II, it has a blade as long as the Lissane one, though rather broader, with an almost identical section (fig. 10a).

The rapiers found in Crete and Mycenae are stouter weapons. Their blades are heavier and generally broader, while the method of fixing the hilt is better. The Celtic rapiers' hilts were fixed on to the flat shoulder by rivets, as shown in fig. 3. This was their weakness, for if lateral strains were put upon them there was little to prevent the rivets pulling sideways through the thin bronze. In fact more than half of the specimens found—the Pens Pits one for instance—have one or more of the rivets pulled away like this. So long as this sort of sword was used for thrusting only, all would be well, but a man's instinct in a fight is to slash at his foe, for his natural blow sweeps round in the segment of a circle centred in his shoulder. To strike out straight is an acquired art, easily forgotten in the heat of battle. Probably because of this weakness great efforts were made to provide a stronger junction between hilt and blade. Many different types of bronze sword have been found in Western Europe, all showing experimental gropings towards a better hilt. A few of them look forward nearly 1,000 years to a system which was perfected in the early Iron Age, where the tang was a narrow rod, made in one part with the blade; it ran right through whatever hilt

26

was fixed to it and was turned over at the top. A very fine example of this experimental type, found in France, is in the Blackmore collection at Salisbury (fig. 4). Here the top of the tang is clubbed, not turned over; maybe the hilt consisted simply of strips of leather bound round between the clubbed end and the blade's shoulders, though the presence of two rivet-holes in the shoulders suggests that something more solid was used. However, by the middle period of the Bronze Age a really reliable hilt had developed; it was in effect similar to the Minoan-Mycenean hilt, and may have been derived from it. Though these Mycenean swords were meant for thrusting, they were quite stout enough to cut with, too. Fig. 5 shows how the blade and the flat tang of the hilt were cast in one piece, with plates of horn or wood, or gold or silver, applied to either side of the tang which was sandwiched between them, and fixed by rivets to make a secure and comfortable grip. This kind of

Fig. 4. Experimental type of sword. Middle Bronze Age (found in France, now in the Blackmore collection at Salisbury).

hilt became universal all over Europe, allied to a blade which has ever since been unsurpassed for the purpose of hand-to-hand fighting, as well as for beauty of outline and proportion. Its purpose was to be

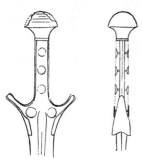

equally effective for cut or thrust, so the point is long and acute enough to be deadly in thrusting while the blade's thickness and the curve of its edge comes in exactly the right place for cutting; the reverse curve, where the edge sweeps towards the hilt, is ideally placed for making a back-handed slash (fig. 6).

Fig. 5. Assembly of Cretan hilt.

Swords of this shape seem to have been used in all parts of Europe throughout the late Bronze Age (1100 to 900 B.C.), and

27

Fig. 6. *Bronze sword from Barrow (British Museum).*

except that some were large and powerful and some small and rather insignificant, the form of their blades, like a long leaf, varied little. Their chief differences, apart from size and occasional ornament, lay in the form taken by the "shoulders" where the blade merged with the hilt. Towards the end of the Bronze Age other kinds of sword became popular; there are three distinctive types in particular which have been found in very wide distribution (fig. 7), two of which can be traced to definite areas of origin. These were the long "Hallstatt" swords, and a rather rare type which British archaeologists have called the "Carp's Tongue", whose origin may have been in Southern Britain, and the swords of the "Swiss" or "Rhone Valley" type.

The Hallstatt swords really belong to the early Iron Age, and though the first swords of this culture were of bronze, it will be more appropriate to deal with them in the next chapter. The "Carp's Tongue" swords were big weapons with curiously shaped blades; their edges ran parallel for about two-thirds of their length, then abruptly narrowed to a point. A very fine one was found in the Thames off Kew (Brentford Museum); it is one of the very few complete specimens of the type, for most have been found in fragments

a   b   c

Fig. 7. *Three Swords of Late Bronze Age:* a. *Hallstatt;* b. *"Carp's Tongue";* c. *"Rhone Valley" type*

28

Fig. 9. Hilt of "Rhone Valley" type sword. Late Bronze Age (from Switzerland, now in the British Museum).

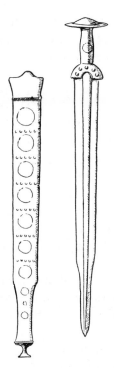

Fig. 8. Bronze "Carp's Tongue" sword from the Seine (Musée de l'Armée, Paris).

among the bits and pieces of bronze-founders' hoards. They seem to have formed an isolated group, for a few have been found in south-east England, and a few more have turned up in France and Italy; so far none has appeared in Central Europe or Scandinavia. Fig. 8 shows one which is particularly interesting as its hilt and its bronze scabbard have been preserved. It was found in Paris in the Seine, and may be seen in the Musée de l'Armée.

The "Rhone Valley" swords are generally rather small; some are more like big daggers, though a few are quite massive. All of them have hilts of an individual pattern made in cast bronze (fig. 9). We see hilts precisely like these again and again grasped in the hands of painted warriors on the Attic red-figure ware of classical Greece, pictures which are 500 years later than the bronze swords, obviously the prototypes of the Greek ones. The pattern probably came to Hellas via the colonial stations at Marseilles and Antibes and other ports near the mouth of the Rhone. These "Rhone Valley" hilts seem to have been the immediate precursors of the "Antennae" and

"Anthropomorphic" swords of the late Bronze Age. In these hilts the ends of the long pommel are drawn out into two long, slender points curved inwards in a spiral, sometimes like the points of a moustache and sometimes in a tight many-ringed coil, or into two branches like human arms upraised. Some of the hilts of the antennae swords are like the "Rhone Valley" type with a sort of short cross-guard, while some are more akin to the Northern and Central European bronze hilts. Swords of this type have been found in Scandinavia, England, France and Moravia, but most of them come from Provence and northern Italy. We shall meet similar swords, also emanating from Italy, in the late Hallstatt period.

We shall have to consider the bronze swords of Scandinavia as a separate group, for they are set apart from all the others by their superlative quality and distinctive forms. Their development from the Minoan-Mycenean swords is more direct than any other of the Bronze Age types. Scandinavia had very close cultural and trading links with the Aegean at this time, and the earliest bronze swords in the north may in fact have been imports from the south.[1] Whether that is so or not, the Danish swords of the early part of the period have hilts which retain many characteristic Minoan features, and all their blades—which tend to be long and very slender—have, like the Mycenean ones, a strong mid-rib running down their centre line. In the north nothing resembling the Irish rapiers has been found, but the practice of swordsmanship seems to have been similar, for the graceful tapering blades of these early swords, and their well-marked central ribs, emphasize their thrusting purpose. Like the Irish rapiers, these gave way to swords with blades which were closely related to the universal leaf-shape, and whose hilts were not made of solid castings of bronze but like the common European type with plates of horn or wood riveted on to either side of a very stout, flanged tang. Towards the end of this middle period we find massive blades which retain hardly a trace of the characteristic leaf-shape; their edges are nearly parallel and their points, though adequate, are in no way acute. The workmanship is still admirable but they are much plainer and are not decorated with the masterly skill and elaboration of the

[1] I have in my possession a bronze sword which seems to provide evidence of trade between the Eastern Mediterranean and Western Europe. It is of a distinctively Mycenean type, yet it was found in the River Thames at Wandsworth.

30

early swords. They were as obviously meant for cutting as the early ones were for thrusting (plate 1).

Thus we see that everywhere man's first swords were meant to thrust with, Mycenae, Denmark and Ireland providing evidence. Then gradually cutting—natural, more untrained fighting—becomes popular and the perfect cut-and-thrust blade develops; then finally the thrust is almost unused and swords are made just for cutting; the latest bronze swords, the Hallstatt type from Austria and the last Danish ones, are proof of that.

In recent years two opposing schools of thought have developed among Scandinavian archaeologists, and much controversy has resulted. Were the swords of the Bronze Age meant for thrusting, or for cutting? The protagonists of each side hold firmly to their extreme views; unfortunately their researches seem to have covered only the Scandinavian swords, yet they seek to apply their theories to all Bronze Age swords irrespective of period or region.

Since the human element in archaeology—the way the original owners used these things which to us are simply "remains"—is so important, and the opposing theories so firmly evade the facts, it will be worth while to examine this question. One thing which even a superficial study of *all* the Bronze Age material shows quite clearly is that in the early part of the period, all swords were made primarily for thrusting; in the middle part of it they were meant to cut *and* thrust; and in the last part of it they were made primarily for cutting. Not just in this part of Europe or in that: everywhere. In fig. 10 I have set out side by side drawings of the nine main types from the earliest to the latest. The weapons themselves seem to supply evidence enough of their makers' intentions. As the exponents of the "thrusting" theory are more emphatic in their assertions, which are themselves more limited and untenable, I will deal with them first.

They base their case on three main points; each of which we will discuss separately:

(1) They say that the swords of the Bronze Age were meant for thrusting "on account of their slender, pointed blades with thin and sharp edges, the strong medial ridge or rib, and the weak connection between hilt and blade". One might think they were referring only to the earliest types, but we are expected to believe that this remark

Fig. 10.

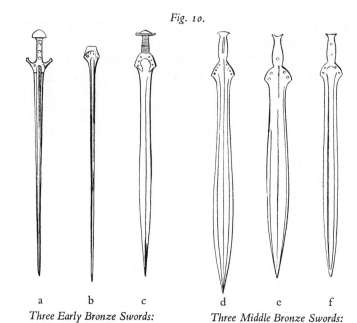

Three Early Bronze Swords:
a. Crete b. Ireland c. Denmark

Three Middle Bronze Swords:
d. England e. Italy f. Mycenae

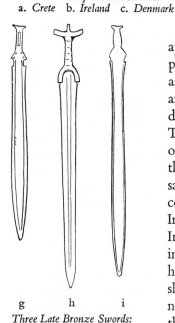

Three Late Bronze Swords:
g. Great Britain h. Denmark
i. Austria (Hallstatt)

applies to all swords during the entire period. Its weakness is obvious as soon as one looks at some of the middle and late Bronze Age weapons which do *not* have slender, pointed blades. Then again, the strong medial rib is only present in the early swords; all the later ones are nearly flat. The same argument applies to "the weak connection between hilt and blade". In the early Danish swords, like the Irish rapiers, this connection was indeed weak, for the short cast-bronze hilts were only fixed on to the blade's shoulders by rivets, in the Irish manner. But in nearly all the swords of the later times the "tang"—which is by itself the grip, only needing to be rounded out for comfort's sake on each face by applied plates—is part of the same casting as the blade; to break it one must break the sword itself, not pull it away from its rivets. So there is the first pillar of the "thrusting" theorists' argument. Had they not tried to make what is indeed true about the early swords apply to all the others, it would have stood.

(2) They say, "No well-preserved sword blade from the Bronze Age shows cuts or any traces of cutting in the edges." This is nonsense. In the museums of Europe are countless bronze swords, very well pre-

Fig. 11. Warriors on a Mycenean intaglio.

served, whose edges are notched and cut in no uncertain fashion; they exhibit also unmistakable signs of grinding and sharpening of the edges. Yet the Scandinavian swords do not. Almost every Bronze Age weapon from Scandinavia, whether axe or sword, bears few traces of wear, and the only shields and helmets which have been found there are thin and flimsy (and undented). It is generally agreed that at this time there was a sort of Golden Age in Scandinavia, peaceful, cultured and wealthy; the unworn magnificence of its swords and axes, and its handsome but flimsy and useless shields and helmets, suggest that it was indeed so; untroubled by war, its arms merely magnificent symbols of ceremony and rank.

(3) They bring forward the Mycenean intaglio gems of gold and stone, whereon scenes of combat are shown; they say "the warriors in all illustrations use long swords for stabbing, and for stabbing only". True. All these gems do that, but they all date round about 1700–1500 B.C., that is during the early Bronze Age when the only method of sword-fighting *was* thrusting, and they show warriors only from an extremely limited area where only thrusting swords were used, so they really add remarkably little to our knowledge and nothing at all to the point at issue. There is another thing we must realize about these illustrations; they all have to fill a small space whose limits are very rigidly defined. If you look at some of them (fig. 11 is an example), you will see at once that the artist *could not* show a man slashing at his opponent without his arm and

33

most of his sword getting clean out of the picture. One can take works of art just a little too seriously, as well as completely disregarding the artist's limitations—limitations imposed in this case by the object he worked on.

Those who uphold the "cutting" theory have a far better case, but they in their turn spoil it by ignoring the early thrusting swords. Paradoxically, it is these very swords which provide one of the best arguments in favour of their theory. As I said before, in nine cases out of ten the hilt rivets on the British rapiers have been wrenched sideways clean through the metal of the blades, *because the swords have been misused by striking cutting blows.* This is concrete evidence of man's natural preference for slashing at his foe. It is worth noting, by the way, that no method of fighting which relied only upon the thrust without the use of cutting blows at all was evolved until the middle of the eighteenth century A.D. Although the Italian and Spanish schools of fence from the early sixteenth century onward relied mainly on the thrust, a great many of their passes involved slashing blows. As we have seen, the first swords developed from daggers; axes and dagger blades set at right angles on to a short shaft were the weapons for slashing. The stabbing sword, though considerable skill was needed for its correct use, was a primitive form of the weapon; its thrusting properties were the result of its weakness and inadequacy, not a manifestation of skilful swordsmanship of a very sophisticated kind on the part of the men who used it. The fashioning of a cut-and-thrust sword which did not come apart in the hand when someone was hit with it was an advance in sword-cutlery, not a regression. More evidence that a deliberate, thought-out advance was made from stabbing to cut-and-thrust is provided by analysis of the metal from which these swords were made. This has shown that in the early Bronze Age the alloy of the stabbing swords contained on an average $9 \cdot 4\%$ of tin, whereas the later ones contained $10 \cdot 6\%$. This alloy may be compared with the gun-metal from which nineteenth-century cannon barrels were made, than which it would be difficult to find anything more tough —an alloy of copper with between $8 \cdot 25\%$ and $10 \cdot 7\%$ of tin. Equally tough, then, were the swords of the later Bronze Age— quite stout enough to stand up to the wear-and-tear of cutting.

Before leaving this question we might consider it in a practical way, by consulting the weapon itself. It has been suggested more than once that you cannot wield these swords unless you have an exceptionally small hand, because their hilts are so short. Now you know well enough that if you hold any implement the wrong way it will feel awkward, almost impossible to use. (Try putting a scythe into the hands of someone who does not know how to use it and watch the fantastic things he will do.) On the other hand, if you grasp it the right way, you seem to know by instinct what to do with it. So it is with swords, more perhaps than with any other instrument made by man. When you pick up a Bronze Age sword, you must not expect it to feel like an eighteenth-century small-sword or a modern foil. If you do, you cannot appreciate what it was meant to do. Neither must you assume that your hand is far too big because all four fingers will not fit into the space between the pommel and the shoulders. These swellings were meant to be part of, and a reinforcement to, the grip; and properly used provide a firmer hold and better control of your weapon. The grip is held by three fingers, the forefinger goes forward and below the shoulder, while the thumb grips it fast on the other side. Now your sword balances properly, it is held firmly, you can control its movements, and it *feels* right in your hand. Held thus correctly, it will positively seem to invite you to hit something with it.

Another thing which is often said in disparagement of these swords is that the weight is too far forward; too near the point; it is ill-balanced and (I quote) [1] "it would be impossible to fence with it". That, of course, is absurd. "Fencing" bears no relation whatever to sword-fighting of the kind these weapons were made for. The nearest thing to it is perhaps the sabre-drill practised by cavalry troopers fifty years ago. No; swords meant to be used as these were —and we can see how, painted on countless Greek pots—needed to have their weight well up the blade either for cutting or thrusting. For cutting it has to be greatest at the "centre of percussion" or "optimal striking point", which simply means that the greatest weight should be centred in the part of the blade which will meet the object struck. For thrusting, having the weight well forward seems, when you lunge, to carry the blade outward from your shoulder; it helps you to aim it, and in striking adds velocity to its

[1] *Land of the Tollund Man*, Palle Lauring, Lutterworth Press, 1957.

Fig. 12. Curved bronze sword from Zealand (National Museum, Copenhagen).

own weight and the power of your arm. This is not just theorizing, but the practical result of having experimentally wielded all kinds of sword over many years in an effort to find out what they were meant to do and how they did it best.

There is one other type of sword which should have mention here. It is extremely rare and so far only three complete specimens, a broken hilt and a flint copy have been found. These swords are one-edged and curved; fig. 12 shows one from Zealand (now in Copenhagen), and you can see what a strange weapon it is—but how effective! The whole thing is cast in one piece; the blade is nearly ½ in. thick on its back and at the curve of it are two bronze pellets, as well as a thick moulding. These serve to weight the blade at its vital striking point. Clumsy, hideous, but probably most deadly. In view of the great popularity of one-edged swords in the north during the whole of the Iron Age, it is odd that they seem to have been so scarce in the Bronze Age. The flint copy is absurd, but fascinating; it seems to suggest that the flint workers were trying against all hope to equal the new metal products; an even greater flint absurdity (also in Denmark, where, perhaps, finer flint implements were made than anywhere in the world) is a copy of a bronze sword, made in several sections, all fitted to a wooden core!

You will notice on the hilt of these curved swords a little ring. At first sight one might think its purpose was to put the forefinger through to get a secure grip, but it is on the wrong side: swords of this shape would not go into a scabbard; the ring is probably some sort of fitting for carrying purposes. This sword is so similar to one from Scania that it seems they must have come from the same workshop. No weapon of like kind has been found anywhere else, so we might conclude that they were an indigenous Danish type, but there is a complication: the decoration on the Zealand sword resembles that on a dagger from Bohemia. However, this does not necessarily mean that they came from there; it is just more evidence of the interrelation of culture.

Chapter Two

IRON COMES TO EUROPE: THE
HALLSTATT PEOPLE

URING THE EARLY part of the first millennium B.C. a new
craft was borne westwards out of Asia to the Bronze Age
people who dwelt in the Danube basin. Whether this involved the movement of migrating tribes is not clear, but its result
was the evolution in the area now covered by Austria and Hungary
of folk groupings more warlike than their predecessors.

At the same time the Mycenean domination in the Aegean was
broken by the invasion of the Dorians, who came down into Greece
from the north. Whether these Dorians were themselves part of a
people moving westwards or whether they were folk who had lived
in the north of Thrace and were now displaced is not certain. The
historians of classical Greece called this invasion "The Return of
the Heraclids", and dated it about 1104 B.C., some eighty years after
the Trojan War.

Archaeology has given some precision to the chronology of these
movements, for types of sword and brooch unknown in the earlier
periods have been found in association with late Mycenean remains.
Particularly significant are some brooches of spiral bronze wire
found in Sparta which are unmistakably connected with those of
the Hallstatt culture of Central Europe. These discoveries in Greece
link with actual personages in Greek history the bringers of iron,
the Hallstatt people. This name is derived from a salt-mining area
in the Salzkammergut in Upper Austria, and the period (about
1000–950 B.C.) marks perhaps the first appearance of the Celts
as well as the real beginning of the Iron Age. Though not the cradle
of iron working, it is the region where objects characteristic of the

culture were first identified in graves which seem to be those of chieftains of a warrior dynasty.

The legendary home of iron is in north-east Asia Minor, in ancient Paphlagonia and Pontus, where the Chalybes (mentioned by Aeschylus in the sixth century B.C.) seem to have had a sort of monopoly, while to the south was Commagene, *Ubi ferrum nascitur*. In the north-east of this area, as well as to the north of the Caucasus, cemeteries have been found which have yielded weapons and other iron objects closely allied to the Hallstatt products; also, and perhaps more significantly, types of bronze horse-bit and bridle mounts have been found in many graves in Hungary and Austria which are closely related in form to types found across the Pontic steppes, beyond the Caucasus and even farther off in Iran. The finding of these objects in graves of the early Hallstatt period (*c.* 1000–800 B.C.) which are clearly those of horse-using warriors suggests that they brought a sort of military stimulus with better weapons of iron and improved horse management; they may even have been veteran mercenaries from the armies of Assyria and Urartu. We shall examine presently some pretty convincing evidence that this was indeed the case.

Herodotus (writing in about 450 B.C.) tells of a people dwelling beyond the Danube and to the north of Thrace called Siggynae. These may perhaps be identified with a people of the Caucasus region called the Siggini mentioned by Strabo, who was writing of a period around 100 B.C., and maybe with the later Sequani of Gaul (Caesar, 58 B.C.) who eventually reached the region of Paris. Both Sigynnae and Siggini are said to have worn Medean costume, trousers; which were of course the usual wear of the Celts. What Herodotus has to say of them is illuminating in the added light of recent archaeological discoveries. He says:

> As regards the region lying north of this country [Thrace] no one can say with any certainty what men inhabit it. It appears that you no sooner cross the Ister [Danube] than you enter an interminable wilderness. The only people of whom I can hear as dwelling beyond the Ister are a race named Sigynnae, who wear, they say, a dress like the Medes, and have horses which are covered with a coat of shaggy hair, five fingers in length. They are a small breed, flat nosed, and are not strong enough to bear men on their backs; but when yoked to chariots are

38

the swiftest known, which is the reason why the people of that country use chariots. Their borders reach down almost to the Eneti on the Adriatic sea, and they call themselves colonists of the Medes; but how they can be colonists of the Medes I for my part cannot imagine. Still, nothing is impossible in the long lapse of the ages.

Nothing, indeed. During the last century the remains of chariots and the bones and trappings of small horses have been found in the graves of the Hallstatt warriors; the trousered costume of the Celts is well known from the Gaulish and Italian sculptures of the Roman period, while Roman writers often speak as eye-witnesses of the swift, shaggy little horses and the trousered charioteers. We may even believe what Herodotus found it hard to imagine; as we have seen, objects of the same culture and the same form have been found in regions very close to the Medean territories (and even within them) as well as in Austria. This at least suggests a cultural connection between the Hallstatt people (the ancestors of the Sigynnae) and the Medes. There is an even closer link with Assyria. In Celtic burials widely scattered in Western Europe—at Avranches, in the Loire valley, near Abbeville, in Baden and the Palatinate and Moravia—have been found ingots of iron, small billets of good quality metal in a handy and portable size. Identical ones have been found at Khorsabad, near Nineveh. Nor is this all, for a distinctive style of sword and scabbard mount is found both in the West and in Assyria.

The objects which are perhaps most characteristic of the Hallstatt culture are the long iron swords, the first iron weapons of any size. During the early period, a new and distinctive sword-form was in use; many examples have been found, made of bronze, in most parts of Europe; these are so similar in shape and detail that it looks as though they come from a single centre of production—one is tempted to say from the same workshop. The iron swords, on the contrary, though they are of exactly the same shape as the bronze ones, have been found in a limited area only—Bavaria, Wurttemberg, Baden, Alsace-Lorraine, Burgundy and Auvergne. The implication is that swords made in the old material were exported to the peoples of the old Bronze Age culture, while the new and presumably more efficient swords were jealously protected and reserved for the use of a dominant warrior-caste.

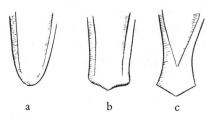

a   b   c

Fig. 13. Three forms of point on the blades of Hallstatt swords.

These swords retain in their form most of the features of the earlier bronze types, but their main purpose was different. They were the long, slashing weapons of a chariot-using people. Their purpose is emphasized in many cases by the point not being a point at all, for it is either of a rounded spatulate form, or cut off practically square, or drawn out into a sort of fish-tail (fig. 13 a, b and c). This last feature became fashionable in a rather similar way seventeen centuries later, when the points of some Italian rapiers of the second quarter of the seventeenth century A.D. were made into little flat tongues at the end of the long slender blades for the purpose of making effective use of a particular pass—the Stramazzone, a slashing blow made at the face—in the Italian mode of fencing.

Some of the Hallstatt iron swords are so large that it has been suggested that they were meant only for ceremonial use, but I do not believe that this is so. They are certainly far bigger than any swords which had preceded them—far bigger than anything which was to follow them for 1,500 years, too—but even so they are by no means too large to be wielded by a tall man; many mediaeval swords of everyday purpose were even bigger. Their manufacture, understandably enough, suggests somewhat experimental methods of forging. This forging seems first to have been carried on in a region known to the Romans as Noricum, roughly within the modern Austrian province of Styria, where the finest iron which was then obtainable was mined; from here came the famous Celtic iron in Roman times, and right through the Middle Ages its products of armour and swordblades (from Innsbruck and Passau) were among the best in Europe. Although it was not the actual cradle of iron working, the region provided a far richer supply of high quality material for the original workers in iron who had probably come from the East, so it can be said to be the birthplace of the European Iron Age.

Over most of the territories influenced by the Hallstatt culture the swords of this first Iron Age show much uniformity of shape in contrast to the many different styles in use during the middle and late Bronze Age. One after the other, three main types of sword were used between about 950–450 B.C. First the transitional long cutting sword of bronze; then the heavy iron sword which carried on the bronze form in the new metal, and in the third and last phase a short iron sword which was derived from the weapons used by the Etruscans and Greeks with whom the Celts had ever-increasing contacts after about 600 B.C.

The bronze Hallstatt sword, despite its distribution over the entire area of influence, shows, as I have said, great uniformity. The only variation seems to have been in length, though this seldom involves more than a few centimetres. Some swords have elaborated points (as I have shown in fig. 13), but in the cross-section of their blades and the shape of the upper parts of these where they meet the hilt there is complete similarity. The hilt was fitted in the same manner as in the Bronze Age, but the form of the blade's shoulders and the tang is different in detail. These differences will be appreciated if you compare fig. 10i with the Bronze Age sword shown in fig. 6.

Several hilts of these swords have been preserved; basically, they are similar to the Bronze Age hilts (plate 1.c.) but they have a very distinctive pommel like a Mexican hat. Most which have been preserved are made of horn or ivory, decorated with gold or amber. A particularly fine iron sword from a grave at Gomadingen in Wurttemberg has a magnificent hilt of horn or bone decorated with sheet gold (fig. 14). This sword is one of the very large ones I have referred to; its total length is $42\frac{1}{2}$ in.[1]

Though this hat-like pommel is the most usual, some have been found which are more similar to the mushroom-like Bronze

Fig. 14. Hilt of sword from Gomadingen, of horn covered with gold foil.

[1] Preserved in the Landesmuseum at Stuttgart.

41

Fig. 15. Late Hallstatt sword of iron, from the Thames (British Museum).

Age pommels; there is, for instance, one in the British Museum which is extremely like the great pommels found in Crete and Mycenae of the period late Minoan III.

The third style of Hallstatt sword, used in the late period between perhaps 600–450 B.C., is clearly either imported from Italy or the Greek colonies or copied directly from Greek or Etruscan models, that is as far as its short, broad and acutely-pointed blade is concerned. Its hilt was as distinctive of the Hallstatt culture (though in a greater variety of forms) as were the Mexican hat hilts. Some were adaptations of the late Bronze Age Antennae hilts, while others were based upon a spread-eagled human figure (and so are generally known to archaeologists as "Anthropomorphic" swords). A good example of one of the former type was found in the Thames in London. Its iron blade is well preserved, and the bronze hilt is furnished with a wide-spreading pair of horns (one of which is missing) in place of a pommel (fig. 15).

The scabbards of the long swords were of wood, probably made like the Bronze Age scabbards[1] with an outer covering of leather and a lining of fur, and were furnished with bronze chapes (the metal terminals at the point ends of scabbards) of a novel and distinctive pattern like a spreading pair of wings or horns. These chapes are splendid objects, though one might think that a finial like this would have been a very awkward encumbrance at the end of a scabbard; but it is reasonable to suppose that they were made that way for a purpose—not, as has been suggested, to serve the same end as the chapes on the sabre-scabbards of nineteenth-century cavalry officers, to trail and clatter along the ground at their wearers' heels. Imagine a barbarian warrior fighting afoot or in a chariot trailing a long scabbard garnished with a seven-inch pair of horns at its tip. No. It is far more probable that the purpose was to assist the warrior to draw his sword from its scabbard. We know from well-preserved

[1] E.g. the sword from the central tomb of Mound 1 at Barkåkra in Skåne.

42

existing remains that in the Bronze Age in Denmark (and probably everywhere else) swords were hung from a shoulder-belt; no trace of any metal scabbard-mount on the upper part of a Hallstatt scabbard has been found, so we may infer that these great swords were loosely carried in the same way. Now, the warrior would almost certainly have a shield on his left arm; if he did, he would have difficulty in grasping the top of his scabbard with his left

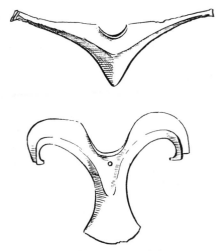

Fig. 16. Hallstatt winged chapes.

hand to hold it down while he drew out his sword with his right. Unless he grasped the scabbard, the tendency would be for the sword to stick and simply pull the scabbard round on its loosely-hung baldric—and here the purpose of the winged chape might appear; all he would need to do in order to hold the scabbard would be to catch one of the wings of the chape behind his leg, thus anchoring it firmly while he drew his sword (fig. 16). Such at any rate is one workable theory; we can be sure that the trailing idea is wrong, partly because it is fatuous, and partly because though a large number of these chapes has been found, none bears any of the marks of wear which such treatment would inevitably make upon it.

The graves of the Hallstatt warriors give no clue as to how these long swords were worn; such fragments which remain are, as I said, without any kind of mount whereby they could be attached to a belt. However, we have the archaeological evidence of those Danish bronze swords, and pictorial evidence may be sought in Assyrian bas-reliefs, for between 900–700 B.C. the Assyrians used long swords which are shown clearly and often in the great bas-reliefs from the palaces of Nineveh and Nimrud. And these long swords are all furnished with winged chapes, like the Hallstatt ones; one type (fig. 17a) is identical with one of the Hallstatt styles. When

43

a   b

Fig. 17. Assyrian winged chapes, from the Nimrud bas-reliefs.

the sword belongs to a monarch or a great official, the chape is formed either of two lions standing upright back to back, their heads forming the wings, or in a simpler form with lion heads alone (fig. 17b). These Assyrian warriors wear their swords loosely on baldrics slung over their right shoulders, but the Great Ones who qualify for the lion-headed chapes wear their swords below the folds of their tunics. In these reliefs it is noticeable how high the sword is generally worn, with the hilt up against the chest. A probable reason for this would be that they were worn in chariots; carried thus, the end of the scabbard would clear the upper rim of the chariot body (fig. 18).

The pommels of most swords in these bas-reliefs present a semi-circular profile indicating a mushroom-like shape, circular in plan, identical in form with the Hallstatt bronze pommel in the British Museum which I mentioned on a previous page.

We have seen how in the latest Hallstatt period, after about 600 B.C., the long sword gave place to a shorter, acutely pointed weapon. Exactly the same change took place about a century before that in Assyria. In all the reliefs dating before 700 B.C., only the long sword with the winged chape is shown; after, no more long ones are seen; their place is taken by short, broad-bladed, acutely-pointed swords without winged chapes. Here may be more corroboration of the fact which Herodotus found it hard to believe, that the Sigynnae of the Danube plains were colonists of the Medes, and for the theory that the earliest Hallstatt warriors were wandering mercenaries from

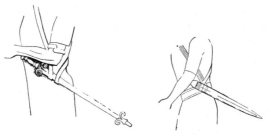

a   b

Fig. 18. Figures from bas-reliefs:
a. *Nimrud*, c. *900* B.C.; b. *Nineveh*, c. *700* B.C.

the armies of Assyria. We may also note that the Assyrians and many of their neighbours wore, between the eighth century B.C. and the fifth, helmets remarkably similar to some which have been found in Celtic graves in Western Europe—tall conical skull caps sometimes drawn out to an acute point at the top, sometimes furnished with a hollow finial to take a

Fig. 19. Assyrian helmets from the Nineveh bas-reliefs.

crest—patterns (particularly the tall spiked ones) found nowhere but in the lands of the Celts and in Assyria (fig. 19): compare fig. 33.

Long or short, the sword was the principal weapon of the Hallstatt warriors; it is unusual to find spears or javelins in their graves. However, there are a few, among which is one distinctive type. It has a heavy head, about 15 in. long; it was fitted to the shaft by a hollow socket, immediately above which the blade widens abruptly in two flat wings, one on either side of a very stout central rib, but they are very small and their edges sweep in to rejoin the mid-rib about 3 in. above the socket; the rib (which is of square section) continues to the spear's point. Thus the spearhead consists of a long stiff and narrow spike swelling out at its base to a small leaf-shaped pair of cutting edges. This sort of spear was often used 1,000 years later in the Viking period, and were it not for one feature, it would be difficult to distinguish a spear of the first period from one of the other: the Hallstatt spears have a small knob of bronze, like a very thick collar, fixed to the top of the socket immediately below the widening of the spearhead.

If spears are scarce in the graves, armour is so far completely lacking. Only one grave has been found which contained remains of a shield (which was a large rectangular wooden one, bound with iron and reinforced with iron rivets, with a double boss of iron), and there is one bronze helmet which was found in an unrecorded Hallstatt grave in Moravia. This is a moderately tall conical cap of the form so familiar to us in the helmets of the Vikings and the Normans of the eleventh century A.D. It has a neat little finial on the top shaped like a golfer's tee.[1] Both shield and helmet were of a shape

[1] An identical helmet of the same period, found near Frankfurt-an-Oder, is in the British Museum.

45

that was to be popular throughout Europe for a long time; the long rectangular shield was characteristic of the Celts from 500 B.C. to nearly 100 A.D., while the helmet was the principal shape in use until about 1150 A.D.

A type of helmet which, though not found in the Hallstatt graves, was in use in Northern Europe during the period is one which is associated with the "Villanova" culture of northern Italy in the eighth century B.C. Several have been found used as lids to the funerary urns of these people; the helmet itself is in the form of a tall rounded cap, with its top drawn out into an acute point. A double row of bronze rivets runs round the helmet just above its lower rim, and from front and back in a central position project groups of three short rods; above these is a flat crest, exactly following the line of the upper part of the helmet (fig. 20). These helmets (as we are shown by a small bronze figure from Reggio in Aemilia which is wearing one) were worn with the crest running fore-and-aft.

Several body defences of hammered bronze have been found in northern Italy and south-western France in association with objects of early Iron Age date, but they owe their origin to Mediterranean patterns and do not directly concern the Hallstatt people.

In the shaft-graves of Mycenae were found several representations of very large shields, shaped a little like a figure eight. On one of the gold-inlaid dagger-blades some lion-hunters are shown with such shields, and we can see others on engraved seals. Until Schleimann found these things, generations of scholars had been puzzled by references in the Iliad to large body shields of a type for which no archaeological or pictorial evidence in classical Greek art existed. Many of Homer's warriors are described as fighting in the familiar equipment of classical Greece, but some of the passages seemed imaginary, like this:

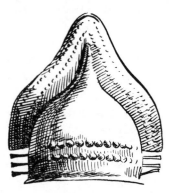

Fig. 20. *Bronze helmet (Etruscan),*
sixth century B.C.

As he walked, the dark leather rim of his bossed shield tapped him above and below, on the ankles and on the back of his neck.

46

Or this: where the Achaean hero Telamonian Aias goes to fight Hector he carries a shield:

Like a tower, made of bronze and seven layers of leather. Tychius, the Master currier, who lived at Hyle, made this glittering shield for him with the hides of seven big bulls, which he overlaid with an eighth layer of bronze.

These clearly covered the entire body, and were unlike any shields depicted in classical times. Where did Homer get this idea from? As with so many things, Schliemann's discovery of these Mycenean pictures supplied the answer (fig. 11). Similar figure-of-eight body-shields were found in Crete, too; they were probably used as a wall-decoration in one of the halls in the Palace of Minos at Knossos.

The helmet and cuirass were common further to the east, how-ever unfashionable they may have been in Central Europe. The helmets and defensive armour used in Greece and the Mediterranean between 1000 B.C. and the end of the Roman period are of so many and such varied kinds that it will only be possible to deal with them in a very broad manner. To begin with we have in the *Iliad* a description of a type of helmet which was common at one time, old at the period of the Great Siege, and non-existent in classical times. Homer seems to go to a good deal of trouble to describe it, and rather stresses that even then it was an old one. It was lent to Odysseus when he and Diomedes made their midnight reconnais-sance of the Trojan camp:

Meriones gave Odysseus a bow, a quiver and a sword, and set a leather helmet on his head. Inside it there was a strong lining of interwoven strips, under which a felt cap had been sewn in. The outer rim was cunningly adorned on either side by a row of white and flashing boars' tusks.

As you see, a careful, practical and convincing description. It seems that it was something of a curiosity, even at the time of the Trojan war; perhaps that is why Homer describes it so minutely, for his usual way with a helmet is to use a single adjective, generally "flashing" or "glittering". He goes on to say:

The helmet originally came from Eleon, where Autolyclus stole it from Amyntor son of Ormenos by breaking into his well-built house. Autolyclus gave it to Amplidamus of Cythera to take to Scandaea, and Amplidamus gave it to Molus in return for hospitality. Molus, in

47

Fig. 21. Small ivory head from Mycenae, showing boar's-tooth helmet.

his turn, gave it to his son Meriones to wear, and now it was Odysseus' head it served to protect.

Thus Homer; and because no such helmet was ever seen on a Greek pot or anywhere else, scholars, historians and archaeologists alike thought it was just another piece of Homer's nonsense. Then came Schliemann, who believed every word that Homer wrote. In the fourth grave at Mycenae he found sixty boars' teeth. He says:

of all of which the reverse side was cut perfectly flat, and had two borings, which must have served to fasten it to another object, perhaps on horse-trappings. But we see in the Iliad that they were also used on helmets.

Then to follow all this came many small ivory plaques showing warriors wearing helmets covered with boars' teeth, just as found in the graves, and later several small ivory heads (fig. 21) with similar helmets.

So much for a type of Mycenean helmet which had passed away when the classical vase-painters got to work. All the "Greek" peoples used helmets of the forms so adequately shown on the Attic vases. These were derived from Cretan and Mycenean forms, and in their turn were the ancestors of all the Etruscan and Roman types. The best way to learn what these helmets looked like, and how

Fig. 22. Greek warrior with kopis from an Attic Hydria in the Museum of Naples. Fifth century B.C.

48

they were made and worn, is to go and look at Greek pots; I have illustrated a few in figs. 22 and 23. A good many actual helmets have been found, quite enough to provide sure evidence that the painters were not pulling the legs of future generations any more than Homer was.

The "barbarians" tended on the whole to favour a conical kind of helmet, sometimes made of a single piece of bronze, but more often of several strips or plates riveted together. We have no pictures to show us what was worn in Britain or Gaul or Germany before the Roman period, but from Persia and Assyria, as we have seen, there is evidence enough.

The body-armour of the classical warrior, Mycenean, Greek or Roman,

Fig. 23. From vases of Attic red-figure ware, fifth century B.C.

consisted of a breast-plate and a back plate, a pair of greaves of solid metal to cover the calves of his legs, and no more. Only a few wore cuirasses of solid metal—wealthy leaders in pre-Roman times, and in the Roman army only high-ranking officers. The defence of the Hoplite or the Legionary was made of leather or of mail, or of overlapping scales of metal fixed to a base of fabric or leather, or in the style of the well-known *Lorica Segmentata* of iron or bronze bands curved horizontally round the body, hinged on one side and buckled on the other, with broad shoulder straps similarly fashioned to hold it up. This sort of defensive coat came into use again for a short time between about 1250 and 1350 A.D.

You will notice that on some of the Greek vases, particularly the Attic red-figured ware of the fifth century B.C. (figs. 22 and 24), warriors are shown wielding large curved swords quite different in shape from the straight ones. The Greeks called these Kopis, or Machaira, and very effective slashing weapons they must have been. In Northern India the form has survived almost unchanged to the present day in the well-known "kukri" of the Gurkhas. If you

49

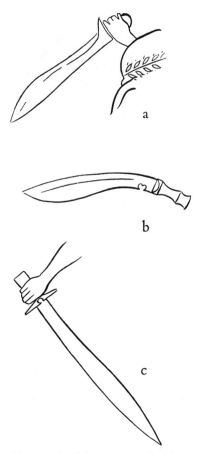

Fig. 24. Greek kopis compared with a
modern Gurkha kukri (b).

compare the kopis I have illustrated in fig. 24a (from an Attic
Hydria in the Museum of
Naples) with the drawing of a
modern kukri from Nepal (fig.
24b), you will see how little the
original form has changed. It is
interesting to observe, too, that
while the blade form has survived in India (whither it was
taken by Alexander's men—I do
not believe the Aryan invaders
brought it), hilts of an obviously
derivative shape were used in
the Levant up to the eighteenth
century. We shall find this
curved variant of the sword re-
curring all through the Middle
Ages. Up to the middle of the
fourteenth century it had much
in common with the kopis,
though by the early fifteenth
century it had developed the
well-known form of the early
nineteenth century cavalry sabre.
We shall see more of this later
on; I mention it here because
it is another example of continuity in the development of arms.

Chapter Three

THE GAULS

THE ROMAN PERIOD provides one of those convenient historical bridges which seem to link one age with another. At its beginning most of the old civilizations of the Eastern Mediterranean were still flourishing; at its end they had all vanished, and the hitherto unknown races of the north, descended from the great people of the Scandinavian Bronze Age, had become dominant. So much has been written of the arms and fighting methods of Rome that perhaps I may be forgiven if I do not take the reader across this bridge but ask him instead to follow me down into the gulf it spans, there to seek out the few clues which show how mediaeval arms developed from those of the Iron Age barbarians.

Mediaeval chivalry owes little to the Roman and nearly everything to the Teuton who overthrew him. We have seem how in Tacitus' time the Germans, ill-armed and primitive though they were, had in their tribal codes many of the abstractions of thought upon which the chivalric ideal was based, however deficient they had been in its material trappings.

Now we shall see how in the first and second centuries A.D. many of the Teutonic peoples from Scandinavia left their homelands, and, moving eastwards and southwards from the southern shores of the Baltic, pressed down into Central Europe and on into Dacia and Scythia: how, after sojourning for generations there in the plains of the lower Danube and the steppes of the Ukraine, ever the cradle of cavalry from the days of the Scythians, they in their turn became horsemen, and how they adapted the weapons and armour which originated in Helvetia and Noricum (roughly Switzerland and Austria). We shall see how, by an apparent paradox, it was the barbarous Franks, descendants of the primitive German tribes described by Tacitus, who under Charlemagne became the catalyst which fused the whole of these people, the kindred races of Goths, Longobards and Vandals, into the nations of modern Europe, and how because of this the Gothic horsemen of the third and fourth centuries became the ancestors of the knights of the Middle Ages.

These Goths, who broke the Roman power in Dacia and finally overran Italy and Rome itself, fought in masses on heavy horses; they wore defensive armour of helmet, mail-shirt, and shield; their weapons were long lances and broadswords. These swords were quite different in shape and purpose from the short stabbing weapon of the Roman legionaries; different, too, from the old leaf-shaped bronze swords from which (via the short Etruscan bronze swords and the Greek iron ones) the Roman weapon developed. What, then, was their origin? To find it we have to go back to the last five centuries B.C., for the weapon which overthrew Rome in the hands of Goth and Longobard was already fully developed while Rome was still at grips with the Etruscans. So, before we consider the Gothic migrations and ultimate victories, we must examine the arms of the La Tène cultures, so called from the type-site where the culture was first discovered.

In the years between 1874–81, the eastern end of the lake of Neuchatel dried out; a Swiss archaeologist, Emile Vouge, found in the muddy shallows the remains of the wooden piles of a bridge; and many dwellings built upon platforms supported by wooden piles. These dwellings had been built on the edges of a watercourse—the former bed of the river Thielle, which long before 1874 had been diverted into a canal. Moving upriver from the shallows (whence the site—La Tène—gets its name) Vouge found more dwellings and another bridge. In the mud around the piles on the principal site of La Tène large quantities of objects, mostly of iron, were found. There were over 100 swords, more than 200 spear-heads, many brooches and fastenings, several iron pots, and many tools and implements of iron—axes, knives, chisels, scythes—as well as a complete wheel, a good deal of harness and some gold coins and some torques and collars of gold. Among all this there was none of the usual domestic debris which turns up in prehistoric dwelling sites, nor any bits and pieces of women's gear such as jewellery, pins, brooches, mirrors and so on (the purpose of such brooches as were found was to fasten the cloaks of men). This complete absence of ordinary domestic life means that the place had been nothing but a military station, and that the material was either in the nature of military stores or goods in transit (for the people of Helvetia and Noricum, further to the east, were the main suppliers of arms to the whole of Europe). All of the swords, for instance, were still in their scabbards. A parallel is given by the hoard of material which was found in 1870 in the bed of the river Saône, at Châlon-sur-Saône. This used to be the ancient Cabillonum, one of the principal towns of the Aedui, and was known to have been a military station and trading post. Here the remains were the same as at La Tène, the wooden piles of a bridge with the objects lying in the mud around them. At this place most of the things were of the La Tène period, though many were Gallo-Roman and several even as late as Merovingian.

The importance of La Tène itself was that it stood at a point of crossing between the valleys of the Rhine and the Rhone, by which the valuable metal-work exported from Helvetia and Noricum could reach the west. The period called after it covers roughly the last five centuries B.C., sometimes called the earlier or Celtic Iron Age: La Tène I, from c. 500–300 B.C.; La Tène II, 300–150 B.C., and La Tène III, 150–0 B.C.

In the preceding chapter we saw how swords which differed from their predecessors appeared at the very end of the Bronze Age in the period of the Hallstatt culture, and how they were superseded by an iron type. The long iron sword of the La Tène cultures which followed this is the true ancestor of the knightly weapon of the Middle Ages. These swords seem to have little connection with the bronze ones, for their outline was quite different; their edges were straight and very nearly parallel, tapering slightly to a rounded point. We have seen that the last bronze types were designed for cutting. At this time the warriors of the West had begun to fight in chariots, and in a chariot it is difficult to do anything with a sword except to slash at your opponent, and you need a long one to reach him. That is one thing, the other is that the nature of the material the sword-smiths worked would have conditioned the shape of the blades they made. You cannot cast a very long, flat and thin blade in bronze, it

Fig. 25. Diagram showing assembly of hilt of a La Tène sword.

has to be solid and rather heavy; nor can it be very long unless (like the Lissane sword) it is also very thick and narrow, and meant only for thrusting. But with iron it is quite different. You do not pour the molten metal into a stone mould, you beat it out flat with hammers; and the more you beat, the harder—and the flatter—it will become. It will also have a certain amount of flexibility, so unless you make it very thick, and thus far too heavy, it will not stand up to thrusting, for a direct thrust will bend it, whereas the breadth of the blade will permit any amount of quite effective cutting. We sometimes hear of how these early iron swords bent in battle, how the warrior using one had to stop and straighten it under his foot. (For instance, we hear of it happening at the battle of Aquae Sextiae in 102 B.C., between the Romans under Marius and the Teutons and Cimbri.)

A practice in sword-making which reappears at the same period (La Tène I) is a method of fixing the hilt to the blade which was tried and rejected in the Bronze Age, but which was successful in the Iron Age and has been used ever since. I believe this too was brought about by the nature of the material—iron as opposed to bronze, forging as opposed to casting—and the nature of the weapon's usage, for it was soon discarded when tried experimentally in bronze, for the thin bronze tang would break too easily. The tang of the blade was drawn out into a long narrow tongue, and the hilt was made in three separate parts, the guard, the grip and the pommel. Each of these was pierced with a hole which corresponded to the size and shape of the section of the tang; these were slipped (in their correct order) over the tang until they settled firmly against the shoulders of the blade; then the short length of tang which projected above the top of the pommel was hammered down and firmly riveted over, holding the whole assembly solidly in position (fig. 25). You can see

54

that however hard you cut, and however solid the opposition your blade meets, only the breaking of the tang itself will cause the hilt to come away.

These La Tène swords of the last five centuries B.C. had an average total length of 36 in. or so; the blades were about 30 in. long and the hilts 6 in. or more. Some blades are as much as $2\frac{1}{2}$ in. broad at the hilt tapering to about $1\frac{7}{8}$ in. at the point. Some are pattern-welded and of excellent quality. Very few of the hilts survive, which suggests that like the later swords found in the Danish bogs they were often made of bone or horn or wood; nearly all of these continental La Tène swords consist now only of the blades and the scabbard mounts; the scabbards themselves were mostly made of wood covered with leather and have perished, though there are a few made of bronze and iron. The reverse was the case in Britain, where most of the scabbards of this period which have so far been found are of bronze. Some of the bronze scabbards from La Tène have the surface pounced in imitation of leather, a form of treatment which has so far not been found in any British specimen.

The British iron swords form a class by themselves, for in the main the blades were far thinner and weaker than the splendid continental ones, but in spite of this the scabbards were, as I have said, mostly made of bronze and often embellished with the most splendid ornamentation; some of them are in fact those great works of art I spoke of. The decoration is of that peculiarly Celtic style, making masterly use of running designs of apparently simple geometrical curves; apparently, because these patterns, though seeming to be repetitive, are in fact extremely complex, as living and subtle as the curves in flowing water; they are drawn with a strength and sureness of touch which only a master could achieve.

The Continental swords are generally large and powerful weapons, and their form differs little throughout their area of distribution. The chief differences are shown in their scabbards. The two principal types are personified by two magnificent and well-preserved weapons, one found in Denmark (now in the Danish National Museum at Copenhagen) and another found at Moringen in Switzerland, now in the Landesmuseum at Zurich. They have much in common, and so clearly demonstrate the main divergences between the northern and southern European types that I shall describe them in detail.

The first was found in a bog at Lindholmgard in Zealand, and is perhaps the best preserved of all the La Tène period swords; its appearance suggests nothing of an immersion in the peat of some two thousand years. The blade is broad (3·5 cm.) tapering very slightly to 3 cm. at the point. To speak of the point in this connection is not really accurate, for there is none. The blade ends abruptly in a graceful double curve, slightly cusped in the middle (plate 3a), and the central portion of the blade is formed of two shallow channels divided by a slight ridge. These channels are decorated by an overall texture made by thousands of tiny shallow holes etched into the surface. The shoulders of the blade are drawn up into a graceful double ogee curve, capped by a hilt guard which follows the line of the blade's shoulders. The tang is very long, and is surmounted by a small spherical pommel of silver, capped by a long pyramidical iron block upon which the extremity of the tang is riveted over. This last feature foreshadows an exactly similar practice in hilt-making of the thirteenth to fifteenth centuries. At the lower end of the tang is a fillet of metal which originally formed some part of the grip, possibly around its middle in the manner of some Romano-British swords and of most European mediaeval swords of the fifteenth century A.D. The scabbard of this sword is with it, most astonishingly well-preserved, made of two convex plates of thin iron. It is quite plain and unornamented, and was suspended by iron rings placed on either edge, one about one-fifth of the way down the scabbard and the other on the opposite edge about 8 in. nearer the point. The "point" end of the scabbard is quite square, finished off with a kind of bronze moulding. The upper scabbard mount, also of bronze, is stuck to the sword's hilt, giving the impression that there is a double guard. There are sufficient scabbards or portions of scabbards of this shape, found in Scandinavia and north Germany, to suggest that it was a distinct local type (plate 3b).

The sword from Moringen in Switzerland has much in common with the one I have just described. Its blade is larger but similar, except that it tapers a little more sharply to a broad spatulate point, and its shoulders are not drawn up into so high an arch. Nothing remains of the hilt, but the tang is about the same length; the riveted bit at the top has been carefully hammered over to form a small sphere. The "locket" or upper scabbard mount of this sword is still in place, and shows a method of suspension quite different from the northern type, for it is formed of a loop

Fig. 26. *Chape of a bronze dagger-sheath from Wandsworth, second or third century* B.C. (*British Museum*).

through which a strap would pass to secure it to belt or baldric. The chape of this particular sword is missing, but many survive on similar swords. These suggest a logical development of the great winged chapes of the Hallstatt period which I described in the last chapter. With the introduction of the strap-loop to suspend the scabbard (which in the Hallstatt swords, you will remember, may have been worn loosely in the Assyrian manner) it was no longer necessary to hook the chape behind the leg or elbow to draw the sword out, so the wings became redundant and were drawn up to lie along the edges of the scabbard, while the central point of the chape was elaborated (fig. 26). This is of course pure theory; we do not *know* that the winged chapes were used in that way or that their successors of La Tène I were developed from them as I have suggested. It simply seems logical to assume that it was so.

Between these two splendid examples found at the extremities of the distribution area of these swords there are a host of others which have turned up in burials or votive deposits. It is an archaeological tragedy that many of these had been destroyed in antiquity. Nothing of this period has been found as yet which can compare with the Danish deposits of the first centuries A.D., but there have been several finds which match the comment of Orosius, writing of the Roman defeat by the Cimbri at Arausia in 105 B.C., who says:

> When the enemy had taken possession of two camps and an immense booty, they destroyed under new and strange imprecations all that had fallen into their hands. The clothes were torn and thrown away, gold and silver thrown into the river, the ring armour of the men cut to pieces, the accoutrements of the horses destroyed, the horses themselves thrown into the water, and the men with ropes around their necks suspended to the trees, so that there was no more booty for the victors than there was mercy for the conquered.

It is worth noting here, incidentally, that Orosius refers to "ring armour".

Then Caesar, writing half a century later of the customs of the Gauls, says:

> When they have decided to fight a battle they generally vow to Mars the booty they hope to take, and after a victory they sacrifice the captured animals and collect the rest of the spoil in one spot. Among many of the tribes, high piles of it can be seen on consecrated ground; and it is an almost unknown thing for anyone to dare, in defiance of religious law, to conceal his booty at home or to remove anything placed on the piles. Such a crime is punishable by a terrible death under torture.

and that "In many states heaps of such objects are to be seen piled up in hallowed spots". One such was at Llyn Cerrig Bach in Anglesey, where over a considerable space of time iron and bronze objects came to light in peat-cuttings. These had evidently been put into a pool, not left out in the open. There were a few swords, all broken and none of particularly good quality, for their blades are narrow and of a weak and poorly defined section. Another such deposit was at Lisnacroghera in County Antrim, where some superlative scabbards came up, and a few smallish sword-blades.

In the later scabbards we find a new feature; all the decoration is put on the strap loop, which is now centrally placed with its ornamental terminals at top and bottom of the scabbard; so the sword must have been worn with the strap loop outwards, unlike all the earlier ones where the loop was on the inner side. A feature of these loops is that a narrow parallel-sided strip was extended above and below the loop itself to carry the ornamental terminals. This foreshadows the design of many scabbard mounts of the later Iron Age, in the first three centuries A.D. Another feature of these scabbards from Britain is that some have two decorative studs, often enamelled, fixed to the scabbard near the hilt; similar appendages have been found in very many of the northern swords right up to the Viking period (fig. 27).

Fig. 27. Decorative motif on scabbard of bronze from Lisnacroghera, first century B.C.

The British swords seem on the whole to be of later date than the Continental ones, few of them being earlier than about 150

58

B.C. The latest among them are perhaps the most interesting, though the decoration is degenerate, so poor in the complete example from Embleton in Durham (fig. 28b) that to call it cheap and nasty would be no exaggeration. However, the blades are good, obviously of Roman manufacture, and several specimens survive where the hilts are complete, or very nearly so. Two from the first century A.D. are illustrated in fig.

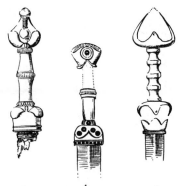

a   b   c

Fig. 28. Three swords from Britain, La Tène III (British Museum).

28a and c. These are really a distinct Romano-British type, not purely Celtic.

In the last chapter I described the Greek kopis. In this period of the last two centuries B.C. we find in Scandinavia and in north and north-east Germany (the lands originally occupied by the Burgundians) a weapon very similar in form to the Greek one, even to the rather odd-shaped hilt (fig. 29). It is, I think, very likely that these swords were derived from the kopis, because the regions where they seem to have been most in use are those whose trade-routes had always run along the southward trending rivers of east Germany and Poland (such as the Oder and the Vistula) into Pannonia, Dacia and Thrace, and whose people must have had a close connection with Greece. This sword type (it was called the Sax, and we shall hear more about it) remained almost unchanged in the north until the end of the Viking period, and survived throughout the Middle Ages as the falchion, and on into modern times under the guise of the sabre.

Fig. 29. Single-edged iron sword, third century B.C., from N. Germany.

59

Since we can trace the kopis' origin back to the ancient Egyptian Kopsh, there is little doubt that the cavalry sabre of modern times has a very respectable ancestry.

Before we leave the swords of this period, a word about the stuff they were made of would not be amiss. It is popularly supposed that steel was unknown until a much later date, but it has been shown by analysis that double shear steel was used for chariot tyres at Llyn Cerrig Bach, and this implies equally good steel for sword-blades. An interesting comment on the effectiveness of the Celtic swords comes from Plutarch, who says that Camillus, campaigning against the Gauls, was obliged hurriedly to have iron helmets made for most of his men in order to resist the Gallic swords.

Evidence for the specialized manufacture of these swords is given by the smith's marks punched on the blades of many of them. These marks are made in exactly the same way as bladesmiths' marks of the fourteenth to seventeenth centuries A.D.; they are stamped into the blade, usually near the hilt, but sometimes on the tang inside the hilt, by means of a punch. These *poinçons* take various forms, mostly naturalistic such as a boar or a crouching man. On a fragment of a pattern-welded blade from the Marne in the British Museum is a deeply imprinted stamp of a half-moon with a face in it, foreshadowing by eighteen centuries a popular German mark of the seventeenth century A.D. We shall meet with marks of this sort later on, together with some of a different kind, when we come to discuss the swords of the first three centuries A.D. which were found in the Danish bogs.

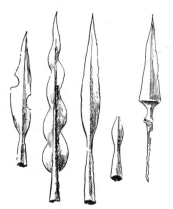

Fig. 30. Spears of the La Tène period.

A spear is a spear whether it is of the middle Bronze Age or the nineteenth century; there is little room for variation and the same shapes of spearhead crop up in every age and in every land. In the La Tène period, most spearheads were made in the same shapes and sizes as they had been before; only the decorative motifs were different. Some were large and leaf-shaped, some small and narrow

60

and some exactly like nineteenth-century lance-heads (fig. 30). One type seems peculiar to this period, with a wavy blade like a Malay Kris.

The shield of the La Tène period was generally oval. Several Gaulish statues show this quite clearly, and in the British Museum is a tiny pewter figure—like a mediaeval pilgrim badge—of a warrior armed with one of them. Two shields found in the bog-deposit at Hjortspring in Denmark (about 300 B.C.) are similar; they are made of wood and have elongated bosses in the centre like those on the monuments. Most of the shields seem to be quite plain and undecorated, but there are exceptions. In Britain there are two shields of the La Tène III period; both are oval in shape, but unlike the Continental ones they have a slight waist; one (found in the River Witham at Lincoln) is fairly large, 3 ft. 8 in. long, and the other found off Battersea in the Thames, is smaller; both are of bronze, and both are decorated. The bronze is only a very thin facing, which must originally have been backed by layers of leather. The importance of these shields is, however, in their decoration. The Witham shield is a fine example of that typically British ornament which is found on the scabbards, chariot trappings and torcs, but the Battersea shield is comparable as a work of art with the finest masterpieces of any age and in any medium. It is not just a superb piece of metalwork; it is a great work of art, and as such has to be judged by the same standards as we would apply to the Parthenon or Michaelangelo's "David". It is quite impossible to do justice to it by an attempt at description; until you see this beautiful thing face to face you cannot possibly appreciate its splendour. Even so there is nothing aggressively striking about it. It is not very big, nor has it any precious metal or jewelled inlay. Its colours are quiet, but the soft ruddy glow of the bronze and the dark crimson of the enamelled insets, combined with the effortless artistry of the design, make an unforgettable impression. Of all the arms of men which have come to light this is the most lovely. Something even finer may still be hidden for archaeologists of the future to find, but it will have to be very splendid to dislodge this shield from its place of honour (plate 2).

Throughout the Celtic Iron Age the noble warrior seems generally to have been chariot-borne in battle. Although most of the vehicles

61

found in the Hallstatt graves were four-wheeled wagons (like those in the Scythian tombs of between 600 and 100 B.C.) some were two-wheeled, and the picture of a two-wheeled chariot on the wall of a Bronze Age tomb in Sweden is clear indication that it was known in the tenth century B.C. in the north as well as the south of Europe. According to Polybius, the Gaulish method of fighting during the third century B.C. was not to press a charge of chariots right home as they did in Britain four centuries later; instead the warriors drove furiously along their enemies' front throwing missiles and making a tremendous and (they hoped) terrifying noise by blowing horns and shouting. After this demonstration they would dismount, their chariots being held in readiness for a quick retreat if necessary, while the warriors went forward on foot to deliver individual challenges to opposing champions, all in a manner strikingly reminiscent of the conduct of Homer's heroes in the *Iliad*.

Polybius, describing the battle of Telamon in 225 B.C. where the Gaulish tide was finally turned back from Italy, mentions a body of troops called Gesatae, a Celtic term meaning spear-men. This force is similar to the later "Fianna" of Ireland, an unattached body of picked warriors who led the roving life of a mercenary band with no specific tribal allegiance. A particular point about the Gesatae was that they fought naked. This seems to have been an old Celtic custom which gradually died out as sophistication spread through the tribes. We find the Cimbri doing this as late as 100 B.C. It was not done out of mere bravado but as an invocation to divine protection. The Viking Berserks behaved in a similar way a thousand years later.

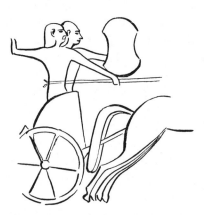

Fig. 31. Hittite chariot from the temple of Rameses III at Thebes.

Wherever men have fought in chariots the same method seems to have been used; the warrior attacks his foe with bow or javelin or with stabbing spear or sword at close quarters—in Britain often running out along the pole between the two horses to get as close as possible—while a second man (not a servant, but a younger man of social standing equal to his principal) controls the horses and covers the other with his shield. It is reasonable to think that such a method of fighting may have conditioned the shape of the shield. There is no doubt that in a chariot an elongated one like those from Battersea or the Witham would be more effective than a round one. It is interesting that in about 1200 B.C. the Hittites used shields in their chariots of a shape not unlike these British ones, with a distinct waist. Fig. 31 (from a bas-relief in the temple of Rameses III at Thebes) shows how they were used.

The shield, as we have seen from Tacitus' comments on the Germans, was particularly venerated; it was considered the ultimate disgrace to lose or abandon it. The same spirit is in the Spartan woman's injunction to her son to come back from battle "with your shield, or on it". Not all Greeks, however, lived up to the harsh Spartan ideal. The Ionian poet Archilochus cheerfully wrote:

> Some lucky Thracian has my noble shield;
> I had to run: I lost it in a wood.
> But I got clear away, thank God. So hang
> The shield. I'll get another, just as good.

The shield of classical Greece was circular or oval in shape, hollowed considerably to afford the best protection. Homeric descriptions of such shields suggest that they were made of bronze, probably backed by leather (though not with the hides of seven bulls, like Aias': these small shields had to be relatively light and mobile). The illustration of the paintings of an Attic vase of 480 B.C. (fig. 32) shows very clearly what these were like, inside and out, and how the warrior used them. The man on the left at the top is in a charging position; we can see the broad loop inside his shield through which his forearm passes; the smaller loop he would grip in his hand is hidden. We can see how hollow the shield is, like a great shallow bowl. The two men who are being attacked have no shields, but the one on the right has wrapped his short cloak over his left hand. (The small circular object slung on his neck is a hat, not a shield.) In the lower part of the picture two men with shields seem to be attacked by one with only a sword and a cloak. The one in the middle holds his shield out, completely covering his body, while the other looks

Fig. 32. Figures from a kylir, fifth century B.C., of Attic red-figure
ware (Boston Museum of Fine Arts).

very awkward, holding it out horizontally in this typical Greek
charging position.

Here, in two painted scenes, we have an admirable picture of the
arms of Greek warriors, and the way they used them; and, just as
we know that this is precisely how the Highlander bore his targe
and broadsword, we may surmise that in the same way the men of
the Bronze Age fought. The reason for the shield being held horizontally while charging—either at a walk or a run—should be fairly
obvious; if you try to run forward with a shield of this size held
vertically close to your body, you are going to hit its rim with your
knees. You hold it well away from you, in a position of instant
readiness for defence, with your sword held low and well back
ready for a thrust below your opponent's shield, or for an overarm
cut at his neck above it (plate 1).

The Roman legionary's shield was rather similar to the ancient
Egyptian's in shape and size; and not unlike the Celtic one; it was
rectangular, reaching from chin to knee and concave to the body.

For its purpose it was the most effective shape possible, though its use was strictly limited to infantry tactics. The Roman cavalryman carried a smaller, round shield, for the large rectangular one would have been quite unmanageable on a horse.

The helmets worn by the Celts seem to be of two distinct classes; one entirely native and the other mainly "classical". The native types are all variations of an ordinary skull-cap of bronze; some found in Britain have a long peak sticking out over the eyes in the manner of a jockey's cap; others found in the Marnian graves in France recall the tall Assyrian helmets, a

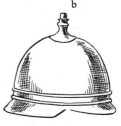

Fig. 33. Gaulish helmets.

skull-cap without any brim drawn out to a tall acute point (fig. 33a). One of these Marnian helmets is remarkably like the old 1914-style German *pikelhaube*, lacking only the spike (fig. 33c). Some helmets from northern Italy are more graceful in shape, and resemble the Italian "Celata" of the late fifteenth century. Here there is only a slight extension downwards of the rear lower edges of the helmet to protect the base of the skull. In the example shown, the lower edges are decorated in a manner which suggests an attempt to simulate hair emerging from beneath the helmet (fig. 33b).

Some of the most interesting of these Gaulish helmets are depicted in sculptures of the Roman period. Two from the triumphal arch at Orange are shown in fig. 34. These, as you can see, are basically Roman helmets, with the typical cheek-guards and backswept rear-plate protecting the neck, but the embellishments of horns and a wheel are entirely barbarian and of most ancient origin. The

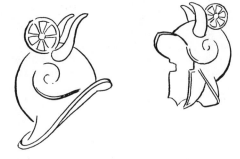

Fig. 34. *Gaulish helmets from the bas-reliefs on the arch at Orange.*

Bronze Age helmets from Viksö in Sweden have similar horns, and the wheel as we know was extensively used in the Bronze Age as a mystical symbol of great (though to us unknown) significance. We shall meet with it again all through this study of mediaeval arms; indeed, if we walk along the pavement edges of our cities and towns we may still come across it chipped as a mason's mark into the granite of the kerbstones, along with various other marks which we shall presently meet with inlaid in sword-blades of the Viking Age.

On the base of Trajan's Column are a number of helmets—captured Dacian trophies—of a type which seems to be a combination of the Roman helmet with neck- and cheek-guards and the conical Gaulish cap. Their skulls are made up from a framework of bands, one horizontally placed round the brow and two others fixed to it at front and back and at each side and crossing at the apex. The spaces between the bands were filled with plates (fig. 35). It is largely from these Romano-Gaulish helmets that the Frankish and Swedish helmets of the sixth and seventh centuries were derived. It is interesting that we find very similar ones in sixth-century Persia, almost indistinguishable from the Frankish helmets and clearly of the same ancestry.

The only body armour remaining from this period is mail; there were several pieces of it among the remains of chariots and other war-gear in a votive deposit of the La Tène III period found near Tiefenau in Switzerland in 1851. A statue of a Gaulish chief of the first century A.D. found at Vachères (Basses Alpes) wears a shirt of mail, and another is figured among the trophies of arms at Pergamum, and there is a third on the base of Trajan's Column. These garments all seem to have

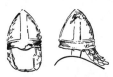

Fig. 35. *Dacian helmets from the bas-reliefs on the base of Trajan's Column.*

66

been of the same pattern, reaching half-way down the thigh with sleeves to the elbow and a round neck; a style which was fashionable until the eleventh century. It is unlikely that the Celtic people wore any other body-armour, for nothing has yet been found which suggests it. Of course they may have used various sorts of defences of leather, like the very effective seventeenth century "buff-coat", of which no trace would remain in the graves. From the comments of the Roman historians we gather that the barbarians did not rely overmuch on armour, though we may believe that they did not all go to the same lengths as the Cimbri, who at the beginning of a battle did not don their armour, but doffed their clothes and went into the fight stark naked—a practice which greatly impressed the Romans. The pewter barbarian in the British Museum wears either a short kilt or a pair of breeches, and cuffed gloves of something which may be meant to represent mail, or may be intended for overlapping scales of metal or horn sewn on to fabric.

We will leave the subject of the armour of the barbarians during the last two centuries B.C. with a question which carries us forward to the next period of the great migrations and the end of the Roman dominion in the West. In Scythian graves of the fourth century B.C. in south Russia at Kertch, Romny and Volkovici were found groups of narrow metal bands or staves, pierced at intervals for metal wires by which they were presumably pulled together until they overlapped. These seem to be pieces of armour made on the Lammelar principle like so much Oriental armour has always been. This Scythian armour is exactly like some which was found at Valsgärde in Sweden in a grave of the so-called "Vendel" period (c. 550–800); it is believed that this was old when it was put into the grave; if it were so, it would bring it back to a date perhaps as early as A.D. 450, some 800 years later than the Scythian stuff. We shall examine this armour in detail in its proper place, but it is perhaps not entirely profitless to speculate; if this sort of splinted armour was used by the Scythians as early as 400 B.C., might it not also have been known to the Celts of Gaul, Dacia and Pannonia? Until some definite evidence is found there can be no answer, but one of the exciting things about archaeology is that there is far more still in the ground than ever came out of it.

Part 2

THE HEROIC AGE

Chapter Four

THE GREAT MIGRATIONS

IN THE NEXT few chapters I shall have much to say about the Scandinavian peoples who spread out from Jutland and Scania and the southern Baltic to cover the whole of Europe—Burgundians, Goths and Vandals, Longobards and Franks, Angles and Saxons. During the first four centuries of the Christian era the migrations and wars of these peoples cut out the pattern from which the whole social, political and military structure of mediaeval Europe was built, yet most people know so little of them. The words "Goth" and "Vandal" are applied to hooligans, and the term "Gothic" to a style of architecture which owes nothing to the Goths, who had disappeared clean out of history 500 years before it first appeared. The derogatory application of these names was put upon them in terror by the late, decadent Romans who were everywhere defeated and overcome by the Goths and Vandals, better men in the main, though lacking the urban polish which still clung to Rome even in decline. The Goths were a great, vigorous people originating in the north, perhaps in south Sweden, who after dwelling and multiplying in the plains of Central Europe and south Russia for about twelve generations, or 300 years, finally overthrew the Roman Empire in the West with fighting methods and battle tactics which were in essence those of mediaeval chivalry. Nor is it generally realized that these people were of the same race as the Anglo-Saxons, who migrated westwards into Britain instead of southwards into Europe like the others.

This period of the Great Migrations used always to be called the "Dark Ages". Historically dark they certainly were, but much light has been shed upon them in the last fifty years, largely by the effects of archaeological research. This darkness was brought about to some extent by the historians of Rome who so brilliantly illuminated the doings of the Roman world that all outside it was hidden, by contrast, in positively cimmerian gloom. Even so, had the historians of the nineteenth century eyes to see, they would have observed that these classical historians, from Tacitus in the 70s and 80s to Procopius in the middle 500s, had something to say about the "barbarians" who dwelt to the north of their frontiers. Neither were the barbarians dumb, for although most of their folk-tales have been lost, much still remained and was available to scholars in the Norse Eddas and Sagas. Unfortunately these were treated as fairy tales like Homer's story of Troy. As the discoveries of Schleimann showed the *Iliad* to be true, so have the amazingly rich Scandinavian finds shown that most of the Norse story material was based on realities. Once this was recognized, this material could be compared with the comments of Roman and Greek writers, and a far clearer picture began to emerge. Now the Dark Ages are, as it were, dotted with an ever-growing number of lights, some still dim and faint but some very bright. The brightest are those which have been lit by discoveries concerning art and war, which were so closely related.

Before I go on to deal in detail with these matters, some sketch of the migrations should be attempted. We have chronologically divided history into two parts, called B.C. and A.D. This division has properly only a religious meaning, for it was caused by an event which, tremendous as it was, only applies to, and is applied by, Christendom. Rome once had her own standard of measuring time, from the date of the foundation of the city; Islam has its own chronology; so have the Jews—theirs the most ancient and unbroken of them all. Even so, Christendom's division of history into A.D.

and B.C. is, quite by chance, appropriate in a much wider sense. In the century during which Christ was born—what we should call between 50 B.C. and A.D. 50—the pattern of the ancient world fell in ruins, and the first shadowy outlines of a new one began to take shape.

In the first century B.C. there was, very broadly speaking, a situation in the world like this: the Mediterranean and much of the Middle East is almost entirely dominated by Rome. Carthage is destroyed, and North Africa and Spain are Roman provinces; Greece has lost all traces of her independence. The 3,000-year-old civilization of Egypt is in the final stages of senile decrepitude, ruled by the last ineffectual sovereigns of the dynasty founded by Alexander's ablest commander, Ptolemy Euergetes. Babylonia and Assyria are no more, and even the once mighty Persia is in decline. To the northward the vast lands of Central Europe, as well as Gaul and Britain, are peopled by the Celts. Though these warlike and highly civilized people have no political coherence, their tribes form a sort of vast loosely-knit empire, of which Gaul and Helvetia are the heart. To the north and east of Gaul, along the right bank of the Rhine, dwell the German tribes, savage, aggressive and mysterious. To the north and east again, cut off from Rome's influence by the great marshes and forests of Germany, are other peoples of whom Rome knows nothing, though four centuries later she will come to know their descendants all too well.

Such, very roughly, was the position when in 58 B.C. a whole people, the Helvetii, one of the most civilized and influential tribes of the Gauls, decided to leave their homeland. (We have met with them before, for they are the people with whom the La Tène culture began, who we may presume were the principal manufacturers and suppliers of arms and metal-work to the Celts.) This was the movement which set off the train of events which ended with the conquest of Gaul by Julius Caesar.

This in its turn opened the gates for the great slow tide of tribes to move down into the Central European plains; with the subjugation of Gaul the loosely-knit dominion of the Celtic peoples crumbled, for Gaul was its heart. Now the Romans stood all along the Rhine, face to face with the Germans, those primitive, ferocious people whose only trade was war. Along the Danube Rome faced other tribes, the Alani and Sarmatians, semi-nomadic horse-breeding people who were successors in these regions of the Scythians.

Then, as Gaul prospered, growing in wealth and culture under Roman rule, the Celts of Austria and south Germany tended to move westwards so that they, too, could share the comfort and prosperity of their kinsmen. Their warriors were enlisted into the Roman forces, joining up with the Gallic auxiliaries. So a sort of power vacuum was created in the heart of Europe. Meanwhile, when these things were going on, the northern peoples were on the move. A tribe called the Burgundians occupied territory on the south Baltic opposite the island of Burgundarholm—Bornholm we call it now—from whence they had come. A little to the eastward another tribe had settled, the Longobards. We shall meet them six hundred years later in France and northern Italy. The name Longobard has usually been taken as meaning long-beard, a connotation given to it by German-orientated scholars. It is more likely that it means "long axe", just as "Halbard" may mean "flat axe".[1] At a time when most barbarians wore long beards—does not the very word mean bearded ones?—a warlike and conquering tribe would more reasonably be named after its own particular weapon.

During the first century both Burgundians and Longobards began to move southward, while still further to the east, where Danzig now is, the Goths (who it is thought had occupied those lands since perhaps 250 B.C.) started on the long wanderings which were to take them to Italy and Spain, and to end in the complete domination of the Roman Empire which imposed their style of fighting upon the whole of Europe for a thousand years.

Such was the position when, in the first half of the first century A.D., the "great migrations" began. These movements are so complex that the simplest way to convey an idea of them is to outline the principal movements of each group, starting with the Anglo-Saxons, whose occupation of Britain had no significant effect upon the art of war, and ending with the Goths and Lombards, whose complete overthrow of the Roman Empire in the West most definitely did. The westward movement of the Angles, Saxons and Jutes did not start in a large way until the fifth century, though it seems pretty certain that settlers in considerable numbers had been in

[1] Though this has often been asserted, it is by no means certain that it is so.

Britain long before that, and we have many accounts by Roman writers of raids carried out by Saxons. Eutropius in his *Breviarum Historiae* says:

> About this time [A.D. 237] Carausias ... was appointed to Bononia [Boulogne] to reduce to quiet the coast regions of Belgica and Armorica, which were overrun by the Franks and the Saxons.

He also records that the Saxons dwelt along the coast and in the marshes of the Great Sea. Later, Ammianus Marcellinus, writing in about 390, says: "The Picts and Saxons, Scots and Attacotti constantly harassed the Britons." Claudianus asserts that they raided as far as the Orkneys. "The Orcades," he writes tersely, "are moist from the slain Saxon."

The starting-point of the Longobards seems to have been from country a little to the eastward of the Saxons; they moved slowly southward, making little impression upon history until the sixth century, when they settled in northern Italy in 568 under their chief Alboin. The fact that they were very closely akin to the Angles and Saxons is shown by the great similarity of the Anglo-Saxon and Lombard languages.

The Franks were the most barbarous and uncouth of all the Teutonic races, and they covered the shortest distance; they were ruled for 250 years by the Merovings, the most bloody and ineffectual dynasty which has ever disgraced a nation, and yet in spite of that they gave their name to the finest flower of mediaeval Europe. During those 250 years of Merovingian rule the Franks were very much less of a menace to the failing Empire than Goths or Vandals, but they in the end overcame or absorbed all the other races—though Goths and Vandals had disappeared from the scene by then—when Charles the Great welded them into the Frankish Empire. They were a confederation of these German tribes of whom Tacitus wrote, who simply crossed the Rhine into Gaul, following up the earlier raids and ravagings of the Alemanni who had broken in when the Roman grip was failing. The fact that it was the Franks who ultimately ruled the whole of Europe and gave their name to its greatest state is hard to equate with their original crudity. The answer is twofold. The original Frankish conquerors of Roman Gaul were comparatively few in number, and they soon (in a generation

73

or two) became fairly well mixed with the Romano-Gaulish population, except for the ruling class who remained completely Teutonic; this had a civilizing effect on the majority of the Frankish people, though the Merovingian rulers were from start to finish an appalling and utterly barbarous lot. Even so, in time this worthless dynasty came to an end, and gave place to an entirely different family. Charles Martel was the first of them, but the one who forged almost all Europe into one mighty whole was Charles—Carolus Magnus—Charlemagne, Emperor of the West. Through this remarkable man the Franks became in the eighth century the dominant power in Europe, but they only did it because Charles absorbed all that was best of other migrated people, the Goths and Longobards, grafting their military system upon the native Frankish one.

The Vandals were the most far-travelled, and for a time the most successful, of the migrants. We know nothing definite of their origin; they appeared in north Germany at about the same time as the Longobards, early in the first century A.D., and settled by the river Oder; they stayed there for nearly as long a time as the Longobardi occupied their first settlements to the south-west of them. They themselves said that they came from Scandinavia, but they lived by the Oder for nearly four centuries, or about twenty generations—a long enough time in one place to make it seem like a permanent home. It is only in the early years of the fifth century that we hear of them migrating westward. On New Year's night between A.D. 405 and 406 they crossed the Rhine and began their great journey. They were led by a most energetic chieftain, Geiseric, who took them southwards through Gaul and Spain as far as the Mediterranean, where in a district which still bears their name— Andalusia—they settled for twenty years, from 409 to 429. Then Geiseric led them across the Straits of Gibraltar into North Africa, to the conquest of the old Romano-Carthaginian province, and the establishment of the astonishing Vandal Empire, which soon became a state every bit as rich and cultured as the great Phoenician civilization of Carthage. This in a way instituted a sort of Viking period in the Mediterranean, for the Vandals were a seafaring folk who sailed all over it on raids very reminiscent of the later Viking raids in the north, or those of their successors on that shore, the Barbary pirates. Their empire soon became a dreaded power which in 455 captured

Rome itself. In 533 it collapsed, defeated by Justinian's great general Belisarius, and the Vandals disappeared from history. Only their name remained, as it does to this day, a word for terror and destruction, a telling reminder of the fearful effect they had on the shrinking Roman world.

The Goths first begin to emerge into the light of history during the reign of Caracalla (c. A.D. 215) when they were already a very powerful race who had dwelt for generations on the plains of eastern Poland and Russia. Their place of origin is as vague as that of the other races, but it is probable that they came from southern Sweden; at all events, according to Pytheas they left this region in about 300 B.C. and passed over the seas to settle in the land where northern Poland is to-day. In A.D. 275 they occupied Dacia, and from that time on settled between the Don and the Danube, where the western group became known as the Visigoths, and the eastern group as the Ostrogoths. The Ostrogoths spread far into western Asia, occupying the territory which had been the land of the Scythians in the last six centuries before Christ. In the year 376 an event of great historical importance occurred. The Visigoths, who had often made raids across the lower Danube against the Romans, now appeared as suppliants; they said that a terrible race whom they were powerless to withstand had invaded their territories. They sought the permission of the Emperor Valens for their people to cross the Danube and settle in Thrace, promising that they would always be faithful allies to the Roman state. Valens (who ruled the eastern half of the Empire) granted this permission on the condition that they came unarmed, gave up their children as hostages and were baptized into the Christian faith. Assenting to these conditions the entire nation (said to have been about a million strong) was allowed to cross the river.

The enemy who had so terrified the Goths was a race of nomadic horsemen, the Hiong-Nu, who had for centuries been roaming in the deserts of North China. They had been gradually pushed westwards by the Han dynasty Emperors of China in wars which lasted from about 207 B.C. to A.D. 39. Gradually moving on, they eventually crossed the Volga, and by the end of the fourth century they were well down into Europe.

Scarcely had the Visigoths settled in Thrace when their kinsmen the Ostrogoths, fleeing in their turn from the Huns (as the Hiong-Nu were called in Europe) appeared in their turn by the Danube, seeking a new home in safety to the south of it. Valens, alarmed already at the vast number of barbarians within the boundaries of the Empire, refused to let them cross; whereupon they crossed just the same, not unarmed and in peace, but armed to the teeth, determined to put the Danube between the Huns and themselves at any price. No sooner were they across than the Visigoths threw off their allegiance to Rome and joined them. Valens sent to Gratian, Emperor of the West, for help; then, gathering the entire available forces in the eastern Empire, marched into Thrace to cope with the situation. Gratian was hurrying to the help of his colleague when he heard of his defeat and death at the battle of Adrianople (378), of which we shall hear more. He at once appointed as his associate Theodosius, afterwards known as the Great, and entrusted him with the government of the eastern provinces.

Theodosius recognized the impossibility of getting rid of the Goths, so he set about the task of absorbing them into the fabric of the Empire instead. While Theodosius held sway in Constantinople the Goths were peaceably contained within the state, but after his death in 395 they began their wanderings again. First the Visigoths, led by Alaric, moved southwards from Moesia and Thrace. They poured through the pass of Thermopylae and devastated almost the whole of the Greek peninsula, but they were driven out again by Stilicho, the commander-in-chief of the West Roman armies. His success in ridding Greece of the Goths only made matters worse, for they did not return to Thrace, but crossed the Julian Alps and spread terror and destruction in Italy. Stilicho cautiously followed, and succeeded in defeating them at Pollentia and again at Verona. Alaric gathered the remains of his army and retreated through the passes of the Alps.

But while Italy was celebrating her triumph over the Goths, far worse things were brewing in the north. In about 400, masses of Germanic tribes—Burgundians, Longobardi, Suevi, Vandals and Heruli—streamed across the Alps into northern Italy. The alarm caused by this invasion was far greater than that inspired by the Goths, who were at least Christians (even though they were Arian

76

heretics), whereas these fresh hordes under their leader the Longobard Radagaisus were not. By vigorous efforts Stilicho raised an army. In 406 Radagaisus was besieging Florence with about 20,000 warriors; Stilicho surrounded them and was able to starve them into surrender.

Fig. 36. Sword from an ivory bas-relief on one wing of a diptych commemorating Stilicho (cf. fig. 45).

Soon after this, the able and victorious commander-in-chief came under the suspicion of the Emperor, the futile and ridiculous Honorius, who had him murdered. Having thus deprived the Western Empire of its only capable leader, Honorius went one step further. He provoked the 30,000 Gothic mercenaries in the Roman army to mutiny by treacherously massacring their families, who were held as hostages. Alaric and his people, who were waiting their chance beyond the Alpine passes, raced back into Italy, joined the mutineers and led the combined forces to the gates of Rome. They laid siege to the city, and very soon the Romans were asking for terms. Alaric left them with their lives, but very little else; he retired into Etruria, where his army was constantly reinforced by bands of Burgundian, Longobardic and Herulian warriors—those who had been enslaved after Radagaisus' defeat in 406. He asked for lands upon which his followers could settle, but Honorius in his usual absurd way treated all his requests—which were in the circumstances very reasonable—with contempt. So Alaric turned again towards Rome, determined this time to make an end. One night in August 410 Alaric's hosts broke into the city, "and the inhabitants were awakened by the tremendous sound of Gothic trumpets". Precisely 800 years had passed since its sack by the Gauls.

Having thoroughly plundered the city, Alaric led his warriors southwards, intending to cross into Sicily and thence to North Africa (which was as yet—in 410—unconquered by the Vandals). The project was prevented by his death.

By now the ruin of the West Roman Empire was almost complete. In his efforts to defend Italy from the Goths, Stilicho had withdrawn every available fighting unit from the outlying parts of the Empire. In 410 the last legion left Britain, and even the fortresses of Gaul were drained of men. The passages of the Rhine were left unguarded—and, of course, the barbarians beyond swarmed across into Gaul. The Vandals pushed right on into Spain and Africa; the Goths, having pillaged Italy to the dregs, re-crossed the Alps and settled in southern Gaul, forming a strong Visigothic kingdom, while to the north-eastwards the Burgundians founded that great power which was to be so important a factor in European politics for centuries to come.

Then for about 200 years there was a lull. Honorius fortunately died in 423, and the general Aetius, Stilicho's successor, was entrusted with the defence of Gaul, whose frontiers he kept from further violations for a couple of decades. Then in the middle of the fifth century the worst terror of all fell upon the Empire. The Huns were on the move again, this time not as a slowly-moving tide of people looking for land, but as a vast organized army under a capable leader. This was Attila, "The Scourge of God". He defeated the armies of the Eastern Emperor and took tribute from Constantinople. Then he turned westwards and crossed the Rhine into Gaul. The Romans and their Gothic conquerors united in the face of the common danger. The Visigoths under their king Theodoric, with Franks and Burgundians, rallied to the standard of Aetius, but even so many of their kinsmen fought with Attila— Longobards, Heruli and Ostrogoths among them. Huns and Romans met near Châlons in 451; the conflict was long and terrible, and though the immediate result seemed to be inconclusive, this was none the less one of the decisive battles of the world. Attila and the remains of his army (contemporary reports—always grossly exaggerated—put its numbers at about 400,000 men, of whom about 200,000 were said to have fallen at Châlons) retired across the Rhine. He left Gaul in peace, but northern Italy suffered again. He threatened Rome, but Pope Leo the Great persuaded him—with the aid of a large bribe from the Emperor—to leave Italy. Added to these persuasions was the fact that plague was devastating his army, so Attila led his Huns northward across the Alps again. Soon after, in 453, he died. Without his vigorous leadership, the Huns scattered and were absorbed by the people they had conquered. Their only lasting monument is the name of the country where they settled most thickly—Hungary.

No sooner had Attila left Italy than Rome had to face a new danger, this time from the south. In 455 Geiseric with a Vandal fleet sailed up the Tiber. Again the great Leo went out to intercede for the city; Geiseric granted the Pope the lives of the citizens, but said that the plunder of the city belonged to him and his warriors. For fourteen days and nights the sack went on; everything of value was taken (it seems quite incredible that anything of value could have been left), and from the Capitol were lifted the great golden candlesticks together with much other treasure which Titus had taken from the Temple at Jerusalem.

The twenty years following Geiseric's raid are a melancholy record of puppet emperors set up by various tribes of the Germanic invaders of Italy. The end came when in 475 a general named Orestes raised his own son, Romulus Augustus, to the purple. He was only six years old, and was known as Augustulus (little Augustus); he reigned for a year, his only claim to fame being that he was the very last of the Roman Emperors of the West. In 476 a Herulian chief named Odovacar dethroned him and abolished the title of Emperor, taking upon himself the government of Italy. At this, the Senate sent an embassy to Constantinople, taking with them the imperial vestments and insignia of office. They told the Emperor Zeno that the West was willing to give up its title to have an emperor of its own, and to request that Odovacar, with the title of Patrician, might rule Italy as his viceroy. This was granted, and Italy became a province of the Empire of the East.

Odovacar was not to enjoy his power for long, for in 493 he was overcome by Theodoric the Ostrogoth, who had brought a large force of Goths from Illyria. Theodoric had spent much of his youth at the court of Constantinople, and was familiar with Roman ways. He and his Goths were for many years vassals of Constantinople, but finally they fell out with the Emperor and left the country. The struggle between the Ostrogoths and the mixed forces under the Herulian Odovacar went on for several years, but finally Odovacar surrendered and was shut up, and finally done to death, in Ravenna.

Meanwhile the main mass of the Visigoths, you will remember, had founded a kingdom in southern Gaul, after helping the Romans to defeat Attila. This kingdom, with its capital at Toulouse, included Gaul between the Loire and the Rhone and all of Spain except a bit of the north-west. It attained its greatest strength and prosperity under Euric (466–485). These Visigoths were Arians, and the orthodox Franks (their neighbours to the northward) regarded them as heretics; in 507 they attacked the Visigoths, whose king, Alaric II, was killed in battle. Gaul was lost to them, but a small Visigothic kingdom persisted in Spain until 711. It is an interesting historical parallel that in the early thirteenth century the Catholic French made a similar attack—the damnable "Albigensian Crusades" —upon the heretic "Albigenses" of Provence, who were tainted with a similar heresy to that of their Visigothic ancestors.

Theodoric the Great's rule in Italy was a time of peace and returning order and prosperity. He was nominally only a viceroy under the Eastern Emperor, but in fact he was an independent ruler. He extended his protection to the Spanish kingdom, partly because he was the brother-in-law of Alaric II and grandfather of his successor, Amalric. He succeeded in ruling over two separate races, Goths and Italians (not to mention the mixture of odd families and groups of Longobards, Suevi, Burgundians and so on, who still dwelt in Italy). Each race lived under its own laws, and it seemed as though a new period of greatness, under a new imperial dynasty, was before Italy.

However, this was not to be. Theodoric died in 526, and in 527 Justinian became Emperor in Constantinople. He was an unpleasant individual, but had the curious power that so many unpleasant rulers have had to attract to himself the most able and admirable servants—like Charles VII of France, the unreliable and quite despicable monarch who was boosted on to the throne by Joan of Arc, and who acquired the nickname of *Charles le bien servi* in spite of his personal qualities. Justinian had the good fortune to have as the commander-in-chief of his forces first Belisarius, and then that surprising personage, the eighty-year-old eunuch Narses. He also had as his consort the redoubtable Theodora, whose personality may have been the chief factor in keeping the loathsome Justinian, who constantly betrayed his generals in the field, and was hated and despised by his people, firmly seated on his Imperial throne. His great desire was to be known to posterity as "The

Great", and to further that end he determined that North Africa and all of Italy must return to Roman rule. Belisarius easily overthrew the Vandals in 534—they were ruled then by Geilimer, a chieftain of different mettle to his predecessor Geiseric. Italy proved to be a very much tougher proposition, for the Goths put up a prolonged and magnificent resistance. They were by this time a first-class military power, but Belisarius, and Narses after him, could outgeneral them every time. In 553 they were so completely beaten that they agreed to leave Italy with all their families and movable possessions.

This was absolute disaster for Italy. Justinian, Belisarius and Narses all died within months of each other in 563, and in 565 all of North Italy was overrun by the Longobards, or Lombards as they came to be called. For generations they had adopted the military usages of the Goths, whose close relatives they were. They occupied the region north of the River Po (called Lombardy ever since) and extended their power southwards; but they were not able to conquer Rome and southern Italy, which remained a province of the Eastern Empire. As time went on the heathen Lombards adopted the religion and culture of the people among whom they lived. For about 200 years the Lombard kings ruled from Pavia, wearing the famous iron crown that had been made in 591 for King Agilulf—partly, it was said, from a nail of the True Cross. In 636 Rothari became king, and reduced the Lombardic laws to a written code. In 652 the crown was seized by Grimoald, Duke of Benevento. An able soldier, he repelled attacks made by the Emperor (Constans II) and by the Franks and the Avars, but soon after his death in 672 a series of revolts began. In 712 Luitprand, probably the ablest of the Lombard kings, came to the throne and reigned until 743. The last king, Desiderius, came to blows with the Pope (in 773) who appealed to Charlemagne. The Frankish king thereupon invaded Italy, beat the Lombards, made an end of their kingdom and assumed the Iron Crown himself.

The Visigothic dominion in Spain lasted longer than any of the other Teutonic kingdoms, for after the death of Alaric II and the Visigothic retirement into Spain, it suffered no serious invasion till the Arabs came in 711. Its greatest king, Leovigild, who began to reign in 568, won back much of the south from the Romans and extended his domain considerably. His son Reccared strengthened his position by forsaking Arianism and embracing the Orthodox faith, after which the Goths rapidly became Romanized.

A succession of kings, all elected, succeeded Reccared. Ruling from Toledo, they made Spain the most flourishing of the new Teutonic kingdoms. Their fall came when the Moors began to attack their coasts. In a great battle (it lasted for a week) near Cadiz their whole army was destroyed, and the king, Roderic, was never seen again.

The Great Migrations can be said to have come to an end with the Lombardic invasion of Italy. After that, Europe more or less settled down to be ruled from end to end by monarchs who were all of the same stock and in many cases closely related to one another. The material was there for a new empire, but a German, not a Roman one. For a short time such an empire existed, for Charles the Great (surely more truly deserving the title than any other ruler before or since) welded nearly all Europe into a political whole; having done so, he assumed the crown and title of Roman Emperor, in St. Peter's Church in Rome on Christmas Day in the year 800. He was the first of a line of rulers of the Holy Roman Empire, which, as Voltaire said, was neither holy, Roman, nor an empire. His death, in 814, marked in effect its end, for its various parts were ruled by his sons; though nominally subject to the new Emperor (Louis the Debonair) they rapidly threw off their allegiance, and by the end of the ninth century the states of mediaeval Europe had taken shape—France, Germany, Italy and Spain, each with its own ruler. The Empire continued in an almost nominal way down to our own time. The only Emperor after Charles the Great who really held sway over the greater part of Europe was another Charles, the fifth of the name, and his dominion was not by reason of his being the Emperor, but because he inherited the throne of Spain and the Dukedom of Burgundy as well as the Empire.

Chapter Five

ROME IN DECLINE: THE GOTHIC CAVALRY

THE MOVEMENTS OF the Indo-Europeans must have been very like these Germanic folk migrations, the gradual spread of a vigorous race whose impact affected the whole of the civilized world. As the Indo-Europeans transformed the ancient world's conception of war by introducing the battle-chariot, so in the same way the Goths transformed their world by the introduction of the heavy cavalryman—the weapon of impact in a new form. We tend to think of the mediaeval knight as a terrible portent of war suddenly appearing for the first time on the field of Senlac in 1066, but in fact this portent made its first appearance seven centuries before Senlac, on a field far bloodier, and as decisive to the Roman Empire as Senlac was to Saxon England. When the Roman army of the East was destroyed at Adrianople in A.D. 378, the old days of the legions' supremacy had gone for ever, and the armoured cavalryman fighting with lance and sword on a heavy horse became for the next 1,100 years the arbiter of war.

This battle was the most crushing defeat suffered by Roman arms since Cannae; for the Emperor, all his chief officers and 40,000 men—practically the whole army of the East—perished on that afternoon.

The political event which led to the battle was Valen's refusal to allow the Ostrogoths to cross the Danube and settle in peace with their Visigothic kinsmen who had crossed into Thrace in 376; its military importance was unmistakable, for it was a victory of heavy cavalry over infantry—the first since the Indo-European chariots had overthrown the forces of the ancient powers in fights of which we know nothing. The archaeological importance was also parallel,

83

for as the art of chariot-fighting set the pattern of war and its implements for more than a thousand years, so did the rise to supremacy of the heavy cavalryman. The battle itself was a terrible affair. The Imperial army found the Goths encamped in a vast "laager" of wagons. Arranging his host in the time-honoured Roman fashion with the legions massed in the centre and the *alae*, squadrons of auxiliary horse, on the wings, Valens attacked the Gothic defences, thinking that they contained the whole of their force. Unhappily for Rome he was wrong, for the bulk of the Gothic horse was away on a large-scale foraging expedition. They had not gone far, however, and as soon as the battle started messengers were sent to rally the scattered parties and recall them as a united force to the field. The fight was raging all along the barricades when suddenly this great detachment charged down upon the Roman left. The cavalry had wasted no time; riding straight for the battle, they crashed down upon the Romans; "like a thunderbolt", writes Ammianus Marcellinus, "which strikes upon a mountain-top and dashes away all that stands in its path."

The squadrons guarding the Roman flank were taken unawares; some stood fast, and were ridden down, though most of them bolted. The Goths swept on down upon the exposed infantry, rolled it up and drove it in upon the centre. Under this terrific pressure the legions were crushed together in hopeless confusion; within a few minutes left, centre and reserve were mixed up in one seething mass. They made a few attempts to stand, but all were broken; Imperial guards, light troops, lancers, auxiliaries and legions of the line were flung together in a confusion that grew worse and worse, for when they saw their cavalry's success the Goths burst out of their wagon-laager and fell upon the Romans in front. Then the cavalry of the Roman right flank saw that the battle was lost. They rode off the field, followed by such individuals of the centre as could break away. Then the abandoned foot-soldiery of the centre realized the ghastly position they were in; beset in flank and rear by the cavalry and in front by the Gothic foot, they had no chance to get away. They simply had to stand wedged together until they were cut down. They were so tightly packed they could not raise their arms to strike a blow; the dead and wounded could not fall, but stayed upright in the weltering mass; many were simply crushed to death or stifled. Into this horrible confusion rode the Goths, slashing and stabbing with their long swords at the helpless Romans. Two-thirds of the men in this army had died before the pressure eased enough to allow stragglers to get out and run for it. When darkness fell a few thousand managed to get off and follow the fleeing cavalry to the south.

Such was the first great victory won by heavy cavalry, which had now shown unmistakably that it must supplant the Roman infantry as the ruling power in war. How was it done? Why did the Goths develop into such formidable cuirassiers, sweeping all the forces of Rome before them for more than a century? Because of two things: one, that by dwelling for generations on the plains of south Russia and Central Europe they had become horsemen; and two, by reason of a simple and obvious piece of equestrian equipment, stirrups, without which horsemen could never have fought as the Goths and their successors did, in heavy armour with lance and sword. Their origin is obscure; it is generally known that Greeks and Romans never used them, and that the Norsemen did. Apart from that simple distinction, no one bothers very much about their early history; however, we can narrow this generalization down a good deal—as it stands it leaves a gap of about five centuries—for there is evidence both literary and pictorial to show that they originated in the East as early as the fourth century B.C., and were an essential item in the military equipment of a conquering race at the very beginning of the Christian era. In the sculptures of the great Buddhist Stupa at Sanchi we find carvings of the second century before Christ where horsemen appear riding with stirrup loops, and similarly on a copper vessel of rather later date from northern India. Then from south Russia comes a magnificent jug made of Electrum, found in a Scythian tomb at Chertomlyk. It is of Greek workmanship of the fourth century B.C., and has engraved round its shoulders a frieze showing various incidents of horse management—Scythian horse-management, not Greek; for though the Chertomlyk jug is of Greek workmanship, it was made for the Scythian market. One horse's saddle is clearly furnished with stirrups or stirrup loops. This may be an isolated case, for there is evidence to show that the Scythians, wonderful horsemen though they were, never used stirrups to any great extent—and they were driven from their land eventually for lack of them. At some time around the year of Our Lord's birth, a race of people moving westwards across the steppes of Central Asia (driven from their home by the first westward movement of the Hiong-Nu, or Huns as they were known in Europe) began to press upon the Scythians. They, too, were horsemen, but they rode heavier animals and their use of stirrups enabled them to fight in armour and with heavier weapons. They were the Sarmatians, and because of their better weapons and more effective methods of fighting, they were able to overcome the Scythians and occupy all the land they had held. These Sarmatians (who were of the same Central Asian stock as the Scythians) were the people displaced in the third century A.D. by the Goths. The Goths ousted the Sarmatians without bringing new weapons or battle tactics; they were probably just better fighters—at least their later record suggests that they must have been. Once they settled down in these horse-breeding regions, they rapidly adopted the customs and acquired the warlike skills of the people in them, while from their own lands in the north they brought a long and heroic tradition of ferocity and efficiency, together with the most excellent weapons. All these Scandinavian wanderers were extremely vigorous people, inquiring and energetic of mind as well as powerful of body; when to their natural abilities were added the traditions and skills of two invincible styles of fighting a very formidable military machine resulted. To say that the whole of the mediaeval military system was based upon the use of stirrups seems a most sweeping generalization, but it is none the less true. None of the deeds of arms of the Goths and their knightly successors could have been done by men riding with their feet unsupported; it is worth pondering on the vast effect of such a seemingly trivial bit of equipment.

The arms of all the wandering Germanic folk during the first five centuries A.D. were very much alike, just as in the first three centuries B.C. the arms of the Celtic people throughout Europe were alike. All of them were made in the same few centres of production and most were decorated with similar art-forms and techniques. Blade-making by its very nature must have been a very rare and specialized craft, probably carefully protected, a closely guarded "mystery" known only to a few families. We know that the Celts were the first great workers in iron, the originators of the intricate and beautiful art of making pattern-welded blades. It is reasonable to suppose, and there are some scraps of supporting evidence, that the Celtic smiths continued to make swords for their Teutonic conquerors in the early part of the Migration period. Some of the names found stamped on blades of the first two centuries have a Celtic origin, though the later ones of the Viking period are purely Teutonic. Be that as it may, the traditions of the Celts survived, possibly in their original home on the Danube in the region where Passau now is, and certainly in the regions of the Rhine and Moselle.

Throughout the period of the migrations and the following Viking Age there was a style of decorative art which pervaded the whole of Europe. It originated with the Scythians, and was adopted by the Scandinavians, both those who stayed at home and those who wandered, when the Scythians were dispersed northward and westward by the advancing Sarmatians. It was based on animal forms, the most popular and widespread motifs being a sort of conventional bird of prey and an elongated snake-like animal form which by complex interlacing appears to devour itself. These forms were applied to pretty well every object which needed embellishment; among the warrior races of Scandinavians, Goths and Vandals these were mostly weapons and personal ornaments, but among the more civilized—or at least more literate—peoples, such as the Celts in Ireland, and Anglo-Saxons and Franks after the sixth century, it was very much used in the decoration of manuscripts.

During the fifth century a technique of decoration was developed, sometimes allied to these "zoomorphic" or animal designs, which also covered the whole area of the Germanic migrations. Its finest and most skilfully made examples have been found in England, so much so that it has been suggested that it may have originated here, among the Jutes in Kent, but it is far more probable that it, too, was Scythian. It consisted of the application of decorative designs by means of small pieces of semi-precious stone (mostly garnets) or coloured glass held together in cells or "cloisons" of gold or bronze. At its worst, it produced decoration of barbaric splendour, but at its best it was jewellers' work of an elegance and beauty which could rival anything produced before or since.

We shall find these zoomorphic designs and this cloisonné technique applied to arms of all kinds from the fifth century to the eighth, from Vendel in Sweden to North Africa and from Ireland to south Russia; that makes it difficult to attribute any particular sword-hilt or shield boss to any particular people within this area unless we know its find-place. On the other hand, we can say with some assurance that weapons found in one part of the area are probably very similar to those used in another—which is a good thing, for vast and very rich finds have been unearthed in the pagan north, while in the Christian south very few objects have come to light. This was because in the period between the first and eighth centuries Goths, Burgundians, Vandals, Saxons, Franks—all the Germanic peoples—became Christianized and gave up the habits of their pagan ancestors of burying arms with the dead or placing hoards of captured gear in sacrificial deposits. But, fortunately for archaeology, those of them that stayed behind in Scandinavia remained pagan and practised these admirable customs until the late eleventh century; in tomb after tomb as well as in the great Danish bog-deposits great numbers of swords, spears and saxes and several helmets, byrnies and shields have been found. These range from the first century to the seventh, and upon them we can base our theories as to the weapons of the conquerors of the Empire.

Chapter Six

THE BOG-DEPOSITS OF DENMARK

BEFORE DESCRIBING IN detail some of the arms found in the Danish bogs, it might be well to glance at the discoveries themselves, for the deposits contained a great variety of objects. From these we can see how people dressed, and we learn much about their riding equipment, agricultural implements, household gear, cooking utensils, wagons and tools, as well as ships and boats and all that goes with them. A lot of these things were of Greek and Roman origin, and many Roman coins were found which supply evidence of date. The state of preservation of most of the objects is remarkable, despite the fact that such a large number of them have been deliberately ruined; they give us cause to wonder at the costly magnificence of these prehistoric warriors' war-gear, though they only bear out the descriptions of such things in the Norse tales. The earliest of these is *Beowulf*, rich in vivid expression of the warrior's love of this arms; never is helm or byrnie mentioned but the poet qualifies it with loving description. For instance:

> Bright were their byrnies, hard and hand-linked,
> In their shining armour the bright mail rang,
> As the troop in their war-gear tramped to the hall,
> The sea weary sailors set down their shields,
> Their wide, bright bucklers along the wall
> And sank to the bench; their byrnies rang
> Their stout spears stood in a stack together,
> Shod with iron and shaped of ash.

Here is not only the feeling for arms, but very useful description as well. Again archaeology has proved that all these pieces of equipment, which in the poem may sound quite imaginary, really existed —do exist still, many of them—exactly as described. For instance:

> Boar heads glittered on glistening helmets
> Above their cheek-guards, gleaming with gold
> Bright and fire-hardened the boar held watch
> Over the column of marching men.

Very poetic; and one might be pardoned for taking it as poetic nonsense. No need, though, to go farther than the British Museum to see a helmet exactly as described here, boar heads, cheek-guards, gold and all (plate 4).

At a time when "chain mail" was thought by antiquarians to be an oriental invention of about A.D. 1100, the many expressions in the poem descriptive of body-armour, such as "hard and hand-linked" or "his war-net woven by cunning of smith" seemed to make no sense. We know now perfectly well what it was—a shirt of interlinked iron rings, a fabric known as *mail*. Not chain-mail; this expression, hallowed though it may be by a century of common usage, is not the word for the thing at all. Mail means a net—"his breast-net"—and is derived from the Latin *macula*, a mesh or net; it was used in mediaeval Italian as Maglia; the French called it Mailles, and we anglicized it into mail. There is no such thing as chain mail, or chain armour, any more than there can be any such thing as "plate-mail". I make this digression deliberately, for we shall hear a great deal more about mail; it is best to clear up this tautologous "chain-mail" nonsense right away.

There are other descriptions which until recently have proved even more baffling. What was one to make of "the battle-blade with its scrolled design" or "with spiral etching and twisted hilt" or "the sword-edge splendid with curving scrolls"? The answer was found on Nydam Moor in 1858, though not recognized until much more recently—the blades of ninety swords were decorated with twisted or coiled patterns wrought in the fabric of the weapons themselves. This shows once more that we can take the poet of *Beowulf* literally, and therefore can trust the tellers of the Sagas too.

It is in *Beowulf* that we first begin to see the high place the sword occupied in men's minds. The note of personal affection creeps in:

> Not the least or the worst of his war equipment
> Was the sword the herald of Hrothgar loaned

In his hour of need—Hrunting its name—
An ancient heirloom, trusty and tried;
Its blade was of iron, with etched design
Tempered in blood of many a battle
Never in fight had it failed the hand
That drew it, daring the perils of war,
The rush of the foe. Not the first time then
That its edge must venture on valiant deeds.

The poet gives almost a living personality, along with its name, to the sword; for what other reason than that his hearers felt that way about their own weapons? The sequel is worth quoting too: Unferth loaned his sword Hrunting to Beowulf when he was about to go down into the depths of the mere to fight the troll-woman, Grendel's mother. During the fight, Beowulf finds that mortal swords are not effective against demons:

He swung his war sword with all his strength,
Withheld not the blow, and the savage blade
Rang on her head its hymn of hate.
But the bold one found that the battle-flasher
Would bite no longer, nor harm her life.
The sword-edge failed at his sorest need.
Often of old with ease had it suffered
The clash of battle, cleaving the helm,
The fated warrior's woven mail.
That time was the first for the treasured blade
That its glory failed in the press of the fray.

Luckily for the hero, on the wall of the cave was a sword to match devils:

Swift the hero sprang to his feet
Saw mid the war-gear a stately sword
An ancient war-brand of biting edge
Choicest of weapons, worthy and strong,
The work of giants, a warrior's joy.

He succeeds in getting this, kills the troll woman and cuts off the head of the dead Grendel. Unfortunately, the demon's blood causes the blade to melt away in "iron icicles" and Beowulf is only able to bring the marvellous hilt back to Hrothgar. Finally, after all was done, Beowulf gave Hrunting back to its owner:

> The hero tendered the good sword Hrunting
> To the son of Eclaf, bidding him bear
> The lovely blade, gave thanks for the loan
> Called it a faithful friend in the fray
> Bitter in battle. The great-hearted hero
> Spoke no word in blame of the blade.

Such was the warrior's respect for a sword; we read of it in Saga, Chanson, Geste and Chronicle throughout the Middle Ages; all arms were important, cherished and revered, but for the sword was reserved a special glory, a particular affection. Later we read of Beowulf's homecoming, when his liege lord Hrethel, king of the Geats, rewarded him:

> Then the battle-bold King, the Bulwark of Heroes
> Bade bring a battle-sword banded with gold
> The heirloom of Hrethel; no sharper steel
> No lovelier treasure, belonged to the Geats.

This is but one of many instances where a sword is given as a rich reward for valour, and is referred to as "ancient treasure" or "costly heirloom", expressions often applied to helmets or byrnies as well:

> The best of mail coats that covers my heart,
> Heirloom of Hrethel, and Wayland's work,
> Finest of byrnies.

This stress on the great age, as well as the value, of swords, helmets and mail runs through all Anglo-Saxon and Norse literature, so much so that in Anglo-Saxon poetry the expression "ancient heirloom" itself is used as a synonym for a sword.

It is an archaeological fact that swords and helmets found in graves of this period are found only in those of chieftains; they are rare and rich. Few which we can date between A.D. 400 and 700 are not "hilted with gold", and often inlaid with jewels as well, or nielloed, or otherwise worked "with cunning of smith" to a rare beauty. Rich jewellers' work though these hilts were, the swords' real value lay in their blades, which were by their nature beautiful and, by all accounts, most efficient too. We get some idea of this from the famous letter which Cassiodorus, the secretary of Theodoric the Ostrogoth, Emperor of Rome, sent to the king of the Varni,

Thrasamund, in A.D. 520, to thank him for a rich treasure of swords he had sent as a gift. He says:

> You have sent us swords capable even of cutting through armour. They are more precious for the iron of which they are made than for the gold that enriches them; with their strikingly perfect polish, they shine so that they reflect the face of whoever looks at them. Their perfectly formed edges are so regular that one would believe they were fashioned with a file rather than hammered in the forge. The admirably hollowed middle part of their blades seems to be veined and patterned. There is the play of so many different shadows that one would think the metal is interlaced with elements of various colours. The beauty of these swords is such that one is tempted to attribute them to Vulcan, of whom they say that he forges with such skill that whatever comes from his hand is not the work of a mortal, but of a god.

We know of course that where Cassiodorus the Roman wrote "Vulcan", Thrasamund the Barbarian would read "Wayland". We know, too, that all that Cassiodorus said of these swords was true, because parts of several such blades have recently been reground and polished, and we find that they look precisely as he said they did fifteen centuries ago.

Small wonder such swords were treasures, not to be cast aside after a decade or two. Then why were they put into graves? The answer is not simple; the belief that the dead warrior would need his arms in another life is the least part of it. The sword's importance to a chieftain as a symbol of his power and to a liegeman as a symbol of his loyalty, and therefore not to be passed lightly on to one not proved worthy of it, is another; the very common human desire to take a loved possession to the grave is probably a third. It is not simply that people believed that grave offerings literally would be taken to another world where life went on as it does here. If you put your father's sword into his grave you act, indeed, like a dutiful son who wishes him to be armed; but you also leave it with him because it is his, and because it has its own soul which can pass over into the realms of the dead with him. If you take it yourself it may not serve you well, for you were not its master. It may fail you in battle, or injure you; or (even worse) the dead man may come to fetch it. He must be given no reason for returning, so his belongings must go with him into the grave. The rich gifts we have found in

93

tombs are not only honours for the dead, but protective measures for the living; we may assume, too, that many of the objects in graves were not gifts at all, but things which the dead man had owned in life. The idea that everything material in this world had a spirit is the basis of most of the ancient belief in an after-life.

There was another reason, too. The hard-headed Norse people had a far more practical idea—that a man should not inherit his father's treasures, but should go out and win his own, lest he grow soft and lazy; though if he is able to prove himself worthy, the tomb may be opened and a part of the treasure (usually arms) given to him.

All the deposits in the bogs of Denmark began to be unearthed at about the same time, the 50s and 60s of the last century, and between them they cover a period between about A.D. 50 and A.D. 450. Many of the objects found in them were unique, but many were of the same types as were found in the graves. As in the burials, the objects were often intentionally damaged. Spear-shafts, bows, arrow-shafts, scabbards are often rolled together into knots or broken in pieces. Mail-shirts and garments are hacked and torn, but carefully wrapped together, and the skulls and bones of horses are cleft. All this follows exactly what was written in the first century B.C. by Orosius and Caesar. Any doubts which one may have that these things were intentionally sunk in these bogs—which in antiquity were meres—is dispelled when we see that clay vessels had been sunk by having heavy stones put in them, and that some things were actually fastened to the bottom by large wooden hooks. In each deposit the area was marked off by fences of hurdles, or by lines of spears or swords stuck upright in the mud. The objects owe their fine state of preservation to the growth of the peat around them in the course of the centuries.

The find at Thorsbjerg (which is in South Jutland, south of Flensburg) was perhaps the most remarkable, for objects were brought to light here of a kind unknown elsewhere. The find was excavated in six years between 1856 and 1862, and its contents date between about A.D. 60 and 200. There were many swords (all double-edged), their hilts of wood covered with bronze and silver, with wooden scabbards mounted with metal—on the chape of one of these is a runic inscription; a sword-belt of thick leather $3\frac{1}{2}$ in.

wide and 41½ in. long; many sword-belt buckles of bronze and some iron ones; some more or less complete bows, the most perfect being 60 in. long, with an inch or so missing at either end; a lot of arrow-shafts, between 26 in. and 35 in. long and about half an inch thick. Unfortunately all the piles have rusted away. There were the remnants of shields, flat and circular, made of several thin boards. The largest shield is 42½ in. across, the smallest 21 in.; the thickness of the middle boards, which are generally a bit heavier than the outer ones, is between ½ in. and ¼ in. The grips and fastenings are mostly of bronze, but a few were of iron. There were many axes, all very perished, but with well-preserved hafts of ash and beechwood between 23 in. and 33½ in. long; a few well-preserved spear-points and others in bad condition, with four shafts, 32 in., 98 in., 107½ in. and 116 in. respectively. There were also many varied riding and driving accoutrements, a good deal of jewellery, many tools, some amber dice, domestic utensils like bowls, spoons, jugs, knives and so on; also two pairs of trousers and a shirt.

Fig. 37. Hilt of Roman sword from Thorsbjerg.

These were the more ordinary things; most noteworthy are the byrnies, the gold-covered circular bronze plates which went with some of them, reminiscent of the Roman *phalerae*, the bronze buckles decorated with gold and silver which fastened them, and a unique silver helmet. As I said, many objects were of Roman origin; a silver shield-boss has the name Aelaelianus engraved on it, and the design of one of the breast-plates is clearly influenced by classical art, for its main decoration consists of reclining Tritons among fish, yet it is obviously of northern workmanship. There is also the hilt of a Roman sword, similar to one found in Pompeii and another (in the British Museum) found in England. An interesting feature of this hilt is its grip, which is covered with fine bronze thread intricately braided (fig. 37) which is well worth noting since it is a form of grip-covering which was popular in the late seventeenth century and the early eighteenth. We shall find, too, that there are mediaeval monuments which show sword grips similarly treated, though with

95

what material the carved stone gives no clue. We have always assumed that the interlacing patterns were formed by flat leather ribbons; maybe we were wrong. At Thorsbjerg 37 Roman coins were found; the earliest of Nero, A.D. 60, and the latest of Septimus Severus, A.D. 194.

In the deposit at Vimose (about 5 miles from Odense, in Fyen) were found 67 swords; some were double-edged and some were single-edged saxes. There were over 1,000 spears, five being complete with shafts, 8 ft. 7¾ in., 9 ft. 2 in., 9 ft., 11 ft. and 6 ft. 6 in. respectively. These shafts are of ash (a fact which is often mentioned in *Beowulf* and the various Sagas) and some of them have the heads ornamented with inlaid threads of gold or silver or bronze in concentric circles. There were also many scabbard-mounts, which I will describe in their proper place. There was some very fine mail in the Vimose bog-find; fine in the sense that it was not only of good quality but made of very small rings, only just over ⅛ in. in diameter; some fragmentary pieces of a byrnie are plated with gold. A large complete byrnie was found there, too. Here the links are of the more usual size—about ¼ in. in diameter; the shirt is about 3 ft. long, with the neck opening in a shallow V in front and with short sleeves. Also there were a great quantity of arrow-shafts (very decayed), about 150 knives, 390 pieces of metal or bone scabbard-mountings, quantities of buckles, buttons and fibulae; some horses' bones; a good deal of harness; scythe-blades, keys, scissors and needles, nails and knives. A millstone, an anvil, 6 hammers, 25 chisels, 3 iron files, 2 pairs of pincers, and plenty of combs, brooches and beads—and four amber dice.

In a small bog called Kragehul, near the city of Assens in Fyen, objects of a later date have been found, belonging to the fourth and fifth centuries. There were the usual small miscellaneous articles, but the principal things were ten swords, most of them with pattern-welded blades, and one of a most unusual completeness. In the deposit much of the material was twisted into knots, and none of it was of Roman origin. A fence of spears bounded the area.

Of all the finds in Denmark, the Nydam bog is the most important, and captures the imagination far more than any of the others by reason of the great ship which was in it. Alas for archaeology, there were no less than four ships when the find was first dug in 1863. Two were small, and it was not possible to reconstruct them, but the two large ones were well preserved. One was of oak, and it was dug out first; a second of red pine was found beside it. This was dug out and its pieces laid in a field near the site of the dig, covered over with bog-mould to preserve it until it was possible to begin work on rebuilding it. Unhappily in 1864 a war broke out between Denmark and Germany, so the boat was left where it was; when the war ended, the Nydam bog was no longer in Denmark, but had passed to German hands. Many pieces of the red pine boat were removed, so that reconstruction was only partial. However, the oak boat is now complete—and I must resist the temptation to describe it here. More to our purpose, this bog contained 106 swords, all double-edged, 93 of them pattern-welded. They had hilts of wood covered with silver, or of bone or massive bronze; several blades bear Latin inscriptions and one has runes inlaid on it in gold. Most of these blades were found without their hilts, and bent, and many had deep cuts on the edges. In spite of this, their general condition is good and much has been learned from them. In addition there were 552 spear-heads, several of them ornamented with gold, and several hundred shafts, as well as the usual arrows (many with personal marks of ownership) and household utensils. There were 34 Roman coins struck between A.D. 69 and A.D. 217, but it is probable that most of the objects date between about A.D. 200 and 350.

It is to the swords found in the Nydam bog that archaeology owes the identification of pattern-welded blades. The patterns of 98 of the Nydam swords were noted, but it was not until about seventy years later that the nature of this form of blade-making was diagnosed and the technique of manufacture appreciated. Originally the patterns were thought to be a form of "Damascene" (which is itself a misapplied word); the technique was generally called "false damascene", though many German scholars described it graphically as *Wurmbunt*. Most of the swords of this period (the first four centuries A.D.) were double-edged, about 30 in. long on an average with blades about $1\frac{1}{2}$ in. broad at the hilt. They tapered very slightly to a more or less spatulate point, and in most cases (though by no means in all) they had a wide and shallow depression, too shallow

Fig. 38. Cavalry sword of
Roman period from Vimose.

to be called a groove, running the whole length of the blade. Quite a number of blades had two, three, and in some cases four shallow grooves instead of this wide "fuller".[1] These swords were mostly far smaller and lighter than their successors in the Viking Age and the mediaeval period, though their shape was the same. There were, however, several swords found in these deposits which were altogether of a different kind, with blades of a shape which we shall not meet again until about A.D. 1350. These are the weapons used by the Roman auxiliary cavalry, long, slender, acutely-pointed blades with a stiff section like a flattened diamond. A rare type, but even so two or three have been found in good preservation. Perhaps the best comes from the Vimose bog. It has a pattern-welded blade with a total length of about 40 in., the hilt being $7\frac{1}{2}$ in. long. Its width is a little over $1\frac{1}{2}$ in. at the hilt (fig. 38). The massive-looking guard of hollow bronze has a pierced decoration of two spirals akin to the La Tène decorative style. The rest of the hilt, originally made of bone or wood, is missing, but it probably was of the same shape as the hilts of the short Roman swords, with a large spherical pommel. In this case, the pommel was surmounted by an elegant little knop of bronze. Two more such blades were found in the Nydam bog. Only one ordinary legionary's sword has been found in Denmark, in comparative isolation at Mollerup.

[1] A "fuller" is the groove or channel running down the middle of a blade. Its purpose is to strengthen and lighten the blade and has nothing at all to do with blood.

98

As I have said, these long Roman cavalry sword blades could very easily be mistaken for swords of the second half of the fourteenth century, for they are exactly alike in size, shape, section and length of hilt. Similar also to late mediaeval swords is a Roman blade in Lincoln. Its section with a very strongly marked medial ridge running along each side from hilt to point, is exactly similar to many swords of the late fifteenth century. (See fig. 150, p. 309.)

Fig. 39. Part of a sword-blade from Nydam showing smith's name RICCIM and built-up shoulders.

Another thing about these swords foreshadows much later practice; the method of applying the smith's mark or name to the blade. We have seen how the La Tène smiths of the early Iron Age stamped their blades with impressed marks; this continued into the fourth century. At Nydam were found swords with marks stamped into the blades, not always as before in the broad of the blade below the hilt, but often upon the tang where it would be hidden by the hilt itself. Among these marks were a star, a crescent moon with three little projections at the back of it, a scorpion and a sort of herringbone. These last two marks appear frequently 1,200 years later—various forms of scorpion marks were in common use from about 1490 until 1700; while the herringbone was not uncommon around 1380. The position of these marks on the tang, too, was used by the fourteenth- and fifteenth-century smiths. Some of these marks had names stamped alongside them—Ricus, Riccim, Ranvici, Cocillus, Tasvit. These names were in small letters punched into a rectangular depression (fig. 39). There is in the Ethnographical Museum at Cambridge a little Saxon sword-blade which bears upon it the firm impression of a small pig with big ears. It was found in the mud of the River Cam, and so its surface (and its pig) are well preserved. It is possible that many of the swords found in Anglo-Saxon graves have marks like this, but owing to the bad state all of them are in it is impossible to see them. After about A.D. 250 this method of marking blades went completely out of fashion for 1,000 years; it is only at the end of the thirteenth century that we find the punched, tiny marks again, while the punched-in names do not return until late in the sixteenth century. What sort of marking took their place in the intervening centuries we shall see in due course.

If you look at fig. 39, you will notice another feature which is not generally recognized as being of great antiquity. The shoulders of the blade, over which the lower element of the hilt is set, are strongly built up. This is found on several of these swords of the late Roman period, and it crops up on swords of different periods all through the Middle Ages; by the end of the fifteenth century it had become fairly common, and during the sixteenth and seventeenth it was the usual practice. This, I think, is an important point, because many mediaeval blades have been condemned either as forgeries or as being of a much later date, simply because they have these built-up shoulders. It would be hard to find swords of an earlier date in the Middle Ages than these from Nydam, which were deposited in the mere a couple of hundred years before the Middle Ages ever began!

You will remember how in the legend of Arthur, the king got his sword Excalibur in a highly improbable way. Here is how Mallory told of it in 1475:

And as they rode, Arthur said, I have no sword. No force, said Merlin, hereby is a sword that shall be yours, an I may. So they rode till they came to a lake, the which was a fair water and broad, and in the midst of the lake Arthur was ware of an arm clothed in white Samite, that held a fair sword in that hand. Lo! said Merlin. Yonder is that sword that I spake of. With that they saw a damozel going upon the lake. What damozel is that? said Arthur. That is the lady of the lake, said Merlin; and within the lake is a rock, and therein is as fair a place as any on earth; and richly beseen; and this damozel will come to you anon, and then speak ye fair to her that she will give you that sword. Anon withal came the damozel unto Arthur, and saluted him, and he her again. Damozel, said Arthur, what sword is that, that yonder the arm holdeth above the water? I would it were mine, for I have no sword. Sir Arthur, King, said the damozel, that sword is mine, and if ye will give me a gift when I ask it you, ye shall have it. By my faith, said Arthur, I will give you what gift ye will ask. Well! said the damozel, go ye into yonder barge, and row yourself to the sword, and take it and the scabbard with you, and I will ask my gift when I see my time. So Sir Arthur and Merlin alit and tied their horses to two trees, and so they went into the ship, and when they came to the sword that the hand held, Sir Arthur took it up by the handles, and took it with him, and the arm and the hand went under the water.

And yet, in view of our present knowledge of these deposits of weapons in lakes, is this so improbable after all? If we allow that the legends of Arthur are probably based on fact, like Homer's tales and the Sagas, we must remember that in his time (about A.D. 500) the idea of depositing arms in lakes was a living reality. When, in the twelfth century, Geoffrey of Monmouth wrote the legends down, it is at least reasonable to suppose that the idea still lived in folk memory, though the romantic additions of the lady of the lake and the arm clothed in white samite had overlaid the old reality of a priest or priestess guarding the sacrificial mere, who for some special purpose might allow a sword to be fished out of the deposit to confer a supernatural power upon a chieftain.

There is a poem composed by Sigvat in the early eleventh century, addressed to his lord, King Olaf the Holy, which illustrates the significance of the sword as a gift binding liegeman to lord:

> I received thy sword with pleasure, O Njord of Battle, nor have I reviled it since, for it is my joy. This is a glorious way of life, O Tree of Gold; we have both done well. Thou didst gain a good follower, and I a good liege lord.

There is more prosaic evidence of this in the "Heriot", the gift of arms (sometimes a war-horse as well) to a man on taking service with a leader. These were in a sense only loaned, for they were usually returned when the man who carried them died, unless he fell in battle for his lord, when (if they were recovered) they might be put in his grave or passed on to his descendants. Many references to Heriot are to be found in the early laws of the Teutonic peoples, as well as in many Anglo-Saxon wills of the ninth and tenth centuries. We have no actual account of the ceremony of the "Treasure Giving", though in an Anglo-Saxon poem we call the "Wanderer" the exiled man without a lord looks back with longing to the time when he knelt before his lord in the Hall; in his dreams

> He embraces and kisses his lord, and lays head and hands on his knee as once he used to do when he enjoyed bounty from the throne in days gone by.

Here is an indication of the sort of ceremony in which a man received his sword. We may add to it a later account from Norwegian Court Law of the thirteenth century, which, based on an earlier twelfth-century version, is likely to go back to a much earlier tradition—the ceremony when a new member of the King's bodyguard (the Hearthmen) took the Oath of Allegiance:

At the time when the King appoints Hearthmen, no table shall stand before the King. The King shall leave his sword on his knee, the sword he had for his crowning; and he shall turn it so that the chape [of the scabbard] goes under his right arm, and the hilt is placed forward on his right knee. Then he shall move the buckle of the belt over the hilt, and grasp the hilt so that his right hand comes over everything. Then he who is to become a Hearthman shall fall on both knees before the king on the floor . . . and shall put his right hand under the hilt while he keeps his left arm down in front of him in the most comfortable position, and then he shall kiss the King's hand.

In the same way, when the King receives a man as a "Gestr", or member of a band of warriors of lesser rank than the Hearthmen, he is directed to put his hand forward over the sword "where the hilt meets the guard". The new man puts his under the hilt, kissing the King's hand at the same time, and thus swears the oath.

The actual touching of the sword was the significant part of the act. Perhaps for this reason, some swords were made with a ring on the pommel in the place where a man would touch it. Several such swords exist, and their quality and richness suggest that they belonged to chieftains. There is much evidence for the importance of the ring as an object upon which oaths are taken as well as the hilts of swords. Incidentally this shows quite clearly that the swearing of oaths on sword hilts goes back to a time long before the hilt could be considered as a Christian cross. There are many instances of "weapon oaths" as well as "ring oaths"; there is one in a poem by Venantius Fortunatus, and another a little later, an oath taken on weapons at a treaty between Franks and Saxons in Fredegar's Frankish Chronicle under the year 633.

A reference to a ring-hilted sword, at a period long after such a form had gone out of use, is in the Edda poem "Helgikvida", in which a sword is offered to a young prince by a Valkyrie who rides through the air to hail him:

I know of swords lying
In Sigarsholm . . .
One among them
Finest of all . . .
A ring's on the hilt
Valour midway,
And fear on the point
For him who wins it.

Here is a sword marked off from the others, the weapon of a leader.

In the Icelandic Sagas we find many stories of how weapons and armour were buried with a chieftain, and how some time afterwards, often a couple of generations, the barrow is opened so that a "sword or spear or broad mailcoat" can be taken out and given sometimes to a grandson or kinsman, sometimes to a stranger who had done the family a service. Generally weapons were handed on to sons or relatives or friends before the owner's death. When they were put intact into the grave, they were most carefully wrapped and preserved with the obvious intention that they might be taken out again, often a century or more later, in a ceremonial manner to be given to a worthy successor. Even so, there were many bold spirits who had no compunction in breaking into a barrow to get the gear out. Such a one was the Icelandic hero Skeggi, who stole the sword Sköfnung from the grave of Hrolf Kraki; Sköfnung seemed to have no inhibitions about being taken out, for it served Skeggi well for many years, and his son Eid after him.

In the Saga of Hrolf Kraki we read of this sword named Sköfnung, "it was the best of all swords which have been carried in the northern lands". We also read that it uttered a loud cry whenever it saw wounds, and that it was laid beside the king in his grave. In a later saga we are told that Skeggi, when he was sailing near Roskilde, where Hrolf Kraki was buried, "went ashore, and broke into the howe of Hrolf Kraki and took out Sköfnung, the King's sword". This was about 200 years after Hrolf's death. We meet Sköfnung again in several sagas; like most other swords of this kind, it had a certain magical quality (or rather, it was believed to have, which after all came to the same thing). Care had to be taken that the charm upon it should be effective, so it had to be handled properly. The

Fig. 40. Sword found in a grave at Klein Hunigen, fifth–sixth century, with a "life stone".

sun must never shine full upon its pommel, nor should it be drawn when a woman was by or in the sight of anybody. There was a "life stone" with it, and a wound inflicted by Sköfnung could only be healed if the life stone were rubbed on it. These life stones were common enough in the sagas, but there is never very specific mention of what they were like or how they were fixed to the swords. It is interesting to note in this connection that in many cases where a sword has been found in a grave of the period between about 200 and 600 A.D., there has been a large perforated bead, sometimes made of stone, sometimes of pottery or meerschaum, sometimes of glass, near the hilt of the sword. The frequency with which these things turn up, and the constant position of all of them near the sword hilt, makes it obvious that they were fixed, probably by a lace or a thong, either to the hilt itself in the manner of the sword knot, or to the top of the scabbard (fig. 40). In the past the historians of Norse literature seem to have had no idea what these life stones were, while the archaeologists were uncertain about the purpose of the large beads. If we put two and two together in this case, it seems that we may obtain a fairly obvious four, except that they only occur on swords of a much earlier period than the Sagas. However, we do know that Skofnung had belonged to Hrolf Kraki, who lived in the early sixth century. But to return to Sköfnung, his owner Skeggi and the headstrong young man Kormac, who borrowed Sköfnung to fight a duel.

There was a man called Bersi in Iceland at that time; he was always "going on Holmgang", which means he was always fighting duels. So much so that he was called Holmganga Bersi (in the modern idiom that would be something like calling him "Basher" Bersi). Kormac got tired of Bersi's boasting at one time, and challenged him. Bersi had a sword called Hviting, which had a life stone with it, and Kormac thought he should have a similar sword to match it. His mother advised him to go to Midfjord and find Skeggi and see if he would lend Sköfnung. Skeggi did not want to do this; he said, "You and Sköfnung are unlike in temper; Sköfnung is slow, but you are headstrong and impatient." However, Kormac's mother told him to try again, and this time Skeggi gave in. He told Kormac, "You will find it difficult to manage. There is a bag with it, and you must not disturb it; it covers the hilt, for the sun must not shine on the pommel, and you must not draw Sköfnung unless you are ready to fight. When you come to the fighting place, go off to one side by yourself, and then draw it. Hold up the blade and blow on it; a small snake will creep from under the guard; incline the blade, and make it easy for the snake to creep back again." Kormac was a bit scornful, and told Skeggi that he must be a wizard; but Skeggi said if he did all this it would help him in his fight. When Kormac got home with Sköfnung he tried to draw it to show his mother, but Sköfnung wouldn't leave the scabbard. Kormac was annoyed: "he tore the bag off the hilt and put his foot on the guard; Sköfnung howled at this; but still would not come."

When the time for the duel came, both Kormac and Bersi rode to the place with fifteen men apiece. Kormac got there first, and told his friend Thorgils that he wanted to sit down by himself for a minute. He sat down and unfastened the sword and took off the bag, but he didn't take care and the sun shone on the pommel; then he tried to draw it, but he couldn't get it out until he put his foot on the guard. "The little snake came out, but it was not handled as it should have been, and the luck of the sword was changed and it came howling out of the scabbard."

Now here we find a lot of things; the charm, the luck of the sword, its own voluntary refusal to work for Kormac, all showing a distinct personality. But what is all this about a little snake? You may think there is enough nonsense in that snake to make bunkum of all the rest of it, life stone and all. So it may look; but it is not—that snake is the one thing which we know to be an archaeological fact as real as the Pyramids. Most of these swords were fashioned in a complicated and wonderful way. Their blades were made up of three separate parts—like the ones which Thrasamund sent to Theodoric; the two edges were forged separately, and the central part was made up of numerous narrow strips of iron. These strips were all twisted together, cold, in various regular patterns and then forged; then they were twisted again, and reforged on to the separate edges. Then the whole thing was with infinite care filed and burnished until the surfaces were totally smooth; the result of all this was that the central portions of such blades had intricate patterns, made up of regularly repeating designs wrought into the fabric of the iron. Most of these patterns are very similar to the markings on a snake's back. In *Beowulf* we read of a sword blade "variegated like a snake", and the snake idea crops up over and over again. The facts about this method of making blades (which goes right back into the La Tène period) are scientifically proven. Many such blades have been cut into sections, and microscopic photographs have been taken and examinations made, as well as x-ray photographs of the integral structure, of dozens of them.

Now you can see—or you could, if you had a pattern-welded sword in pristine condition in your hands—what Kormac should have seen if he had done what Skeggi told him. If you blow on the cold surface of one of these blades, the faintly etched patterns will suddenly show up clearly and seem to wriggle as your warm breath condenses in passing over it.

Another thing we find in the Norse tales is that all swords (and most spears and many axes, too) are named. This is undoubtedly a custom going very far back, and in its earlier forms at least must have been closely associated with magic, and the belief that all objects, as well as men and animate beings, had souls, and that a name had great power in it. This belief, which we know was still firmly held in all the northern lands before Christianity came to them, explains all these lively references to the personalities of swords. The practice of naming swords persisted throughout the Middle Ages, even though official Christian doctrine denied any sort of spirit to anything save man; but man has always been reluctant to abandon his ancient beliefs, and the sword's personality seems to have stayed with it, though it was not so often written about.

Chapter Seven

THE ARMS OF THE MIGRATION PERIOD

THE SWORDS OF the Migration period have been classified into a most complete typology by a Swedish scholar, Elis Behmer. For our purpose it will, I think, be enough to summarize and simplify this typology to give some indication of the development of the weapon from the Roman period to the age of the Vikings. Behmer takes into account variations in the styles of scabbard mountings as well as shapes of hilts, but for the sake of simplicity we will concentrate here on the hilts alone. Fig. 41 sets out four types; there are well-preserved examples of each, worth describing in detail.

Swords of Type I are characterized by grips which follow the pattern of the regulation Roman infantry sword-hilt, with ridges to give a secure hold for the fingers. The guards, upper and lower, are of about equal shape and size and there is only a rudimentary pommel, sometimes lacking altogether, set on top of the upper guard. Some of these hilts were made of plain horn or bone or wood, while some were of these materials covered with silver or bronze. There is one made of horn (it is in the British Museum and was found in Cumberland) whose decoration consists of small plates of gold covered with minute filigree work and set with tiny garnets—decoration which looks far too dainty and delicate for such a robust thing as a sword hilt. The type clearly was in use by about A.D. 150,

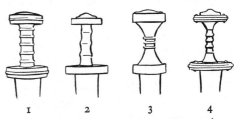

Fig. 41. Sword types of the Migration period.

Fig. 42. Sword hilt of Type 1 from Thorsbjerg. Wood covered with silver. First–second century A.D.

for a splendid silver-covered hilt was found in Thorsbjerg Moss (fig. 42). Two more of identical form, with their blades, were found in the Kragehul bog. This shows that a hilt-type either went on being used without change for 200 years—the Thorsbjerg objects, you will remember, all date before A.D. 200, while the Kragehul ones are all after A.D. 400—or that old swords remained in use. The latter is more likely; the repeated evidence of the Sagas about swords being handed on is too clear to be passed over. For instance, the sword Aettartangi which Grettir the Strong had: "She (Grettir's mother) took an ornamented sword from under her cloak; it was very costly, and she said, 'This sword my grandfather Jokul owned, and the old Vatnsdaelir. It used to give them victory. I will give it to you; use it well'." (*Grettis Saga*, Chap. 17.)

On the grounds of its decoration, the Cumberland hilt has been said to be of the late seventh century, but there is a similar one, of undecorated bone, in Copenhagen which came from the Nydam find (A.D. 250–350), and Oslo has one, found in a grave at Evebo which dates from late in the sixth century. Here there are several possibilities. The Nydam hilt is evidence enough that the type was in use in the fourth century; while the Evebo grave shows it in the sixth; whether in the Cumberland specimen the decoration—which could quite well be of the sixth century rather than the late eighth— was added to an earlier hilt is an open question. These three hilts give more evidence (if more is needed) of the longevity of weapons in this period.

A prototype of type 2 is one of the best known swords of the Migration period; it was found with a sax in the grave of the Frankish king Childeric 1 who died in A.D. 481. It was discovered in the seventeenth century, and in 1665 was presented to Louis XIV. The hilts of both when found were in pieces, and until very recently the two fragmentary hilts have been made up as one, which is shown in many illustrations looking most improbable. This hilt is decorated with garnets inset into cloisons of gold; the grip is ridged like those I have just described, but it is covered with gold. Swords of this style have been found in wide distribution; one of the best of them is from the village of Klein Hunigen in Switzerland. Its hilt is not so well preserved as the Childeric sword, but it has its complete scabbard and all its mounts, including what may be the problematical "life stone" which we read of in connection with Hrolf Kraki's sword Sköfnung. Both the guards of this sword have perished, which is a great pity as the rest of it is so well preserved that were it complete it would give us a very clear idea of the appearance of the swords used by the Goths at the time of Theodoric. It has a small pommel of bronze with "zoomorphic" heads at its ends, and a handsome grip of thick gold similar to that of the Childeric

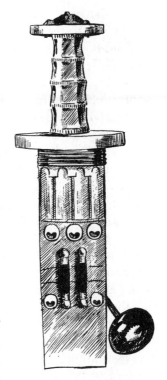

Fig. 43. Reconstruction of the hilt of the Klein Hunigen sword.

sword. There is a passage in Magnus Barefoot's Saga (Ch. 26) which might refer to just such a weapon:

> He [King Magnus] was girt with a sword called Leggbitr [Leg-biter]; its guards were of walrus-tusk, and its hilt [grip] was covered with gold. It was one of the best of weapons.

It is illustrated in fig. 40 in its present condition, but here in fig. 43 is a reconstruction of it as it would have been. The general shape of the hilt is very similar to Childeric's, and the scabbard-mounts are interesting for their completeness. The mouth of the scabbard is finished with a band of gold, worked into seven longitudinal ridges, three narrow ones between four broader ones. The wooden surface below it is carved with a sort of low-relief arcade, very reminiscent of the panels on late mediaeval chests and coffers. We find this sort of "architectural" idea for the decoration of the tops of scabbards again in the period 1350–1420. Below this are three circular gold studs, each pierced with a sort of flattened heart-shaped aperture. These seem to have had no function apart from a purely decorative one, and are reminiscent of the studs on some La Tène scabbards. Below the studs are two strap-loops placed side by side. They are of a shape different from most of their predecessors, being cylindrical and double, decorated with inlays of gold wire. The lower end of each loop is flanked by another stud of the same pattern as the upper ones, though one is lacking. The chape is a single band of metal bent over in a U section to enclose the edges of the scabbard; one side of it extends nearly two-thirds of the way up towards the hilt, on the side of the scabbard which, in wear, would knock against the leg of the wearer when riding, a very practical feature. The lowest extremity of the chape is decorated by three diamond-shaped garnets set in gold—an admirable little work of art on its own (fig. 44). There are several other scabbards with mounts exactly like this, one from Alter Götterbarmweg in Switzerland (very near Klein Hunigen) and six more from Germany. Some of these are so like the Klein Hunigen sword that they may have come from the same workshop.

Fixed to the top of the Klein Hunigen scabbard at the back is a large, flattened sphere of polished stone mounted with gold. As we have seen, many swords of this period have been found with stones of this kind near their hilts; here is one still actually in position, maybe like the life stone on Hrolf Kraki's Sköfnung. No sword belonging to the actual period of Skeggi's life (ninth century)

has ever been found with a stone with it, whereas in this earlier period of the fifth and sixth centuries there are many. We have to remember that Sköfnung was in fact a sixth-century sword—or at least, its owner Hrolf was a sixth-century chief, and his sword may have been old when he had it—so there is nothing at all odd about its life stone being with it still in Skeggi's time, three centuries later. I think it not unreasonable to suppose that the stones, or

Fig. 44. Decorative finial on scabbard of the Klein Hunigen sword.

beads, often beautifully marked, polished and mounted, which have been found alongside swords were in fact these "life stones "which the Sagas so often speak of in connection with weapons of an age prior to that of the Saga itself.

Of the same type as this are the few Gothic swords from south Russia. Their general shape is similar, though they have pommels of a different kind made of large pieces of stone, usually chalcedony, or of bronze with cloisonné decoration. They clearly owe some part of their origin to the Sarmatian swords of the first few decades of the first century. One of these, from Janusowice, is of the period of the battle of Adrianople; it is very plain, completely without decoration, with a large mushroom-shaped pommel of bronze similar in shape to one in the British Museum of the Hallstatt period; its blade is very long, and a good deal of its leather scabbard remains. Other Gothic swords have decoration on their lower guards (most of which are very deep and far shorter than those of the north) carried out in the cloisonné technique; it is worth noting, incidentally, that the Goths seem to have had a taste for heart-shaped cloisons, and all the swords of the kind of the Klein Hunigen one have similarly shaped openings in the gold studs on their scabbards, suggesting a com-

Fig. 45. Gothic sword from Taman in S. Russia.

mon origin. The strap-loops on these Gothic swords are unlike the others, being of direct descent from the Sarmatian ones; which in turn are of the same form as, and could be derived from, ancient Chinese sword-mounts of the Han dynasty. The only Gothic sword (of about the second half of the fifth century) which has its strap-loop still in position is a pretty complete one. It was found at Taman, in the Kuban, and is now in the Wallraf-Richartz Museum at Cologne (fig. 45). The lower ends of the long gold strips which flank the strap-loop are in the form of predatory birds' heads; we shall meet something very like these in the next sword we have to examine.

The distribution of finds of Type 2 swords suggests that they were used mostly by the Germanic peoples of central and eastern Europe. Type 3, on the other hand, seems to have been almost entirely northern, most examples having been found in Denmark. The two which I have chosen to illustrate the type (plate 3) were both in the Kragehul deposit; they are so complete that it takes little imagination to appreciate how they appeared before being "sacrificed" in about 450. They are similar except for one thing—one has a broad, blunt-ended blade but the other is slender and quite acutely pointed. That this slenderness is not due to the edges of the blade having corroded away is proved by the narrowness of the bronze chape, which is still in position. The hilt form seems to be a modification of the Type I hilts, brought about by the stretching-out of the upper and lower ends of the grip between the two guards, and the consequent squeezing together of the ridges into the narrow waist at the centre. These grips look clumsy, but actually they are very flat, and surprisingly comfortable to hold. Many of them are made of wood covered with bronze or silver or gold, but some are of solid massy bronze. The whole sword has a rather ponderous appearance, for not only is the hilt very solid, but the distinctive kind of chape is large and important. There are swords of quite recent date from the Sudan which have hilts of almost exactly the same shape. Everyone knows of the swords of the "Fuzzy-Wuzzies" of 1880 which were of the cross-hilted mediaeval shape; it is less usual to find one similar to a fourth century Scandinavian hilt. I have sketched in fig. 46 one which I found in a North Devon hotel while on holiday.

The method of fixing the scabbard to the belt is quite different from that of the Type 2 swords, for it was effected either by means

Fig. 46. Nineteenth-century Sudanese sword-hilt.

of double hooks (like little anchors) fixed to a ring on either side of the "locket", or by rings similarly placed. These presumably hooked into rings fixed to the end of straps in a fashion very popular in the fifteenth century; but the slender upward and downward prolongation of the middle part of the locket is still reminiscent of the old Celtic strap-loops. On the mouth bands of these scabbards we find the same bird-of-prey heads which decorate the Gothic sword from Taman.

Swords of Type 4 are found all over Europe, and date from about A.D. 500 to 700. It is no exaggeration, perhaps, to say that practically every sword of this period is of Type 4, and it includes the very many Anglo-Saxon specimens which have been found in innumerable English graves. Its principal feature is the emergence to a dominant position of the pommel, which in the preceding types was only an elongated block to give a firm backing to the clinching of the tang rivet. Now it emerges in its full "cocked-hat" form, set upon the top of the upper guard. In most cases now the tang does not pass through the pommel, which is secured by long rivets which go right through the guard, but is riveted over on top of the guard below the pommel itself. The guards are made in three parts—a narrow band of metal, generally bronze but often of solid gold, on either side of a broader "filling" of hard wood or horn.

There are many very splendid swords within this type, but perhaps the finest is one of our own, the sword from the Anglian ship burial at Sutton Hoo in Suffolk. The burial, though in the form of a pagan ship-grave, contained no body; it seems that it was in fact a memorial deposit to a king (or a line of kings) of East Anglia. It was probably made in about A.D. 670, perhaps by the Christian king Aethelwald to commemorate his brother, the pagan Aethelhere, who was killed fighting against the Northumbrians at Winwaed in Yorkshire, or as a memorial to his predecessors. Whoever made the burial, or whoever it was for, one thing seems certain: the objects in it were mostly of earlier date than the deposit itself. So the sword, though we do not know precisely who owned it, undoubtedly was a "costly heirloom", like the one which Hrethel, king of the Geats, gave to Beowulf. Its design is simple, not nearly so lavishly adorned with goldsmith's work as its Swedish contemporaries, but it is perhaps all the better to be so. Its pommel is an outstanding work of art, in the same class as the Battersea shield. Like the shield, it defies description, and owes much to the soft red colour of the garnets set off by the bright gleam of the gold. The jewellery of the sword-belt which went with it is the very finest expression of pagan European art known to archaeology. These mounts are the only things of their kind which have survived from this period, though when the belt was found crushed into the ground by the collapsed burial chamber they were scattered, and it was impossible to tell how they were placed on the belt.

The blade of the sword is not very long, about 28 in., but it is quite broad (about $2\frac{1}{2}$ in. at the hilt); its exact form cannot be discerned for it is inseparably corroded into its scabbard. However, it has been possible to see it clearly by means of an x-ray photograph; this has shown the design of the pattern-welding of the blade. The scabbard was made of wood in the usual way, but it seems to have been lined with leather. Some scabbards of this period were lined with fur; we find mention of this in the Sagas, and there are a few swords where it can still be seen. There is one from a Norwegian grave (Find No. 110 from Snartemo), and an English-found fragment of a blade clearly shows the imprint of fur on the corrosion of its surface.

The only mounting on the scabbard is a pair of dome-shaped studs—there is neither band nor chape. It is unlikely that they have perished, for they would certainly have been of imperishable gold like all the rest of the sword's mountings, but it may be that they were lost when the find was being taken out of the ground. But the studs are superlative, each one a masterpiece of jeweller's art. It is a thing common to nearly all these Type 4 swords that the scabbards are very simply mounted; chapes are very plain, generally just pieces of metal of a U section enclosing the two edges of the scabbards, while mouth-bands are no more than finials, often magnificently wrought, with no function for suspending the sword. The explanation may be given by a scabbard of the very end of the period, about 700, found at Oberflacht in Wurttemburg, which has a very simple strip of wood with a slot behind it fixed to the side of the scabbard, like the Celtic strap-loops—and like the Sarmatian scabbard-mounts and the jade mounts of ancient Chinese swords. This may be the answer to the total lack of these fittings on swords at this time; such wooden pieces would easily be lost in getting a sword out of the ground, even if it were possible to recognize them, for if they had perished to anything like the extent to which the wood of the scabbards has perished they would simply have merged with the soil round them. On the scabbard of the

Sutton Hoo sword there is a long shallow groove where such a fitting may have been.

Of this period—and type—were the ring-swords. The most splendid of these have been found in Sweden and Lombardy, but perhaps the most interesting were found here in England, for they are the earliest. As I have said, a ring in this heroic age was something to swear oaths on; we read of ring-oaths as well as weapon-oaths. Here in the ring-swords we find the two combined in the swords of chieftains, swords upon which oaths of fealty were sworn. At one time scholars believed that these rings were for the purpose of attaching the "fridbond" or "peace-strings" of which we hear so much in the Sagas—laces fixed to a sword-hilt whereby it could be tied into its scabbard to hinder hasty unsheathing and hot-tempered killing. Such, at least, was the idea and purpose of the fridbond; how successful it was we can judge by the countless hot-blooded (and often extremely cold-blooded) killings of which the Sagas tell. For instance in the Gisli Surssons Saga we read how Gisli's brother Thorkel went to the Thing (council meeting) very well turned out:

He wore a hat from Gardariki and a grey cloak with a gold brooch at his shoulder, and carried a sword in his hand. Two boys walked up to him. The older boy said, "Who is the noble-looking man sitting here? I never saw a better-looking or more dignified man." Thorkel answered, "You are right, I am called Thorkel." The boy said, "The sword in your hand must be very precious; may I have a look at it?" Thorkel answered, "This is strange, but I will let you look." The boy took the sword, turned aside, unloosed the peace-bands, and drew it. When Thorkel saw this he said, "I didn't say you could draw the sword." "I didn't ask you," replied the boy; and he swung the sword and struck at the neck of Thorkel, taking off his head.

No. The ring-hilted sword was one set aside for the use of a chief (that is why they are so rare); the fridbond undoubtedly were used, but no trace of them has so far been identified anywhere.

Most of the English sixth-century ring-swords have been found in Kent; there are several in the Maidstone Museum, and all are characterized by the ring being a small, loose ring, rather smaller than a finger-ring, set into another ring or loop of metal fixed at the side of the pommel above the upper guard. The ones from Bifrons

and Gilton (fig. 47) are the most complete. Another from Faversham, in the British Museum, was found with its ring divorced from its hilt, and it does not seem possible to fix it on in any way, for the ring and its holder are shaped exactly like a certain type of picture-frame ring (fig. 48). The hilt was at one time put together with the ring fixed to the pommel and the stalk of the holding-ring sticking out at an angle. Fortunately it has now fallen apart again and not been replaced, for that way it was absurd. In a magnificent sword from Snartemo in Norway the ring was fixed to the bottom of the lower guard, the stalk of its holding-ring passing through the lower plate of the lower guard and fixed into the horn or wood core. This sword is the only one known with a ring in this position, unless the Faversham one might perhaps have been the same. It was this sword from Snartemo, incidentally, which gave rise to the theory that the friðbond were tied to the ring, for in that position it does indeed seem that such might have been its purpose.

Fig. 47. "Ring sword" from the Anglo-Saxon cemetery at Gilton, Kent (sixth century).

Other ring swords were found in a number of chieftains' graves at Vendel and Valsgärde in Sweden, while several more of the same kind have come from graves in Germany. They date between about A.D. 650 and 750, and are all far more elaborate and rich than the Jutish ones from Kent, whose hilts are mainly of bronze or silver. They differ, too, in the style of the rings, for now the loose ring has merged with its holding-ring so that the whole thing becomes a single piece of solid metal. In the Sutton Hoo burial an isolated ring was found; it could have been from a sword, though no other sword or part of one was in the ship; perhaps it adorned a drinking horn, for we read of horns being garnished with rings, and in one of the Valsgärde graves was a horn with a ring on it. Very similar in shape and style to the Vendel swords are some from Lombardy, swords of those

Fig. 48. The detached ring from one of the Faversham swords (British Museum).

116

Longobards of whom we hear so much from Procopius and Paul the Deacon. A passage in Paul gives us the armament of a Lombard knight—helm, mail-shirt, shield and greaves—the last a piece of equipment which, though it was common in ancient Greece, we do not generally expect to meet with in the Middle Ages until the thirteenth century. In another we read of the great lance (*contus*), so strong that a Lombard champion who had pierced a Byzantine horseman through the body lifted him from his saddle and bore him aloft wriggling on the point of it (Paul V : 10). The other great weapon of the Lombards was the broadsword, which they wore at all times, not just in war. In Paul VI: 51 we read of it worn at the king's council board, and in VI: 38 at a feast. There are several of these Lombard swords, some like the Vendel ones and others with much in common both in form and decoration with the Sutton Hoo sword, for they use the garnet and cloisonné technique. Two very fine ones which were found in Perugia have it, and in the British Museum there is a ring-pommel from Lombardy, most beautifully wrought, which is decorated in a manner remarkably like the Sutton Hoo belt mounts. There is no doubt that Lombard and Anglo-Saxon were closely akin, for the two languages were remarkably similar.

A weapon nearly as popular as the sword in this period was the sax, a comparatively short, single-edged weapon which seems to have descended directly from the ancient Greek kopis. Saxes were known in the early Iron Age in Scandinavia, as the finding of two or three of them in the boat burial of about 300 B.C. at Hjortspring in Denmark shows. We have seen already the evidence that something like the sax was used in the north during the Bronze Age, but it is during the Migration period that its popularity seems to have been greatest. Many saxes were found in the bogs, though most of them were in the Vimose and Nydam deposits. There is a very complete one with its scabbard from Vimose, interesting because it shows a type of scabbard quite different from most of the sword-scabbards among the Danish finds. Its nearest parallel—a very close one—is a sword in its scabbard found in the ditch of the great Brigantian earthwork fortress of Stanwick in Yorkshire. This fortress was overthrown by the Romans between A.D. 71 and 74 and never used again, so the sword most probably dates within the

first century. The Vimose weapons are mostly of the late Roman period, so this particular sax may be coeval with the Stanwick sword. The scabbard is made up of many longitudinal strips of wood bound at intervals with metal bands (fig. 49). Some of these saxes have simple geometrical patterns incised on their blades.

One of the best-known saxes we read of is the one Grettir the Strong had. He got it when he broke into the mound of Kär, the Norwegian chief. He was staying with Thorfinn, the son of Kär, and when he had rifled the barrow (a thing which Thorfinn himself feared to do) he brought a good deal of property back to Thorfinn's home:

> Late at night he returned to the house, and placed on the table before Thorfinn the property he had taken from the mound. Among the treasures was a sax, such a good weapon that Grettir said he had never seen a better. He wanted to have it very much, but produced it last of all. Thorfinn's face brightened when he saw the sax for it was a great treasure and had never been out of the family; he asked how Grettir got it, and he told him. Thorfinn said, "You must do something that I think famous before I

Fig. 49. Sax and scabbard from Vimose.

will let you have the sax, for my father never allowed me to use it."

Grettir got his sax in the end; he carried it all his life, and always used it in preference to his sword Aettartangi, which had a tendency to bring bad luck.

Most of the saxes in the Vimose and Nydam finds were very broad-bladed weapons, slightly curved on the back and more strongly curved on the edge, with an acute point; the hilt is curved, a continuation of the back of the blade; except that it was never furnished with a knuckle-guard, it is remarkably like the stirrup-hilts of early nineteenth-century cavalry sabres, as well as being so similar to the kopis hilt. It was always made on the sandwich principle, like some of the Bronze Age hilts, secured with several rivets. Some had more slender and less strongly curved blades; one such was in the Kragehul deposit with its scabbard and a good deal of its hilt remaining. The scabbard is made more on the lines of an ordinary sword-scabbard, with two rings for suspension. The decoration is interesting because its main motif is a cross within a circle, the old Bronze-Age sun-symbol which we shall meet as a decoration on arms all through the Middle Ages.

To the warriors of the Sagas the spear was nearly as important a weapon as the sword; we read of many different kinds of spear, every one which has been found in the bogs. There was the hewing spear (Höggspjøt), the javelin (Gaflak), the string-spear (Snoeris-Spjøt) which was used for throwing with a loop of cord fastened to the shaft; the pole-staff (Pal-staf) which was a pole furnished with a long spike; the "cord-shaft" (Skepti-Fretta) which was probably another version of the string-spear; and the "Atgeir", a kind of halberd.

There was considerable variety in the forms of these spear-heads, as well as in the length of the shafts. Those found in the bogs were all of ash, and though the lengths differed few were more than 1 in. thick. There were several string-spears with the loop of cord still in place, and others had the centre of gravity marked by cord bindings or nails, so that the thrower could instantly give the spear the right position in his hand. One may wonder a little at the great length—over 11 ft.—of some of these spears; such a length suggests the great lance of the mounted warrior, but we never hear of these Norsemen fighting like the Goths or the Longobards; they rode horses to get about, but generally fought afoot. These spears were probably used as pikes—we read in Tacitus' *Annals* how the Germans in A.D. 17 were greatly hampered in one of their battles against Germanicus by the great length of their spears.

Many of the sockets were richly decorated with designs, usually one variation or another of the interlace patterns, inlaid in gold or silver wire or of gold or silver foil wrapped round and engraved or nielloed. Some spear-heads are pattern-welded,[1] and may have been reforged from broken sword-blades, like the famous spear Grasida

[1] There is a particularly fine pattern-welded spear head in the Reading Museum.

which started in the eighth century as a sword, was re-made as a spear and was still in use in the thirteenth century.

The javelins and string-spears had smallish, narrow heads; the hewing-spears long and blunt-ended heads, and we may perhaps equate the "Atgeir" with a curious form of head with a broad cutting edge on one side and a sort of barb on the other which is reminiscent of some of the very early Swiss halberds of about 1350.

Axes were used a good deal, but only a few are really distinguishable as weapons from others which could equally well have been designed for the humdrum purpose of cutting wood. Axes have often been found in the graves, but I believe one should not because of that assume they were always weapons of war; to any kind of householder or landowner in those days an axe was such an absolutely essential tool that its presence in the grave is not surprising. In the sagas we often read of war-axes, but it seems that they were more used in later times.

Innumerable pieces of shields of this period survive—mostly the large central bosses—and quite a number of more or less complete ones. The finest of them all is, of course, the one from Sutton Hoo (plate 5). This, like all the other gear, was in fragments, but it has been reconstructed so that one can appreciate its original splendour.[1] When found the pieces comprised the heavy iron boss ornamented with gilt bronze and garnets, and gold and gilt bronze mounts and fittings in the form of stylized animals, or decorated with bird-of-prey heads. There was a gilt bronze rim all round the edge, decorated at intervals with little dragon heads. This rim gave the diameter of the shield, which is 33 in., considerably bigger than some of the shields found in the bogs; to the right of the boss is a strip of gilt bronze, an ornamental survival of a once useful metal brace, while to the left are two studs, the heads of rivets holding the leather arm-strap. Above the boss is a purely ornamental fitting in the form of a bird-of-prey on the wing. There is a decorative strip of garnet inlay above and behind the bird's eye, and another pear-shaped inlay of garnets in its hip in the form of a simplified human face. Both head and leg are of bronze, but the lappet at the back of its head is of

[1] Some doubts have recently been expressed by Swedish scholars as to the accuracy of this reconstruction; the suggestion is that in its original form this shield was oval.

plaster, covered with gold leaf. Below the boss is another decorative fitting in the form of an eight-legged (or eight-winged) dragon. This is of bronze, but its last two pairs of legs or wings are also of plaster covered with gold leaf. So, too, were several of the twelve animal heads round the shield's rim. These plaster pieces are repairs carried out in antiquity, probably to replace pieces lost or damaged in battle; they indicate that it was already of considerable age— probably a family heirloom—when it was placed in the grave. The reverse of the shield (plate 5b) shows how it was carried. The left forearm passes through the leather strap while the hand grasps the metal bar which crosses the back of the hollow boss. This iron grip is deliberately put off centre to allow the knuckles to fit into the cavity of the boss, and the forearm to lie flat against the shield. This bar is extended above and below by gilt-bronze strips with bird and animal heads with garnet eyes. The boards of the shield were covered with leather, upon which the ornaments rested. Below the grip-extension on the back is a silver-plated bronze fitting with a ring, to which a strap-end is still fixed. The upper end of this strap was found attached to the upper end of the grip-mounting. Its purpose was to suspend the shield round the owner's neck when in use (a forerunner to the mediaeval "Guige-strap"), or to the wall behind his high-seat in his hall when it was not. This Sutton Hoo shield, like so much of the other material, is very similar in character to objects found in the earlier of the Vendel graves in Sweden.

In this period, as in the following Viking age, shields were often painted as well as richly bedecked. For instance in Egil's Saga (ch. 82) we read:

When the Jarl heard the poem he gave Einar a most costly shield; it was painted with the old sagas, and all the spaces between the paintings were covered with plates of gold and set with stones. When he was ready he went to the seat of Egil and hung the shield there, telling the servants he gave it to Egil, and then rode away.

And in Volsunga Saga (ch. 22):

Sigurd rode away. His shield was of many layers, covered with red gold, and on it was painted a dragon; it was dark brown on the upper part and light red on the lower, and in the same way were coloured his helmet, saddle and armour. He had a gold coat of mail, and all his weapons were ornamented with gold and marked with a dragon, so that everyone who saw the dragon might know who the man was, if he had heard that Sigurd slew the dragon which the Voerings called Fafnir.

This painting of the warrior's entire equipment in different colours is yet one more foreshadowing of a usual mediaeval heraldic practice. Many of the sagas tell of shields painted in sections of different colours as well as with designs or animals. The mention of Sigurd's gold byrnie may strike the reader as an exaggeration, but it is reasonable enough, as the byrnies with gilded plates from Thorsbjerg and the one with gold-plated rings from Vimose prove. The form of these shirts seems to have been the same as it was centuries before in the Celtic Iron Age, though some were very short, only covering the shoulders and chest.

We do not know a great deal about the helmets of this age, for though many magnificent ones have been found—notably at Sutton Hoo and in the Vendel and Valsgärde graves—all are the rich equipment of chiefs. We know from the poems that ordinary men wore helmets, but only a few fragments have survived. There is one from a small ship-burial at Ultuna near Uppsala in Sweden which is a simple skull cap made of interlacing bands of metal riveted to a band encircling the head horizontally. Even this comparatively common type of helmet is "beset with the boar", for it has an ornamental crest running across the top with a stylized head in front similar to the Sutton Hoo boar or dragon heads.

The earliest of the more magnificent helmets is the silver one from Thorsbjerg. This has an extremely classical look about it—in fact it is even reminiscent of the golden helmet of Mes-Kalam-Shar, the First Dynasty ruler of Ur, about 3000 B.C., for it is made in the same way with a visor covering forehead, cheeks and chin (all in one piece) and a separate skull with simulated hair.

The helmets which are considered as more or less typical of the Heroic Age are those of the "Vendel" or "Sutton Hoo" type. These stem directly from Roman, and so ultimately from Etruscan, Greek and Minoan-Mycenean types. They are not unlike the Gaulish helmets of the first century shown in the sculptures on the triumphal arch at Orange, and may indeed stem from a common Frankish prototype. They have neck and cheek guards of the same

kind, but a feature which sets them apart
from all others is the visor; and instead of
the horns used as a crest, we find a stout
ridge running fore-and-aft across the skull,
usually ending in a conventional beast's
head. There is a deep-rooted idea in the
minds of most people that the helmets of
Anglo-Saxons and Vikings were invariably
adorned with horns, or wings; contrari-
wise, there is a tendency at present for
scholars to affirm that this was not so—as

*Fig. 50. Helmeted figure
from Sutton Hoo helmet.*

indeed most of the (extremely scanty) archaeological evidence
suggests. However, there may have been helmets so adorned.
Some bronze plaques for stamping out the embossed figures on the
thin metal plates with which the Vendel-type helmets were decorated were found at Øland in Sweden, showing fully armed warriors,
one of whom wears a helmet with two huge curved horns. The
Sutton Hoo helmet is adorned with similar embossed bronze plates,
one with a figure wearing a horned—or perhaps winged—helmet
(fig. 50). Other similar helmet-plates depict warriors wearing the
more usual variety of helmet corresponding very closely with the
Sutton Hoo type, except that they have very large complete boars
as crests, and no visors.

The Sutton Hoo helmet is made entirely of iron; the crown, like
the Swedish ones, was covered with thin bronze plates, parts of
which survive; originally they were tinned. Narrow ribs of tin,
fluted and gilded, were riveted over the joints between these plates,
covering the junctions between them and dividing the skull into
panels. The lowest row of these were embossed with figured
designs in a semi-naturalistic style; depicting god-like personages
and warriors in battle scenes. Only fragments of these survive, but
individual scenes are repeated several times. The panels on some of
the helmets from the Vendel graves agree so closely with the
Sutton Hoo ones that it seems likely that they came from the same
workshop. The panels in the upper part of the skull, as well as the
visor and the cheek and neck guards, are decorated with interlace
ornament. The crest running across the top of the skull is covered
with silver, grooved in a chevron pattern, and below it are eyebrows

of bronze inlaid with silver wire in vertical lines; at the outer end of each eyebrow is a small gilt bronze boar's head; and the under edge of each is picked out with a line of small square-cut garnets set in metal cells. The visor, covered like the skull with bronze plates, has a gilt bronze nose, mouth and moustache. The nose is in full relief and the moustache is a remarkably modern-looking affair, close-trimmed in a military style. This is decorated—made to look very bristly and realistic, too—by wires of silver inlaid vertically. The lower lip is decorated like the eyebrows with a row of square-cut garnets. The cheekguards are large and cover the ears, to accommodate which they are hollowed; and the neck-guard, which is shaped in its upper part to follow the line of the base of the skull, abruptly changes its angle and sticks out sharply, extending some way down between the shoulders. The rear end of the crest comes down on to the upper part of this neck-guard, where it ends in another animal head. This helmet looks very large, like a crash-helmet—a thing which we find in all helmets until the early seventeenth century. This was to accommodate the padded lining which held the metal of the helmet itself a good way away from the head, and without which it would be practically useless. The same thing is to be found in any modern tin hat. Like the Roman helmets which were their prototypes, they were all fastened by chin straps, probably attached inside the lower edges of the cheek-plates.

In one of the graves at Valsgärde (grave 8) together with one of these splendid helmets and other war-gear was a wooden box containing twenty-one iron staves or splints, which show signs of having been joined in three groups, two long and one short, by means of transverse riveted leather straps. The shorter ones are decorated on their thinner ends with conventionalized animal heads testifying to their Scandinavian origin. All of them are connected at one end to fragments of mail. As they were in a box, and not on a body, it has been a matter of great scholarly controversy as to the precise manner in which they covered what portion of their wearer. As is customary in such cases, not a little scholarly nonsense has been written about them, but the final result, well supported by contemporary pictorial evidence, shows with reasonable certainty that the long staves 'made up' into a pair of greaves, with sock or spat-like mail appendages to cover the insteps, and the short set formed the cuff of a single gauntlet. It is not feasible here to go into the arguments about the nature of this armour, let it suffice to show the final conclusion (fig. 51). Armour of a very similar kind was (you will remember) found in some Scythian graves of about 400 B.C. The greaves are not a pair, for though the size is the same the method of attaching the mail is different on each. It seems, therefore, that like so much grave-furniture of this period, the armour was already of some antiquity and defective when it was buried. The fact that there is only one gauntlet is not necessarily so odd as it might seem, for few warriors went without a shield, and it would be a severe handicap to carry a shield on the left fore-arm if you had a stiff metal cuff; quite apart from the inconvenience, extra protection of the arm would be unnecessary.

Fig. 51. Reconstruction of probable appearance of splinted armour found in one of the Valsgärde graves.

Strong support for the correctness of this reconstruction comes

Fig. 52. Figure from a golden vase found in the Nagyszentmiklos treasure.

from a gold vessel found at Nagyszentmiklos in Hungary, upon which is embossed the figure of a mounted warrior wear-ing the usual long byrnie of mail with the addition of splinted greaves and gauntlet cuffs (fig. 52). He also appears to wear mail breeches on his thighs, but this may be intended to represent the lower part of the long byrnie, slit up fore and aft for convenience in riding. We shall find exactly the same

Fig. 53. Gauntlet with splinted cuff, from the Sutton Hoo helmet (British Museum).

thing shown on the Bayeux Tapestry, where all the Norman warriors seem to be wearing voluminous "shorts". The treasure of which this vessel was a part is dated at about 860, considerably later than the Valsgärde splints, but the armour of a well-equipped warrior had changed hardly at all since the period of La Tène III, about 100 B.C. Futher evidence for the gauntlet cuffs is found on the helmet-plates from Sutton Hoo and Uppsala (the east mound) and Vendel, Grave 1 (fig. 53). A very interesting parallel with these figures has been found in some gold plates of Longobardic origin, figures of warriors similar to those on the Sutton Hoo and Vendel helmets, more proof of the close cultural links between all these Scandinavian peoples. Though none of these Longobardic figures show splinted greaves or gauntlets, we do know from the descriptions given by Paul the Deacon (in about A.D. 600) that the Longobards at that period did in fact wear greaves.

These items of war-gear I have described are the equipment of chieftains, but, as the Sagas show, such gear was often used by less high-ranking warriors. These things were meant to be used, and no gift bestowed more honour, and none were more hardly earned.

I have concentrated rather much on the arms of the Scandinavian races, because I believe them to be representative of the arms of the majority of the migrating peoples. We have seen from the Sutton Hoo material that the gear of the kings of East Anglia was in nearly every respect identical with that of kings of Sweden. By the same token it is likely that Goth, Longobard and Vandal were similarly armed. But what of the Franks? We have much information about them, but from sources literary rather than archaeological. It is clear enough that they were not nearly so well equipped as their contemporaries—a fact which matches their general crudity. There were lavishly armed chiefs, as we know from the recently discovered Frankish grave of a sixth-century warrior at Morken in the Rhineland. Here the main interest centres on the helmet, which was extremely well preserved. It has some features in common with the

Sutton Hoo and Vendel types, but far more which are quite different: the skull is more conical in form, made of several panels set vertically between the spaces of a framework of bands springing from a horizontal band round the brow and joined at the top (fig. 54) in a point, where the skull terminates in a little hollow fitting into which a crest—probably a plume—could be stuck. The cheek guards are narrower and closer to the Roman type in form, while instead of a neck-guard there is a short "curtain" of mail hanging from a series of holes round the lower rim of the framework of the

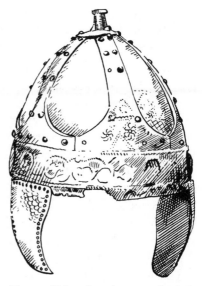

Fig. 54. *Helmet from the grave of a sixth-century Frankish chieftain. Morken, Rhineland.*

skull. It is in fact identical with those Dacian helmets of the second century so clearly shown on the base of Trajan's Column (fig. 35). This helmet is also remarkably similar to others which have been found in Persia, dating from the period of the Sassanian rulers. With its little plume of feathers at its apex, it was the regulation headgear of the Byzantine cavalry of the fourth to the seventh centuries.

The other object of particular interest from the Morken grave is the "life stone" which was lying near the sword, for it is a very handsome thing made of meerschaum and mounted with gold.

The Frankish tribes which overran the valleys of the Seine and the Loire, united by the strong arm of Chlodovech (Clovis) were still very like their ancestors described by Tacitus when Sidonius Appolinaris wrote of them in 460, and over a century later Agathius uses almost the same words, which shows that even their conquest of Southern Gaul had made very little difference to their military organization and customs. Telling of the defeat of their king Clodion by Aetius, Sidonius says:

They are a tall race, clad in close-fitting garments with a belt encircling the waist. They hurl their axes and cast their spears with great force, never missing their aim. They manage their shields with great skill, rushing on their enemy so fast that they seem to fly more rapidly than their javelins.

Procopius says much the same describing their terrible raid into Italy in the sixth century; Agathius, in the seventh, says that the arms of the Franks were very scanty, they wore neither mail-coat nor greaves; but he speaks of their characteristic spear, the Angon. This, he says, is used either for thrusting or throwing, its shaft covered with iron so that very little of the wood is showing; the head is furnished with two barbs. The Frank hurls this as he charges forward; it sticks into the shield of his adversary, who cannot pull it out because of the barbs nor cut off the head because of the iron haft; the weight of the spear drags down the shield. The Frank closes in, puts his foot on the spear butt, and finishes off his foe who is deprived of his shield.

This type of spear, the angon, is a weapon similar to the Roman Pilum, and must, I think, be derived from it. The Franks (who had very early and close contact with Rome) may have been the first of the barbarian peoples to make use of it, but they were by no means the only ones; Anglo-Saxons and Scandinavians used them too, particularly the former. There were seven angons in the Sutton Hoo grave, and very many more have been found in countless graves from Norway to Spain. Most of those which have been found have heads considerably larger than the ordinary pilum head, and the iron shafts are not, as Agathius seems to suggest, very long sockets covering the wood of the shaft, but are themselves forged in one piece with the head; there is an ordinary socket, from 4 in. to about 8 in. long; this merges with a long slender solid iron neck, of anything between 10 in. and 30 in. long, at the end of which is the broad barbed head (fig. 55).

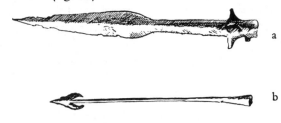

Fig. 55. a. Winged spear: b. Angon.

Fig. 56. Frankish throwing axe.

The other typical weapon the Franks had was the short light throwing-axe. This was always referred to as "Francisca" by the Latin writers, and it is hard to say whether the weapon was named after the people who used it, or whether the people were named Franks on account of their favourite weapon; we read of it being called "Frakki" as well. Probably the latter reason is more likely, for it seems reasonable to suppose that the Longobards were so named on account of a characteristic weapon, just as the Saxons may have been because they were characterized by their fondness for the sax. It is a curious reflection that the proud name of France may owe its origin to a little battle-axe used by the most barbarous of the Teutonic races (fig. 56).

The first mention of horsemen among the Franks is by Procopius, who says that when Theudebert invaded Italy with a vast army in 539, he had a few horsemen whom he kept about his person. During the next two centuries the composition of Frankish armies, like their armament, remained much the same—a large mass of undisciplined and ill-armed, unarmoured foot soldiery with a small guard of mounted men around the king. The number of these seems to have increased somewhat by the end of the Merovingian period, but it was still a very small proportion of the whole.

This was the age of the heroes, some legendary, some historical; of Sigurd Fafnisbani and Arthur, of Beowulf, Hrolf Kraki, Cuchulainn and Cadwalader, Clovis and Geiseric and Belisarius; the misty borderland of history where fact and legend mingle. From now on we shall be on solid historical ground, for with the Viking period history, as it were, came to the legendary north. Even so, the task of the student of the Archaeology of War becomes harder, for as documented history becomes more and more plentiful, so the archaeological material becomes less. Gone are the sacrificial deposits and the pagan burials after the Viking period; all that remains of the hardware of war is what we are fortunate enough to recover from the beds of rivers and from battlefields.

Part 3

THE VIKINGS

Chapter Eight

SWORDS IN THE VIKING PERIOD

T HE VIKING PERIOD (roughly between A.D. 750 and 1100) is generally treated as a separate age on its own, for though it is the historical continuation of the legendary centuries, its political effects were profound. It saw a final life and death struggle between the Christianized Germanic peoples whose ancestors had migrated from their northern homelands, and the pagan descendants of those who had stayed at home. Though it is given its name by the terrible raiders from the north, its truest significance was the cultural and political growth of Europe, from Charlemagne at the beginning of the period to the Normans and the First Crusade at the end of it. The Normans were the descendants of Vikings, and chivalry was the offspring of a marriage between the old heroic ideals and the Christian ethos.

No one really knows what caused this great series of raids and invasions which went on without a break for 300 years; it began (so we are told) in 787 with three black ships sailing into Poole harbour and up to Wareham, disgorging a fearful band of heathen warriors who sacked the peaceful town, and then sailed away again; and it ended in 1066 on the field of Senlac when William the Norman overcame the Saxon kingdom of England. Although the period of active roving and raiding had ended over a century before, the Norman invasion was, in a sense, the culminating adventure of Vikingdom.[1] Between these two events Iceland, the Shetlands and Orkneys, the east coast of Ireland, the Western Isles, the Isle of Man and a great part of Scotland and northern England were conquered and occupied by the Vikings; France was raided again and again, until finally Normandy was won and settled by Rollo. From Sweden they penetrated far into the heart of Russia, founding many great towns like Kiev. They raided up and down the Mediterranean like their Vandal predecessors and became for centuries the pampered *corps d'élite* of the fighting forces of the Emperors of Constantinople, the famous Varangian Guard. They founded a colony in Greenland (then far more habitable than it is to-day) and another, we have reason to believe, in America.

Our knowledge of the first appearance in England of Vikings in 787 comes from the late tenth-century historian Aethelward and the author of an entry in the Anglo-Saxon Chronicle, who describes the raid as, "The first ships of the Danish-men which sought the land of the English nation." Even if this assertion is literally correct, we cannot entirely discount the evidence of the Sagas, which over and over again tell of Scandinavian connections with England, of a political, plunder-seeking and trading kind. This is supported by archaeological evidence from a period as early as the fifth century. We read, for instance, in Fornmanna Saga:

> When Sigurd Hring (late seventh century) father of Ragnar Lodbrok (Hairy Breeks) king of Sweden and Denmark had made peace in both ... he bethought himself of the kingdom which his kinsman Harald Hilditonn (War-Tooth) had possessed in England, and before him Ivar Vidfadmi (Ivar of the Wide Embrace).

The outburst of Vikingdom seems to have been a final tremendous birth-giving by the vigorous and fertile genius of the north; for since then Scandinavia has produced no more Goths or Vandals or Vikings to shake the world and mould it to their own energetic and hard-headed pattern.

The Vikings used a great variety of sword-hilt types, though their

[1] R. E. M. Wheeler, *London and the Vikings*, 1927.

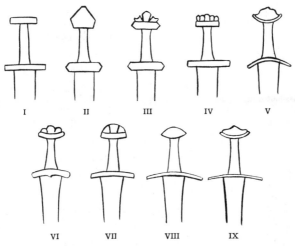

Fig. 57. Viking sword types.

blades varied very little. These hilts have been most thoroughly classified into 26 types by Dr. Jan Petersen, but it will be more convenient if we use a simplified typology worked out by Sir Mortimer Wheeler in 1927. He reduced Petersen's 26 types and sub-types to 7 basic styles, to which I have added two more. This, much abbreviated, is adequate to cover the whole range of hilt styles in use during the period (fig. 57). All of these are logical developments of the styles of the preceding period; but they are more massive, to balance the larger blades which began to come into use during the eighth century. Two basic factors are common to all of them—the continuing use of the combined upper guard and pommel, and the extreme development of the latter. The most characteristic Viking pommel is made up of three lobes, upon which basic form there are an infinity of variations. Laking [1] worked out a quite untenable (but ingenious) theory as to the reason for this pommel-form's emergence; unfortunately he seems to have ignored any earlier hilt-types except such as were incomplete, or had only the upper guard without the pommel. Upon this simplified hilt-form (which seems to have been used extensively in Norway between about 750–950) he built up a fantastic theory: that the Vikings in their early days, having a liking for charms, fitted such charms into little bags, and

[1] Sir Guy Laking: *A Record of European Armour and Arms through Seven Ages*, 1921, Vol. I.

Fig. 58. Sword found in the River Witham, ninth–tenth century (British Museum).

tied them with strings on to the tops of the upper guards of their swords. This theory is, I believe, quite wrong; though it is logical, the more because several of these tri-lobed pommels have twisted wires like strings in the depressions separating the lobes. And of course there is literary evidence for the use of bags on hilts like the little one which covered the pommel of Sköfnung, though we are told clearly enough that it was to keep the sun off, not to keep charms in. (Incidentally, it is not illogical perhaps to wonder whether the beautiful and elaborate jewelled hilts of pre-Viking days were not as a matter of course covered up when at sea, or on the march.) The Vikings themselves had much more down-to-earth decorations upon their swords—inlays or platings of silver, bronze, tin, copper and brass—which must have been far more hard-wearing. They would have been easier and less expensive to make, too; gone are all the elaborate jewelled inlays and delicate goldsmith's work; swords in the Viking age were in much more common use, and though some are very splendid, many have hilts of plain unadorned iron.

Yet they are, as swords, far more beautiful as well as being stouter and more terrible. The marvellous swords of the Heroic Age, with both blade and hilt works of lovely craftsmanship, often look ugly and clumsy, but the swords of the Vikings mostly have that austere perfection of line and proportion which is the essence of beauty. Compare the drawing of the Klein Hunigen sword in fig. 40, for instance,

134

with fig. 58, a Viking sword of about A.D.
900 which was found in the River Witham
near Lincoln. The one is garnished with
gold and jewellery, but it is not beautiful;
the other is plain, its only decoration being
simple geometrical patterns, rather crudely
executed, inlaid in copper and brass upon
its hilt; yet it has a very splendour of
beauty. It lives in your hand, too. As your
fingers close round its hilt you feel the
character of the weapon; it seems positively
to woo you to strike. There is no mistaking
its message or its purpose, even after an immersion in mud and water and weeds of
eight or so centuries. This sword is in the
British Museum. Look at it when you go
and see the Battersea shield and the Sutton
Hoo treasure; I believe you will not be dis-
appointed in it.

In this period we are able for the first
time to assign certain styles of sword hilt to
specific peoples by reason of the distribution of the specimens which have been
found. Types I and II, for instance, we can
assign with some certainty to the Norwegians. Over 330 examples of Type II
have been found in Norway (most of them
on one-edged swords (fig. 59), for which
the Norwegians seem to have had a prefer-

Fig. 59. Norwegian Long Sax.

ence), some have been recorded from Sweden, and none at all from
Denmark. In the British Isles they occur along the line of the early
Norwegian raids—Orkney and the Western Isles (four examples in
the Scottish National Museum in Edinburgh) and in Ireland—
fifteen or more in the National Museum in Dublin—where they are
characteristic of the Viking cemeteries. From England, which was
attacked mostly by the Danes, only one example has been recorded,
and that not for certain, from the River Lea at Enfield, near
London; a single-edged blade from the Thames at Mortlake is

135

of Norwegian character and may have had one of these hilts. This type lasted from perhaps about 775 to about 900.

Type III has a three-lobed (occasionally five-lobed) pommel, often with zoomorphic ends, and straight guards. The central lobe is always the largest. It is the normal type in north-west Europe during the ninth and tenth centuries, where its main development seems to have taken place in north-western Germany and southern Scandinavia under the influence of the zoomorphic pommels which were characteristic of this region during the fifth and sixth centuries; it is, in fact, in all its forms simply an enlarged development of the cocked hat pommels of Type 4 of the Migration period (fig. 41). This type is rarely found in the British Isles, though it occurs in Scotland (on the island of Eigg) and in Dublin.

Type IV is perhaps rather a sub-type of III. It has an almost flat pommel with five lobes, generally all of the same size; the lower edges are usually straight, as are the guards, but occasionally both are slightly curved. The distribution of the type is wide; many were found in graves at Knin and elsewhere in Jugoslavia; some in Norway (one with curved pommel-base and guard) and others in Ireland, and one magnificently decorated pommel of nielloed silver was found in Fetter Lane in London. This is in the British Museum. Also in London (in the Wallace Collection in Manchester Square) is another, but it was acquired in France and was probably found there. This type is generally held to be Frankish, though the Fetter Lane example may suggest an English influence upon the development of a Viking type; it was in use between about 850 and 950.

Type V is a distinctive group, dating between about A.D. 875 and 950, with a very high peaked central lobe and sharply curved pommel-base and guards. One from the River Thames at Wallingford (from which the type has been named) and others found in Norway bear English ornament (in the "Trewhiddle" style) of late ninth century date. This, combined with the fact that more have been found in England than anywhere else, suggests very strongly that it is a native English type.

Type VI may equally well be said to be a Danish type of the tenth and early eleventh centuries, for its greatest concentration of finds seems to be in Denmark and those parts of England where the Danes under Sweyn Forkbeard and Knut were concentrated upon London and south-east England during the first quarter of the eleventh century. Most, in fact, have come out of the Thames. The type is lacking in Scotland and Ireland, and its main concentration in Europe is to the south and east of the Baltic.

Type VII has an almost semi-circular, flattish pommel in the shape of a tea-cosy. Most examples have grooves or beaded lines which divide the surface into three parts, vestiges of the threefold division characteristic of the pommels of Types III and VI, though many have only one horizontal groove, suggesting a division between pommel and upper guard, and some have none at all. It is found in fairly wide distribution, and its associations in Scandinavia suggest that it belongs mainly to the tenth century. Many examples have been found in rivers along the western coasts of France; there is a particularly fine one from the Scheldt in the Tower of London,[1] and another in the same collection from the Thames at Bray. There are two in the museum at York, found in the city—which was captured by the Danes in 867—and another in the British Museum from the River Lea at Edmonton in London, and others—one complete with its scabbard and grip—from the Seine at Paris, relics probably of the great siege of 885–86.

The two types which I have added to Wheeler's typology are transitional forms which link the Viking sword, with its generally short guard and lobated pommel, with the later mediaeval sword, the knightly weapon of the Age of Chivalry. Type VIII has a pommel which is, I believe, nothing but a much simplified development of Type VI. The divisions between the upper and lower parts have vanished as well as the lobes, leaving a form just like a brazil nut. Nearly all swords with this form of pommel have slender guards, much longer than the usual Viking ones and generally curved towards the blade. The earliest swords with these hilts have been found in Norwegian burials of about A.D. 950, and its latest forms belong to the thirteenth century. Its distribution (in its earlier form within the Viking period) tended to be confined to northern and central Europe, with isolated examples in Norway. So far none has been found in the western parts of Europe, with the exception of one which just possibly may have been found in England. This is in my own collection and has a story which I shall recount later.

[1] On loan from the collection of Sir James Mann.

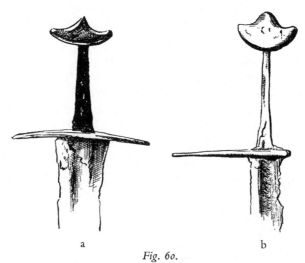

Fig. 60.

a. *Sword from Flemma in Norway inscribed* INGELRIIMEFECIT.
b. *Thirteenth-century sword from Denmark with pattern-welded blade.*

Type IX is, I believe, a bye-form of VIII. The general shape of the hilt is similar, but the pommel at first retains the division into upper and lower parts, the upper part taking on an exaggerated cocked-hat form. The one illustrated in fig. 60a was found in a Norwegian grave of about 1000. It is much less common than Type VIII, and one cannot say that it is found more in one locality than another, for only isolated examples have been found widely separated. Its greatest popularity, in a more massive form, was in Germany during the period 1250–1300 (fig. 60b).

There is one further pommel-type, which can be included in the latest of the Viking hilt-styles. This is in the form of a thick disc, sometimes with the edges bevelled off. Now in nearly every work in any language which discusses mediaeval swords, you will come across phrases such as: "The disc-shaped pommel did not come into use until the twelfth century." There is pictorial evidence to show that this is quite wrong; it was used in the eleventh and even in the tenth century, but archaeological support was lacking until about 1950, when a series of late Viking graves—dating between 1000–1100—was opened in Finland. In these graves were found a number of swords with disc pommels, a discovery which enables us to say with certainty that this, the most common type of mediaeval sword-pommel, popular right up to about 1550, was in use by about 1050.[1]

The Viking swords give the impression that their decoration was wrought by the swordsmith, not by a jeweller. In nine cases out of ten it consists of simple designs applied to the iron in various ways; in the earlier part of the period a thick plating of silver, often covered all over with small punched dots, or crosses (fig. 61) or small geometrical figures, was popular; during the ninth and tenth centuries this plating was often engraved with running interlace patterns of the kind used in book decoration (the Lindisfarne Gospels, for instance) to which niello was sometimes applied (fig. 62). Towards the period's end we find geometrical patterns inlaid in brass on a background of tin, each figure outlined by a strip of copper wire. A simple and much-used decoration all through the

Fig. 61. Sword with massive silver-covered hilt (Bergen Museum).

Fig. 62. Sword of Type 3 with decorated silver hilt (Bergen Museum).

[1] I had this information in the course of correspondence with Dr. Jorma Leppaho of Helsinki, who was concerned in the clearing of these graves.

Fig. 63. Sword of Type 2 with hilt decorated with vertical strips of silver. Found in Switzerland (Zurich, Landesmuseum).

period consisted of the whole surface of guards and pommel being covered with closely placed vertical strips of copper and tin alternately, running from edge to edge (fig. 63) of each element. This was sometimes elaborated by little herringbone patterns inlaid between each vertical strip in a different metal. These decorations are often finely executed, works of real craftsmanship which give an effect of splendour which in its way is far more effective than the older jeweller's work, for the direct simplicity of the ornament is well-matched to the grim dignity of the sword's shape.

The plating was applied to these hilts by hammering or burnishing thin sheets of gold, silver, copper, brass or tin foil on to the surface of the iron which was covered all over with a close network of fine cuts; the softer metal of the plating was forced into these cuts and held securely. In some cases where plating was decorated with interlace or other patterns or by geometrical designs, the ground would be of tin or silver, the pattern itself of brass or gold, outlined with copper or bronze. Sometimes the pattern was not inlaid in metal but filled with black niello. Fig. 62 is an example of this sort of work, while the sword from the Witham in the British Museum (fig. 58) which I described earlier is decorated in the latter style, the motif being diamond-shaped insets of brass outlined with copper on a ground of tin. This sword's long immersion in the mud has worn away the pattern on the hilt so that we can see very clearly the method by which it was applied. There is another tenth-century sword hilt similarly decorated in the museum at Dorchester (Dorset)—and very many more all over Europe. This copper-brass-and-tin ornament seems mostly to have been used late in the period (*c.* 950–1050), whereas the more elegant and often far richer interlace patterns often of gold-silver-bronze are earlier (*c.* 800–900).

The swords of Type V, which as we have said are probably Anglo-Saxon, have decoration applied in thick embossed or engraved plates of silver or bronze; one or two have been found with medallions like coins (but not actual coins) inlaid in the centre of the pommel. Some of the Type IV swords have a quite different sort of decoration, like sprays of foliage (fig. 64); this is a typically Frankish ornament of the ninth–tenth centuries, and strengthens the supposition that these swords are of a Frankish fashion.

Fig. 64. Hilt of sword from Gravraak in Norway, with Frankish decoration.

There are a few Viking hilts which bear the name of their maker. In the British Museum is a "lower guard" which was found near Exeter, upon which is written "LEOFRIC ME FEC". We might be tempted to think that this referred to the whole sword, not merely the hilt, were it not for two swords of Type IV which were found in Ireland. On the lower guard of one is the name HARTOLFR, but on its blade is another name, ULFBEHRT, that of the smith who made it. This sword was found at Kilmainham, and the other was found at Ballinderry Crannog in 1928; its guard is inscribed HILTIPREHT, while its blade also bears another name. In Norway is one signed HLITER, and in London (the Type IV sword in the Wallace Collection) is one where the guard has on one side of the blade the letters HLI, and on the other letters which are not clear, though they have been read as TR. From this we may assume that these names applied only to the makers of the hilts.

Yet it is by no means certain that all these "names" on hilts were

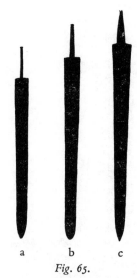

a   b   c

Fig. 65.

a. *Roman Iron Age (first–fourth centuries A.D.).*
b. *Migration Period (fifth–ninth centuries).*
c. *Viking Age (eighth–twelfth centuries).*

in fact names at all. "Hliter" for instance is extremely reminiscent of a word in Old Norse for protection, while "Hiltipreht" is more likely to be a compound of words meaning "hilt" and "ready". "Hartolfr" does at first glance seem like a name, and of course the Exeter guard with "Leofric me fec(it)" is not open to any doubt.

At some time during the Viking Age the sword-makers evolved a new technique of bladesmithing. In the first part of it—say between A.D. 700 and 850—sword blades had tended to become larger and heavier than their predecessors, but somewhere about 900 blades of a far handier shape began to appear (fig. 65). These were not pattern-welded, yet were tougher and lighter; they tapered more sharply away from the hilt so that the point of balance came nearer to it, thus making them swifter and more manageable in the hand than the older, almost parallel-sided blades with the point of balance well down towards the point. These swords are all right for making heavy, slashing blows, but with the newer type you can thrust as well, and make a far quicker recovery from a blow, or turn a forehand stroke to a back-hander without having to use nearly so much force. The first appearance of these swords seem to have coincided with the emergence of a new style of marking blades, and a new name, ULFBERHT. This name is inlaid in countless blades found in every part of Europe.[1] Philologists have stated that it is a mixture— Ulf is Scandinavian, while Berht or Bert is Frankish; the H in Behrt denotes an early period, before about 900. The name, in connection with the known centres of blade-making from which all these swords have emanated from the La Tène period onwards,

[1] Until 1959 it was not known whether any of these blades had been found in England. In March of that year I was able to identify, by means of an x-ray picture, that the blade of a Viking sword, found at Shifford in the Thames and now in the Museum at Reading, was inlaid with that name.

suggests the Ulfberht was a smith who lived in the later ninth century and worked in the region of the Rhineland where Solingen—a famous centre of sword-making up to this century—now is. There are so many blades bearing Ulfberht's name, and which cover so long a period (more than 200 years) that Ulfberht himself cannot have made all of them. The obvious inference is that he was the founder of a firm, probably a family affair like the great blade-smithing families of the later Middle Ages, which flourished for a very long time. Like the later smiths he seems to have his imitators. In the River Nene near Wisbech was found a sword of the late Viking period, upon one side of which appeared a mis-spelt form of the name Ulfberht, while upon the other is an even more garbled version of another great smith name of the tenth century, Ingelri.

Many swords by this firm have been found, though not in such numbers as the others nor covering so long a period. I shall have more to say about these later, but I must return to Ulfberht and the new fashion of inlaying the name in the blade. None of these blades is pattern-welded, for they relied for their toughness not upon the age-old, complicated structure afforded by that technique but upon the fact that they were of hard, elastic steel; steel all through, not iron stiffened and strengthened by countless twisted threads of steel woven (as it were) into the iron fabric of the blade. Tests were made as long ago as 1889 on three pattern-welded blades from Norway, which showed that they had 0·414%, 0·401% and 0·520% of carbon content, whereas an Ulfberht sword from Norway had 0·75% of carbon. This is only an indication, for much wider testing will be needed before one can be dogmatic about it.

These smiths did not modestly stamp their names in tiny letters like Ranvic and Tasvit and the others of the fourth and fifth centuries; they inlaid them in large, untidy letters sprawling right across the middle of their blades, letters often an inch high. Even so, they were probably as unobtrusive as their predecessors, for they were made of iron inlaid in the steel of the blade. The smith, having finished his blade, would mark on its surface the letters he intended to inlay. Then he would follow his marks with strong cuts of a cold chisel. Little pieces of iron wire twisted like string would then be cut to fit into the chiselled grooves; the blade would be made white-hot, and the cold bits of iron hammered into the grooves;

Fig. 66.

after which the whole thing would be re-heated to welding-heat—say about 1,300°C.—and the safety of the inlay insured by careful hammering. Finally it would be filed smooth, and the whole blade burnished like a mirror till the letters were scarcely visible. Yet all the potency of the name would be there, an integral part of the sword.

In every Ulfberht name so far identified a cross is incorporated with the name; occasionally there are two, one preceding the u and the other either between the r and the h, or between the h and the t (fig. 66). The second one is invariably present, even if the first is omitted.

The other side of each of Ulfberht's blades is inlaid similarly with a pattern, no two of which are identical. These patterns consisted of arrangements of upright strokes, diagonal crosses, interlaced bands and isolated letters. We have no clue as to their meaning, though there can be no doubt at all that they *had* meaning, for we must remember that at this period names and words and symbols had a great and god-like potency. Some of these symbols, particularly the ancient cross-within-a-circle and a diagonal cross with a small dot between each arm, are to be seen roughly hammered into granite kerbstones at the present day.

There were many other smiths of the period who marked their blades in this way, but their swords have only appeared in isolated examples. At first it was thought that the name denoted the sword's owner, but when so many Ulfberhts were identified it became obvious that this was impossible; some scholars believed that the name referred to the place or district where the blades were forged, but then a sword was found in Sweden marked INGELRIIMEFECIT. Another (see fig. 60a) was found in Norway with the same inscription; while in the region of Strassburg a sword was found which told that Banto made it; so it became clear by analogy that Ulfberht also was the name of a maker. Even so, there were swords which bore the name of their owner. One of the best known of the early Viking

INGELRII

HOMODEI

Fig. 67. *Inscription on sword of Type X from Dresden.*

swords, from Saebo in Norway, has runic characters (inlaid in these big iron letters) saying "Thormud possesses me"; and there is a little sax of the tenth century in the British Museum (it was found in the Thames) with a silver plate inlaid in its blade which reads + BIORTEL-MEPORTE (Bjortelm carries me), and on the other side, inlaid in silver letters in the blade itself, SIGEBERTMEAH, which seems to mean nothing except that Sigebert had a hand in the knife's being in some way or other, probably in its making. There are other cases in the twelfth and thirteenth centuries of swords with owner's names on them which we shall discuss later.

The sword which first gave the clue that these inlaid names were those of smiths was found in the Sigridsholm lake in Sweden; it is of Type VI and dates about the middle of the tenth century. All the other Ingelrii blades (so far only about twenty have been identified) are of the later tenth and the eleventh centuries. They differ from the earlier Ulfberht blades in that their inscriptions are more neatly done, and are without crosses. For instance, a sword found near Dresden has the name INGELRII inlaid in big letters on one side, but on the other, in much smaller, neater letters of iron, appear the words "Homo Dei" (fig. 67). The men who went on Crusade in 1099 called themselves *Homines Dei*, Men of God, and here is an eleventh-century sword which we may presume was borne by one of them. There is an almost identical sword in my own collection; on one side it bears the name (or part of it, for the final letters are not visible), but on the other is an odd-looking pattern of lines and triangles which was inlaid in copper or latten, not in iron. This is the sword I mentioned which had a story. Actually it has two, one quite unimportant, of how I came by it, and the other, far more significant, which its own fabric tells us.

It was bought by a friend of mine in 1936 in the Caledonian Market in London, where he saw it lying on the cobble-stones, bundled together with two or three brass-hilted Waterloo-period swords. It still had upon it a lot of the hardened mud which had encased it when it was dug up, no one knows where, though the fact that this mud had not been chipped off suggests that it might have been found recently, and in England. He bought it (with the brass-hilted swords) for four-and-sixpence. When he took some of the mud off, he found clear traces of a diapered pattern inlaid on the cross-guard in a yellow metal, and some traces of yellow metal inlaid in the pattern on the blade. Not being particularly interested in mediaeval swords, he parted with it soon afterwards to a collector who unfortunately cleaned it with a rust-removing substance, with the inevitable result that all traces of the decoration were removed with the rust. In 1947 it was sold at Sotheby's, where I had the good fortune to get it (owing to a thick fog which prevented another friend of mine, who wanted it too and had far more money than I had, from reaching the sale-room in time to examine it).

Since I have had it, some very interesting facts about it have been revealed. Firstly, I was able to clear and read the letters INGEL . . . which told of its origin. Then the pattern on the back was identified as a rather crude representation of the "Caroccium", a type of war-standard on a wheeled car used by the free cities of the Rhine and of northern Italy. This standard consisted of a tall flag-pole set upon a car, with the banners of the wards of the city, or of the leaders of the host, hung upon it from gaff-like poles projecting from the main staff; at the top was a spherical container wherein the Holy Sacrament was placed before going into battle, and a large cross surmounted the whole. Here upon this sword-blade is the whole thing (fig. 68). This type of standard appears to have been invented by Heribert, Archbishop of Milan, in 1035. The inlays on these two blades (the Dresden one and my own) are interesting because they help us with dating not only the swords themselves but others with inlays in similar technique. For instance, the small neat letters of the Homo Dei inscription are of a style which seems to have become popular during the twelfth century,

Fig. 68. The "Caroccium" mark on the blade of a sword of Type X in the author's collection.

146

for many blades which date before about 1150 have similar inscriptions (a most beautiful sword, in nearly perfect condition, lies upon my writing table at this moment with an inscription of this style on each side of its blade; this will be described fully later). The fact that a sword which can be dated by its form and its maker's name to the eleventh century has upon it an inscription in a style popular in the twelfth only gives evidence that the new style came in before the old one went out, but the words of the second inscription gave us a date showing that the new style was probably in use before 1100.

The other sword shows two separate styles of inlay in use on the same blade, the old iron-inlaid smith-name on one side and a copper or latten inlaid pictograph on the other. This style of inlaying "pictorial" designs on blades in fine lines of copper, latten, silver or pewter was much used during the twelfth and thirteenth centuries, but here we have it on a sword of the eleventh. It is unlikely to have been applied to the blade before 1035, for we are told that the "Carrocium" was not used before then, while the style of the sword is such that it is very unlikely that it was made after 1100. So the inlay helps to date the sword, and the sword helps to date a style of inlay. Actually inlays of yellow metal, gold or copper, were used (though not often) all through the Roman and Migration periods. There is a blade from the Nydam bog with runic letters inlaid in gold, and there are many saxes inlaid with designs of copper or brass (or latten).

Further facts about this sword of mine came to light when the Ancient Monuments department of the Ministry of Works became interested in it. I have said that the last letters of the name are obliterated. This is because a small patch has been welded into the blade at this point. It is obvious from the patination of the blade that this patch was put in in antiquity; it is no modern repair. The question was, why was it there at all? An x-ray photograph of the blade gave us the answer. A severe blow on the sword's edge about four inches below the hilt had caused two fractures to run into the centre of the blade. These are not visible on the surface, but they must have caused the inlaid iron of the final letters to fall out, leaving a weak patch in the blade. Now a good sword was a costly thing; one would not discard it unless it was quite unusable.

Presumably the damage did not seem too bad, for the patch was put in—not very well, certainly not by a swordsmith. The inference must be that the damage was done on campaign (what would be more likely?) and that a hasty repair was made by the nearest armourer. The mark of the blow which caused the damage is still clearly visible on the edge of the sword—a gently curving depression about 3 in. long—with the metal of the edge burred over on either side. Presumably this curving dent would fit the curved surface of some long-perished helmet—only a helmet would have been hard enough or would have presented a large enough surface to make such a mark on a sword's edge, for at this period no other plate armour was worn.

The introduction of these new-fashioned blades in the early tenth century did not mean that the older styles of pattern-welded ones were abandoned, for we find many of them mounted in hilts which are unmistakably of the tenth and eleventh centuries—indeed, in Copenhagen there is a sword which cannot be earlier than 1250, with a fine pattern-welded (though broken) blade in it (see fig. 50b); and in Zurich there is a "Landsknecht" sword of the last years of the fifteenth century which has one. These, of course, were old blades re-hilted. There seems to be no doubt that the making of these blades had ceased by A.D. 1000. The Zurich sword is particularly interesting, for the hilt is of a most distinctive form (see plate 20, D) which was only used for a very short time between about 1490 and 1530, and there can be no doubt that the ancient blade was fitted with a modern hilt in 1500-odd; it is no nineteenth century collector's pastiche.

The sax underwent a complete change during the Viking period. No more do we find the stout, broad-bladed weapons of the fifth century; instead, we have two kinds of sax; a long, single-edged sword—one much favoured by the Norwegians—and a shorter, more slender weapon like a knife, used extensively by Anglo-Saxons and Franks and called nowadays a Scramasax. Some of these scramasaxes were quite long (one in the British Museum from the Thames

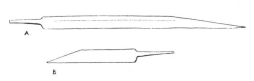

Fig. 69. Scramasax blades, eighth–tenth century.

148

in London is 28 in. long) but most are short—"Handsaxes", the Saxons called them. Fig. 69 shows types of sax-blade in use during the ninth and tenth centuries. They are unlike their large fifth-century predecessors for the tangs are always straight, springing from the middle of the blade, and do not show the shape of the hilt itself. It is curious to note that the Sinhalese for the last three centuries or so have been producing very beautifully decorated little knives remarkably like these handsaxes.

Chapter Nine

THE VIKINGS AT WAR

NORSE LITERATURE is full of poetic allusions to arms, most of which were held to be pure fancy until the archaeological evidence of the weapons themselves became available. There are, for instance, four words meaning "sword", but each denotes a different type. "Svaerd" is the most common, and refers to what we nowadays would call the broadsword—a two-edged blade without much of a point, meant mainly for slashing. "Maekir" is a slightly less common term, and seems to refer to a weapon similar to the sword, but with a more slender and acutely tapering blade ending in a sharp point. The two swords from the Kragehul bog illustrated in plate 3 are admirable examples of *svaerd* and *maekir*. Then, of course, there is the sax, and one of its varieties, the *skolm*, a short one-edged sword like a knife (fig. 69b is probably a skolm.)

The word "hilt" (Hjalt) denoting the whole of the handle of the sword was used in its modern sense by the Saxons, but in old Norse it denotes only the cross-pieces, the upper hilt (Fremir Hjaltit) and the lower hilt (Efra Hjaltit).[1] The grip was called the middle piece, Medalkafli. The metal fillets which we see on the grips of so many swords of the Migration and Viking periods were the Vettrim (meaning "lid-formed rim"), and we may suppose, though this is by no means certain, that the leather or vellum or linen covering

[1] For this reason I always refer to a sword as if it is looked at point downwards, for it is evident from this and many other literary allusions that it was so regarded and described in antiquity. Modern writers tend to refer to it as if it was seen point upward, which would make nonsense of the Viking's references to upper and lower hilts.

Fig. 70. Blade-patterns which may equate with the descriptive terms "Ann" and "Blodida".

of the grips was called the Valbost. This means literally "foreign covering", but originally it denoted any thin membrane covering any object. In one of the Edda poems direction is given to cut runes *a vettrimum ok a valbostum*; in another, the Helgakvida, there is a reference to a sword with a serpent sign on the valbost. The long slender guards—or lower hilts—which occur on many late Viking swords of Type VIII were called "Gaddhjalt" spike hilt, for Gaddr means a spike.

The decoration is called Mal or Moel, but it was really used far more often in describing the blade of a sword—one of the things which baffled scholars a good deal before the identification of pattern-welding. There is frequent mention of the wave-sword (Vaegir in Old Norse and Waegsweord in Old English), but even more obscure seemed the descriptive terms for certain blade-patterns: "Blood-eddy", for instance (Blodida), or Ann, which is an old Norse word for swathes of mown corn (the same word as the Middle High German Jan). Both these terms are perfectly apt when we apply them to the patterns shown in fig. 70 a and b. Of a more robust character are two other terms occurring in a poem as features or parts of a sword: Blodvarp and Idvarp. This could (and probably does) refer to a style of pattern-welding where the pattern is made up of long parallel stripes running lengthwise down the blade. Varp means a warp in weaving, and the long lines down the blade are likened to the warp of a web which is completed when the blade is imbrued with blood or vitals. (Blod is blood, and Idr means intestines.)

Many and picturesque are the descriptive phrases used for swords: Odin's Flame, the Ice of Battle, Serpent of the Wound, the Dog of the Helmet, Battle-snake, The Fire of the Shields, The Battle-Fire,

Torch of the Blood, The Snake of the Byrnie, The Sea-King's Fire, Tongue of the Scabbard, The Byrnie's Fear, Harmer of War-Knittings. Similar colourful expressions were applied to other arms as well; the byrnie (which in the Viking Age was a garment of the same cut as in the preceding Migration period) was called The Grey Clothes of Odin, the Weft of Spears, Blue-Shirt and Battle Cloak, Cloak of Kings and War-Net, and, as we have seen, War-Knitting. In view of this constant reference to nets and webs and knitting it seems quite extraordinary that even now it is a commonly held belief that mail was unknown in the West until "the Crusaders brought it from Palestine in the twelfth century".

Some of these byrnies the Vikings wore were very short, only covering the upper half of the torso, while there is a reference to another type called Spanga-Brynja which means a byrnie with plates. This may possibly be a garment like the mail-shirt with gold plates which was found in the Thorsbjerg bog.

Shields were much the same as in the preceding period, and the description on p. 120 of the Sutton Hoo shield would in the main hold good for those of the following four centuries. That they were often as large may be inferred from references such as "Then the king . . . selected a resting-place for the night where all his men came together and lay in the open under their shields" (St. Olaf's Saga, Ch. 219) and "When Olaf was in the Syllingar (Scilly Isles) a hermit prophesied to him 'that he would get severely wounded in a fight and be carried on a shield on board his ship'." (Olaf Tryggvason's Saga, Heimskringla, Ch. 32). Shields seem to have more poetic phrases bestowed upon them even than swords: The Sun of Battle, The Sun of Odin, (or the Moon of either), the Net of Spears (spears being referred to as the Fish of the Shield), Board of Victory, The War-Linden, The Wheel of Hild (a Valkyrie) and Hild's Wall, The Sun of the Sea-Kings, The Land of the Arrows, The Spears' Path, Battle-Shelterer, the Hall-Roof of Odin, the Burgh of Swords, and so on.

Helmets, on the other hand, do not seem to have been favoured with such specific allusive phrases. Sometimes we read of them having names, like king Adils' helmet which he called Hildigölt (War-Boar); as we can see from the few bits of *Beowulf* which I quoted in chapter VII, the boar usually figured prominently on helmets as crest or decoration, with a strong protective symbolism, and allusions to boars generally indicate helmets. From the Viking period there are practically no helmets surviving. In Laxdaela Saga (Ch. 63) we read:

> He had a spanga-brynja (q.v.) and a steel cap, the brim of which was as wide as a hand's breadth, and a shining axe on his shoulder, the edge of which seemed to be two feet long. He had black eyes, and was very Viking-like in appearance.

Fig. 71. Carolingian helmet, from "Vivians Bible", c. 850 (Paris, Bib. Nat. Cod. Lat. 1)

Here is a type of helmet which was very popular all through the Middle Ages. Illustrations of these war-hats abound, and in many Frankish manuscripts of the Carolingian period we see brimmed iron hats. A particularly good example is shown in fig. 71 from a manuscript of about 850 now in the Bibliothèque Nationale in Paris. These helmets, probably derived from a Roman type of cavalry helmet, are remarkably like the late sixteenth-century morions which are so familiar.[1] It is possible that the reference to the steel cap with its wide brim told of one of these, for though we only find pictures of them in Frankish manuscripts, it does not follow that they were not worn elsewhere than in Frankland (we cannot speak of France or Germany at this period, for the two were at that time united). Indeed, it seems extremely likely that most of the Vikings' helmets—like all the sword-blades they used—were made in "Valland", as they called the countries of the Franks, for over and over again we find in the Sagas such comments as

> He has on his ship one hundred men, and they had on coats of mail and foreign helmets.
>
> St. Olaf's Saga, Ch. 47.

Generally on the front of helmets was painted a "War-Mark"

[1] Some of the war hats illustrated in these Carolingian manuscripts are so close to those shown in late Roman art that one wonders whether they were not debased copies of these, and not of actual contemporary helmets—yet most other arms such as swords, spears, shields, saddles, stirrups and byrnies are clearly not Roman at all, but ninth-century Frankish.

(Herkumbl), a badge whereby men following one leader could recognize their comrades, a sort of Viking regimental cap badge.

During the Viking period axes became far more popular and were held in greater respect than formerly. We read of costly decorated axes being bestowed as gifts, in the same manner as swords:

> As they parted, the Jarl gave Olaf Hoskuldsson a most costly gold-ornamented axe.
>
> *Laxdaela Saga, Ch. 29.*

These axes were far more effective weapons than the ones which belong to the earlier centuries. You have just read of the very Viking-like warrior who wore the iron cap and carried an axe whose "edge seemed to be about two feet long". He who made that comment was a herdsman, warning Helgi Hardbeinsson of a band of men who were out to kill him; it may well have seemed to him that this weapon really was as formidable as he said it was, for these Viking axes (there are many such from the Thames, in the British Museum and the London Museum) are enormous and terrible weapons (fig. 72) whose edges are often as much as 12 in. long. These were indeed battle-axes; we cannot confuse them, like the earlier ones, with domestic axes. They had their poetic names, too: the Fiend of the Shield, Battle-Witch, the Wound's Wolf— but "Fiend" and "Witch" were applied to them almost exclusively, as "Witch" of the Shield, of the armour, of the byrnies, of the helmet, and so on. The great two-handed axes which Harold's Huscarles wielded at Senlac were of this type, as we can see most plainly in the Bayeux tapestry.

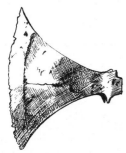

Fig. 72. Viking axe head from the Thames (London Museum).

In the same way as axes were usually called witch, spears were "Serpent", Serpent of Blood, or of anything else the poet fancied; sometimes, as we have seen, a spear was called the Fish of the Shield, or of the war-net; at other times we find it called—an excellent name this, nearly as good as Homer's "long-shadowed spear" —"the flying dragon of the fight". The actual spears used seem to have been hardly different from those found in the great bog-deposits, except that in the later part of the period they tended, like the later swords, to have a fairly simple kind of decoration in the form of narrow bands of alternate white and yellow metal running (like a cord binding) round and round the socket, often with little herringbone insets between each band.

The Vikings (and there is no doubt their forbears also) had as strict a code of rules governing duelling as did the French in the 1720s. There were two sorts of duel, a more informal "single-fight" (Einvigi), and a most punctilious formal one called Holmgang. This means literally "going on an island", and wherever possible such duels were fought on small islets, but where this was not possible a space (like a boxing ring and of much the same size) was marked out on the ground. These Holmgang duels were often used as a legal method of settling disputes about property or women, in the same way as the mediaeval trial by combat. Unfortunately they were much abused by tough individuals like professional duellists and Berserks to get possession of someone's wife or land, though occasionally such men would challenge another to a Holmgang merely to get his loose property; or sometimes, like Holmganga Bersi of whom we read in Kormac's Saga (see ch. 6), p. 105, just for the fun of it. It is in this Saga that we find one of the best descriptions of the Holmganga law. You remember how Kormac borrowed Sköfnung from Skeggi of Midfirth for his duel. Here is what happened:

A cloak was spread under their feet. Bersi said: "You, Kormac, challenged me to Holmganga; but instead of it I offer you Einvigi. You are young and inexperienced, and at Holmganga there are difficult rules, but none whatever at Einvigi!" Kormac answered, "I shan't fight better at Einvigi, and I'll risk it, and be on equal footing with you in everything." "You shall have your way, then," said Bersi.

This was the Holmganga law: that the cloak should be ten feet from one end to the other, with loops in the corners, and through these loops should be put pegs with a head at the top. These were called Tjosnur. Then three squares, their sides each a foot beyond the other, must be marked round the cloak. Outside the squares must be placed four poles called Hoslur (hazel-poles). It was called a Hazelled Field when it was prepared thus (fig. 73). Each man must have three shields, and when these where made useless he must stand upon the cloak, even if he had moved out of it before, and defend himself with his weapons.

Fig. 73. Diagram of the Hoslur, or Hazelled Field.

He who had been challenged must strike first. If either was wounded so that blood came upon the cloak he was not obliged to fight any longer. If either stepped with one of his feet outside the hazel poles he was held to have retreated; if he stepped outside with both feet he was held to have fled. One man was to hold the shield before each of the combatants. The one who received most wounds was to pay as Holmslausn (indemnity for being released from the fight) three marks of silver.

Thorgils held the shield for his brother, and Thord Arndisaron that of Bersi, who struck the first blow and cleft Kormac's shield. Kormac struck at Bersi in the same way. Each of them spoiled three shields for the other. Then Kormac had to strike; he struck, and Bersi parried with Hviting. Sköfnung cut off its point, and it fell on Kormac's hand and wounded him in the thumb, whose joint was rent so that blood fell on the cloak. Thereupon the others intervened and did not want them to go on fighting. Kormac said, "It's not much of a victory Bersi has got from my accident, though we part now."

Kormac's Saga, Ch. 10.

That particular Holmgang was a tame affair, but in most of them far more blood was spilt than the drops from Kormac's cut thumb —this, for instance:

There was a fine field not far from the sea, where the Holmganga was to be. There the place was marked out by a ring of stones. Ljot came thither with his men, prepared for the Holmganga with shield and sword. He was very large and strong, and when he arrived on the field at the Holmgang place the Berserk frenzy came upon him, and he howled fiercely and bit the rim of his shield.

Egil made ready for the Holmganga, having his old shield, with his sword Nadr girt to his side and with Dragvandil (his other sword) in his hand. He went inside the marks of the duelling place (i.e. the squares marked out round the cloak) but Ljot was not ready. Egil raised his sword and sang.

After the song Ljot came forward and pronounced the laws of the Holmganga, that whoever stepped outside the stones which are set around the place of Holmganga should ever afterwards be called Nithing (coward).

Then they rushed at each other, and Egil struck at Ljot, who covered himself with his shield while Egil dealt blow after blow so that Ljot could not strike back. He drew back to get room to swing his sword, but Egil went just as fast after him and smote most violently. Ljot went out beyond the mark-stones and to and fro on the field. Thus went the first attack. Then Ljot asked to be allowed to rest, which Egil granted.

Egil bade Ljot make himself ready; "I want this fought out," he said. Ljot sprang to his feet, and Egil ran forward and at once struck him; he went so close that Ljot stepped back, and his shield did not cover him. Then Egil smote him above the knee and cut off his leg. Ljot fell, and at once died.

Egil's Saga, Ch. 17.

There are a number of interesting points here which are worth noting. Egil came to the fight with two swords, one at his side and another, his famous Dragvandil, in his hand. In just such a fashion did men arm themselves in the fifteenth century when engaging upon a judicial duel. In the actual attack we see firstly that they fought alone, without the seemingly impossible necessity of each having another man—his second—to hold his shield. Egil had the first blow, but (and this seems a little unfair) he did not, having struck, wait for Ljot to have his turn but pressed his attack until he pushed Ljot back on to the ropes and clean out of the ring. Nor did he give him a chance in the second round: undoubtedly the most effective way of dealing with a Berserk. (You noted the curious way in which we are told that Ljot behaved, howling and gnawing his shield rim? This seems to have been the usual Berserk practice before a fight, to work themselves up into that sort of psychopathic frenzy which makes men quite impervious to caution or pain or any thought at all save the will to slay. Very terrifying it must have been, and very effective.) It must have taken some doing, to rain blows thus without giving time for an opponent to reply. These swords were quite heavy, weighing two and a half to three pounds —but they are not, as so many people seem to think, so heavy "that a man to-day could scarcely lift one from the ground, let alone wield it". That—a view widely held and often expressed—is utter nonsense; as I say, they weigh comparatively little and with practice could be wielded easily enough. A Viking of the tenth century would have been used to wielding a sword every day of his life from the time he was about seven, and there is nothing extraordinary in the statement that Egil cut off Ljot's leg above the knee with one blow. By a similar stroke was Harold's life ended at Senlac (the arrow in his eye did not kill him); if we are to believe the chronicler, it was Duke William himself who dealt the blow.

Most people are to some extent familiar with sword-play—stage sword-play. In these days this is usually well enough done, but all of it is based more upon modern fencing practice than upon the realities even of eighteenth-century rapier fighting. When it comes to combats between mediaeval warriors we see a tremendous clashing of sword against sword and not much else. The real thing was, I believe, quite different. If we carefully read and correctly interpret what we are told in the Sagas about sword-fighting, and co-relate that with the archaeological evidence plus—and this is essential—a practical knowledge of the "feel" of the swords themselves, we may arrive at some reasonable conclusions as to how it was done. To begin with, one combatant would strike at the other. As we have seen, in formal duels this first blow was the privilege of the man who was challenged, but in the rule-less Einvigi either could strike first. In such fights we may take it that, as in modern wrestling or boxing, a good deal of preliminary manœuvring and feinting took place before one combatant or the other saw his opportunity and smote. The other would then defend himself either by taking the blow on his shield, or by evasive action such as ducking or dodging or leaping aside—often he would leap right over the stroke, for it was always a good idea to go for your opponent's leg below his shield. Then came the turn of the second man, while the first was recovering from his stroke and preparing for the next. This blow would be parried or evaded in the same way, and so on. It was very important to be able to change the direction of your stroke at the instant you saw that it was going to miss its target, even if this meant turning a downward blow into an upward one, or a forehand to a backhand. It was their great mobility and handiness which made the "new" style of blades produced in Ulfberht's time so much better than their predecessors; an Ulfberht was to an eighth-century blade what in 1940 a Spitfire was to a Gladiator—it combined greater speed and mobility with greater striking power. Naturally enough, there would be many occasions in a fight of this kind when both combatants would strike at the same moment, and there would probably be quite long spells while both jockeyed for position and neither smote at all. It was only when the shield had been so cut up that it was useless that one used one's sword to parry with, and then one would try only to use the flat of it, for if sword-edge clashed with edge much damage resulted. This is in fact what happened to Kormac, for he parried the stroke of Bersi's Hviting with Sköfnung's edge; Hviting's point broke off, and Sköfnung got a bad nick in the blade, which caused Kormac a deal of worry (because it was Skeggi's sword) and greatly annoyed Skeggi.

Even pitched battles between armies were often conducted with much of the punctilio of the Holmgang—at their beginning, any-how. In the Saga of Egil Skallagrimsson we read a very full account of the great battle fought in 938 at Brunanburgh in northern England, where King Aethelstan, Alfred the Great's grandson, defeated a great host of Scots and Welsh who came down from the north to invade and overrun England. They seem to have had much initial success, and we are told that while Aethelstan was raising men in the south of England, he left Egil and his brother Thorolf and an earl called Alfgeir in charge of his forces in the north. A little later on:

> They sent men to Olaf (the Scottish King) with the message that Aethelstan would fence a field with hazels to offer it as a battlefield to him on Vinheidi (Vin Heath); that he did not want them to ravage in his land, and that the one who gained the battle should rule over the land of England; they were to meet there in the course of one week, and he who should arrive there first was to wait one week for the other. It was customary then, after a battlefield had been enhazelled, to consider it a disgrace for a king to plunder until after the battle. Olaf therefore stopped his host, and did not ravage, but waited until the appointed day and then moved his host up to Vinheidi.

Then Aethelstan arrived with his host, and a good deal of nego-tiation went on in the hope of averting a great slaughter. However, Olaf's requirements were too much for Aethelstan, and the negotiations were broken off. Then the Scots king planned a preliminary surprise attack, sending part of his host (the Welsh contingent under its leaders Adils and Hring) to beat up the quarters of Alfgeir and Thorolf and their men in the early morning:

When it became light Thorolf's sentries saw the host; a war-blast was blown, and the men got into their armour, and Thorolf began to array them in order of battle in two fylkings (what would have been called "Battles" in the later Middle Ages). Alfgeir commanded one of them, and had a standard carried in front of him. In this division was the force which had followed him; it was much larger than Thorolf's division. Thorolf had a wide and thick shield, a very strong helmet on his head and a sword which he called Lang (the Long One), a large and good weapon. He also had a spear in his hand, the blade of which was four feet long, the point four-sided, the upper part of the blade broad, and the socket long and thick. The handle was no longer than one could reach with the hand to the socket, but very thick; there was an iron peg in the socket, and the whole handle was wound with iron. Spears of this kind were called Brynthvari (Mail-Piercer). Egil had the same gear as Thorolf. He had a sword which he called Nadr (Viper) which he had got in Kurland; it was an excellent weapon. Neither of them wore a coat of mail. They set up their standard, and Thorfinn the Hard carried it. All their men had Northern shields, and their whole outfit was Norwegian. All the Northmen who were there were in their ranks.

Adils set forward against Alfgeir's division, which broke and fled. Alfgeir and his companions rode off to the south. He feared to face his king, so he pressed on southwards and took ship for France, where he had relatives, and "he never since came back to England".

Adils first pursued the fleeing men, but not far. He returned to the battle and advanced to attack. As Thorolf saw this, he sent Egil against him and ordered the standard to go forward. He bade his men follow each other well, and stand closely together. "Let us move toward the forest," he said, "so that it can shelter our rear, so that they can't attack us from all sides." They did so, and a sharp fight followed. Egil advanced aginst Adils, and they had a hard encounter. The difference in numbers was very great, but even so more fell on Adil's side. Thorolf became so furious that he slung his shield over his back, and taking the spear in both hands rushed forward and struck and thrust on both sides; men turned away from him, but he killed many. Thus he cleared a way to the standard of Hring, and nothing could stand against him. He cut down the man who bore it and cut down the standard pole. Then he thrust his spear through the breast of Hring through the coat of mail and his body, so that it came out between his shoulders; he raised him on the spear over his head, and struck the shaft down into the ground. The Jarl expired on the spear, in sight of foes and friends. Then Thorolf drew his sword and dealt blows on both hands. His men also made an onset; many of the Welsh and Scots fell, and some fled. When Adils saw his brother's death, and the great fall and plight of his men, finding himself severely pushed he turned and fled, running into the forest as did his men.

Egil's Saga, Ch. 51–56

Here is a vivid though entirely credible and reliable account of a skirmish preceding a great battle—in the same way as the Quatre-Bras affair preceded Waterloo—which is itself less vividly described because it did not so intimately concern Egil; though Thorolf was killed in the course of it, and Egil avenged himself by slaying Adils.

Another account of a battle which ought to be included here describes a much earlier affray, fought two centuries before Brunan-burgh in about A.D. 700. It was between Harald Hilditonn (War-Tooth) and Sigurd Hring, and was fought on Bravoll in Eastern Gotland. Harald Hilditonn was king over Sweden and Denmark and part of England and other lands, but he was old. Sigurd Hring was his nephew, and

When old age was heavy upon the king, he made Hring king over Uppsala and gave into his power the whole of Sweden and West Gotland, but himself retained the rule over all Denmark and East Gotland.

Harald became very old indeed, so

Some chiefs resolved when he was having his bath in a tub to cover it with timber and stones, intending to smother him in it. When he saw that they wanted to kill him, he asked to be allowed to get out of the bath. He said, "I know that you think I am too old. That is true, but I would rather die my fated death. I don't want to die in a bath tub, but in a much more kingly way." A little while after he sent word to his kinsman Hring in Sweden, that he should gather a host from all the lands he ruled over and meet him on the frontier and fight against him; and he told him all about the reason, that the Danes thought him too old.

Hring gathered men from his lands, and many came from Norway, while many warriors from Ireland and "Saxland" (Frisia) came to the aid of Harald, as well as some from Koenugard (which was Kiev). There follows a long list of the champions who followed the two kings. Among those of Harald we find:

> There were the shield-maidens Visma and Heid, each of whom had come with a numerous host. Visma carried Harald's standard. . . . Another shield-maiden was Vebjorg who came from the south from Gotland and many champions followed her.

These formidable ladies, the shield-maidens, are a striking feature of Norse military life. What induced them to be the ferocious warriors they were is never clearly stated, but their deeds match those of their brothers. The names of some of the champions of Hring are worth noting for their vivid and interesting variety: Erling the Snake, Hrut the Rambler, Odd the Wide-Travelling, Egil the Squinting, Hrolf the Woman-Loving, Dag the Stout, Gerdar the Glad, and Glismak the Good.

Harald sent Herlief with the Saxon force to King Hring "in order to stake out the field chosen for the battle and declare the truce and peace broken". When these formalities had been concluded, the two hosts drew up on Bravoll.

> When these hosts were ready for battle, both had the war-horns sounded and raised the war-cry. The arrays met, and the battle was so severe that it is said in all old Sagas that no battle in the Northern lands was ever fought with so many or so valiant picked men.

The battle raged for a while, and Ubbi, one of Harald's champions, began to take a terrible toll of Hring's leading men:

> When Hring saw this, he urged the host not to let one man overcome all, such proud men as they were. He shouted: "Where is Storkud who till now has always borne the highest shield?" Storkud answered, "We have plenty to do, Sir, but we will try to gain a victory if we can, though were Ubbi is a man may be fully tried." At the urging of the king he rushed to the front against Ubbi, and there was a great fight between them with heavy blows; each of them was fearless. After a while, Storkud gave him a large wound, and himself received six, all of them severe, and he thought he had rarely been so hard pushed by a single man. As the arrays were dense they were torn apart

and so their hand-to-hand fight ended. Then Ubbi slew the champion Agnar and cleared a patch in front of himself, dealing blows on both hands; his arms were bloody up to his shoulders. Thereupon he attacked the men from Telemark. When they saw him they said, "Now we need not go elsewhere, but let us shoot arrows at this man for a while, and as everybody thinks little of us let us do the more and show that we are valiant men." The most skilled of the Telemarkians began to shoot at him, namely Hadd the Hard and Hroald Toe. These men were excellent archers and they shot twenty-four arrows into his breast; this much was needed to destroy his life. These men slew him, but not before he had slain six champions and severely wounded eleven others, and killed sixteen Goths and Swedes who stood in the front of the ranks.

Vebjorg, shield-maiden, made hard onsets on the Swedes and the Goths; she attacked the champion Soknarsoti; she had accustomed herself so well to the use of the helmet, mail-shirt and sword, that she was one of the foremost in Chivalry (the word used here is Riddara-skap, meaning literally equestrian exercises) as Storkud the old says: she dealt the champion heavy blows and attacked him for a long while, and with a blow at his cheek cut through his jaw and chin; he put his beard into his mouth and bit it, thus holding up his chin. She performed many great feats. A little later Thorkel the Stubborn, a champion of Hring, met her and they fiercely attacked each other. Finally with great courage she fell, covered with wounds.

And so on. Finally the aged Harald (who fought in the battle in a cart, as he could neither walk nor ride) was killed.

When Hring saw Harald's wagon empty he knew that he had fallen. He had the horns blown and shouted that the hosts should stop fighting. When the Danes became aware of this the battle ceased, and Hring offered truce to the entire host of King Harald, which all accepted.

Sögubrot, Ch. 9.

A good deal of this is remarkably similar to many of the mediaeval chronicles and Chansons de Geste. In very similar terms the chroniclers like De Joinville or Froissart record the fights of the champions of their own day.

Chapter Ten

FROM CHARLEMAGNE TO THE NORMANS

T HE ACCESSION OF Charles the Great to the Frankish throne
in 771 marked the beginning of a new era, in the art of war
as in all else. At the start of his reign each Teutonic nation
had its own military customs; at its end he had welded all these
peoples into a single state, with the exception of the English and the
Visigothic remnant in Spain. Until the formation of this empire,
these diverse peoples had little contact with one another, but after
800 all of them were directed towards the same political ends under
the same rulers. The unity of purpose imposed by this long and
triumphant reign was never quite lost by the countries of Western
Europe. In spite of all national divergences, from that time on they
developed according to the same pattern, which provides the unity
of thought, of religion and art and letters and military usage which
is such a striking and remarkable feature of the Middle Ages. And
of course it explains why Charlemagne replaced the old battle
tactics and arms of the Franks, so crude and inefficient, with the far
better ones of the Longobards. There had been some movement
towards a better way of fighting before Charles' accession; under the
later Merovings and the great Mayors of the Palace the Franks had
begun to build up, from the small mounted bodyguards of the
earlier period, an aristocratic force of cavalry, clad in a certain
amount of defensive armour. This process was stimulated by the
sudden appearance of the Saracens in the south of France in 725–32.
Charles Martel defeated them decisively at Poitiers in 732, but the
extent of the danger can be appreciated by the distance to which
they had penetrated into the heart of the Frankish kingdom. For
forty years after this there were a series of aggressive wars against

the Saracens and Longobards as well as the Saxons in the north. Both Saracens and Longobards were horse-soldiery; in their wars against the Emirs of Spain and Aistulf the Longobard the Franks must have developed their cavalry arm in order to cope with such adversaries.

Charles the Great, however, undertook wars on a far bigger scale, and he began at once to increase the amount of mounted men in his hosts. His first military ordinance shows how anxious he was to keep as much war material as possible within his realm. In 779 he ordained that no merchant should dare to export byrnies. This order was repeated in the Capita Minora Cap. 7 and in the Aachen capitulary of 805. In this the trade in arms with the Wends and Avars is particularly denounced. Any merchant caught conveying a mail shirt outside the realm is threatened with forfeiture of all his property—more evidence that within his boundaries there were centres of armour-making whose wares were eagerly sought beyond them. Charles conquered the Lombards in 774, and immediately issued military legislation imposing upon them the Frankish regulations for compulsory military service, making for instance the fine for neglecting the king's "ban" sixty solidi, and the penalty for desertion in the face of the enemy death, or at least to be placed at the king's disposal both for life and property. It is interesting to find in the Lombardic capitulary of 786 that the Lombards who are to swear obedience to the royal mandate are one and all described as cavalry. They are:

> Those of the countryside, or the men of the Counts, Bishops and Abbots or tenants on royal demesne or on Church property, all who hold fiefs or serve as vassals under a lord, all those who come to the host with horse and arms, shield, lance, sword and dagger.

Thus the obligation to serve with armour becomes a matter of compulsion and ceases to be voluntary.

The possession of this great force of horsemen was of the greatest value to Charlemagne in his wars, particularly those against the Avars, a people of the same stock as the Huns, largely composed of descendants of the survivors of Attila's hosts who had settled down in Hungary. The comments of Paul the Deacon in the seventh century and Einhard in the eighth give us a clear picture of the

Lombardic warrior; it was his absorption into the Frankish Empire, of whose hosts he became the backbone, which made him the mould from which all the knights of the Middle Ages were cast.

As the reign went on, so was the organization of the war-machine extended and improved. It became statutory that all men owning certain amounts of land should serve with the host, each equipped according to his holding and status; the Feudal System was getting into its stride. There are many "capitularies" dealing with this organization. A clause in one (Capitulare Aquisgranense of 813) lays down that all the "men" (landed retainers) of Counts, Bishops and Abbots must have both helm and mail shirt; in another (section 10) we get a glimpse of the existence of a military train; on the wagons are to be picks, hatchets, iron-shod stakes, pavises, rams, and mechanical slings; the king's marshals are to provide stones to be cast from these *fundibuli*. Of all these documents, perhaps the most interesting is the one which calls Fulrad, abbot of Altaich, to the host in 806:

> You shall come to Stasfurt on the Boda by May 20th with your men prepared to go on warlike service to any part of our realm that we may point out; that is, you shall come with arms and gear and all warlike equipment of clothing and victuals. Every horseman shall have shield, lance, sword, dagger, a bow and a quiver. On your carts you shall have ready spades, axes, picks and iron-shod stakes and all other things needed for the host. The rations shall be for three months, the clothing must be able to hold out for six. On your way you shall do no damage to our subjects and touch nothing but water, wood and grass. Your men shall march along with the carts and the horses (it appears that this refers to remounts), and not leave them till you reach the muster-place, so that they may not scatter and do mischief. See that there be no neglect, as you prize our good grace.

Similar orders were to be sent out, almost word for word, by rulers all over Europe for the next seven centuries.

There is a vivid account of the entry of one of Charlemagne's hosts into Pavia in the Italian campaign of 773. Unfortunately it was not itself written by a contemporary, but by a monk of St. Gall who had it, he tells us, from those who remembered the Emperor and had served with him. Quoting these, and borrowing perhaps from a lost poem of Charles' day, he describes King Desiderius and his henchman Ogier the Dane watching as the invading host approaches. As each column comes in sight the king asks if his rival Charles and the main body have not now appeared. Again and again Ogier replies that Charles has not yet come—the masses of warriors who have passed are only his vanguard. At last the plain is darkened with a column still mightier than the others.

> Then appeared the Iron King, crowned with his Iron Helm, with sleeves of iron mail on his arms, his broad breast protected by an iron byrnie, an iron lance in his left hand, his right free to grasp his unconquered sword. His thighs were guarded with iron mail, though other men are wont to leave them unprotected that they may spring the more lightly upon their steeds. And his legs, like those of all his host, were protected by iron greaves. His shield was of plain iron without device or colour. And round him and before him and behind him rode all his men, armed as nearly like him as they could fashion themselves; so iron filled the fields and the ways, and the sun's rays were from every quarter reflected from iron. "Iron, iron everywhere," cried in dismay the terrified citizens of Pavia.[1]

In the original Latin the words for the king's helm are *ferrea cristata galea*, which implies that the helmet was a crested one, perhaps like those in so many contemporary manuscript drawings, such as that shown in fig. 71, or maybe it was of an earlier pattern like the Morken helmet. The sleeve is spoken of as if it were a separate piece of armour; such mail sleeves were common in the later Middle Ages; they may in the eighth century have been long ones to supplement the usual elbow-length byrnie sleeve.[2] Greaves seem common, and remind us of the Valsgärde splints and the figure—almost contemporary with Charlemagne—on the Nagyszentmiklos vase, which shows a figure very like the monk's description of Charles' men (see fig. 52). A century later we have more evidence of the wearing of iron greaves.

And what of Charles' "unconquered sword"? Everyone has heard of the immortal Joyeuse, and most people have heard of the

---

[1] This translation is open to question in certain details; there is no corroborating evidence, for example, of shields made of (or even covered with) plain iron.

[2] We see in the Bayeux tapestry tight-fitting sleeves of mail under the loose byrnie sleeves.

sword in the Louvre, the Coronation sword of the Kings of France, which has always been called the Sword of Charlemagne. Until about fifty years ago it was accepted that this had indeed belonged to the great Emperor, until the niggling scepticism of some late nineteenth-century antiquaries set to work to prove that it was nothing of the kind, but a sword made in the twelfth century "to replace an earlier one". There can be few cases where the form and decorative treatment of an object so clearly point to a particular period; in this case it is the ninth century which is indicated, not the twelfth. Apart from this fact, there is no reason why this lovely weapon should not have been at least connected with Charlemagne in his lifetime or immediately after his death. The solid gold hilt was furnished with a new grip in 1803 when Napoleon had it done up for his coronation—and the blade (a type quite consistent with a ninth-century date) has been polished and rubbed for so long that it has become very thin and much narrower than it originally would have been. It would be too much to try and persuade oneself that this is in fact Joyeuse; but there need be no doubt that it was made within a few decades of Charles' coronation in Rome on Christmas Day, A.D. 800.

There is another very splendid sword attributed to Charlemagne in Vienna. Tradition has it that it was a present to him from Haroun el Raschid, Caliph of Baghdad, but it is not an oriental weapon in spite of its curved blade and oddly shaped hilt, which are very reminiscent of seventeenth- and eighteenth-century Persian or northern Indian swords; early oriental swords were invariably straight. It is of a type much used in Hungary during the ninth and tenth centuries, a fact proved by the finding of many similar ones in graves of that period. The most similar is from the grave at Tarczal in the Tokay Mountains; this had silver scabbard mounts similar to Charlemagne's, but it—or at least the grave—was of a later date (tenth century).

It has a slightly curved blade, double-edged to a point a little short of half its length; the cross is short with knobbed ends, made of hollow silver-gilt embossed and chased with arabesque designs; the pommel, in the form of a slightly bulbous cap, is similarly made. The grip is covered with fish-skin and encircled with three jewelled gold bands, later mediaeval additions (fig. 74). This sword was used, in a similar manner to the one in the Louvre, at the coronations of the Emperors.

In 814 the reign of Charlemagne ended, and immediately his tremendous presence withdrew from the scene his empire began to fall apart, and during the next century the separate states of France and Germany took shape.

In 936 a descendant of the German side of Charlemagne's line, Otto I, became King of Germany. In 962 he was crowned in Rome as Emperor of the West, and from that time until 1806 the title was held by a King of Germany. He also was deservedly called the Great, and founded a line which provided some of the most colourful and potent monarchs of the Middle Ages. Under his rule and that of his immediate successors Germany became the leading partner in the great family business that Charlemagne had founded. So much so that they have given their name to a cultural period—we speak of Ottonian art in the same way as we do of Carolingian art. And with reason. While the Vikings were providing Saga-material for the Skalds of the North, the lamps of Christianity as well as of the old pagan learning were kept alight in great monasteries like Fulda and Reichenau and St. Gall, deep in the heart of Germany, far from the seaborne ravagings of the Norsemen. To these retreats came scholars and artists driven from

Fig. 74. The Sword of Charlemagne (Imperial Treasury, Vienna).

Iona and Lindisfarne, from Clonfert and Bangor and Clonmacnoise, from Liège, St. Trond, and Malmedy. They left their abbeys roaring red to heaven behind them, but many of the precious books went with them as they fled. In the scriptoria of these quiet places of refuge many artists worked alongside the scholars, illustrating the

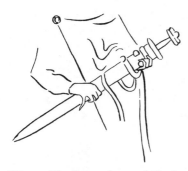

Fig. 75. The Armour-bearer of Charles the Bald (c. 870).

manuscripts they wrote or copied. While Norwegian heroes fought Scots and Irishmen, and Dane battled with Saxon and Frank, they peacefully illustrated the wars of Saul and David and the Maccabees. By a blessed dispensation of providence they knew nothing of these ancient warriors other than was contained in the Old Testament, so they drew them in modern dress. Otto sits as a model for David, and his barons and knights for the hosts of the Philistines. So because the artists of Reichenau knew nothing of archaeology, they have been able to show us exactly how the warriors of the tenth century were dressed and armed.

In the eyes of the Victorians these drawings seemed quaint and immature, as indeed they must if one judges them against the work of men like Millais or Holman Hunt. To-day they are easier to understand and appreciate, for we are much more inclined to see things as the tenth century did, and to the devil with perspective. The artists of St. Gall and Reichenau were fine draughtsmen and by no means immature; nor were they shut away from the world, seeing nothing beyond the abbey walls and knowing nothing of the captains and the kings. They knew their world very well, and what went on in it; they noted everything they saw, and down it went on to the vellum just as it was. This literal approach was characteristic of all the artists of the Middle Ages. We may be sure that what they drew was what they saw, and they saw things as they really were. True enough that some drawings are bad and unreliable, but there are so many extremely good ones of all periods from Charles the Great to Charles V that we are embarrassed by the choice offered for study. From this point on, nearly every piece of military equipment I shall describe can be seen in manuscript illustrations, many of which can be cross-checked for accuracy against surviving originals.

For example, look at fig. 75, from the Codex Aureus of St. Emmeran, written in 870 for Charles the Bald. It shows the figure of the royal armour-bearer from a full-page illustration of the king's enthronement. The sword he holds is a very clearly-drawn example of Type III, and there on the scabbard are two large dome-shaped studs such as survive on the Sutton Hoo sword. From the way the belt is wrapped round the scabbard, it looks as if the bosses were buttons to hold each an end of a strap. In a MS. of St. Gall (the "Psalterium Aureum"), known to have been completed before 883, is a drawing which shows another, simpler form of the Frankish brimmed helmet (fig. 76). It is a figure of Saul, very lively and vigorous. He is about to hurl a long lance at David (who is dodging behind a tree on another part of the otherwise practically blank page); an interesting weapon, for its head is exactly like many "winged" spears found in the graves. His byrnie is tucked round his thighs, looking like short trousers. In other drawings in this MS. we see groups of warriors, some dismounted; they are not foot-soldiers, for they are standing by (or have fallen off) their horses; in every case their byrnies hang free to the knee, like skirts, so they were obviously not made like trousers. A different treatment was given to the Norman hauberks in the Bayeux Tapestry, as we shall see. In another St. Gall manuscript of the first half of the tenth century we find a very spirited drawing of a battle-scene from the Book of Maccabees. Here are swords of the kind we have found in the

Fig. 76. Figure of Saul, from the "Psalterium Aureum" of St. Gall: before 883.

Fig. 77. From a battle-scene in a MS. of St. Gall, c. 900–950 (Cod. Perizoni 17, Leyden).

Viking graves, but seen in their proper milieu. Fig. 77a is a broken sword lying on the battlefield; b is wielded by a horseman (note how he puts his forefinger over the lower guard); c shows how instead of the forefinger over the lower guard, the warrior has his little finger over the pommel — a curiously awkward grip shown in very many of these tenth-century drawings; it is hard to see why, for if one tries to hold a sword of this kind thus it is most uncomfortable. All the same, a man with large hands would have to have one finger outside the grip itself, for generally this is too short (only about $3\frac{1}{2}$ in. to 4 in. long) to accommodate four large fingers. The pommels of these swords are, however, generally very flat, and fit quite snugly into the heel of one's hand. Another of these Maccabean warriors wields his sword with both hands (fig. 77d), one clasped over the other. He wears a helmet very similar to the sixth century one from the Morken grave, with the same sort of ear-flaps. In another picture from the same MS. are some warriors wearing similar though far less acutely pointed helmets; they are dome-shaped and the spaces between the bronze bands are coloured solid black. In the Swiss National Museum in Zurich is just such a helmet; the skull is made from a single plate of iron, unlike the earlier pointed "Spangenhelm". The bronze bands running crosswise over the skull are for reinforcement and decoration, not to hold separate plates (*spangen*) together. The bands are decorated with a simple running design of tendrils, which is very similar to the decorative motifs which began to appear in manuscripts during the ninth century—similar, too, to the decoration on the hilts of some of the Type IV swords (those from Gravraak in Norway and Kilmainham in Ireland particularly) which are thought to be Frankish. This helmet (it was found in Switzerland in 1927 at Chamoson) is regarded as being Saracenic by the museum authorities in Zurich, though so many things seem to point to a Frankish origin: its find-place, its similarity to the drawing in the St. Gall MS., and its very Frankish decoration. It seems to be a transitional style half-way between the old Spangenhelm of many plates and the far better helmets of the eleventh century made from one piece of metal. There is a remarkably good Spangenhelm in the Tower of London. On loan from the Liverpool Museum, it was obtained in Prussia in 1854, and is similar to the Morken helmet without the cheek guards (see fig. 54).

The Sagas often tell of shields painted in different colours, either in halves or quarters of the shield. In this MS. of St. Gall are several shields with alternate light and dark quarters. They have very odd-looking bosses, long and acutely pointed, sticking out about 8 in. from the boards of the shield. Many such bosses have been found (fig. 78), though it is a rather rare

Fig. 78. Painted shield from MS. of St. Gall, Cod. Perizoni 17, c. 900–950, and shield boss.

type. In one of the battle pictures—still in the same MS.—there is a drawing of a riderless horse, its stirrups hanging free (fig. 79). Compare these with fig. 80, a stirrup of the ninth century found in London. We are doubly fortunate that while the Vikings could tell such lively stories of their heroes with so much circumstantial detail, in another part of Europe far away from them and their works there were artists who could draw the arms they so loved to talk about; and from the way the arms in the drawings tally with the descriptions in the stories, and both with the surviving pieces, we can be sure

Fig. 79. From a battle scene in a MS. of St. Gall, c. 950.

Fig. 80. Viking stirrup from London (London Museum).

that even in the ninth and tenth centuries all European warriors were clad alike.

Little more than a century after the Northmen had settled down in the lands granted them in northern France by the treaty of 911, the old roving spirit asserted itself for the last time. In 1038 the sons of Tancred de Hautville led a war-band into southern Italy, where in a remarkably short time they made themselves masters of Apulia and Sicily, founding a kingdom that was to endure and flourish for 200 years. On a much larger scale was Duke William the Bastard's invasion of England in 1066. In chapter 10 I called this (in a phrase I could not resist borrowing from Sir Mortimer Wheeler) the culminating adventure of Vikingdom, though perhaps it should not be regarded in isolation as such, for there was the great raid of the Norwegian king Harald Hardrede, so valiantly broken by Harold and the English at Stamford Bridge only three weeks before Senlac. With these two expeditions, one such a disaster and the other so triumphant, the Viking Age comes to an end, but before we leave it, it will be appropriate to consider the arms and fighting methods of the Normans. We have two documents which provide ample information about these—the Bayeux Tapestry, and a long poem in Norman French, the "Roman de Rou", which is a sort of Frenchi- fied Saga, for it tells the story of Hrolf (Rollo) and his successors in the Dukedom of Normandy, reaching its climax with the battle at Senlac. It was written ninety years after the battle, in badly rhymed verse which necessitated an inexact use of words, so it cannot be taken too literally, though it is very lively and picturesque.

The Bayeux Tapestry is known to everyone, and is in itself a most important object in the Archaeology of Weapons. It would be pedantic to call it by any other name, though in a literal sense it was not a tapestry at all; the figures are embroidered upon the material, not woven into it. It is embroidered on coarse linen in two kinds of woollen thread in eight colours—three shades of blue, one so dark as to be nearly black, a bright and dark green, red, yellow or buff, and grey. The design is very close in style to contemporary (or slightly earlier) book illustration. It is the principal, though not the only or the best, source of information about the way men armed during the late eleventh century. It was probably made about twenty years after the Conquest to the order of Bishop Odo of Bayeux for the new abbey he was building there, and all the indications are that it was made in England. It is the only thing of its kind which has survived, though we read of other instances of similar works—in Volsunga Saga, for instance, that Brynhild, in her bower at Hlymdale:

> sat, overlaying cloth with gold, and sewing therein the great deeds which Sigurd had wrought, the slaying of the Worm and the taking of his wealth, and the death of Regin.

An even closer parallel must have been the hanging presented to Ely Minster by Aethelflaed, the widow of Byrhtnoth, who fell in the battle at Maldon in 991 which inspired the last and noblest of Old English poems—the one which ends with the splendid couplet:

> Thought the harder, heart the bolder,
> Mood the more as our might lessens.

a sentiment which was equally true on the fields of Poitiers and Agincourt, as it was in the air over Kent in 1940.

The "Roman de Rou" was written by Robert Wace in about 1160. He was a prebendary of Bayeux, and may have used the Tapestry as one of his sources. Another source, he tells us, was his father, who was able to provide some first-hand information.

The armour worn by both Norman and Saxon is exactly the same as had been fashionable for a century before 1066 and was to remain in vogue for nearly another century after: the conical helmet, with or without the noseguard or nasal, the long kite-shaped shield, and the mail byrnie with elbow length sleeves, its skirt—divided fore and aft for convenience in riding—falling to the knee. In all the scenes of the Senlac battle, Duke William wears a garment we have not met with hitherto—the calves of his legs are protected by mail *chausses* instead of the hose or cross-gartered linen trews worn by all the others.

In the "Roman de Rou" the byrnie is called "haubert", and as the *hauberk* we shall refer to it from now on, for its French name became correct usage over most of Europe except Scandinavia after about 1100. Another garment, which has sometimes caused confusion, appears in the "Roman"—the "Haubergeon". Wace tells us that Duke William, arming for the battle, *son bon haubert fist*

175

demander, while his cousin Bishop Odo with *un haubergeon aveit vestu*. The Duke was armed with lance and sword (though once or twice in the Tapestry we see him armed with a club, but not in the poem) whereas the Bishop *un baston teneit en son poing* which suggests that he was lightly armed; and the poet makes specific mention of his white tunic appearing prominently under his haubergeon. This suggests that it was a short garment, reaching only to the waist and not to the knee like the hauberk. I would like to refer back again to the St. Gall MS. (Cod. Perizoni 17) of about 900, for in the battle scenes from the Maccabees are some warriors with long hauberks, and some with short haubergeons with white tunics falling to the knee below them. Some of the Vikings' byrnies, you will remember, were referred to as being very short. In mentioning the hauberks in the St. Gall MS. I said that when worn by dismounted men they ceased to look like trousers. Not so in the Tapestry: here they are shown as if they fitted quite tightly round the thighs, except where they are being stripped from the dead. In view of the almost overwhelming evidence that in the late tenth century there were no such mail combinations, we must assume that the ladies who worked these figures (or perhaps the artist—for an artist he was, and a good one, too—who drew the figures for the ladies to embroider) were uncertain as to the best way of depicting long hauberks divided up the back and front.

The Norman kite-shield was in use at the end of the tenth century, as we can see by a picture from a page in the Gospels of Otto III,

which was made between 983 and 991 (fig. 81). Here is a warrior who might well be mistaken for one of about 1150; he wears the conical helmet, with a coif which appears to be of linen, a byrnie a little shorter than the Norman pattern, under which is a kilt of linen or some similar material; and a great kite-shaped shield covering him from his knee to his shoulder.[1] Behind him is another man holding a sword with a circular pommel,

Fig. 81. Figure of one of Herod's guards, from the Gospels of Otto III (983–991).

[1] It is in a picture of the Visit of the Kings to Herod. The soldiers are part of Herod's bodyguard.

the centre of which is painted red—an instance, as I mentioned in chapter nine, of the early use of this sort of pommel. A warrior dressed almost exactly the same appears on a font of black marble at Liège, which can be dated about 1120.

Fig. 82. The shield adapted to fit the space between a rider and his horse's neck.

The shield shaped like a kite is a horseman's shield, its form directly derived from the shape of the space between a horse's neck and its rider's thigh (fig. 82). It is plain that a circular shield would afford poor protection to the left side of a rider, particularly when the lance was used. The long shield fills the gap as well as protecting his leg.

In the Tapestry many of the English are shown fighting on foot with long shields, though some still use the old round pattern. One feels that if Ljot had had a shield like this he would not have died of the stroke Egil dealt him. It may have been this sort of shield which was spoken of in St. Olaf's Saga, where the king was warned that he would be carried aboard his ship on his shield; though it seems unlikely that kite shields would have been used at sea; one might think that a long shield would be as cumbersome and inconvenient aboard a ship as a round one would be ineffectual on a horse.

The great English axe, of which so many specimens have been recovered from the Thames, is well shown in the Tapestry; in every case we see that the haft is a good four to five feet long. In the "Roman" we read:

> ... un Engleiz vint acorant:
> Hache noresche ont mult bele
> Plus de plain pié ont l'alemele.

which reminds us of the herdsman who told Helgi Hardbeinsson of the axe blade which seemed to be two feet long. An objection to

this great axe was that you need both hands to wield it, and must do without your shield. As Wace has it:

Hoem ki od hach: volt ferir
Od sez dous mainz l'estuet tenir
Ne pot entendre a sei covrir
S'il velt ferie de grant air.
Bien ferir e covrir ensemble
Ne pot l'en faire, ço me semble.

Both Norman and Saxon use the same arms—spear, sword, and—rarely—clubs and maces. Most of the charging Norman knights carry their spears at arms' length, either in an overarm position as if they were going to throw them like javelins, or

Fig. 83. Dragon standard. From the "Psalterium Aureum" of St. Gall. Before 883.

with their arms held low. In only a few cases are they couched under the elbow as we should expect to find a lance being carried when charging.

In the MS. of St. Gall (the "Psalterium Aureum") to which I have already referred, we have a horseman (armed exactly like Saul in fig. 76) whose long winged spear is couched under his elbow. Perhaps the most interesting thing that this particular drawing shows, however, is that another horseman riding in front of him carries a standard—not a flag or a banner, but a flat figure of a dragon fixed upon a staff (fig. 83) in the immemorial manner of the Roman Eagles and the standards of the nomes of Egypt and the regimental ensigns in the armies of the Pharaohs. Very like this dragon is Harold's standard in the Tapestry, the famous Dragon of Wessex. This use of a dragon is found among the Continental Saxons, too. Of Witikind (Charlemagne's adversary) we read:

Hic arripiens signum quod apud eo habebatur sacrum, leonis atque draconis desuper aquilae volantis insignitum effigie. . . .

The people of Burford in Oxfordshire used to carry a figure of a dragon each year "up and down the town in great Jollity, to which they added the picture of a Giant", until about a century and a half ago, in memory of a victory over Aethelbald, a king of Mercia, in which he lost his "Banner, whereon was depicted a Golden Dragon".

In the description of the fight before the battle of Brunanburgh in Egil's Saga we have read how Thorolf caused the war horns to be sounded and the war-cry raised, and his banner advanced. We are not told what this war-cry was, and the Sagas as a whole tend to be silent on this point. Not so the "Roman de Rou". In his passage concerning the battle at Val-es-Dunes in 1047, Wace writes:

> *De la gent donc esteit emmie*
> *Poinst li cheval criant " Tur aie"*
>
> *Cil de France crient " Montjoie"*
> *William crie "Dex aie"*
> *C'est l'enseigne de Normandie*
> *E Renouf crie o grant pooir*
> *"Saint Sever, Sire Saint Sever"*
> *E Dam as Denz va reclamant*
> *"Saint Amant, Sire Saint Amant."*

In the fight between Lothaire, King of France and Richard Duke of Normandy:

> *Franceiz crient " Montjoie" e Normanz "Dex Aie"*
> *Flamenz crient "Azraz" e Angevin "Valie"*
> *Et li Quens Thibaut "Chartres et passe avant" crie.*

He who at Val-es-Dunes cried upon Thor to aid him was Raoul de Tesson, unhorsed and surrounded; so what was probably one of the most usual war-cries of the pagan Vikings still seems to have been used in moments of stress by their Christian descendants. The Saxons at Senlac took a very different style of cry at the start of the battle: "Holy Cross" they shouted, and "God Almighty", but as the fight grew hotter they simply cried "Out, out". Wace tells us of these cries:

> *"Olicrosse" sovent crioent*
> *E "Godemite" reclamoient*
> *Olicrosse est en Engleiz*
> *Ke Sainte Croix est en Franceiz*
> *E Godemite altretant*
> *Com en Franceiz Dex tot poissant.*

William's tactical use of the bow undoubtedly hastened the Saxon defeat, for had Harold not been put out of action at a critical point of the battle when his steadiest troops were being galled beyond endurance by the rain of arrows falling from the sky, they might have held the shield-wall round the standard till nightfall, and maybe the end would have been different. But Harold was struck, and cut down by a Norman sword when William's knights burst through the Huscarles to trample down the Dragon standard and Harold's banner of the Fighting Man. As the evening drew on a few groups of Huscarles fought to the end around their dead king and his fallen standard. Their valour brought generous tribute from their opponents: "The valour of the English and all their glory raged", says the Draco Normannicus, and William of Poitiers: "They were ever ready with their steel, these sons of the old Saxon race, the most dauntless of men." With the dusk of October 14, 1066, fell the twilight of that race, and the Age of the Vikings was ended. The Conqueror and his warriors were themselves Northmen, but it was not the arms and battle-tactics of their Viking grandfathers which gave them victory, but those of the Goths who had broken the power of Rome seven centuries before. From that moment on the hilltop at Senlac the armoured horseman was to be the supreme instrument of war for nearly 300 years. With the slaughter of Harald of Norway's host and the destruction of the army of England there was no disciplined force of foot soldiery in the old Norse tradition left anywhere in Europe; only in the East did such a force survive for a few years more—the Varangian Guard of the Emperors of Constantinople, and they were to be cut to pieces by Norman horse near Durazzo in 1096.

So the change in the pattern of war which first appeared at Adrianople had spread until it covered the whole tapestry. For seven centuries the power of the armoured horseman had been growing, and for three more he was to dominate every battlefield in Europe. By one of the ironies of history he was to be stripped of that dominance by the descendants of the Saxon ceorls he had cut down at Senlac, for after the chivalry of France had been mown down by English arrows on the field of Crecy in 1346 his real supremacy was at an end.

Part 4

THE AGE OF CHIVALRY

Chapter Eleven

THE "GAY SCIENCE" OF CHIVALRY

Taillefer the minstrel knight bestrode
A gallant steed, and swiftly rode
Before the Duke, and sang the song
Of Charlemagne, and Roland strong
Of Oliver and those beside
Brave knights at Roncesvalles that died.

THUS THE PREBENDARY of Bayeux begins the immortal story of Taillefer, part Berserk, part Jogeleur, riding to a hero's death on the Saxon shield-wall at Senlac. Wace was probably more concerned with telling a splendid story than in recording an historical fact, and Taillefer's deed of arms must be regarded as legendary; but the "Song of Roland" which he chanted as he rode, throwing his lance in the air and catching it as it fell, is real enough. Its only literary parallel is the *Iliad*, and it became to mediaeval France what that was to ancient Greece: a national epic not only in its subject but in its origin. It tells, like the *Iliad*, of an historical event which fired the blood of ordinary men—though the affair in the pass of Roncesvalles was a little thing compared with the great siege. And like the *Iliad*, its final form was the production of a poet who idealized a less heroic foundation-story and welded into a harmonious whole the rough materials of ballad, lay and legend originating among the men of the generation which played a part in it. Behind the "Chanson" are several centuries of song and story, as the "Homeric Cycle" lay behind the *Iliad*. In its present form it is probably contemporary with the Bayeux Tapestry: if Taillefer had really sung it at Senlac, it would have been an earlier version. Whoever composed it must have gloried in the result of his work, for it became at once the national hymn of France, and the gospel of chivalry. The listeners for whom it was sung cared nothing for the sober facts of history: it was not the Roland who had commanded Charlemagne's rearguard on the march out of Spain in 778 that appealed to them; it was the Roland of the poet's creation. The eighth-century warrior was transformed into a national hero who reflected all the ideals and aspirations of the nascent age of chivalry.

By the time the "Chanson de Roland" had begun to be nationally popular in the middle eleventh century, feudalism had done its work. As a military system it had come into existence in the ninth century, as the best means of defence against the invading hosts of Vikings, Saracens, Magyars and Slavs which threatened the extinction of Christendom. Based upon the armoured horseman and the fortified castle, it had sprung up more or less spontaneously as a system of local defence when governments were too weak to organize national resistance. The knights who were needed to cope with such assailants "were not courteous gentlemen full of pity and piety, but tremendous bullies overflowing with energy and martial fury"—like Thorolf at Brunanburgh—who, though Christians, were as ferocious as their opponents. A knight was simply a freeman who owned a horse: *Omnes pagenses Franci qui caballum habent vel habere possunt* were commanded by Charles the Bald to bear arms. By about 1030 the work of these people was finished. All the invaders had been absorbed or driven back. The Danes had settled down and become good Catholics in France and eastern England; the Saracens were safely bottled up in Spain; the Magyars and the Slavs were back beyond the Oder: but the feudal nobility remained; invincible with its terrible cavalry, impregnable in its castles, and as much of a menace as its foes had ever been. The problem of every monarch and prelate was how to find something for it to do before it tore

Christendom to pieces. The solution was given at the Council of Clermont in 1095, where Urban II proclaimed the Crusade which fired the imagination of the whole of Europe—not the noble classes alone—and sent knights, burghers and peasants off, aflame with holy zeal, to rescue Jerusalem from the hands of the Heathen.

So the Church found a job for the unemployed brigandage of Europe. At the same time Urban issued a general injunction that every person of noble birth on attaining the age of twelve should take a solemn oath before a bishop that "he would defend to the uttermost the oppressed, the widow and the orphan, and that women of noble birth should enjoy his especial care." This was no new ideal: according, for instance, to the Greek geographer Strabo in about 20 B.C., the Gauls:

> Are easily roused, and always ready to fight. If they are angered they march straight at the enemy and attack him boldy in the open; they can therefore easily be overcome by cunning. They can be made to fight when one likes and where one likes, the motive matters little. They are simple moreover, and spontaneous, and willingly champion the cause of the oppressed.

The papal injunction fell upon ears well attuned to receive it, for such a stock as the French nobility was favourable for the growth of the chivalric ideal; it is not surprising that it first appeared in France and came to its finest flower there, for it belongs to the same civilization which illuminated Western Europe with its learning— even during the otherwise rather desperate eleventh century—and won for the French the name of "God's chosen people", like Judah of old. It was a product in its finished form of the period 1080–1130, the period of William of Poitiers and his troubadours, of Abelard and William of Champeaux, when Suger was making St. Denis the centre of European art.

> C'est alors [says Joseph Bedier] aux alentours l'an 1100 qu'apparaissent, comme tumultuairement, le premier Croisade—et encore le premier arc d'ogive—et encore le premier vitrail—et encore le premier drame liturgique, et encore le premier Tournoi—et encore le premier charte de liberté d'un commune—et encore le premier chant du premier troubadour: toutes creations inattendues, jaillies à la fois du sol de la France.

The fullest expression of the chivalric ideal in its early stages is found in the "Chansons de Geste", in which it is closely connected with the land which gave it birth. The "Chanson de Roland", the "Gesta Francorum", the "Chanson d'Antioche"—all have as their dominant motif God's choice of Charlemagne and his Franks to be his champions in a perpetual Holy War against the Infidel. Loyalty is its keynote. The knight must give unstinted loyalty to God, his liege lord and his chivalry. The ideal was harsh and bloody, but magnificent, a consummation blessed by the Church of the old Teutonic warrior virtues wedded to the impetuous, generous *élan* of the Celt. It is expressed in many parts of the Song of Roland; for instance when Roland sees the huge army of the Saracens approaching he is anxious above all to prove himself a worthy vassal of the Emperor. He says to his friend Oliver:

> The Emperor gave us this host of Frenchmen, twenty thousand picked men amongst whom he knows there is not one coward. A man must endure great hardships for his lord; for him he must suffer both cold and heat, for him he must sacrifice both flesh and blood. Strike with your lance and I will smite with Durendal, my good sword which Charles gave me. If I die, he who inherits it will say, "It was the sword of a noble vassal."

At the same time Archbishop Turpin addresses the barons and prepares them for battle.

> "Barons," he says, "Charles gave us this task; we must die for our king. Christendom is in peril; lend it your aid. You will now have battle, for you see the Saracens before you. Confess your sins and ask God for pardon. I will absolve you to save your souls. If you die, you will be holy martyrs and will win a place in Paradise."

Whereupon, in a scene reminiscent of many during the Crusades, the warriors fell on their knees and are blessed by the Archbishop, who bids them smite the enemy for their penance.

The knight in these years between 1090 and about 1150 had a religious mission; from the beginning of his career to its end he was the Church's servant, and the first article in his code was the defence of Christendom. Etienne de Fougères, Bishop of Rennes, in his "Livre des Manières" written in the twelfth century, says that St. Peter brought two swords to Christ: one for the clergy, who were to punish the evildoer by excommunication; the other for the

(a)   (b)   (c)

1. Three Bronze Age swords from Denmark (*National Museum, Copenhagen*). (*a*) Thrusting sword, *c.* 1000 B.C. (*b*) Cut-and-thrust sword with hilt of bronze, *c.* 900 B.C. (*c*) Cutting sword with hilt of bone or horn, *c.* 850–700 B.C.

(*d*) Combat between Memnon and Achilles, from a krater of Attic red-figure ware, fifth century B.C. (*British Museum*).

2. Shield from the River Thames at Battersea. Bronze, once perhaps gilded, decorated with insets of red enamel, first century A.D. (*British Museum*).

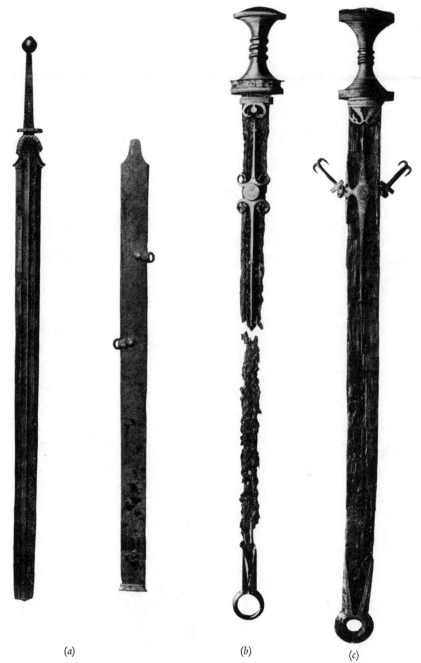

3. From left to right: (*a*) Iron Age sword and scabbard, *c*. 300 B.C., from Lindholmgard, Denmark. (*b*) Sword with hilt and scabbard-mounts of silver, from the Kragehul Bog in Denmark, fourth–fifth century A.D. (*c*) Sword with hilt and scabbard-mounts of bronze, from Kragehul, fourth–fifth century A.D.

4. Helmet from the ship grave at Sutton Hoo, 7th century.

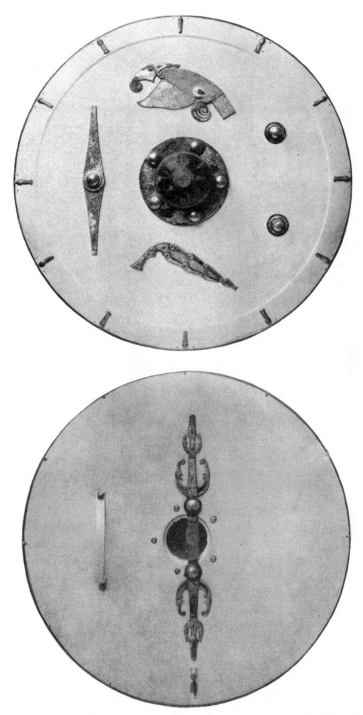

5. Reconstructed shield from the ship grave at Sutton Hoo: (*top*) outside of shield; (*bottom*) inside.

6. (*a*) Viking sword from River Thames at the Temple. Type VII, *c.* 1000 A.D. Blade with iron-inlaid inscription INGELRII. (*b*) Sword (Type X) of late Viking type, *c.* 1050. Blade with iron-inlaid inscription INGEL(RII). (*c*) Sword (Type XI), *c.* 1130–70. Blade with iron-inlaid inscription GICELINMEFECIT. (*d*) Sword (Type XI) from Fornham, site of a battle fought in 1171. Blade with inscription inlaid in white metal SESBENEDICTAS.

(*a*)　　　　　(*b*)　　　　　(*c*)　　　　　(*d*)

7. (a) Sword (Type XI) found in Denmark, *c.* 1150–1200. Blade with inscription in yellow metal SESPETRNUS. (b) Sword (Type XII) from the River Witham near Lincoln, *c.* 1250–1300. Blade inscription inlaid in latten + HDXOXCHMDRCHDXORVI+ . (c) War sword (Type XIII) from River Thames near the Temple in London, *c.* 1300. (d) Sword (Type XIV) with hilt of iron overlaid with silver, *c.* 1300.

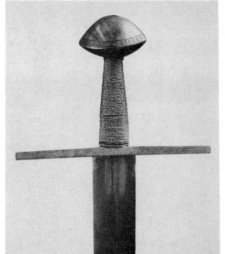

8. (a) Hilt of "The Sword of St. Maurice", Imperial Treasury, Vienna. Engraved in the silver-plated pommel are the arms of England and of Otto IV. Type XI, c. 1200.

(a)

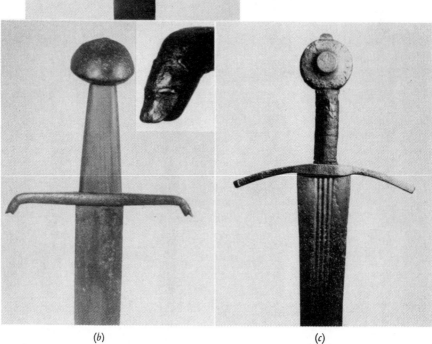

(b)

(c)

(b) Detail of plate 6c showing (inset) beast's head on end of cross. (c) Hilt of sword of Type XIV (c. 1300). The pommel and cross are plated with silver. The grip of beechwood is original and retains part of its leather covering, which shows the impression of a thong or cord binding.

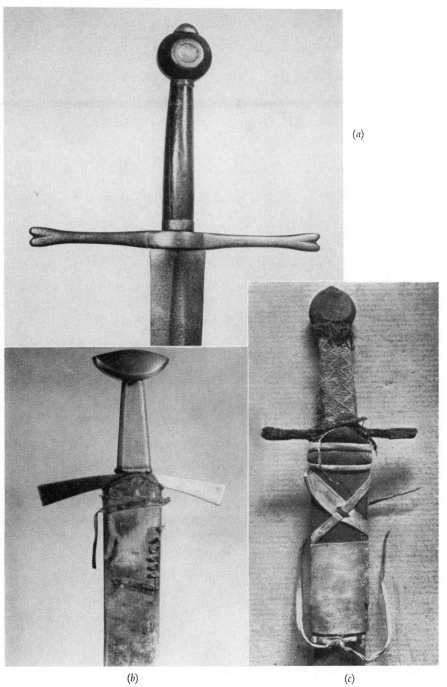

9. (*a*) War sword, *c.* 1300, Type XIII, with original wooden grip. (*b*) Copy of the "Sword of St. Maurice" from the Royal Armoury at Turin. (*c*) Sword (Type XII) from the tomb of Fernando de la Cerda (ob. 1270), in the convent of Las Huelgas, Burgos.

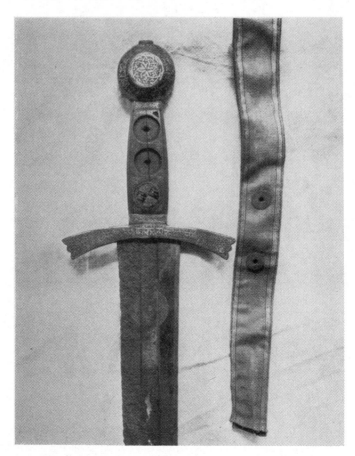

10. (*a*) Sword (unsheathed) of Sancho IV of Castile (see frontispiece), showing part of the belt.

(*b*) Gilt bronze spurs of Sancho IV of Castile.

et aliquo inter feceriint. quod accidie ipei iiam dei qui propar p̄ es̄ uoiac
omnes uiii ui ca occiderentur. Vroiq: ipi.i iiii.uicina.a cet nec ce preda quicquam ab aliqua tan
rerur. Vnus autem filiorum ishtabel contra preceptum dei aliqno ex pꝛ
(top border text, partially legible)

11. (*a*) "The Israelites repulsed from Hai." Painting from the Maciejowski Bible (fol. 10A).

(*b*)   (*c*)

(*b*) Seal of the Guild of St. George, Ferrara (*c.* 1290). Note the greaves and the coat of plates.
(*c*) Impression of the seal of Roger FitzWalter (1235).

12. Monument above the tomb of Can Grande Della Scala (ob. 1329), Verona. Note the closed greaves, the war sword of Type XIII, and the high saddle. It is unlikely that the helm would be carried this way while riding; its representation on the monument is the result of incorrect reassembly after the statue fell from its pedestal in the nineteenth century.

(a)

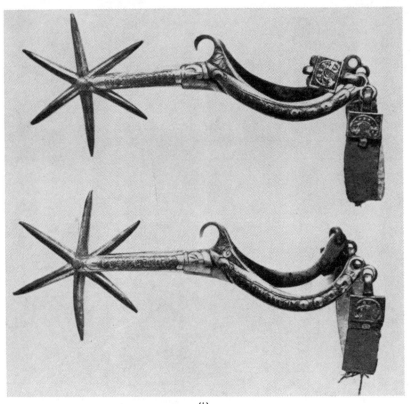

(b)

13. (a) Sword-hanger from a late fourteenth-century hip belt of copper-gilt, with fifteenth-century roundels of silver gilt. (b) Pair of spurs of gilt bronze, with their original cloth-of-gold straps; they are decorated with an engraved pattern in the form of a strap and buckle with the word "Esperance", a device adopted by Louis II, Duc de Bourbon (1356–1410). They were found, together with an enamelled horse bit, in an oak chest in the dry moat of the Chateau de Bonchat, near St. Dourçain sur Sioule, Allier.

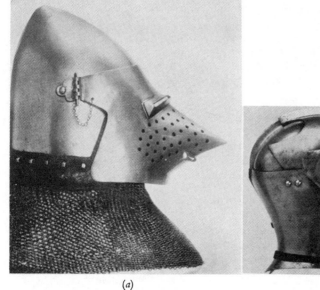

(a)

(b)

14. (a) Bascinet, c. 1390, with snouted visor (the mail aventail is a restoration).

(b) Armet, probably Italian, c. 1470.

(c)

(d)

(c) Barbute, Italian, c. 1440.

(d) Sallet, German, c. 1450.

15. Complete armour made between 1497 and 1503, in Nurnburg, for Kunz Schott von Hellingen (the sabatons are restored).

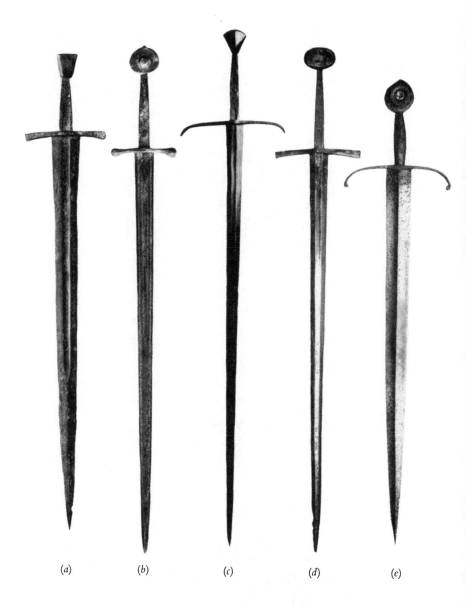

(a)   (b)   (c)   (d)   (e)

16. (a) Sword (Type XVI) blade with inscription inlaid in yellow metal; +NnDIC+.
(b) Sword (Type XVI) found in London, c. 1320–50. (c) Sword (Type XVII) found in the
River Cam, c. 1375–1410. (d) Sword (Type XVII), c. 1360–1400. (e) Sword (Type XVIII)
probably part of the funeral furniture of Henry V; it is a well-used fighting sword and may
have belonged to him in life.

17. *Right*: Sword (Type XII) (*c.* 1310–30) of doubtful origin, preserved in the treasury of Toledo Cathedral. This may have belonged to the Infante Don Juan of Tarifa (son of Alfonso X), killed in 1319 fighting against the Moors. His seal bears the same arms as those on the sword.

Left: Sword of Can Grande Della Scala (ob. 1329), Type XII. Found in his coffin, now in the Archaeological Museum in Verona.

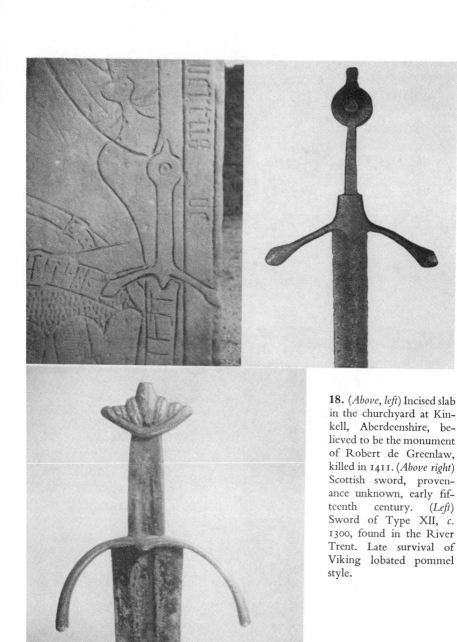

18. (*Above, left*) Incised slab in the churchyard at Kinkell, Aberdeenshire, believed to be the monument of Robert de Greenlaw, killed in 1411. (*Above right*) Scottish sword, provenance unknown, early fifteenth century. (*Left*) Sword of Type XII, *c.* 1300, found in the River Trent. Late survival of Viking lobated pommel style.

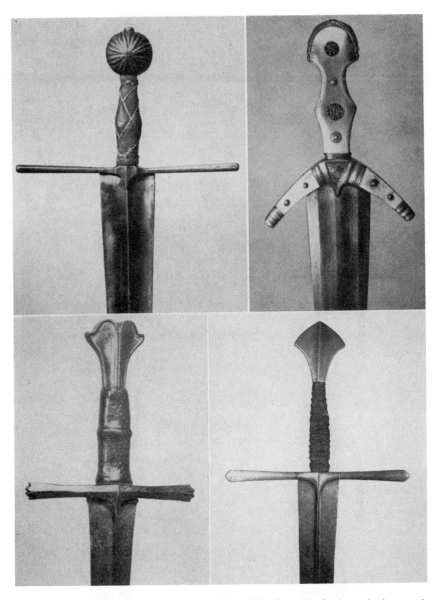

19. (*Above left*) (*a*) Sword, Italian, *c.* 1460–80, Type XV. The original grip retains its covering of red velvet bound with silver and steel wire. (*Above right*) (*b*) Sword, Italian, *c.* 1485–1500. The hilt is of mammoth ivory and bronze, fashioned in the style of a cinquedea. The blade is 31 in. long. (*Below left*) (*c*) Sword, perhaps Flemish, *c.* 1450–75, Type XVIII. Hilt of gilded iron. (*Below right*) (*d*) Sword, Italian, *c.* 1450–1500, Type XV.

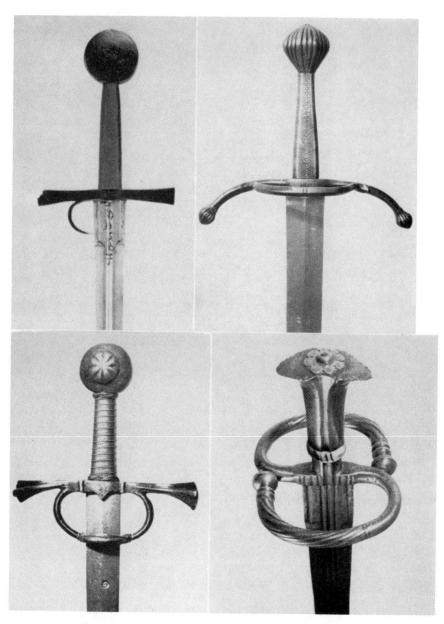

20. (*Top left*) (*a*) Sword (Type XIX) with blackened hilt and finger-ring, dated by an arabic inscription in the blade: A.H. 836 = A.D. 1432. (*Top right*) (*b*) Sword (Type XVIII) with side ring, *c.* 1420–50. (*Below left*) (*c*) Sword with blackened hilt "Pas d'Ane" and ring. The cross is curved horizontally. Spanish, *c.* 1480. (*Below right*) (*d*) "Landsknecht" sword, *c.* 1520.

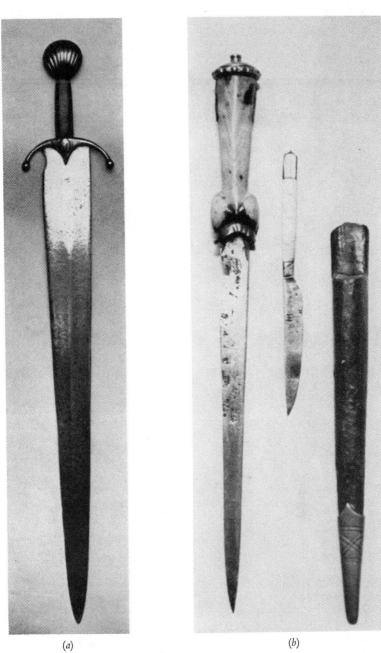

21. (*a*) Short sword, Italian, *c.* 1470–90. (*b*) Dagger and sheath, *c.* 1450–80.

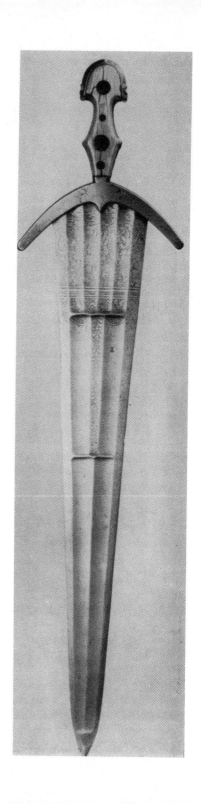

22. (*a*) Cinquedea, the hilt of gilded iron, the blade blued, etched and gilt in the manner of Ercole Grandi of Ferrara. The arms are those of Colonna and Malvezzi of Mantua, *c.* 1490. (*b*) Cinquedea, *c.* 1490, the blade etched in the manner of Ercole de Fideli.

knight who was to smite the enemies of the Church. The mission of the clerk was to pray, that of the knight to defend the faith; hence a knight's sword was sacred. It was consecrated at the altar for the defence of Christ's people, and on the death of its bearer it was to be restored to the altar. (This comment has a bearing on archaeology, as we shall see later.)

In the "Chanson d'Antioche" the knights are "*li Jhesus Chevalier*", and the troubadour completes this definition by saying that they are "*cil qui Damedieu servent de loial cuer entier*".

At the same time the knights had a more matter-of-fact role in society; they constituted a definite rank in it, set there for a purpose. "The knighthood," says John of Salisbury, "is the armed hand of the state." Its numbers must be carefully selected, hardy, disciplined, virile warriors bound by oath to serve their king but never to the exclusion of their duty to protect the Chuch. At all times this is their first task. Vincent of Beauvais elaborates:

> The use of an organized knighthood lies in protecting the Church, attacking disloyalty, reverencing the priesthood, avenging the wrongs of the poor and keeping the country in a state of quiet.

Such was the Church's view; knights are not courtiers, or members of an upper class justified by its own culture, but responsible officials, the armed policemen of the state.

The epic poems tell only of war and the devout loyalty of the knighthood to their God and their liege lords; there is no mention of the love of women, which was soon to become a predominant feature in chivalry. "These warriors," it has been said, "thought less of a beautiful woman than of a good lance-thrust or a fine charger." Practically the only mention of a woman in the "Song of Roland" is in the few lines telling how the beautiful Aude, Roland's betrothed, hears of his death and herself dies of it. When the hero is at the point of death and thinks of the things most dear to him, Aude is not included. He mourns that he will see fair France no more and that his lord Charlemagne must lose a good vassal and that his lovely sword will be masterless. This indifference to women is notable in the Chansons, but they reflect only one aspect of knightly thought. We cannot believe that the gently-born heard nothing but these warlike epic songs and were unaffected by the popular lyrics of their day, any more than that they cared nothing for love nor had any decent and refined feelings about it. Among the innumberable Latin "Scholars' Lyrics" originating in France and Germany we find, in the tenth and eleventh centuries, verse as lovely as any the troubadours made in the twelfth and thirteenth. For instance, written in the fearful Viking-ridden tenth century we have one of the most romantic and charming love-songs of all time, the "Iam, Dulcis Amica", from which I quote four stanzas:

> Come, sweetheart, come,
> Dear as my heart to me,
> Come to the room
> I have made fine for thee.

> Here there be couches spread,
> Tapestry tented
> Flowers for thee to tread,
> Green herbs sweet scented. . . .

> Alone in the wood
> I have loved hidden places,
> Fled from the tumult
> And crowding of faces.

> Now the snow's melting,
> Out the leaves start,
> The nightingale's singing,
> Love's in the heart.

This was being sung in hall and castle and court all over France and Germany (and in the streets, too), while the Skalds of the north were singing of Beowulf and the frightful doings of Ragnar Hairy-Breeks' sons. As sincere and direct as the Chansons, it is immortal in a way that the epic can never be, for its sentiment and expression would be fresh and real in any age. Even amid the lightnings the blackbird sings; fire and blood and battle were not the only things men dreamed of.

The inevitable development of what we might call the official knightly attitude towards women began to take hold in the middle of the twelfth century. It was given impetus by the poets of southern France, particularly after Eleanor of Aquitaine (one of the most glamorous women of the Middle Ages, who later married Henry II of England and became the mother of Richard Lion-Heart and John) came from Provence to Paris to become for a while the Queen of Louis VII of France. The mingling of the tongues of "oc" and "oui" in overseas expeditions strengthened it.

Henceforth the influence of women dominates chivalry, and religion and feudal loyalty take second place. Only war, a glorious and exciting pastime and a stimulating way of winning wealth, kept its high place as a gentleman's most cherished occupation; but the influence of love as the mainspring of warlike aspiration gave a much lighter rhythm to it, and to literature and life itself. Poets sing now only of their ladies' perfections, crave their pity and strive to merit their grace. The knight fights as hard as he ever did (he was not to be deprived of his business or his fun) but it is to win his lady's favours, and the word *amoureux* comes to mean more than it does today, for it covers the entire range of knightly virtue. The idea has prevailed that:

> Hee never were good werryoure
> That cowde not love aryghte

"He who loves not is but half a man" and "*por l'amor des dames devient li vilains courtois*". This is the essence of it, for what society needed more than anything was an influence which would make villains courteous. Like *amoureux*, the word *courtois* had a wider meaning than we give it today, and covered the whole field of gracious living and behaviour.

This "amorous" aspect of chivalry has caused furious controversy among historians. Because of it, those two nineteenth-century colossi, Freeman and Green, condemned it utterly. To do them justice, chivalry looks fearful when judged by the standards of their time, for its main supports were both abhorrent to late Victorian society in England—the Roman Catholic Church, and illicit love. For let us not mistake it: the love the troubadours sing and the knights fight for is not to be found in the bonds of marriage. Marriage was, and remained, not the consummation of *L'amour courtois*, but its most dangerous and formidable obstacle. Ladies were encouraged to find the emancipation of illicit intrigue, and were carefully instructed in the devious ways by which their

187

husbands could be outwitted; while knights and squires were expected to gain the favour of a lady (whether married or not was immaterial) and having won it to make it the lodestone of their lives. In theory this love was intended to be entirely pure; the knight expected no practical favours from his lady other than gifts of arms, or horses or cash. In this way chivalric gallantry could—and frequently did—become a colossal system of bigamy in which every lady was expected to have a husband and a lover *par amours*, and every proper knight, as well as the wife to whom he was bound for business reasons, a goddess whose cause he upheld against all comers, and whose every demand he unhesitatingly obeyed. Even so there are many instances—in the marriages of Edward III and Philippa of Hainault, for instance, and of the Black Prince and Joan Holland—where wife and goddess were one.

The Church frowned upon this system of gallantry and struggled against it, not so much because it was immoral, but because it diverted the attention of the knighthood from its task of fighting the infidel and recovering the Holy Land. Even so it very rapidly succeeded in becoming established as the third and completing element of chivalry. It has been said that the distinctive qualities of a knight were at their best honour, piety and love; at their worst ferocity, superstition and lust. The virtues of chivalry were courage, faith and devotion; its vices murder, intolerance and adultery. Unless we are prepared to take neither one side nor the other, to see more than just the black or the white, to allow chivalry to be a fantastic mixture of vices and virtues, of good, bad and indifferent like all human institutions, we shall get a very mistaken idea of it.

There was one further obligation laid upon those who would be perfect knights: at all times and in all circumstances they must be cheerful; the very science of chivalry itself became known as the *Gai Saber*, and gaiety, even in the grimmest situations, became the hall-mark of knightly behaviour. That this was no idle injunction to be forgotten in the general ferocity of war is proved by innumerable instances, not only in the Age of Chivalry itself but in all later ages including our own. Because of it, we can forgive much which we may not approve.

One of the most striking characteristics of mediaeval society is its formalism and love of ceremony. The respect for names and words, definitions and regulations which were regarded as the vesture of realities, stems from the prehistoric awe of the magic of words and symbols. The symbolic character of chivalric institutions is recognized by all, but it is easy to forget that the knights themselves lived, as it were, in an allegory, and that what to us seems fantastic and even absurd was not so to them. Knighthood was a discipline never relaxed through life, its object to make a man complete and free in himself but obedient to the rules of knightly conduct. In the ceremonies of conferring knighthood everything was symbolical, actions, arms and dress. The ancient ceremonial was simple, and we may believe primaeval. The formal arming (the Adoubement: Adoubs is the group of arms making up a warrior's equipment) was the core of it. This became greatly enlarged under the Church's influence.

When knighthood came to its prime early in the twelfth century the symbolism which accompanied it became more elaborate. On the eve of his admission to the Order, the aspirant to chivalry was solemnly stripped of his clothes by his fellow squires and put into a bath, a symbol of purification. Then he was dressed in a white tunic, emblem of purity (analogous to the chrisom of baptism); and a scarlet mantle, the emblem of nobility; and hose and shoes of black, symbolic of death and the earth in which all must eventually lie. He was girt with the white cingulum, for chastity, and led to the church or the castle chapel where all night he would keep solitary vigil in prayer, his arms lying before the altar. In the morning he would make his confession and hear Mass. Then comes the great moment. After the Alleluias of the Gradual he hands his sword to the priest who lays it on the altar and prays for a blessing upon it; he returns it with the words: "*Accipe gladium istum in nomine Patris et Filii et Spiritus Sancti et utaris eo in defensam tuam et sancti Dei Ecclesiae et confusionem inimicorum crucis Christi ac fidei Christianiae.*" Virtue has passed into it; he receives it back from the priest and brandishes it three times, sheaths it and hands it to his sponsor—who might be his liege lord or simply another knight, for all who had received knighthood might bestow it—and makes his vow of knighthood to him. Then he is armed in his complete war-gear by his friends and attendants, but it is left to his sponsor to gird on his sword and give him the colée or accolade. This could either be a blow across the shoulders with the flat of a sword, or a buffet with a clenched fist. Finally he received four injunctions: he must never traffic with traitors; never give evil counsel to a lady, whether married or not; he must treat her with great respect and defend her against all. He must observe fasts and abstinences, and every day must hear Mass and make an offering in Church.[1] This last is the point of a highly moral tale of a knight overdue at a tournament who, in spite of his impatient squire, insisted on hearing Mass first, wherefore he was miraculously aided in the fight by Our Lady.

Tournaments have always appealed to the imagination, and (perhaps partly because of that) have been soundly drubbed by Freeman and his followers as another aspect of chivalric absurdity, but in their heyday (the twelfth and thirteenth centuries) they were important social events providing a necessary outlet for martial ardour and an indispensible "battle school" of military training. A tournament was the great social event of the age, bringing together knightly folk from all countries and keeping alive the spirit of international brotherhood in arms which was such an essential part of the chivalric ideal. It was a useful source of knightly revenue, too, for successful combatants carried away rich prizes of arms and horses —though sometimes the prize was less valuable, even downright embarrassing: after the Barons of England had made King John sign Magna Carta on Runnymede in 1215, they decided to hold a tourney at Staines—it seemed too good an opportunity to miss as so many of them were gathered there anyhow: the prize, jousted for and presented by a lady, was a bear! The "Fabliaux" often tell of the pathetic plight of knights complaining of the Church's prohibition of tournaments which deprives them of their only means of livelihood.

Throughout Europe the tournament and the exercises which prepared for it were the most serious occupation of knightly people when they were not engaged in hunting and hawking. To a man of this class, unless he were a clerk or a churchman, war was not only his job but a most thrilling and absorbing pastime, and tournaments were like race meetings; the royal and important ones like

[1] These ceremonies were not, of course, always followed. It was perhaps the ambition of every squire to receive his knighthood on the battlefield. In such cases the *colée*, given usually by his lord or captain, was all that was needed.

the Derby and the Grand National, and the small local ones organized by provincial barons like country point-to-points. All the merriment and fun of mediaeval life was brought out at the fairs which were an essential part of them; all sorts of people were made welcome—wandering players and poets, Jogeleurs, tumblers and musicians. (In John's reign a certain John de Rampagne disguised himself as a Jogeleur and went and beat a tabor at a tournament in France.) Naturally enough, these junketings which brought all kinds of people together gave plenty of opportunity for gambling and drunkenness and riotous behaviour; no doubt this was one reason why the Church objected to them. Also, in the early days of chivalry particularly, too many noblemen lost their lives in them, like Geoffrey de Mandeville, Earl of Essex, who was killed in London in 1216 in a tournament *more Francorum*. (The phrase shows that they were still regarded as a French custom.) According to the letter of the Church's ban, all who died thus were to be denied Christian burial; there are visions of knightly souls excluded from Paradise, but we may believe that the knightly folk did not worry unduly:

> "For to Hell," says Aucassin, "go the good clerks and the goodly knights who have died in tourneys and in the great wars; and the good soldier and the true man. With these do I wish to go. And there go also the fair courteous ladies who have two loves or three besides their lords; and there go also the gold and the silver and the rich furs; and there also go the harper and the minstrel and the kings of the world."

Paradise, it seems, had only arid attractions to offer.

The origins of the tournament, like those of chivalry itself, are primaeval, but we may assume on the evidence available at present that its immediate ancestor was the Roman *Ludus Troiae* (Troy Game), which was a warlike exercise played by two mounted teams; it is believed by some that the word "Torneamentum" is derived from it. The Gauls—many of whom were matchless horsemen— took kindly to it, and the Goths and Lombards had similar ideas of their own. We have seen how the Northmen had formalized their single combats, and it is reasonable to suppose that similar formalities governed the duels of their kinsmen in southern Europe. However it was, the first historical record of a tournament in the mediaeval sense (reported by Nidhard, who was there) was when the two sons of Louis the Debonair, Charles and Louis the German, met at Strassburg in 875 to divide between them the kingdom of their brother Lothair. Here the vassals of both kings engaged in combats on horseback. Henry the Fowler (876–936), father of Otto the Great, is said to have brought the tournament from France into Germany, and in the Chronicle of Tours the death is recorded in a tournament in 1056 of Sire Geoffroi de Preuilly, a baron of Brittany, who is said to have invented it (*Torneamentum invenit*); though what is probably meant is that he drew up the rules of the game. In the thirteenth century Matthew Paris calls it "*conflictus Galliae*"; like chivalry itself it seems to have originated in France. We hear of Stephen being severely criticized because he was too weak to prevent tournaments taking place in England, but Henry II very firmly put a stop to them —his knights had to go overseas if they wanted to joust. Count Geoffroi of Brittany left the English court and rejoiced in the opportunity of "matching himself with good knights on the borders of Normandy and France". Richard I permitted them again in England, partly so that "the French might not scoff at the English knights as being unskilled and awkward" ("*tamquam rudibus et minime gnaris*", says Matthew Paris), and partly to raise money for his crusading war-effort. He did this by granting licences to barons to hold tournaments in specified places. We may look back from our own licence-ridden age across seven centuries with fellow-feeling for one Robert de Mortimer, who "*tornerverat sine licentia*" and was heavily fined for it.

During the thirteenth century tournaments became more popular than ever, and towards its end they begin to show the first signs of their ultimate declension from purely warlike exercises fought with real weapons[1] to the elaborate and comparatively harmless pageants which they became during the fifteenth century. The earliest record we have of the use of special armour for the tournament is in the accounts for the royal tournament held in the park at Windsor on

[1] At some date before 1200 a slight concession was made to the needs of safety by the introduction of a rebated lance-point—often in the shape of a crown— which would grip on an opponent's armour sufficiently to unhorse him, but not penetrate his armour to hurt him. Later these became known as "lances of courtesy".

July 9, 1278. All the armour mentioned in these accounts is of leather—even the helms—nothing tougher being needed against the whalebone swords also mentioned.

The passion which the knights felt for tourneying is reflected in the frequency of efforts made to prevent them—to prevent unlicensed ones, that is. Edward II, for instance, issued a number of letters forbidding all persons

Torneare, burdeire, justus facere, adventuras quarere, seu alias ad armas ire . . . sine licentia nostra speciale.

It may seem a little hard that individuals should be forbidden to joust or seek adventures or ride "at arms" without his special licence. The reason given is for fear of "breach of the peace and terrifying quiet people". No tournament, for example, is to be held within six miles of Cambridge to protect "*Tranquillitatem ibidem studentium*". Naturally enough, sovereigns were jealous of anything that would exalt their vassals overmuch, for undoubtedly unlicenced tournaments gave opportunity for the meeting of disaffected people and making the barons' castles schools of private war. They also tended to infringe the sovereign's own prerogative.

From about 1250 and all through the fourteenth century the tournament enjoyed perhaps its golden age, for much pageantry was involved, and much gallantry. Knights fought each other both *à outrance* (to the death) or *à plaisance* (for fun), and though formality and organization took away a little of their warlike character, tournaments were gay and glamorous affairs, where brave men fought each other "on foaming horse, with swords and friendly hearts" and lovely ladies watched with all the enthusiasm of the bull-ring (fig. 84). A most attractive account of a tournament in the thirteenth century tells how the ladies give away their scarves and chaplets to be worn as favours by their chosen knights, but as the excitement grows they tear off and throw into the lists "wimples and caps, mantles and tunics ('chemises' is the word in the original text), sleeves and dresses, until they all sit there with their heads bare (*le chef pur*) and laugh at each other's disarray".

With the beginning of the fifteenth century and the accession to the English throne of the usurping and businesslike House of Lancaster, a new spirit begins to appear in the attitude taken in this

193

Fig. 84. Jousting (from an unfinished drawing in the "Willehalms Codex" Cassel), c. 1335.

country to tournaments. Our puritanical hero Henry V considered them frivolous and time-wasting. He refused to hold jousts when he wedded Katharine of France; "rather", he said, "let the King of France and his servants besiege the town of Sens" and there:

jouster et tournoyer et montrer sa prouesse et son hardement

to some useful purpose. War had become a serious matter, and the end of chivalry was in sight. The French went to the opposite extreme, and the tournament—by the middle of the century—became a more or less senseless pageant which can be seen in all its silliness in the accounts of the tournaments of Charles the Rash and René of Anjou.

I said just now that to Henry V war was a serious business. Then had it not been so before, to Henry II in his constant tussles with his unruly vassals, to Edward I trying to subdue the Scots, to Edward

III seeking the crown and the fair land of France? Yes, serious it was perhaps to kings and political prelates, and certain great lords who were responsible for organizing war and raising the money to pay for it. Deadly serious it was to the townspeople and peasants who were constantly being killed and raped and burned in it; but for the ordinary gentlemen who fought in it, we may believe that if it had any seriousness at all it was of a very different kind, the sort of seriousness that professional footballers and athletes give to their profession, save that to the mediaeval professional it was all spiced and laced with a most high and terrible glamour. Even such wandering mercenary swords as the knights errant, to whom war (any war, so long as they had a lord to serve who would pay for their service) was a business, and whose swords themselves, which they thought of as "Gagnepain" or "Wynbrod", had to win their livelihood for them—even they lusted for the glamour of battle. We are not reading romantic fairy tales when we are told how a knight would camp out by a bridge for a month, and hold it against all comers. Such things were constantly happening until late in the fourteenth century. Even more drastic events took place: in 1350 there was a truce in France. No one was at war, and the small garrison of the castle of Josselin in Brittany was bored. The seneschal, Sire Robert de Beaumanoir, who held Josselin for France and the Duchess of Montfort ("*vaillant chevalier durement et du plus grand lineage de Bretagne*", writes Froissart) sent an envoy to the neighbouring castle of Ploermel, held for England and Count Charles of Blois by a freelance captain whose English name baffled Froissart; he called him "Brandebourg" but who he really was is obscure—and a small force of knights and men-at-arms. Beaumanoir's message called upon Brandebourg to send him forth one champion or two or three to joust with swords against an equal number for the love of their ladies. "No," says Brandebourg, "our ladies will not that we adventure ourselves for the passing chance of a single joust; but if you will, choose twenty or thirty of your companions, and let them fight with us in a fair field." So thirty champions on each side were chosen. They heard Mass, armed themselves and went out to the place of arms, a field midway between Josselin and Ploermel. Twenty-five of each side went on foot and five on horseback. Then they fought, and after some time they were quite exhausted and each captain drew his men off to rest. Beaumanoir (he was short of two front teeth, and in a fashion reminiscent of Viking times was called "Gap-tooth Beaumanoir") was heard to say he longed for a draught of water. "Drink your own blood, Beaumanoir," croaked one of his companions. Then they went to it again and many were killed on one side and on the other, and at last the English had the worst of it, and all who were not slain were made prisoners, and courteously cared for until they were healed of their wounds, when they were ransomed. Froissart saw, sitting at King Charles VI's table, one of these champions, a Breton knight named Yvain Charuelz, and "his face was so cut and slashed that he showed how hard the fighting had been".

We may wonder at this useless bravery and lust to fight for the sake of it, but we should not laugh at it—nor scorn it. War is beastly, but such incidents lessen the weight of woe that is inseperable from it. These warriors, little as we may be able to understand their feelings, wanted to fight and to die if need be, and they gloried in it. They fought without personal animosity; if they died, they were honoured; if they were wounded, they were cared for—whether by friend or foe was immaterial. (The remedies used to heal wounds in the Middle Ages were very much more effective than those Florence Nightingale battled with at Scutari in 1854.) If they were made prisoner they were usually treated as friends and made much of until they raised the money for their ransom. It was a rule of knightly conduct that a captor should not seek to extort from a prisoner a ransom that would ruin him. He should say what he could afford, and his captor would accept it. There were, alas, many occasions when captured knights were thrown into dungeons "where rats and mice," as Du Guesclin says, "are more plentiful than singing birds", but happily such unknightly actions were not too frequent; a notable example is the imprisonment of Richard I by Archduke Leopold of Austria and the emperor Henry VI.

The tournament included two kinds of encounter: the single combat or joust on horseback or afoot, with lance, sword, pole-axe, axe or dagger, and the tournament proper which was a general melée like a miniature battle. The "Battle of the Thirty" was a tournament in this limited sense. At a tournament at Chauvency in 1285 the contests were arranged thus; on the first day, a Sunday, there was a general fête while all the contestants and visitors assembled; Monday and Tuesday were devoted to jousts. Wednesday was a rest-day, and sides were picked for the tournament which took place on Thursday. Each evening after the fights were over the whole company joined in singing, dancing, feasting and general jollity.

We often read of courteous and gallant deeds of arms in accounts of the more serious occasions of war. In the chronicle of the ill-fated crusade of Louis IX (St. Louis) in 1250, written by the Sire de Joinville, Seneschal of Champagne and a close friend of the king, we find many outstanding examples of the knightly spirit in action and at its best. One episode, for instance, reminds one of the scene in the "Chanson de Roland" in which Roland refuses to sound his horn to summon Charles to his aid, and shows that the poet's ideal of knightly honour is not diminished by its reality in a desperate situation. A large force of Saracens had surrounded Joinville and a party of knights and serjeants, and as many of them were sorely wounded he saw little hope except in the saints. At this critical point one of his knights saw the Count of Anjou and his following not far off in the field, but would not seek their help without asking his leader if he thought it consistent with his honour to do so. Joinville tells how this knight came to him—a ghastly figure, for he had been fighting without a helm and had been hit in the face so that his nose hung down over his lip—and said, "Sire, if you think that neither I nor my heirs will incur reproach thereby I will go and seek help from the Count of Anjou who I see yonder in the field." "My lord Everard," replies de Joinville, "meseems you would earn great honour if you went to save our lives; your life, too, is in great danger." He adds that he spoke truly, for Sire Everard died soon after of his wound.

Elsewhere Joinville tells of a valiant man, Lord James of Castel, Bishop of Soissons:

> when he saw that the French were retreating towards Damietta, he, who had a great desire to be with God, felt no wish to return to the country where he was born, so he hastened to be with God and set spurs to his horse, and fell single-handed upon the Saracens, who killed him with their swords and put him in God's companionship and amongst the number of the martyrs.

Fig. 85. From an early fourteenth century "Romance of Lancelot de Lac".

The chronicles of the Hundred Years War abound with stories of how single knights would ride forward when two forces were drawn up for battle and summon a champion from the other side to run a course with him for the love of their ladies. At Cocherel in 1364 an English knight rode out

> *pour demander a faire un coup de lance contre celui des Francois qui seroit assez brave pour entrer en lice avec lui.*

Roland deBoy answered the challenge "*pour lui prêter le colet*" and had the best of it. Another, before Cherbourg in 1379, invited three champions, "the most amorous knights of the enemy, to fight with three amorous knights on his own side, for the love of their ladies". So Gareth in the "Morte d'Arthur" rides abroad and to please Linet kills or spares knight after knight, red, green or black.

The principal failing of chivalry to a modern eye, one of the reasons why Freeman denounced it so uncompromisingly, is its emphasis on noble birth and the privilege of rank, and its apparent utter disregard of all who were not of gentle blood. Like a certain lord in Shakespeare's *Henry IV*, the knight regards the disturbance of the knightly melée by infantry (who were called ribauds, brigans, vileins) and archers as "great pity". The Flemish knights at the great battle of Bouvines in 1214 refused to charge a body of infantry "because they were not gentlemen" and so lost the battle. Yet on the other hand we read of countless occasions when knights put themselves in great peril in order to bring the "ribauds" under their command safely out of dangerous situations, or refuse to run away and leave their infantry in the lurch. This was particularly the case with the English, for in this country the lower classes were far more independent and less down-trodden than their continental fellows, while the average English knight from the twelfth century to the fifteenth was a simple country gentleman, looking after his land and his tenants, serving in the county courts, on juries and inquests, or doing his work as sheriff or in Quarter Sessions. When knight and yeoman went to war together, there was a comradeship between them which was found nowhere else in chivalric Europe. Even so, the French were not unaware by any means of the duty of a lord to his folk. Joinville tells us how deeply impressed he was by the remarks of a cousin of his before he sailed for Egypt with St. Louis.

"You are going overseas," he said, "now take care how you come back, for no knight, whether poor or rich, can return without shame if he leaves in the hands of the Saracen the meaner folk of our lord, in whose company he went out."

Chapter Twelve

SWORD TYPES AND BLADE INSCRIPTIONS, 1100–1325

E VEN A SUPERFICIAL sketch of military archaeology as a whole during the last four mediaeval centuries would fill a sizeable book; so in dealing with this period I shall concentrate on those aspects of it which have received the least attention. There is a great mass of scholarly and reliable work on mediaeval armour published in the English language, much of it very recently and all in easily accessible form, but correspondingly little dealing with the mediaeval sword. For some reason this most beautiful and important object has been disregarded in this country, though there are many learned papers and articles concerned with it in continental journals; but these are hard to come by and often misleading. So in this section I shall discuss armour only enough to complete the picture, paying far more attention to swords, daggers and spurs, with some of the many varieties of weapon which came into use for fighting on foot.

For more than 2,000 years the sword had been an emblem of power and chieftainship when the advent of chivalry brought it to its fullest glory. By about 1150 it had attained a complete symbolism; to all the ancient traditions was added the final touch of Christian sanctity. The form it had developed during the Viking Age was easily adapted and made holy by the Church, and the Cross which it formed became a protection against sin, a reminder that its owner must use it well in the protection of the Church and to the confusion of the enemies of Christ. Its two-edged blade stood for truth and loyalty, one side for the strong who persecute the weak and the other for rich oppressors of the poor.

In the Viking period a chieftain would often give gold rings to his followers as a reward for valorous service, presenting them on the point of his sword. In German poems of the eleventh and twelfth centuries we occasionally read of swords being similarly used in the marriage ceremony: the priest would bless the ring, taking it from the flat of the bridegroom's sword. In one of these poems we find that the essential and binding act of the marriage service was the placing of the bride's thumb upon the pommel of her groom's sword. In this particular instance the girl was forced to marriage against her will. They got her to the altar, but they could not by any effort get her clenched hand open and her thumb placed upon the sword pommel. The end of the poem is lost, but it looks as if the girl's wishes prevailed in the end.[1]

Preserved in nearly every major museum in Europe will be found a few swords of the period 1100–1500, most having been found in rivers and ditches and fields, offering no objective information by which they can be dated. For example, in the City Museum of Lincoln is a series of swords dredged from the River Witham during works carried out in 1788. They all come from a comparatively short stretch of the river, and it would be tempting to assume that they all got into it at the same time, perhaps during the first Battle of Lincoln in 1141. Yet one is a Roman blade, and another is a fragment of a back-sword of the Civil War period of the seventeenth century! The principal swords, a very handsome and well-preserved group of six, date between about 1120 and 1320. In 1952 another came up—at the end of an angler's line—in a nearby part of the Witham, this time a Viking period sword of Type V.[2] This is a good example of what has happened everywhere. Isolated specimens have been found without associated datable objects, most of them before the science of stratigraphy had come to the archaeologist's aid, and they were often passed from hand to hand for a generation or two before finally coming to rest in museums, so that even the knowledge of their find-place is lost. The only way by which such finds can be dated is by the internal evidence of their form, inscriptions

[1] *Journal of the Arms and Armour Society*, "The Ring on the Sword", Vol. 11, No. 10, June 1958. Dr. H. R. Ellis Davidson, M.A., Ph.D., F.S.A.

[2] The magnificent Viking Type VI sword from the Witham in the British Museum came from a different part of the river.

and marks, or by comparison. Fortunately there are a number of swords which have been found in clearly datable contexts; in tombs, on battlefields, or on sites which are known only to have been occupied between certain dates. Others can be dated to within a decade or so—even to a year or two—by means of the armorial bearings upon them. With these we can establish certain fixed points, the accuracy of which is confirmed by reliable—and often datable—comparison provided by the skill of contemporary sculptors and painters. Even so, there are many difficulties in the way of accurate dating, for although fashions in hilts changed as they did in the preceding periods, swords may have had similarly long lives. It is not until the time when the universal wearing of plate armour forced the bladesmiths to evolve a new form of sword blade that function is a help in dating (and the new shapes were only prehistoric ones revived, as we have seen). In the period 1120–1320 such changes as there were in the shape of blades did not affect their purpose, which was the same as it had been for nearly a thousand years.

In the course of years of intensive research I have worked out a typology for the neglected swords of the later Middle Ages similar to those of Dr. Elis Behmer and Dr. Jan Petersen. It is not possible to present this in full here, so I shall do for my own typology what I have done for Behmer's and what Sir Mortimer Wheeler did for Petersen's—offer a boiled-down version which, though ignoring the innumerable variations and sub-types, will yet give a general idea of the placing of the main types within the framework of archaeology and history (fig. 86). In describing and illustrating examples of each type I shall use wherever possible one of these "fixed point" swords together with comparable examples in sculpture and painting. Inscriptions are a necessary adjunct to the dating of swords, but for the sake of clarity I shall deal with them separately as I did for the Viking period. With the Viking swords, and to a lesser degree with those of the Migration period, it was possible to say that such-and-such a type was Danish or Norwegian. This can no longer be done, for after 1100 swords were alike—though in infinite variety—from Finland to Spain and from Britain to the Caucasus. There are, it is true, certain characteristics which allow us to say a sword is of German or Italian style, but no more. This will be seen as we go on.

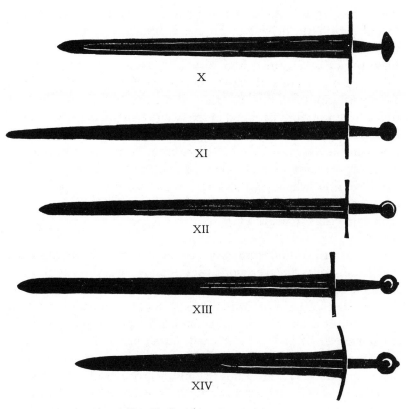

X

XI

XII

XIII

XIV

Fig. 86. Sword types, 1100–1325.

The sword typologies worked out by Behmer and Petersen were based mainly upon styles of hilt, and hilt and scabbard ornamentation, taking little or no account of the shapes of blades, but when we consider the sword types of the later Middle Ages we have to reckon with many differing blade forms which have an all-important bearing on classification: this is further complicated by a great variety of pommels and cross-guards—or lower guards as we have been calling them hitherto. This feature is generally referred to nowadays as "the Quillons", which is a term that came into use only late in the sixteenth century; there is no scrap of evidence for its use during the Middle Ages, when it was always called the Cross, and sometimes, perhaps harking back to earlier usage, the hilt. Between the fourth and the eleventh centuries there was very little variety in the form of this feature, but after the first quarter of the twelfth there are infinite diversities of shape, size, length and weight—diversities which probably were the result of personal fancy, for they cannot be classified into periods or regions. For this reason, the shape of the cross of the mediaeval sword is of little value as a dating criterion: forms which may seem to be exclusive to the later fifteenth century can be found in the twelfth, and shapes which have been considered characteristic of the thirteenth will be found belonging to swords of the late fourteenth. However, allowing for the great variation of detail, they do fall into certain basic types in use during the whole period of 1100–1500. To my abridged sword typology I have added a shortened classification of pommel and cross types (figs. 106 and 113).

In numbering the sword types I shall go straight on from the nine Viking ones, for the sword's development was directly onward from these. Thus the first type for the later Middle Ages will be X. This is a development of Type VIII with slight modifications. It was in use from the late tenth century until perhaps the first quarter of the thirteenth. It had a wide brazil-nut shaped pommel, a rather wide-spreading cross which was nearly always straight (though there are a few curved examples) and a broad blade of the same shape as the Ulfberhts, with a wide and shallow fuller. The earlier ones were inlaid with iron letters, large as in the Ingelrii and Ulfberht blades, but with one very notable difference; on the side opposite to the one which bore the smith's name, instead of the old patterns of lines and diagonal crosses and various patterns appears a new slogan: INNOMINEDOMINI. This is often mis-spelt and garbled, but unmistakeably indicates a date when Christianity had gained the upper hand over the old gods of the north. There is in the Museum of Archaeology at Cambridge a most splendid sword of this type; its maker's name was Constaininus, which is inlaid in the bold straggling letters of the Viking Age, with the religious invocation similarly inlaid on the reverse. There are two reliable fixed points for dating this type, one pictorial and the other archaeological. The picture is from "The Gospels of Otto III", a very fine manuscript made in Reichenau between 983 and 991 (Munich, Staats Bibliothek Cod. Lat. 4453); it shows the sword held by an armour-bearer in a scene of the Emperor enthroned receiving the homage of the four nations (fig. 87). The archaeological point is the sword in Dresden with the name INGELRII on the one side and the phrase HOMO DEI on the other, which gives it a date around 1100. My own sword with the mark of the Caroccium gives a date within the eleventh century, though less reliably.

Type XI, which seems to have been popular between perhaps 1120 and 1200, shows a completely different style of blade, slender and rather elegant, tending to be longer than its predecessors. It always has a rather narrow, well-marked fuller beginning just inside the hilt, on the tang, and running to within an inch or two of the point. Many of these blades have inscriptions inlaid in iron in the small neat letters of the Homo Dei style, but many of them show another new type of inscription, consisting of very neatly drawn letters, inlaid in very fine lines with white or yellow metal—silver, tin and pewter, or copper and brass. (Not, as some have asserted, gold.) These were simple and clear, the finely made letters spaced widely, forming religious invocations, such as BENEDICTUS DEUS MEUS, or SES (Sanctus) PETRNUS, or again IN NOMINE DOMINI. No longer does a smith's name appear; both sides of the blade are devoted to sanctity.

Many swords of Type XI have rounder, more contracted forms of the brazil-nut pommel, but many have disc pommels. There are at least two fixed points for the type: a sword found on the site of a battle fought in 1171 between Henry II and the Earl of Leicester at Fornham in Norfolk (plate 6d) which has a disc pommel and inscriptions reading SES BENEDICTAS and IN NOMINE DOMINI, with a small mark of an extended hand at the point end of each inscription; and a magnificent weapon used until recently as part of the coronation regalia of the Empire. It is known (no one knows why) as the Sword of St. Maurice, and is preserved in a quite remarkably pristine condition

Fig. 87. The Emperor's armour-bearer, from "The Gospels of Otto III", 983–991 (Munich, Staatsbibliothek. Cod.Lat. 4453).

205

in the Imperial Treasury at Vienna (plate 8a). Its value as a dating point lies in the arms engraved upon the thick silver plating of its pommel: on one side the three leopards of England and on the other the arms of the Emperor Otto IV. This gives a date between 1200 and 1214, for Otto had a treaty of alliance with King John against Philippe Auguste of France, ending by the defeat of himself and his allies at Bouvines in 1214.[1]

Type XII, dating between about 1180 and 1320, has a large blade, very similar in shape to the Ulfberht ones but generally with a more acute point, and a well-marked and slightly narrower fuller starting in the tang and running about halfway along the blade; this occasionally is of two or more grooves. The pommel is generally in the form of a thick disc, sometimes with the edges bevelled off, sometimes of the so-called "wheel" form. Its cross is generally straight, circular in section and widening at the ends, but it may be of a square section; or it may be curved or have decorated terminals. Inscriptions on examples of these swords dating after about 1220 are slightly different again; the letters are closer together, often so close that it is nearly impossible to make them out; and instead of the clearly legible religious phrase there is a jumble of repetitive letters which seems meaningless.

Fixed dates for this type are given by a sword found in a brook where a battle was fought in 1234, at Altenesch near Oldenburg, and an extremely interesting sword preserved with its leather scabbard and belt-fittings, and all the cord bindings of its grip. This was found upon the body of one of the sons of King Alphonso the Wise of Spain, Fernando de la Cerda (ob. 1270), when his tomb was opened in 1943 (plate 9c). There are innumerable sculptured figures and manuscript paintings showing swords of this type, but one of each must answer here. Fig. 88 is the sword held by a magnificent figure, made in about 1265, of Count Dietrich von Brehna, one of the benefactors of Naumburg Cathedral. Its pommel is one of the rarer styles. A sword with an identical hilt was found in Hungary, and there is another very similar in the Museum of Archaeology at Cambridge.

[1] Engraved upon the silver plating of this sword's cross are the words CRISTUS VINCIT . CRISTUS REINAT . CRISTUS INPERAT, the war-cry of the Christian hosts under Philippe I during the Third Crusade.

Plenty of excellent pictures of these Type XII swords come from the Maciejowski Bible, one of the very best sources of information about thirteenth-century military gear from Mangonels to tent-pegs. It is a magnificently illustrated book of Old Testament stories made in about 1250; more than one artist illustrated it; all are good, but one is superlative, and at some time he must have been a soldier, for no one without practical experience could have depicted military gear, manners and actions so faithfully and vividly. Most of his swords are of Type XII, and they show practically all of the different styles of pommel and cross prevalent in the thirteenth century (plate 11a). This book is generally known as the Maciejowski Bible because it was once in the possession of a certain Polish Cardinal, Bernard Maciejowski, during the seventeenth century. He made a present of it to Shah Abbas of Persia, and it eventually found its way into the Pierpont Morgan Library in New York.

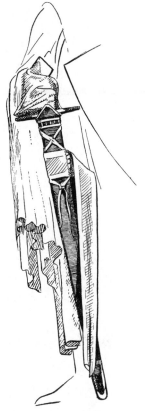

Fig. 88. The sword of Dietrich von Brehna, Naumburg Cathedral.

Swords of Type XIII are of a very striking and individual shape; some of them are very large—"swords of war" they were called in the time of their popularity between about 1280 and 1340. These *Epées de Guerre* are massive weapons, but are not to be confused with two-handed swords. There were a few such as early as 1350, but they were considerably bigger and were always referred to as *Epées a deux Mains* or even "Twahandswerds". The War Sword had a blade some 36 in. to 40 in. long with a very long hilt, from 6 in. to 8 in. between cross and pommel, but it can be wielded in one hand, though provision is made for using it with both. Most Type XIII swords are large like this, but there are several of more ordinary dimensions, though they have hilts

207

long in proportion to their blades. These are broad and flat, with edges running nearly parallel to a spatulate point; they might seem to be very ugly and clumsy, but their ugliness is redeemed to some extent by a slight but very distinct widening below the hilt, while their clumsiness is perfectly suited to the work they had to do—to deal enormous, slow, sweeping, slashing blows from the back of a horse. It is a type which seems to have been characteristically German, though many are to be seen in English manuscript paintings of the late thirteenth and early fourteenth centuries. A very fine specimen was found in England, in the River Thames

Fig. 89. Figure from an Apocalypse of St. John, English, c. 1300.

opposite the Temple,[1] but unfortunately it cannot be used as a fixed dating point (plate 7c). There is, however, a nearly identical sword in the National Museum of Denmark in Copenhagen which was found on the site of a battle fought in 1340 at Nonnebjerg, which gives a date anterior to 1340. These two swords are very big; the London one has a blade $39\frac{3}{4}$ in. long and with a grip of $7\frac{3}{4}$ in. The Danish one is within an inch or so the same size; both have very heavy and deep "wheel" pommels. In the centre of the London sword's

Fig. 90. "Sword of War" from an Apocalypse of St. John, English, c. 1300.

[1] Now in the Guildhall Museum in London. Fully described in the *Journal of the Arms and Armour Society*, Vol. 1, No. 8, December 1954. R. E. Oakeshott: "A War Sword of the XIV Century in the Guildhall Museum."

pommel is a small cross inlaid in copper. It is widely held among Continental students that such a cross in a sword-pommel indicates that its owner was a member of one of the military orders. There is some reason to believe that the weapon from the Thames may indeed have belonged to a Templar.

There are some excellent pictures of these swords in an English manuscript of the early years of the fourteenth century (B.M. MS. Roy. 19.B.XV, an Apocalypse of St. John) two of which I have reproduced in figs. 89 and 90. Another of an earlier date is to be found in an admirable little drawing of a knight fighting a giant upon a page of a small psalter made for the eldest son of Edward I of England, Alphonso, who died in 1284. The sword is so accurately depicted (fig. 91), that it is safe to take it as a dating point, for the manuscript is known to have been completed before the prince's death. This most attractive little figure may be seen in the British Museum, for the manuscript is one of the few displayed and is usually open at that particular page.

Nearly every German military tomb effigy of the period between about 1280 and 1350 has one of these big swords and several are shown on English effigies, as for instance at Astbury in Cheshire. One very good example on an English tomb is difficult to see—a little mounted figure high up on the canopy of Edmund Crouchback's tomb in Westminster Abbey. (He was the Earl of Lancaster, second son of Henry III, and died in 1296.) You can just see it if you climb up into the Islip Chapel in the North Choir aisle, for this is raised about 30 ft. above the level of the floor; look across the aisle over the parapet of the chapel which spans the arch containing it and there is this small knight with a great war sword girt to his waist (fig. 92).

Fig. 91. Figure from the "Alphonso Psalter", before 1284 (British Museum).

Fig. 92. Figure in the canopy of the tomb of Edmund Crouchback, Earl of Lancaster (1296), in Westminster Abbey.

Type XIV is very different, tending to be quite short, with a broad, flat tapering blade fullered in its upper half (plate 16a). Its cross is generally long, slender and curved, its pommel of "wheel" form but very flat and wide. There are not very many remaining specimens, but in its period—from about 1280–1320—there are perhaps more sculptured and pictorial examples than of any other type. I know of no actual sword which can give a dating point by the circumstances of its finding or by arms or associations, so it can only be dated by representations of it. To begin with, perhaps eight out of ten English military effigies of *c.* 1290–1330 have swords of this type (though it is very difficult to be certain in some cases, as the hilts are often missing; however, the short tapering blades are clear enough). Then again, nearly all the effigies of Alsace and Lorraine and the Rhineland dating between 1300 and 1330 have this kind of sword. A particularly good example is the effigy of Robert d'Artois (ob. 1319) at St. Denis (fig. 93). There is a figure in relief which used to be on the former Kaufhaus at Mainz, made in the early fourteenth century, with one of them, and it is interesting to note that a second figure from the same frieze wears a big sword of Type XIII. On the tomb of Edmund of Lancaster in Westminster Abbey, at its base, is a sort of frieze of painted knights, all of whom have Type XIV swords, and one of the best known brasses in this country, that of Sir Robert de Bures, from Acton in Suffolk (he died in 1302), has one (fig. 94).

Though one or two of these swords have been found in Germany (both in the ground and in sculptured figures) it is a style more generally Italian, and judging by the

Fig. 93. The sword-hilt from the effigy of Robert d'Artois (1319) in the Abbey of St. Denis.

210

numerous representations of it in sculpture and manuscript pictures
it was popular in France and England. A well-known Italian example is in the hand of one of the figures in the cloister of the
Annunziata Convent in Florence; a small mounted knight, one
Gulielmus Balnis. This figure has acquired a good deal of fame
since it is an early representation—it was made in about 1320—of
plate armour worn upon the legs. This aspect of it will be dealt
with later. It is worth noting that from the earliest times southern
Europeans and particularly Italians have preferred a thrusting kind
of swordplay, while northerners and Teutons preferred to slash;
the swords of both races always reflected this. Very few of the
Hallstatt swords, for instance, have been found in Italy, while the
short Italian bronze thrusting sword tended to supersede the Hallstatt
long sword during the last phase of
that period. In the same way the
Italians were the originators, in the
middle years of the sixteenth century,
of the use of the long, slender rapier.
During the fourteenth and fifteenth
centuries we find that Italian swords
were nearly always as suitable for
thrusting as for
cutting. In spite
of the Teutonic
penchant for
slashing blows,
the thrust was
certainly used in
sword fights.
Fig. 95, "The
Victory of Humility over Pride",
from a manuscript in Trier, called
"The Young Ladies' Mirror,"[1] of
about 1200, gives a very spirited
rendering of a useful gambit in
swordplay, and there are very many
equally convincing examples of

1 "Jungfrauenspiegel."

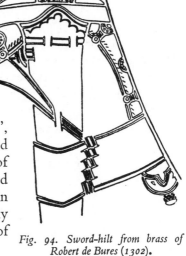

Fig. 94. Sword-hilt from brass of
Robert de Bures (1302).

Fig. 95. "The Victory of Humility over Pride", from the "Jungfrauenspiegel", c. 1200.

similar effective thrusts. Sometimes we see (and read of) the sword tucked up under the right armpit and used like a lance.

Before dealing with the various kinds of pommels and crosses, one thing about these sword-blades needs to be said: the variations in their form for the most part are very subtle, especially between Types XII and XIV; many surviving swords cannot be pigeon-holed into a type at all, because the shape of their blade's outline has been changed either by corrosion or by grinding. Where such blades bear smiths' marks or inscriptions it is possible sometimes to classify them, but there are not many which are furnished with these aids to analysis. Another thing to remember is that certain types—particularly XIII and XIV—lasted for a very long time. In the last two decades of the fifteenth century, for instance, Type XIII became very popular again, so much so that many old blades of the early fourteenth century were re-mounted in fashionable hilts; and Type XIV is found in the mid-fifteenth century. Generally there are clear enough differences in these later swords to distinguish them from their predecessors of the same type, but it all adds to the confusion.

Inscriptions on hilt or blade are the best guide to period, for the styles both of the content of the inscription and the form of the letters composing it changed with the years. The styles of these inscriptions are as many and as varied as the styles of pommel and cross, but there were certain basic trends in fashion by which they can be classified. The first style to come into use after the old Viking iron inlays was the insetting of small iron letters in the manner of the "Homo Dei" inscription in the Dresden sword. There is a small group of swords with inlays of this kind on each side, the last blades to be marked with a smith's name until the sixteenth century. On one side of each blade is the phrase +INNOMINEDOMINI+ and on the other the name + GICELINMEFECIT +. "Gicelin" is perhaps a variant spelling of the name Jocelin, which in the Middle Ages had many spellings, such as Gozelin or Gizelin. Nothing is known of him, of course; he stands in the same shadow as Ulfberht and Ingelrii; his only memorial this group of blades, so far only five in number.[1] Unlike the products of the other two workshops, all had the same inscriptions, the name on one side and the invocation on the other, and all are of Type XI. A hitherto unknown specimen (and the finest of them all) is beside me as I write. It was acquired (not alas by me) in circumstances of extreme good fortune, a collector's dream all too seldom realized.

A friend of mine bought some books in Shaftesbury during the spring of 1958. While he was waiting for them to be wrapped up he noticed a bundle of nineteenth-century swords sticking out of an umbrella stand in a gloomy corner. Being interested in swords of all periods, he had a closer look—and saw in the middle the black nut-shaped pommel and straight cross of what was apparently a mediaeval sword. He asked the price of the bundle and was given a figure not unreasonable for fourteen nineteenth-century swords—it worked out at about 7s. 6d. each. After an appropriate and well-acted pause for thought, the cash changed hands and the bundle went into his car, whereupon he drove out into the country a little way, then stopped and disentangled the black sword from its unworthy neighbours. Little imagination is needed to appreciate his unholy joy when he gazed upon what he had got. Even then he did not realize he had quite such a rare and beautiful weapon (plates 6c, 8b and figs. 96 and 98).

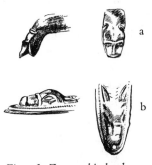

Fig. 96. Zoomorphic heads: a. from the cross of the twelfth-century "Shaftesbury" sword, b. from a pommel of the sixth century found in a grave at Finnestorp in Sweden.

Some weeks later he brought it to me for a thorough examination. At that time the inscription was illegible, though

[1] Three from Germany, one from Finland and recently one from England. The Finnish example was found in a late Viking grave of c. 1100, a fact which was imparted to me in the course of a private correspondence by the finder, Dr. Jorma Leppaho of Helsinki.

Fig. 97. Ornamental head from the Cross of Cong, made for Toirdelbach Ua Conchubhair, king of Connacht, in 1123 (Nat. Museum of Ireland). Note the similarity to Fig. 96a.

it was obvious that there were letters inlaid in the blade. The cross, with its sharply down-turned ends, was of a form rarely found in twelfth-century swords (except in manuscript paintings) though common enough in the fourteenth and fifteenth centuries. Even more rare were the terminals, each simply, but with absolute artistry, carved in the form of a beast's head (fig. 96 and plate 8b). These heads, and the style of their chiselling, stem directly from the old Norse zoomorphic pommelends of the fifth-century Type 3 swords—there are several of these practically identical, made in the same manner with similarly placed chisel cuts. Similar too, though a little more elaborate, are the ends of the cross on the Sword of Charlemagne in the Louvre. As if this was not enough, there still remains quite a lot of gold plating on the pommel.[1] The exact find-place is unknown, but it seems certain that it was found locally. I cleaned the sword—not that it needed much; it has a splendid blue-black patina, but a certain amount of rust had accumulated on top of it. Otherwise the blade is like new; on the edges are a few nicks, got in use, and the unevenness of sharpening, but the surface is quite unpitted and unspoilt. The inscriptions on each side were carefully cleaned until the original surface of the steel was free of the black deposit. At that stage it was possible to see only that the inlays were of small letters, in iron. The letters IN . . E were visible on one side, and an O, but no more. However, after leaving it for two months or so, the slight natural etching of the surface brought both inscriptions clearly to light (fig. 98).

There are three more swords in England, all of Type XI, with these small iron inlays, and a few on the Continent. Two are in Lincoln. The first is the earliest in date of the group, found in 1788 in the Witham. In shape it is similar to the Fornham sword, though

[1] The owner very properly refused to believe that this was original plating until it was analyzed in the laboratories of the Ancient Monuments department of the Ministry of Works.

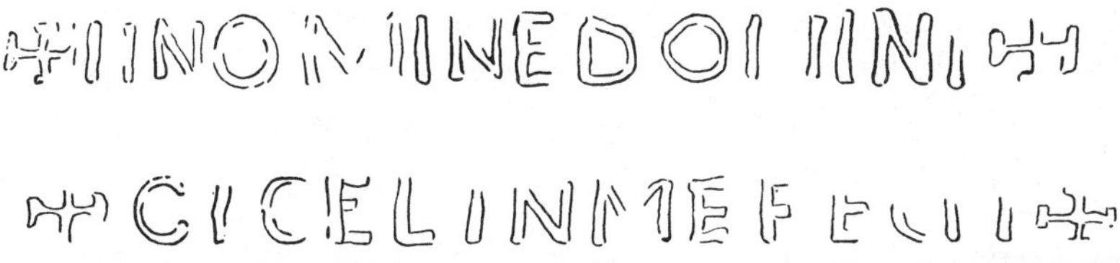

Fig. 98. Inscriptions inlaid in iron on the blade of the "Shaftesbury" sword.

a rather lighter weapon; dating from about the middle of the twelfth century, it could be a relic of Stephen's battle at Lincoln in 1141. The surface of the blade is so corroded that only a few upright strokes of the letters are visible on one side, and the blade has been broken in the middle of the inscription. It was mended in antiquity by having another two-thirds of a blade (of poorer quality) welded on to the stump in the same manner as the patch was put into the blade in my collection. The other is also in the Museum at Lincoln, but it was bought in London and has no known provenance. It is in good condition, but the inscription is hard to make out. I have tried, unsuccessfully so far, but I believe that with care and in time it will be elucidated. A third is a magnificent sword which has been in English private collections for the past sixty years or more. It has been published more than once (in fact in nearly every work, long or short, on the subject of arms written in the English language during the past half-century), but never has the inscription been given. Photographs show clearly enough that there is one— INNOMINEDOMINI—but not once has any writer (and the most eminent have featured it) mentioned this or what is on the other side. Something must be visible, for the sword seems to be in near-perfect condition. This is another example of the indifference English scholars have shown towards mediaeval swords. Unfortunately I have never been able to see the sword, so I can do no better for it.

Some of the Type XI swords have religious invocations inlaid in white or yellow metal, the best known of these being the Fornham sword (before 1171, q.v.), but there is one in the National Museum at Copenhagen with a similar inscription and a hilt like that of the so-called St. Maurice sword in Vienna. This inscription is executed in the same style as the Fornham one, and the invocations are very

215

similar: SANCTUS PETRNUS and BENEDICATNTIUS ET MAT (fig. 99),
though the spelling of the second inscription is vague and seems to
be a movement towards the very greatly abbreviated inscriptions of
the thirteenth century.

SƲSPETRNꞀƧ

BENƐDIGATNTIVꞄET·MA·T ꝃ

Fig. 99.

The first group of these abbreviated invocative inscriptions is
based upon the letters o and s. Most of these are very small, simply
consisting of the letters OSO or SOS, or sometimes a larger o with a
tiny s within it. Some are so small that they get overlooked, the
letters being sometimes only about $\frac{1}{8}$ in. in height, inlaid in extremely
thin wires of brass or silver so that in a corroded or heavily patinated
blade they tend to vanish. There are a few larger and more elaborate
inscriptions of this kind, however, which give a clue to their
meaning. A sword found in the River Peene in Pomerania (it dates
from the first half of the thirteenth century, a very late example of
Type X) has a most beautiful inlay on each side of the blade. On one
side is a running design of foliated scrolls (fig. 100) in the manner

Fig. 100.

of manuscript decoration and almost exactly the same as the patterns
upon the lower guards of some of the Frankish Type V swords. On
the other are the letters SOSMENCRSOS. The N, C and R are run together, the second upright of the N forming the upright of the R, and
the C forming the little loop at its top; round the uprights of the M
and N are twined little s's, with others within the o's. This inscription
is a small work of art, for the letters are beautifully formed, and
stand out most valiantly against the smooth black patina of the

blade's surface. The o and s could be interpreted as standing for O Sancta; it would be not too wild a guess to suggest that the m is the initial letter of the name Maria and the cr as Cristus. The en might be *Eripe Nos*; as the Psalmist says (Psalm 30: 16), *Eripe me de manu inimicorum meorum*. Thus the whole invocation could embody a cry to Christ and His Mother for help in battle.

Another inscription in this group, of even better quality, is in a blade traditionally held to be the "Lobera " sword of St. Ferdinand.[1] Here are four i's separated by foliated scrolls (fig. 101), and NONON

Fig. 101.

with an s across the diagonal of the middle n. This is generally interpreted as being a sort of jingle, a motto reading, "Si Si, No Non" meaning "Let your yea be yea, and your no, no", but this seems to be out of character with the spirit of the period. Besides, the first inscription consists of only four i's; the designs separating them are not s's, and there *is* an s in the NONON part. No, I believe the i's stand for Iesus, and the other letters for O Nomine Sancti: O Nomine Sancti Iesu; which makes sense and is in keeping with thirteenth-century feeling.

Fig. 102.

Later in this century the sword inscriptions developed into long and apparently meaningless strings of letters, yet they too must have concealed invocations, religious or maybe cabalistic. The sword from the Altenesch battlefield has a very well preserved (and well executed) inscription which has had a meaning ascribed to it (fig. 102). It has been interpreted as being the initial letters of the phrases

[1] In the Royal Armoury at Madrid.

Nomine Eterni Dei Regis Caeli: Nomine Eterni Dei Regis Universi: Sancti Dei Regis Caeli: Nomine Eterni Dei Regis Universi Initiatus. A great number of swords (mostly of Types XII and XIII) have been found bearing inscriptions of this kind, many of them incorporating the letters NED or DIC several times repeated; most defy elucidation because apart from the recurrent NED and DIC all are different and cannot be classified or made to fit any recognizable phrases.

Towards the end of the thirteenth century and during the earlier part of the fourteenth these long inscriptions gave way to shorter ones consisting mostly of three or four letters, generally widely spaced so that they fill the entire length of the fuller.

In the Kunstgewerbermuseum at Dusseldorf is a late thirteenth-century sword with a totally different kind of inscription, inlaid in tiny silver letters (less than ¼ in. high), which forms the correctly spelt words of four moralizing mottoes or proverbs in Latin: *Qui falsitate vivit animam occidit. Falsus in ore, caret honore.* (Who lives in falsehood slays his soul, whose speech is false, his honour.) And on the other side: *Qui est hilaris dator, hunc amat Salvator. Omnis avarus, nulli est carus.* (The Saviour loves a cheerful giver, a miser's dear to no one.) The style of the lettering of the inscription is akin to that to be seen on a sword in the British Museum, which was found on Canwick Common in Norfolk; here the inscription is just a repetitive series of letters: ANTANANTANANTAN. . . . Both inscriptions are curious because they read from the point of the sword towards the hilt, instead of the other way about as in almost every other mediaeval inscription. The tiny silver letters of each are exactly alike, so much so that one is tempted to think that both swords must have come from the same smithy.

This weapon is altogether something of an oddity, for it has always been classed as a Viking sword. It is indeed very like one, having a five-lobed pommel and a short, thick cross. The pommel is similar to a Viking style, a mixture of Types IV and VI, but has definite differences which would make it very hard to place within the Viking grouping. The cross, on the other hand, is identical with one, for instance, on a fine tenth-century sword of Type VII found in Poland. But the blade with its narrow fuller and its inscription is most definitely not Viking; the sword is one of the very rare examples of the late survival of Viking hilt styles, which lasted in popularity in the British Isles (as well as in Scandinavia) until the beginning of the fourteenth century. Another particularly good example of this survival is a sword which was found about a century ago in the River Trent near Cawood Castle. For several years it was on loan to the armouries of the Tower of London, but unfortunately it left there during 1956 and was sold in London (incidentally making saleroom history in achieving the highest price to be paid for a mediaeval sword for a generation) and is now in private hands (plate 18c). Its very fine well-preserved blade has an inscription (in the NED group) exactly paralleled by a more conventionally-hilted late thirteenth-century sword found in the old town moat of Perleberg in Germany. There are several effigies in Britain showing these lobated hilts, all dating between about 1250 and 1320; most of these are in the north and east, where Danish influence was strong.

This has brought us a long way from the rhyming doggerel of the Dusseldorf inscription. This is a sort of thing one would expect to find upon the blade of an Elizabethan sword rather than one of Edward I's time, yet though it so far seems to be unique in its form and its lettering, there is another example somewhat similar. This is a sword of enormous dimensions (the blade is over four feet long) which was dug up late in the sixteenth century in the "Welfsholze" near Mansfeld in Germany. It is a "bearing sword", that is a weapon similar in size and application to the swords so prominent among the civic regalia of many cities; during the Middle Ages private individuals, particularly great nobles, often had special out-size swords carried in front of them wherever they went. Froissart tells of an Esquire who was severely taken down by the Count of Flanders for having a sword carried before him.

Upon the blade of this great weapon is a four-part inscription in German:

+ CHUNRAT.VIL.VERDE.SHENKE   + VOR. VINTERSTETER.HOHGEMUT
+ HIE.BI.OV.NIR.GEDENKE   + LA.GARZ.DEHAINE.IISENHUT

Its meaning is obscure, but its doggerel style equates it to some extent with the Dusseldorf example, and the name Konrad von Winterstetten is clear enough. This was an historical personage, a great baron who stood high in the favour of the Emperor Frederic II, "Stupor Mundi". It is perhaps not surprising that a sword which

was made to serve a ceremonial function for a great baron should bear upon it his name embodied in a complimentary verse. More unusual, because it is upon a sword which, despite a decorated and inscribed pommel and cross, seems to be an ordinary fighting weapon, is the inscription "Gladius Rotgieri" in the blade of a fine sword of Type XII, dating from about 1300. It is possible that very occasionally the owner of a sword had his own name upon it; there are one or two shown in manuscript pictures so inscribed. In the Eneide of Heinrich von Veldecke for instance, the sword with which poor Dido is transfixed has "Dido" written on its blade; and on a sandstone bas-relief of the late eleventh century from the Groszmunster at Zurich there is depicted a battle scene, whereon a warrior is being run through with a sword on which the name GUIDO can be read plainly.

There are a few other

Fig. 103.

notable examples where pictures of swords show inscriptions similar to the real ones found upon existing blades. A very finely executed "Tragaltar" (a sort of small portable altar) of copper gilt, made in 1118 by one Rodkerus of Helmeshausen, and now in the Franciscan church at Paderborn, has engraved on it a spirited series of scenes showing the martyrdom of SS. Felix and Blasius. They were done to death with swords, and Rodkerus has armed his killers with weapons having brazil-nut-shaped pommels and inscriptions or marks such as we find on the reverse sides of ULFBERHT blades—a plaited-band ornament, a St. Andrew's cross between two sets of vertical strokes, the marks o + o, and so on. Another rather similar example, though much later, is the sword in the hand of a knightly figure of the early fourteenth century—the brass of Guillaume Wenemaer (+ 1325) in Ghent. He carries his sword naked (fig. 103) and on its blade are the words, in a style exactly similar to the Dusseldorf inscription: HORREBANT DUDUM REPROBI ME CERNERE NUDUM, which could be freely translated as "Time was the wicked quaked to see me naked".

Most of these lettered inscriptions had marks of one sort or another at each end; the earliest a simple cross, as in the ULFBERHT blades; later (in the CICELIN ones for instance) this developed into a cross potent; the earlier silver or latten inlays had crosses and sometimes an additional mark—like the little hand at the end of the inscription on the Fornham sword—was put in. By the turn of the twelfth–thirteenth century, these terminal marks began to become elaborated. There is a sword of *c.* 1200 (of Type XII) which has an inscription in the same group as the Fornham sword (fig. 104). Here

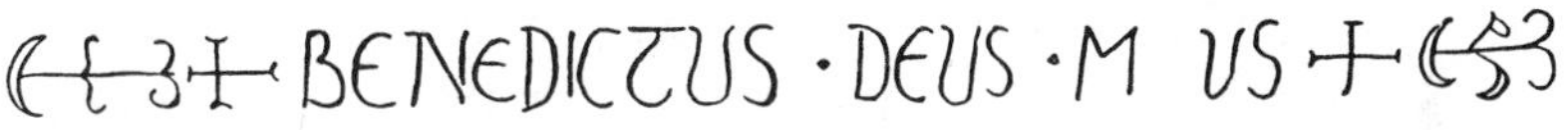

Fig. 104.

the terminal crosses have turned into decorative motifs; the sword from the Altenesch battlefield (see fig. 102) has almost identical terminal decorations, but the style of its inscription belongs to the next "period". The later inscriptions of this NED group, as well as those with the repetitive DIC, have decorations which appear to be obvious elaborations of the simpler ones which preceded them.

Some of these marks had a different origin; once or twice we come upon heraldic inlays—a lion Passant and an eagle Displayed, for example, upon a particularly fine sword of the DIC group in the Pomeranian Museum of Archaeology at Stettin (Type XII, *c.* 1270). A few blades of the late twelfth–early thirteenth century have flying birds inlaid in them; the souls of the faithful were often thought of as birds, flying into the Church's bosom for protection against the instruments of the devil. A sword-blade was no doubt considered an appropriate place to put a flying bird, being such an effective liberator of souls. Such birds are to be regarded in that light, I believe, not as heraldic beasts. Where heraldry was intended, correct heraldic forms were used.

During the thirteenth century bladesmiths began again to inlay in their products marks of a personal kind. It is generally possible to distinguish "trade-marks" from religious symbols; the s within a circle, for instance, belongs to the "O Sancta" group of invocative inscriptions; a cross within a circle is similarly religious in intent—incidentally it is precisely the same mark as the old Bronze Age symbol, which was used all through the Iron Age up to the fifth or sixth century. After going out of use for 800 years, it suddenly became popular and was inlaid upon countless sword-blades after perhaps about 1250. It is difficult to draw a line between religious and trade marks: hearts, for instance, whether on their own or within a circle might be either; but where we find a helm, or a shield, or a sword (there is a sword inlaid in the blade of the Type XIII war-sword in the Guildhall Museum, q.v. plate 7c), or a bull's head (on a sword *c.* 1300 in Copenhagen), or of course the famous "Wolf" which is first found on thirteenth-century blades.[1] A mark which can easily be mistaken for the "Wolf" of Passau is a unicorn; since both wolf and unicorn are only very summarily sketched with a few inlaid strokes, it needs the eye of faith to distinguish an animal at all; the examples of the unicorn which I have met with look exactly the same as the wolves except that they have a long straight stroke sticking out in front (fig. 105b). A rarer mark in the same

---

[1] An excellent example dating from *c.* 1300 is on the blade of a Type XIII sword in the Armouries of the Tower of London, on loan from the collection of Sir James Mann. Another, of slightly later date, was found in the Thames in London in February 1959 and is in the Guildhall Museum.

category is a pelican. These early makers' marks were inlaid in slender lines of white or yellow alloys in the same manner as the inscriptions, not stamped into the blades with punches in the old style of the Roman Iron Age, which came back into use again late in the thirteenth century.

a   b

Fig. 105. The "Running Wolf" and "Uni-corn" marks of Passau swordsmiths.

Chapter Thirteen

SWORD HILTS AND FITTINGS

I HAVE TREATED THE very complicated subject of these inscriptions in a most summary fashion, omitting much and dealing arbitrarily with many things, but lack of space precludes a deeper study of it here. Maybe I have done enough to show how valuable such inscriptions can be in dating otherwise undateable material, and how greatly they add to the human interest of the sword. I shall deal even more shortly with the matter of pommels. I have roughly divided the styles in use between 1100 and 1325 into three groups: A–F developments of the late Viking styles of Types VIII and IX: G–K the disc-form and its variants: and L–S sundry odd styles which belong to neither of the main groups. There is no

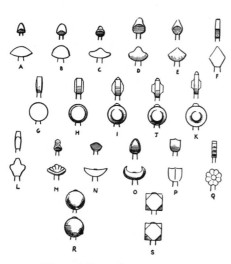

Fig. 106. Pommel types, 1100–1325.

need to make more than brief comment on each style. Fig. 106 first, then, shows the six styles springing from the late Viking pommels:

Type A. In use frequently between c. 980 and 1120. More rarely up to c. 1200 on Type X swords.

Type B. Development of A. Popular between c. 1150–1250 on swords of Types XI and XII.

Type C. Development of

Viking Type IX pommel. Popular *c.* 980–1100 on Type X swords.

Type D. Development of *C* and used between *c.* 1230–1280, generally on Type XII swords, but occasionally on Type XIII.

Type E. Same as *D*, another variety. Excellent example in hand of one of the Benefactors of Naumburg Cathedral (Conrad).

Type F. A style unknown in Viking times. Popular *c.* 1120–1350; though rare. Examples in hand of figure of Dietrich von Brehna at Naumburg, in the Siebenburg Museum in Hungary and Archaeological Museum of Cambridge.

Then the five variants of the disc-form:

Type G. First used in Viking period. Popular *c.* 1100–1200; still used until *c.* 1380 particularly in Italy and Spain. Returns to favour between *c.* 1450–1550.

Type H. Development of *G*. Found in Viking graves in Finland. Popular *c.* 1180–1350 and 1420–1500.

Type I. Development of *H*. Also found in Viking graves in Finland. Popular *c.* 1180–1500. This and the preceding type were perhaps the most-used pommels of the later Middle Ages.

Type J. Development of *I*, with the bevelled faces strongly hollowed out. Popular between *c.* 1250–1400. Occasionally used up to 1450 or 1460.

Type K. Combination of *G* and *J*. Possibly originating in Italy. Found mostly on Type XIV swords, though sometimes on XIIIs and XIIs. Popular *c.* 1270–1350, and again in south Europe, *c.* 1450–1550.

Then the last eight types which are oddities, only a few examples of each being known so far, either in pictorial form or more solid reality:

Type L. The most notable example of this is upon the so-called "Sword of St. Ferdinand" in the Armeria Real in Madrid. There are several representations of similar maple-leaf shaped pommels in Spanish manuscripts dating between *c.* 1150–1250.

Type M. Last survival of Viking principle of lobed-pommel set above an upper guard. There are examples from Norway, Denmark and Germany as well as from England, but they are rare and mostly date before 1300. There are pictures of them in Scandinavian manuscripts up to the late fourteenth century, though.

Type N. A rare type, obviously a bye-form of *A*, characterized by extreme breadth. The only two actual examples are a large war-sword (Type XIII) in Zurich and another, even larger, in Bucharest, found in Rumania. One of the Naumburg benefactors (Wilhelm von Camburg, fig. 107) has one on a short sword of Type XIV.

Type O. Curiously enough, nearly every sword (and there are many) carried by carved warrior-figures in the Cathedral of Freiburg has a pommel of this unusual form—St. Peter in the Garden of Gethsemane (fig. 108), SS. George and Sebastian (these two have long-gripped war swords), on the West Front and one of the sleeping guards of the Holy Sepulchre. All these figures were made about 1300. There is one pommel of this sort in the Maciejowski Bible. The only actual example I know of is on a sword which was in the Gimbel collection earlier in this century,

Fig. 108. St. Peter in the Garden of Gethsemane, from the tympanum of the main door of Freiburg Cathedral.

226

but I have no knowledge of its present whereabouts: it was found in Germany.

Type P. I know of only one isolated example of this pommel—carried by yet another of the Naumburg benefactors, Dietmar von Kisteritz (*c.* 1270, fig. 109).

Type Q. Appears in many manuscript pictures of about 1280–1320, but I know of no actual examples. In the manuscripts they are generally fitted to swords of Type XIV (fig. 110).

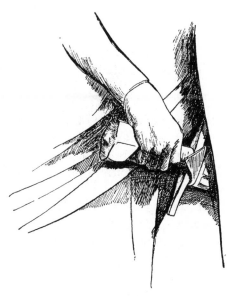

Fig. 109. The sword-hilt of Dietmar von Kisteritz, Naumburg Cathedral.

Type R. There are several examples of globular pommels, the best known being a sword of Type XII found in Cannon Street, London, now in the London Museum. The sword of Goliath in the Maciejowski Bible (see fig. 129) has a pommel almost exactly like it, with two incised lines running parallel round its circumference (like an equator) and a series of lines above it like parallels of longitude.

Type S. This particular form, a cube with each corner bevelled off, has few examples, all dating around the year 1300. There are three Type XIII swords in Stockholm (all found in Sweden) which have them, and a similar but far finer one which was

Fig. 110. Sword of Type XIV from an East Anglian MS., c. 1310 ("GREGORA MORALIA SUPER JOB", Emmanuel College, Cambridge).

227

found in Switzerland was in the Boissonas collection in Geneva. There is an exactly similar one, on a well-preserved Type XIII sword, on an English effigy of about 1310–1320 at Halton Holgate in Lincolnshire (fig. 111). These seem to be the only examples so far found.

Each or any example of these basic pommel styles may have been varied or modified in the matter of decoration by its maker's customer, though here again some generalization is possible. The Nut- and Hat-shaped pommels, judging by those which have survived and those which are adequately shown in sculpture and manuscript painting, tended mostly to be quite plain. The long brazil-nut pommels of Type A never seem to have any trace of gilding or silvering or embellishment with arms—the latter probably because they had rather gone out of fashion before heraldry came in— though there is an isolated example in a sword of Type X found at Zalecino in Poland with a large Maltese Cross in its pommel. The pommel of my INGELRIUS sword gives no reliable indication that these pommels were decorated, for though there were many traces of decoration on its hilt these were only observed on the cross-guard.

Several pommels of Type D, on the other hand, are shown in the Maciejowski Bible with shields of arms on them, and of course there is the pommel of the Vienna St. Maurice sword, silvered, inscribed and bearing arms, and the gold plating on the pommel of the newly-found GICELIN sword described above. Such gilding of the pommel was the most usual form of decoration applied to sword hilts during the twelfth and thirteenth centuries; usually only the pommel was so treated, the cross being left plain. Some pommels of Types H, I and J were made of bronze, and these were nearly always gilded. There are a very few still showing clear traces of gilding, but they are very rare. A few pommels of Types I and J still survive made of

Fig. 111. Sword from an effigy at Halton Holgate, Lincs, c. 1320.

228

hard stone such as jasper and rock crystal, though of the former material only dismounted specimens are known. That swords fitted with such pommels were in ordinary use, not kept for ceremonial purposes, we may infer from an entry in the inventory of the effects of Raoul de Nesle, Constable of France, who fell in the battle of Courtrai in 1302. Several items refer to swords: "Item, a sword and a black sheath with a green belt garnished with silver. Item, another, a pommel of crystal."

Fig. 112. The sword of Joab, from the Velislav Bible, c. 1380, showing the leather "chappe" over the mouth of the scabbard.

In the same inventory are other swords which give an indication of the sort of decoration used; we have "Item, a sword garnished with hide" and "item, another garnished with the arms of Nesle in needlework". That these "garnishings" refer to the sword and not the scabbard is clear from other entries, such as "Item, another sword with a red sheath garnished with silver" and "another with a green silk sheath powdered with escutcheons". Presumably "garnished with hide" means the sword had a hide grip, and the arms of Nesle in needlework might also have been upon the grip, though in both these cases the reference may have been to the "chappe", a sort of flap of leather or fabric placed between the bottom of the grip and the cross, falling over each side of the central portion of this and covering the top of the scabbard, partly, no doubt, as an embellishment and partly to prevent rain from running into it (fig. 112). Surviving examples are rare—indeed I only know of one, a broken sword of c. 1250 in the British Museum whose leather chappe is still in place, though the grip has gone. We shall meet other swords with arms on the grip (only in more durable materials) later. Two other entries are interesting: "Item, to X swords without silver garnish: cs. Item, a sword of Genoa, garnished with silver: xl." It gives some indication of the disparity in value between ordinary plain swords—ten of them at 100 shillings—and a special single one with silver garnishings at ten pounds. An example of such a sword—indeed it could almost be the very one, for it is Italian of about 1300, garnished with silver—is in my possession (what pleasure

229

it gives me to write this), and the circumstances of its appearance are worth recording, for it could possibly lead to the unmasking of other silvered hilts hitherto looking just like blackened iron, as this hilt of mine did when first I had it. The entire hilt (plates 7d and 8c) was covered with a dark blue-black patina. The sword is an excavated one, though unusually complete and very well cleaned and cared-for by a previous (unknown) owner and by its finder. The blade had been freed of its black patination by electrolysis, and as you can see has regained most of its pristine brightness; its edge, too, remains, not so sharp as a razor but far sharper than I can ever edge a carving-knife. The hilt had not been touched, wisely, for it retains its original grip of wood covered with leather, the latter bearing upon it (as you can also see) the marks of the spirally-wound cord or thong which decorated it, impressed into the leather and the wood beneath by the hard grip of its owner's hand. When I examined the surfaces of this hilt it seemed to me that the patination was the wrong colour for plain iron, so I needled a small bit clean, not rubbing or scraping it but poking it with the sharp point of an awl, held at an angle of about 45° to the surface, and pressed hard. This caused small flakes of the patina to fly off, revealing bright white metal below it. When a larger area was cleared, I could see that it was tarnished heavily in places with an almost prussian-blue discoloration such as one gets on silver. So I carried out this flaking process all over one side of the pommel and cross-guard, following it with applications of a silver cleaner—and a fine sword (which incidentally I had been outbid for at a London sale in 1945, and had coveted and watched for ten years) turned out to be a particularly splendid one. The roughness of its surface below the plating, showing clearly in the photograph, is caused by a certain amount of corrosion of the soft iron of the hilt, which is noticeably absent in the flint-hard steel of the pyramidal rivet-block on top of the pommel. An exactly similar condition may be observed in the heavily gilded iron pommel of a lovely little sword found in the River Gué in Normandy.[1] As I have said, it is possible that there may be other swords whose silver-plated hilts are similarly obscured.

I believe that in some cases where sword hilts were not gilded, silvered or tinned they may have been painted; no such paint

[1] Illustrated in Laking, Vol. 1, fig. 169, p. 135.

survives on any actual sword I know of dating from the period we are considering, and nearly every hilt shown in paintings which is not gold is coloured with the same grey tint used for mail and helmets and other items of ironwork; but even so, many paintings (particularly, again, in the Maciejowski Bible) show helmets[1] painted red and blue and green (or all these together) and sword pommels too. Often in these coloured examples the tint only covers part of the pommel, such as the central part of a disc pommel.

Many disc and "wheel" pommels have shields of arms inset in coloured enamels, or engraved upon small plates of silver let into the iron. In the Metropolitan Museum in New York there is a disc pommel of Type G with, on one side, the enamelled arms of the famous Count Peter of Dreux, friend and companion and fellow prisoner-of-war of St. Louis in the disastrous crusade of 1250, and on the other a red cross.[2] This is an isolated pommel, long since broken away from its sword. What a pity this is, for although the pommel of so notable a Baron's sword is well worth having, what a treasure the sword itself would have been! This pommel was bought in Damascus, and acquired by the Metropolitan Museum in 1939. On the effigy of Count Peter in the Abbey of St. Yved at Braine near Soissons he wears a sword with these arms on the pommel.

The many styles of cross-guard in use between 1100 and 1325 are subject to the same infinity of modification as the pommels, but in the same way can be classified into seven basic forms, upon which personal taste has been exercised to vary detail. These, though particularly relevant to the period we are considering, are applicable to the whole of the later Middle Ages. Certain fashionable trends become noticeable after the mid-fourteenth century, and in rare cases we can say that cross-guards of such and such a style or with this or that kind of decoration may be of Danish or Flemish or Italian fashion.

[1] Froissart mentions the use of vermilion-tinted mail worn by the Champion at the Coronation of Henry IV.

[2] Roger de Hoveden, writing under the year 1188, tells us that the leaders against the Saracens "for the purpose of recognizing the various Nations, adopted distinguishing signs for themselves and their people. For the King of France and his people wore red crosses; the King of England and his people, white crosses, while Philip Count of Flanders and his followers wore green crosses."

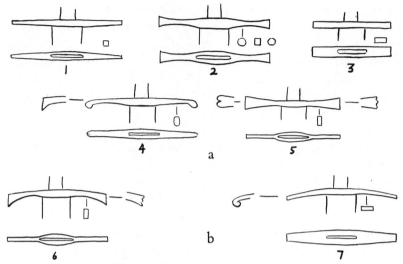

Fig. 113. Cross-guard styles, 1100–1350.

I have divided my seven styles into two groups, those which are straight (1 to 5) and those which are curved (6 and 7), but I would emphasize that whether any particular kind of cross-guard was straight or curved was a matter of taste, not in any way at all of region or period. A straight cross-guard can easily be made to curve, if so desired, and we find that except for two styles all the curved crosses are simply straight ones, bent.

Fig. 113a shows the five straight forms:

1. This is a simple, easily made and obvious style which first appears in tenth-century Viking graves (in straight or curved form) and is still in use in the Renaissance.

2. Is more elaborate and can be said (though with reservations) to have been popular between 1200 and 1350. Its section could be circular, square or octagonal. In general terms one might say that a circular section indicates a date between 1200–1270, a square section one between 1250–1350 and an octagonal section one after 1350.

3. Is generally short and thick, and is not very common, dating up to about 1260.

4. Is a rare style, similar in plan and section to an elongated Viking lower guard, but most examples have decorated ends. The

GICELIN sword from Shaftesbury with its abruptly down-turned beast-headed ends is one example; another, with knobbed or clubbed ends is on a sword in the Maidstone Museum (which was not found in Kent, but in the Gudbransdal in Norway). It is a style rarely found in actual examples but is very often depicted in twelfth- and thirteenth-century manuscript paintings.

5. Looks like a bow-tie. In elevation it is broad with expanded ends, but in section it is flat and ribbon-like. Crosses of this form can be seen on a few swords dating before and about 1200—one of the GICELIN swords in Hamburg has one—but they do not seem to have been common until about 1300. Sometimes they are quite long, in which cases they are slender and light-looking. This, incidentally, is an obvious principle of hilt design: if a long cross-guard was made as thick and heavy in section as a short one, the hilt would be overweighted; the longer a cross is, the more fragile-looking it must be. Here again I believe that the length of a cross was a matter of personal choice.

Fig. 113b shows the only two curved styles which are not simply bent variants of the straight forms.

6. Looks at first like a bent variety of the "bow-tie" style (5) but it is not. Always its upper edge curves in a single regular arc, while its lower edge is like a four-centred arch. It was used from the late twelfth century to the end of the fifteenth, but its greatest popularity seems to have been between about 1280 and 1370. Crosses of this style, and of (5) as well, are often decorated with one or more nicks filed in each end, producing a fish-tail or a foliated effect. Manuscript pictures of the early fourteenth century very often show swords with crosses treated thus (e.g. figs. 85 and 91) and a few are found on effigies, perhaps the best known being the Brass of Humbier Corbeare at Awans, near Liège. In my collection I have a large war-sword of Type XIII with a cross of Style 5 having fish-tail ends (plate 9a); in the Swiss National Museum at Zurich is one of Type XIV with a Style 6 cross decorated with a double nick at each end, and there is in the Cathedral Treasury of Toledo a

233

Fig. 114. Sword of Type X, c. 1150–1200 (Musée de l'Armée, Paris).

superb sword (splendidly decorated and complete with its scabbard and belt, which will be described later) with similar cross-ends (plate 10a and frontispiece).

7. A style which is generally assumed to belong only to the late fifteenth century, but in fact it was used in Viking times. When seen in elevation it appears to be exceedingly thin, but in plan it is broad and flat, always curved, and many have each end curled under in a little roll. Viking examples are found generally on swords on Type V, and are usually quite short. There is a fine sword in the Musée de l'Armée in Paris with a longish cross of this style, with plain ends. It is an example of a Type X sword with a disc pommel; its blade is broad with a very wide and shallow fuller (fig. 114). Viollet-le-Duc illustrates this weapon, dating it about the middle of the twelfth century. Laking illustrates it too, but gives it a rather later date. Judging by the early form of its blade and the extreme similarity of its hilt to many swords in manuscript pictures of the early twelfth century, I am inclined to think that Viollet-le-Duc's date is nearer the mark. Crosses of this style are to be seen in many manuscripts of thirteenth century date, but because all of them are seen in elevation we can only assume that they have the flat ribbon-like section of Style 7 because the arms look so very thin.[1] Fig. 115 shows a particularly good example (note also the long grip and trilobate pommel) from a manuscript of about 1250 in the library of the Duke of Rutland.

Fig. 115. Sword from the Rutland psalter, c. 1250.

There is a possibility, slight enough, that

[1] A case in point may be seen on a Lenten altar-front, made between 1374–8 for the chapel of Charles V of France at Narbonne. Here are two swords with crosses of Style 7 with turned-over ends. (See also Chapter Seventeen.)

certain kinds of decorative treatment may denote regional origin. For instance, there are in England four swords and a monumental brass which have cross-guards of Style 6 with a single small perforated cross in each end. Three of these cross-guards were found in East Anglia, where the

Fig. 116. Falchion, splinted gauntlet and kettle-hat from an Apocalypse of St. John, c. 1300.

brass is also (at Gorleston, Suffolk), while the fourth (a sword in the Wallace Collection at Hertford House) was probably found in France and so may very likely be English. The brass dates from about 1320, while the three swords (two from the River Witham at Lincoln and one—a falchion—from Thorpe near Norwich) all belong to the late thirteenth–early fourteenth century. The cross-guards of these weapons are not just similar, they are identical. Unfortunately one of them is now missing, and only the blade which belonged to it is in the Museum at Lincoln. Drawings of all the Witham finds of 1788 were made, however, in about 1854, and at that time the missing cross was still with its sword so we know what it was like. The weapon in the Wallace Collection is not so clearly related to this group, for it is later by 100 years and is a sword of a totally different type with a long, slender and stiff thrusting blade rather like the Roman swords from Nydam and Vimose. Its cross-guard is of Style 5 and the perforated crosses are a lot smaller. Even so, it does seem rather as if this kind of cross-guard may have been popular in England, and it is an odd coincidence that no less than three real examples and one pictured one should be found within such a small area.

One of these weapons is a falchion. This is a development from the old Norse sax, particularly the long Norwegian sax, which was popular all over Europe during the eleventh and twelfth centuries, as we can see by its frequent appearance in manuscript paintings. During the thirteenth century its form altered considerably: the blade became extremely broad at its "optimal striking point". This is clearly shown in many pictures (fig. 116 for instance), but there are at least two surviving examples as well. One of these was found in 1861 on the site of the Chatelet in Paris, and bears the arms of the Grand Chatelet upon its bronze pommel. The other is a much finer weapon, and is kept in an almost perfect state of preservation in the Library of Durham Cathedral. It has a large blade similar to the one shown in fig. 116, but its end is rounded and lacks the sharp point. This may be due to continual grinding and sharpening having worn it away, but since it is unlikely that it was ever used for fighting (we shall see why) it is more probable that it was made without a point in the first place. Its hilt is made of copper gilt, with considerable traces of the gilding still visible. The pommel is of Type H, the cross-guard of Style 4, or rather a somewhat flattened modification of Style 4 with the extremities of the lower edge abruptly turned down. Both pommel and cross are decorated with moderately well-executed incised patterns of foliage, with a little dragon or wyvern tucked into each end of the cross. The pommel is further enriched with an enamelled shield of arms on either side—on one the three leopards of England, and on the other arms which would be read as: Or, an Eagle displayed Sable—in other words the black eagle of the Empire. It may seem odd to find this on a weapon whose origin is entirely English, but its form suggests a mid-thirteenth century date; the leopards at that time had a close connection with the eagle in the persons of Henry III and his brother Richard Earl of Cornwall, who was also his chief minister and principal supporter (and incidentally supplied the brains and stability of character to the royal cause which the king himself so sadly lacked). Richard of Cornwall was also from 1257 to 1272 King of the Romans, a title second only to the Emperor himself, which carried the right to bear the arms of the Empire.

Why, then, is this sword so definitely English? Even the fact that it has been preserved in one place in England for seven centuries need not necessarily imply that it originated in this country. The real reason why this seems certain is that it is a Tenure Sword; by it the family of Conyers held the manor of Sockburn in County Durham. This manor was first given to the family in the time of Bishop Flambard, the grant subsequently being confirmed by Henry II. The terms of its tenure were that every time a new Bishop Palatine entered his diocese for the first time, the holder of the manor should present himself with the falchion at the bridge over the Tees across which the Bishop was to pass. There he handed the falchion to the bishop, who thereupon handed it back, and so confirmed the family in its tenure until such time as the next bishop should come to Durham, when the whole ceremony was enacted again. The present falchion is certainly not the original one of Henry II's time. We cannot know why a new one, perhaps some time between 1250 and 1270 or thereabouts, should have been made for the Conyers; or more probably, as the arms on the pommel suggest, presented to them by the king or his brother. There are infinite possibilities here for romantic speculation.

There is mention of this ceremony in the records of an Inquisition on the death of a Sir John Conyers in 1396: "Tenuit manerium de Sockburne per servicium demonstrandi episcopo unam fawchon, ita quod postea dom episcopus illud viderit restituit ostentendi, pro omnibus aliis serviciis." The last time the ceremony took place was when the falchion was presented in 1826 to

Fig. 117. The Conyers Falchion (The Library, Durham Cathedral).

Dr. Van Mildert by Sir Edward Blackett, into whose family the manor had passed. Recently the falchion was presented to the Dean and Chapter of the Cathedral Church of Durham, who now preserve it in a glass case in their library (fig. 117).

This, I believe, is the only case where we still have not only the history of a "weapon tenure" but the weapon itself. It is possible that the Chatelet falchion may have had a rather similar application, for otherwise it might seem odd to have found a weapon bearing the arms of the Provostship of Paris on the site of the seat of that juridical function. There are many examples of lands held in this way, for it was quite a common thing in the Middle Ages. There is the immortal story—which, like so many good tales, has to be

Fig. 118. The Thorpe Falchion (Castle Museum, Norwich).

taken with a very large pinch of historical salt—of John de Warenne, Earl of Surrey, and his appearance before the Royal Commissioners during Edward I's examination of "Quo Warranto" when he was regularizing and codifying the tenure of all lands and manors in the realm. The Earl came before the Commissioners, slapped an out-of-date sword on to the table under their noses and said, "My ancestors held my lands by this; and by God so will I!" with which the commissioners had to be content.

The blade of the falchion from Thorpe differs from the Durham and Chatelet ones, for it is very similar to a sabre blade (fig. 118). How this blade form developed is not clear; we rarely see it in manuscript pictures before about 1290, and it seems to have no direct kinship, like the Durham type, with the old Norwegian long sax. It may have developed under an Eastern European influence, for it is very closely akin to the Sword of Charlemagne —the Hungarian one—in Vienna (see fig. 74), a type which had been in use in Eastern Europe since the ninth century. Whatever the origin of its particular form, as a falchion it is still a direct descendant of the sax, the Greek kopis and the ancient Egyptian kopsh, and its form remained in use from the early fourteenth century till the mid-eighteenth, with modifications, while the Durham type is seen no more after about 1300.

Chapter Fourteen

THE SWORD IN WEAR

URING THE TWO centuries between 1100 and 1300 the fittings and belt attachments of swords and their scabbards were in the main very simple and austere, even those of royal personages or great nobles. The magnificent gold and silver, jewelled and nielloed mouth-bands, chapes, belt-loops, studs and buckles of the Migration period had already become simplified in the Viking age, but even the average member of a Viking war-band had a great deal more adornment to his scabbard and sword-hilt than the average mediaeval knight, whose sword and its fittings were generally all of steel and leather. We have to rely largely on the evidence of monuments and pictures for this assumption, but there are enough actual examples of surviving scabbards and sword-belts to prove its accuracy.

We have seen how in these two centuries the form of the sword varied very little; so it was also with scabbards and the methods of attaching them to the person. One of the best documents showing how this was done is the sculptured figure (of about 1265) of Dietrich von Brehna in Naumburg Cathedral (see fig. 88). A broad belt of leather or buckskin—more probably buckskin as this does not shrink or stiffen after getting wet—was fixed round the scabbard about five or six inches below its mouth; this passed round the wearer's body from right to left. A second short, broad flap of leather was fixed immediately below the mouth of the scabbard going in the opposite direction, across the front of the body from left to right. The free end of the belt was divided into two tails while the flap was provided with two slits. When the belt was girt round the hips, the two tails were drawn through the slits in the flap in front and tied in a knot. There are innumerable representations of this simple and effective method of girding on a sword, some of them as early as the tenth century (for we find it in the Gospel of Otto III, 983–991). It should be noted that while the knotted belt was almost universally used in Scandinavia and all the German lands, it never seems to have been popular in England, France or the south of Europe. In these countries an ordinary buckle replaced the slitted flap, and the free end of the belt was carried round to fall on the left side of the sword hilt (see figs. 92 and 94). There were various ways by which the belt was fixed on to the scabbard, but all were modifications of the same principle, which is shown in fig. 119. In English paintings and monuments we always find that instead of the divided ends of the flap or buckle section being brought across the front of the scabbard in a diagonal cross, only the piece running downwards from right to left goes across the front; the other piece presumably going across the back. This is shown very clearly on the brass of Sir Robert de Bures (1302) from Acton, Suffolk (fig. 94). This method of applying belt to scabbard made a secure fastening which held the scabbard at an angle when worn round the hips, and yet if any part of the belt was damaged, as it so well might be, it could very easily be replaced. The purpose of the diagonal straps between the main bands which held the ends of the belt to the scabbard was to prevent these from sliding apart.

About a century ago a sort of leather ball was found in the library of Bamberg Cathedral, yet it was clearly not just a ball, but something rolled up and sewn into one. When it was unravelled, it turned out to be the upper part of a twelfth-century sword scabbard and its belt, which was of the tailed belt and slitted flap variety. In this case the two sections of the belt were fitted close together near the mouth of the scabbard without any of the elaborate lacing and thonging which was usual. A similar belt fitting can be seen on a tenth-century sword in the Gospels of Otto III.

The best known mediaeval sword scabbard belongs to a sword now in the Royal Armoury at Turin, which has for centuries been called "The Sword of St. Maurice" (not to be confused with the sword with the same attribution in Vienna). This is a very fine and perfectly preserved fighting sword of the late twelfth century, of

Type 12 with a brazil-nut pommel of Type A and a cross-guard of Style 6. Its scabbard

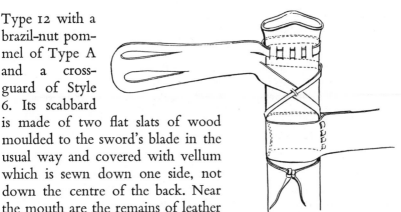

Fig. 119. Diagram of belt-fitting, c. 1220–1320.

is made of two flat slats of wood moulded to the sword's blade in the usual way and covered with vellum which is sewn down one side, not down the centre of the back. Near the mouth are the remains of leather thongs, some of them threaded through slits cut in the vellum covering. This is clearly a remnant of a belt fitting made somewhat on the principle shown in the diagram in fig. 119, but with very definite differences which are difficult to interpret. No good photograph of this scabbard seems ever to have been published, though one or two very indifferent ones of the sword have, but I am fortunate in possessing a scrupulously accurate copy of both sword and scabbard. It once was in the collection of Sir Guy Laking, and before he had it there is reason to believe it was owned by—indeed, made for—the famous architect and antiquarian Viollet-le-Duc. Plate 9b shows a photograph of it. I should have preferred to illustrate the actual sword, but as this is not possible the copy must do; however, its inequalities and blemishes have been copied most faithfully, so it gives a clear idea of the real one.

The next two swords I shall describe are of the greatest archaeological importance. The first is very little known, for it was found in 1943 and was not published until 1946, in Madrid. The second has been published in 1959,[1] and yet is virtually unknown. Both belonged to princes of the House of Castile and Leon.

The first was found upon the body of Fernando de la Cerda (he was the eldest son of Alphonso X of Castile) when his tomb in the Convent of Las Huelgas at Burgos was opened in 1943. The

[1] *Journal of the Arms and Armour Society*, 1959. Claude Blair, "Medieval Swords and Spurs preserved in Toledo Cathedral".

Infante's body lay in its coffin completely clothed in garments appropriate to his rank—cloak, super tunic and tunic of gold tissue woven in all-over design of the quartered arms of Castile and Leon. On his head was a cylindrical cap (of a type often seen on sculptured figures) richly decorated with the same arms. Hose and shoes were on his feet, and his gilded spurs were strapped to his heels. In his hand was his sword, and round his waist was a splendid belt which is not, as has been generally believed, a sword belt—but more of this later.

The sword is of Type 12, in itself a weapon no more remarkable than many another, for it is perfectly plain without adornment of any kind. The pommel (Type H) is of ungilded bronze, and has oxidized to a blue-green colour; the cross (Style 2) is of iron and, since the dead hand of the Infante had rested upon it for nearly seven centuries, is very much corroded. The blade has rusted immovably into the scabbard, but the binding of the grip, being of cord, has perished hardly at all, neither has the scabbard and belt fittings of white buckskin (plate 9c). These are exactly similar to those of the Naumburg figures and to the diagram in fig. 119. The curious thing is that the belt itself has been cut off. It has been thought that the reason for this was the presence of the other belt, magnificently enriched with coats of arms, but as I have said this was not a sword-belt. It is over six feet long and $1\frac{3}{4}$ in. wide and consists of a flexible portion made of embroidered gold galon, finished with silver gilt mounts—a buckle and chape or tongue, a frog or hanger (for a dagger or pouch: it is far too fragile to support the four pounds or more which a scabbarded sword weighs) and crossbars set at regular intervals along its length. These serve to divide the belt into twenty panels of alternating design closely embroidered with sapphire beads and seed pearls. The arms with which the whole length of this belt are decorated are fully discussed in a paper published in 1955 by the Heraldry Society,[1] and are beyond the scope of this work, but it must be mentioned that the three leopards of England appear on it three times, as well as the arms of Richard of Cornwall and of France, Navarre and the County of Champagne. It is believed that it was originally given by Henry III of England to Count Thibant V of Champagne, king of Navarre, on the occasion

[1] Bertha Collin, " The Riddle of a 13th Century Sword Belt".

of Richard of Cornwall's coronation as King of the Romans in 1257. The question of how it got into the coffin of the Infante of Castile is unresolved, though it seems possible that his sister-in-law, who was wife of Count Thibant, may have given it to him after her husband's death in 1270.

I have said it is not a sword-belt. Why? For one thing it is too long; also it equates with no known pattern of sword-belt; and the "frog" or hanger is too delicate to hold a sword; but these arguments are only negative. On the positive side, it not only equates with, but is

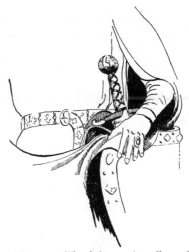

Fig. 120. The belt on the effigy of Wilhelm von Groitsch, Wechselburg, (c. 1240.)

exactly like, the long belts upon several effigies of the thirteenth century, the best known being the figure of King John on his tomb in Worcester Cathedral. He is not shown in armour, though he has a sword in his hand and spurs upon his heels. His effigy is in fact clothed precisely as the body of Fernando, and round his waist —girt tightly, not slung loosely round the hips as a sword-belt would be—is a long, narrow belt, its free end, furnished with a long tongue or chape, falling well below his knees. In it are the shield-shaped spaces where shields of arms were once inset. Another effigy of about the same period (c. 1240) is that of Wilhelm von Groitsch (fig. 120) in the Cathedral Church of Wechselburg in Germany. He, too, is clothed in ordinary "civil dress" though he is spurred and holds a shield and has a sword at his hip and a lance beside him. His over-tunic is girt tightly round the waist by a belt like John's, divided into partitions by small mounts of exactly the same shape as those upon the belt of Fernando. Then also the two Naumberg figures which show waist-belts (Count Ekkehard and Wilhelm von Camburg) have exactly similar ones, divided into sections by these metal mounts.

Identical belts are shown upon the effigies of great ladies; the figures in Fontevrault Abbey of Isabella of Angoulême, wife of King

243

John, and Berengaria of Navarre, Richard I's queen, are particularly apposite. Queen Isabella's girdle (which is of the same length, and worn in the same way as her husband's) is divided into sections by metal mounts, identical with those on Fernando's belt, and in each section is a lozenge-shaped pattern, also identical with the pattern alternating with Fernando's shields of arms. Queen Berengaria wears a belt with identical mounts with cross-shaped patterns between them, but the particular interest of this one is that in the same position to the left of the buckle as on Fernando's belt is a little metal fitting, a frog or hanger, from which the Queen's purse hangs on two long cords.

Here, I believe, is conclusive evidence that the belt in Fernando's coffin is not a sword-belt, but the only surviving example of that supreme badge of rank, worn by knightly folk of both sexes, the "cingulum Militaire". Hitherto the natural assumption that this is a sword-belt has been taken for granted; its magnificence and the fascination of its heraldry have obscured its true purpose.

During the thirteenth century many knightly figures, whether tomb effigies like those of John or Wilhelm von Groitsch or monuments like the Naumburg figures, are shown in ordinary dress, carrying their swords as one might carry a rolled umbrella. This is particularly the case in Germany where nine out of ten effigies on the tombs of knights were not shown in armour until after 1300, quite contrary to the practice elsewhere. It was not customary in the Middle Ages for gentlemen to go about in civil dress wearing swords as they did from the sixteenth century to the end of the eighteenth. Sometimes they would have a dagger at their belts, but seldom, if ever, a sword. If they

Fig. 121. The sword of Count Ekkehard, Naumburg (1260), showing belt wrapped round the scabbard.

carried one, as they did on special occasions, it would be loosely in their hands, with the belt wound round the scabbard (fig. 121), unless —as is really more probable—a page or a squire carried it for them. The plainness of Fernando de la Cerda's sword is in striking contrast to the richness of his garments and his belt, and serves to emphasize the severity of all swords meant for use rather than ceremony. In the manuscripts the swords of kings—Saul, David, the Maccabees, as well as contemporary princes—are rarely shown with more ornament than a gilded pommel, and their sword-belts and scabbards are as plain as those of their humblest followers. This, of course, is entirely in keeping with the universal brotherhood of chivalry, in which the simple knight is the equal of kings and of which the sword is the symbol. This does not, however, mean that there were no ornamental swords; the hilt of Sir Robert de Bure's sword, for instance, is decorated with incised foliage upon its pommel in the same style as the Conyers falchion, and similar ornament is to be seen on many brasses. Frequently we read in inventories and wills entries such as *Unum Gladium ornatum cum Argento*, or *IIIj espees: lun des armes le dit Counte, lautre de Seint George, et le tierce Sarziney: le quarte de Guerre.* The sword ornamented with silver was probably not uncommon, neither would be "one with the arms of the said Count", or "the other of St. George" (i.e., with the cross of St. George painted or enamelled in the pommel—this was an Englishman's sword, Humphrey de Bohun, who died in 1319 and from the inventory of whose arms this item is taken), but "the third Saraceny" is puzzling; it clearly denotes a decorative style which was Saracen or Moorish; maybe the explanation can be found in the sword of Fernando de la Cerda's brother, King Sancho IV of Castile and Leon. (Plates 10a and frontispiece.)

This is the finest and most beautiful mediaeval sword known to survive. It was found in the Capilla Mayor of Toledo Cathedral in 1941 during a search undertaken at the request of the Portuguese government for the remains of the Portuguese king Sancho II (1223–48). In the course of this search the tomb of Sancho IV (el Bravo) was opened. In it was found the mummified body of the king lying under a rich pall with the head resting on a cushion richly decorated with coats of arms. He had been clad (in a manner reminiscent of John of England) in the habit of a Franciscan friar;

245

on his head was a remarkable crown of silver gilt decorated with the arms of Castile and Leon, antique cameos and sapphires; on his feet were a pair of magnificent spurs (plate 10b) and his hands rested on the hilt of his sheathed sword.

This is known to be in the Treasury of the Cathedral at Toledo, yet, unlike another complete sword of about 1320 which will be described later, it is not on view. A provisional note based on such information as has been obtainable and upon the two photographs of it (the same as those reproduced here in plate 10 and the frontispiece) has been published recently; previous to this a short article on the tomb and its contents appeared in *ABC*, a Spanish popular magazine. This showed a rather poor photograph of the sword, which however does at least give a view of the whole length of its blade and scabbard.

It is of Type XII, with a pommel of Type H and a cross of Style 6; each tip of this has been notched twice. The grip, of some hard black wood (perhaps ebony), is of oblong section chamfered at the angles and swelling a little in the middle; it is fitted at the top and bottom with a narrow metal collar. Each of its broader faces is recessed for three circular plaques (two of which are missing on one face). These bear the arms of Castile quartering Leon; they have been described as enamelled but are in fact of painted glass. Between the plaques are similarly inlaid pairs of small chequered squares, while at top and bottom are little triangles of the same design.

All of the metal parts of the hilt are decorated with engraved *Mudejar* ornament, incorporating Cufic characters which are apparently purely decorative. The pommel, cross and collars are of iron, the background to the engraving being gilt. They are, as you can see, quite undamaged; being of iron it is remarkable that the dead hands of the king have not caused them to corrode in the same manner as the cross of Fernando de la Cerda's sword.

The blade has suffered a certain amount of corrosion, but parts of it retain their original mirror-bright polish. Engraved on one side of the blade near the hilt is a circular design of running foliage; the central section of this was originally carried across the depression of the fuller on a small plate; this is missing now, but the hole for the rivet which secured it is still to be seen. In the fuller on each side of the blade is a lettered inscription which, like those on other Spanish

246

swords, reads from the point up to the hilt instead of the other way about as was more common. These inscriptions have been partly obscured by rust; they are composed of very finely executed Lombardic letters, the following only being visible: on the one side GL . . . IARA and on the other M . . . N ?AS.

The perfectly preserved scabbard is made in the same way as that of the Turin St. Maurice sword, of two thin slats of wood covered in this case with rose-coloured leather decorated with a few tooled lines. It terminates in a simple U-shaped chape of silver similar to the one on the effigy in Salisbury Cathedral of William Longespée, Earl of Salisbury (c. 1240). The belt is attached by two black leather bands, one set about 1 in. below the mouth of the scabbard and the other about 3 in. below that; they are laced tightly round the scabbard and are joined by a diagonal strip of leather. The belt is of light green galon with narrow borders of red silk decorated with a cable pattern. Like all belts of this kind, it is of two parts of unequal length, each laced to one of the leather bands on the scabbard. The buckle and chape of this belt are missing, but the eyelets are of silver.

The crown found on Sancho IV's head is known to have belonged to his father, Alfonso X, El Sabio (1252–84); it is possible that the sword too was his. It is of a type much used between 1250 and 1300, and although it can be no later than 1295 it is not impossible that it could be as early as about 1260.

There is, as I have said, another complete and splendid sword in Toledo Cathedral, of rather later date (c. 1320) to be described in another chapter; another which belonged to St. Ferdinand is preserved in the Cathedral of Seville as a relic of him. It is a sword of Type XII, with a hilt fashioned of garnet and rock crystal mounted in silver. The pommel (Type I) is of crystal, and the grip and most of the cross-guard of garnet. The silver mounts are decorated in the same Moorish style as the hilt of the Sancho IV sword. This weapon is mounted with its point embedded in a stand made of gold or silver-gilt so that it stands free like a cross.

Part of a thirteenth-century sword-scabbard was found recently in a mediaeval cess-pit in Coventry, and is now in the City Museum. Only the upper part of the leather covering remains, all the wood having perished (cess-pits have splendid properties for preserving leather). Tooled upon the outside face of the scabbard is a diagonal cross about $3\frac{1}{2}$ in. deep set between two pairs of horizontal lines, suggesting the shape of the usual thirteenth-century belt fitment which may at one time have been with it. Similar tooled lines are clearly visible in the photograph of the Sancho IV scabbard. Below these marks is a row of six vertical slits each about $\frac{1}{4}$ in. long. These slits are entirely in conformity with the thirteenth-century method of threading the belt fitting through the covering of the scabbard, though in this case they are some 4 in. lower down the scabbard than is usual; a scabbard fitted in this way may be seen on the effigy of a knight in the church at Ash-by-Sandwich in Kent (c. 1300).

The swords in the cathedrals of Toledo and Seville are among the very few remaining in the church where they were originally deposited. It was quite usual in the Middle Ages for swords to be placed in churches, either as votive offerings (like the sword which Joan of Arc took in personal combat from a Burgundian man-at-arms on the walls of Paris and later caused to be hung upon a pillar in St. Denis) or to be placed upon or above the tombs of knights, or put inside them. It is worth noting here that when King John's tomb was opened in 1797 his body was found clothed in garments identical with those on the effigy above it, except that the head wore a monk's cowl instead of a crown. At the left side was a sword: as Stothard says, describing the appearance of the body:

> His left arm was bent towards his breast and the hand had grasped a sword in the same manner as on the tomb. The cuff of this arm still remained lying on the breast. The sword was much decomposed and its parts found at intervals down the left side, the scabbard was much more perfect.

It would be very desirable to know what this scabbard was like (for there is none on the effigy). Stothard does not say what was done with these relics (he mentions considerable portions of the royal garments, as well as the sword and the famous monk's cowl) so we may assume that they are still in the tomb. It is a fascinating possibility that in many of the military tombs of Europe there may still be swords like John's and the Infante Fernando's.

The innumerable swords which once hung above mediaeval

tombs have all vanished; there was one among the achievements of the Black Prince in Canterbury Cathedral, but it has been missing for over 300 years, and in Dart's description of the Chantry Chapel of Henry V in Westminster Abbey we read that in the year 1721 there was a sword and a dagger preserved with other "warlike furniture"; there is no trace of any dagger now, though the sword is most probably the one which is still preserved in the Muniment Room.

One or two accessibly placed swords or helms are known to have been removed from churches, and from this we may surmise the rest of the story of respectable plunder. Mr. (later Sir) Justinian Isham visited the church at Holdenby, for instance, in 1717, and mentions in his diary "an old monument of a person in wood, who I was told was a Holdenbie; a helmet and a sword lies upon it". The same effigy was mentioned in Bridge's *Northants* and that there were "an iron sword and a helmet laid by him". There was earlier in this century a local tradition that many years ago (i.e., some time during the mid-nineteenth century) the effigy, sword and headpiece "were taken away by a gentleman who came in his carriage for the purpose". We also know the fate of the helm which until early in the nineteenth century hung upon a staple above the tomb of Sir Richard Pembridge (ob. 1371) in Hereford Cathedral. This was given by the Dean of the time to Sir Samuel Rush Meyrick, the famous collector who was the Herodotus of the history of armour and arms. From his collection it passed eventually to the Royal Scottish Museum in Edinburgh, where it may now be seen. So until recently the staple which originally supported it might have been seen in Hereford Cathedral above the plundered tomb of Sir Richard.[1]

It is quite clear that many swords now in public or private collections (I have two myself) were once preserved in churches; it is possible to deduce this from the condition of the swords themselves. All surviving swords of the mediaeval period fall into three groups: those which have been dug up out of the ground or from the beds of rivers (the great majority); those which have been preserved in churches (very few); and those which (like the Conyers Falchion)

[1] Even this old staple has now gone, swept away presumably for the sake of tidiness.

have been cared for continually since they were used, and never been allowed to rust.

Excavated swords are either extremely perished or very well-preserved, saved from rusting away by the protective covering of black scale (containing, as a rule, principally Goethite: $FeO(OH)$) which was formed upon the steel by the action of chemicals in the soil, though of course there are many which come between these two extremes of corrosion and preservation. "Church" swords are as easily distinguishable. They have been exposed to the air and to a certain amount of damp and dust; originally they would have been well greased, but from the time of their being hung above or placed upon a tomb, would probably never have been cleaned. In this way they have acquired a distinctive sort of patination, consisting of a very close powdering of small rust-pits covered over with a hard black patina. These close, tiny pits were probably caused by a layer of dust sticking to the original grease; the dust particles would hold damp, which would eventually penetrate the grease and oxidize the surface of the metal, but not seriously owing to the protective effect of the grease above. This grease and dust would, during the years, harden into a more or less impenetrable patina, upon which layer upon layer of dust would accumulate, forming fresh rust upon the patina; thus the oxidization would tend to grow outwards, forming thick layers of rust, instead of inwards to eat the metal away. The few pieces of armour which remain in churches[1] all show this sort of surface.

In 1939 I was lucky enough to obtain a sword which had been preserved in this way (plate 9a). I hasten to add that I bought it respectably in a sale in London and that its previous owner (a gentleman of Somerset) had got it in the same way and at the same sale-room four years before, where it was among the "property of a Viennese collector". We may wonder from what church in Austria *he* had got it. Luckily neither of these persons had cleaned it at all. In 1939 it was black, and thick with rust, its wooden grip covered with layers of centuries-old dust and a few fragments of leather or linen which had once covered it. Unfortunately it was impossible to preserve these when the dirt was taken off the grip.

[1] The helm of the Black Prince at Canterbury, and those of Henry V and Henry VII (or Sir Giles Daubeney) in Westminster Abbey are the best known.

Literally months of work were needed to get down to the surfaces of the rest of the sword. The rust on the outside was loose and dusty, but below it was very hard and dark; the black patination was as hard as flint, and could only be removed on one side of the blade; it came away more easily from the softer iron of the pommel and cross, though only partially. After the war the grip was examined in the research laboratory in the British Museum. I had been a little doubtful whether it was contemporary with the sword (which is of c. 1300, a war-sword of Type XIII) or a later replacement. Everything about it had suggested from the start that it *was* the original, but it was desirable to have this scientifically confirmed. It is certainly original, and of beech-wood.

The third group, swords which have been cared for and cleaned continually, is extremely small. There are a few swords of the fourteenth century so preserved, and a surprisingly large number of the fifteenth, apart from special weapons like the two swords of St. Maurice (Turin and Vienna), the Conyers Falchion, or the Toledo and Seville swords.

The reason why swords were preserved in churches may be that every knight's sword belonged in a sense to the Church. It was sanctified on the altar at his knighting, and was supposed to return to the Church's keeping at his death. It was probably this intention, rather than a mere vainglorious seeking after immortal fame, which caused so many swords and spurs, helms and gauntlets to be hung above tombs, and for so many swords and spurs to be put into them. The warrior had finished with them; he had used them (or should have) to defend and uphold the Church, and so their work, like his, was done, and they too should rest. This sentiment is exactly the same, though Christianized, as that which caused the swords of the Vikings and their predecessors to be put into their graves.

The attitude of many thirteenth- and early fourteenth-century military effigies in England seems to reflect this feeling. The knight, recumbent on his tomb, is shown in the act of sheathing his sword. A few such effigies look so vigorous that it is generally assumed that they are drawing their swords, though this seems quite contrary to the idea of rest and of work well done. Many of these knights, however, have their right hands resting upon the top of their sword-pommels, as if they had just given them a final pat to drive the sword home in the scabbard. Though it is opposed to the general belief that these knights are shown in an attitude of instant readiness, even in death, to fight for Mother Church, I believe that they are intended to be at peace in the Church's bosom, their fighting done for ever.

Brass from the tomb of King Eric Menved (†1317),
Ringstead, Denmark.

Chapter Fifteen

"THE COMPLETE ARMING OF A MAN"
1100–1325

THE DAGGER DURING the twelfth and thirteenth centuries was not so important an item of the warrior's gear as it became during the fourteenth and fifteenth. Very few are shown in manuscript illustrations or upon monuments before the end of the thirteenth century, and such as do appear are in the process of being used in combat rather than worn upon the person. In the Maciejowski Bible, for instance, there are several battle scenes where daggers are almost as plentiful as swords, but there is no indication here or elsewhere in this manuscript where they were kept when not in use.

From documentary evidence it seems that the dagger was developed from a weapon used by foot soldiery, or by peasants in defence of their homes. It was in fact simply the descendant of the short sax or "skolm" of the Viking age, though, with the complete abandonment of Norse terms in England and Normandy, we find it everywhere called Cultellus or Coustel. That this term was used for the dagger is made clear by a passage in a statute of William, king of Scotland (1165–1214), which says: "*Habeat equum, habergeon. capitum e ferro, et cultellum qui dicitur dagger.*"

From their use of this weapon bodies of foot soldiery came to be called "Coustillers", and even as early as the middle of the twelfth century the term was applied in an entirely derogatory sense to bands of brigands. We read in a statute of the Count of Toulouse in 1152: "*Si quis aliqem hominem malum, quem Cultellarium dicimus, cum cultellis euntem nocte cause furandi occiderit, nullum damnum patiatur propter hoc.*" Another indication of the use and shape of the cultellus is found in Rigord's description of some Imperial troops at the

a   b

Fig. 122. Daggers, second half of the thirteenth century (author's coll.).

battle of Bouvines in 1214. *"Habebant cultellos longos,"* he says, *"Graciles, triacumines quolibet acumine indifferentur secantes a cuspide usque ad manubrium, quibus utebantur pro gladius."*

In one of the scenes of an Apocalypse (illustrated in about 1230) in Trinity College, Cambridge, a man is shown wielding a long and slender weapon such as this, which he wields daggerwise, though it is almost as long (about 20 in. in the blade) as a very short sword. In the Maciejowski Bible the daggers are short (with blades of about 8–10 in. long) and held daggerwise, though there are a few held in what seems to be a far more effective and practical way for knife fighting, with the blade projecting upwards from the fist instead of downwards. Most of these daggers have short, sharply arched cross-guards and pommels either in the form of a crescent (like the sculptured sword pommels of Freiburg Cathedral described on p. 226) or like an upcurving pair of horns, very reminiscent of the "anthropomorphic" daggers of the late Hallstatt and La Tène I periods. There are quite a number of daggers of this type still in existence; several, for instance, have been found in London and are in the Guildhall Museum and the London Museum. I have one myself, also from London, which, as it is fairly complete, I use to illustrate the type (fig. 122b). Their blades are short and double-edged with a flattened diamond section, and their hilts have a curved guard at each end, each of the same size and made flat like a ribbon about $\frac{1}{2}$ in. wide with the axis of its width set at right-angles to the plane of the blade; the ends of these guards are rolled over; in mine, the hollows in the rolls are filled with little pieces of silver.

A few daggers with crescent pommels survive but they are rare. Again I am fortunate in having a good specimen which is also believed to have been found in London (fig. 122a). The blade of this dagger is longer (10 in.) and has one edge, the section being triangular.

There is another type of dagger which was used in this period, long, slender and acutely tapering with two edges. Here again I must use one of my own to illustrate the type, for there are exceedingly few of them (fig. 123). It is later than the preceding ones (late thirteenth–early fourteenth century against mid-thirteenth) and is distinguished by a curiously shaped pommel of bronze, once gilt. This is lozenge-shaped, with a little lug sticking out of each side. There are arms upon it—a fleur-de-lys on one side and two chevrons on the other—and it is one of a group of daggers with similar pommels of which only a very few fragmentary bits survive; one was found in England and several more in Germany. The provenance of mine—the most complete of them—is unfortunately not known.

Fig. 123. Dagger with bronze pommel, c. 1300 (author's coll.).

In the Inventory of the arms of Raoul de Nesle which I quoted a few pages back are several entries relating to daggers which provide additional evidence of differing forms: "Item, an axe and several cutting knives" (*plusieurs coutiaus à tailler*); "Item, to VI stabbing knives (*pour VI coutiaus à pointe*) whereof one is garnished with silver"; "Item, ii swords and ii small misericordes". The *coutiau à tailler* would be a single-edged weapon—there are several well preserved daggers of this period (1302) in Switzerland which have single-edged blades quite broad with curved edges rather like worn bread-knives (fig. 124); and the *coutiau à pointe* would perhaps be the long needle-like blade such as fig. 123.

Fig. 124. Dagger with single-edged blade (*Historisches Museum, Berne*).

The word "misericorde" applied to a dagger is found as early as 1221, for in the Charter of Arras of that date we have *Quicumque cultellum cum cuspide, vel curtam spatulam, vel misericordiam, vel aliqua arma multritoria portaverit.* And in 1303 Guiart has a nice little passage:

> *Fauchons tranchans, espées cleres,*
> *Godendas, lances émolues,*
> *Coutiaux, misericordes nues.*

It seems to have got its name from its use in single fights when the uplifted dagger of the victor suggested to his fallen adversary that it would be advisable at that point to sue for mercy. So this murderous little weapon was by the poets assigned to pity as the emblem of her benevolence; Jean de Méun writes in the "Roman de la Rose":

> *Pitiez, qui à tous bien s'accorde*
> *Tenoit une misericorde*
> *Decourant de plors et de lermes*

As I have said, we seldom see it shown as being worn before the thirteenth century. An effigy of a knight in the Church of Ash by Sandwich in Kent shows the lace or thong by which a dagger was hung, not from the broad sword belt slung round his hips, but from the narrow girdle at his waist. The dagger itself has been so thoroughly broken away from the monument that there is no other trace of it. Another English monument of *c.* 1325 gives us one of the earliest representations of a type of dagger which was very popular during the late fourteenth and the fifteenth centuries, but which seldom appears before 1350. It is generally referred to in published works by the politely euphemistic name of "Kidney Dagger" or *Dague à Rognons* by reason of the two globular swellings with which the base of its cylindrical hilt is furnished, but in the more realistic and robust Middle Ages it was called by its proper name of "Ballock Dagger". The inhibitions of the nineteenth century seem to be wearing off, for daggers of this type are to be seen in many of our public collections correctly labelled. That is by the way; the monument in question is one which has several interesting peculiarities of great archaeological value which we shall return to. It is in the church of Minster in the Isle of Sheppey, and commemorates Sir Robert Shurland (see fig. 132).

Fig. 125. From a MS. at Bury St. Edmunds (1121–1148).

The axe was widely used during the twelfth and thirteenth centuries. In the eleventh it had been regarded as rather an ungentlemanly weapon by Continental warriors; only Saxons and Scandinavians considered it fit for any save churls, but by the early twelfth century it has become respectable and we find knightly warriors wielding it. The chronicler Roger de Hoveden, describing the battle at Lincoln in 1141, tells how Stephen, that most valiant and efficient knight but most ineffectual king, fights with an axe:

> "Then was seen the might of the king," he says, "equal to a thunderbolt, slaying some with his immense battle axe and striking down others. Then arose the shouts afresh, all rushing against him and he against all. At length, through the number of his blows, the king's axe was broken asunder. Instantly drawing his sword with his right hand he marvellously waged the fight till the sword too was broken. On seeing this, William de Kahamnes, a most powerful knight, rushed upon the king and seizing him by the helmet cried with a loud voice, 'Here! all of you, come here! I have taken the king.'"

There is a warrior in a manuscript at Bury St. Edmunds made between 1121 and 1148 (fig. 125) who might be King Stephen himself. His great axe is just the same as those in the Bayeux Tapestry and of which many were found in the River Thames (see fig. 72) and which we read about in the Sagas. These great axes continued in use right up to the end of the thirteenth century, but during the twelfth a lighter axe-blade became fashionable. This had an edge nearly as long as the old "Danish" axe, but the whole head was lighter. Fig. 126 shows a good example of this type of axe-head (which incidentally was used in Viking times as well as the larger type). It was found in the bed of a stream in

Fig. 126. Axe head from Northumberland: mid-thirteenth century.

257

Northumberland, together with a sword of Type XII and the bones of an exceptionally large man. You can see how the back of the axe has been developed to form a hammer-head. Most battle-axes in this period had long hafts and were wielded in both hands, though short hafts are frequently shown.

The war hammer, such a popular weapon during the Hundred Years War, was in use (though it seems infrequently) during the thirteenth century. The best known of the rare pictorial examples perhaps is a tomb-effigy of an unnamed warrior in Malvern Abbey Church, Worcestershire. He wears the knightly armour of the middle thirteenth century, but he is armed only with a short hammer and a small round shield of the kind known as a buckler. Maces were used too; during the thirteenth century we find representations of much more sophisticated types than the bludgeons of earlier periods, such as are so often shown in the Bayeux Tapestry. They tended to be massive things, sometimes with large flanged heads cast in bronze, sometimes made of six or seven wings of steel brazed on to a central core. There are two good thirteenth-century sculptured figures showing maces—both, curiously enough, of the sleeping guards at the Holy Sepulchre. One of these is in Lincoln Cathedral, and though the mace is much perished it is clearly distinguishable; the other, very similar and better preserved, is in the Cathedral at Constance. There are a few survivals of these mace-heads; one in the London Museum for instance (fig. 127) and a

bronze one in the Blackmore Collection in the Museum at Salisbury. This is in the well-known collection of Bronze Age weapons, and may be of the Bronze Age itself, though its form is exactly similar to many thirteenth-century ones, as for instance some in the Maciejowski Bible and others which have been found in Germany and Switzerland.

The knightly lance in this period remained the same as it had been since the fourth century—a long, stout spear between 9 and 11 ft. long, its shaft of uniform thickness throughout its length, its head

Fig. 127. Mace-head, thirteenth century: found on the site of the Bank of England (London Museum).

small and leaf-shaped. It was not until the fifteenth century that this weapon acquired its tapered form, with a narrowed hand grip near the butt-end protected by a steel disc called a Vamplate, though vamplates on a shaft of the old form were in use during the fourteenth century. The kind of spears used by foot-soldiery seem also to have been like those used in the preceding four or five centuries. The heavy spear like the old Carolingian "winged" spear was probably one of the most usual types for well-equipped infantry, though it may have lacked the wings or lugs; we read in Rigord's account of the battle of Bouvines in 1214 how the career of the King of France, Philippe Auguste, was very nearly brought to an end by some such weapon. The Imperialist foot had broken the French infantry. King Philippe, who had about him the flower of the French chivalry, met them with a desperate charge which carried him and his knights far into their ranks. William des Barres and most of the knights pressed on, cutting their way deep among the enemy, but the King got left behind. He was surrounded by the German foot, and though he laid about him most valiantly he was at last pulled off his horse because the lug or wing of a spear got caught in his mail coif; if he had not been able to get to his feet again it would have been all over with him; as it was, he fought on until some knights who were near by succeeded in reaching him. Pierre Tristan leapt from his horse and mounted his master on it, while Walo de Montinguy signalled for help by alternately raising and lowering the banner which he bore until des Barres and his men cut their way back to the King.

There are a great many names given by the thirteenth century chroniclers to the long-hafted weapons used by infantry, but it is practically impossible to say categorically which referred to what. We are confronted with the names Gaesa, Godendac, croc, Faus, faussal, Pikte, Guisarme and Vouge. In manuscript paintings we see a variety of staff weapons, but all seem to be more or less variants of what could equally well be called a bill or a halberd or a pole-axe. The true halberd was not invented before about 1300, and the credit for it must probably go to the Swiss. The pole-axe was simply what it is called, an axe on a pole, and is only a descendant of the Vikings' hewing-spear. It was not until the fifteenth century that the pole-axe became specialized, and was promoted from the common infantryman's use to become a very knightly weapon indeed.

Of all these names "Godendac" is the oddest, and it has given rise to much speculation, partly as to why a weapon should be called a Good Morning and partly as to what precisely that weapon was. Almost its only claim to fame is its use in the battle of Courtrai in 1302, when the burghers of that city inflicted a terrible and most bloody defeat upon the chivalry of France.

Guiart gives an account of this battle, and describes the Godendac thus:

A grans baston pesans ferrés
Avec leur fer agu devant
Vont ceux de France recevant
Tiex baton qu'il portent en guerre . . .

Cil baton sont long e traitis
Pour férir a deux mains faitis.

At one time it was believed that the mystery surrounding this thing's precise shape had been solved. A great oak chest of fourteenth century date in New College, Oxford, has carved upon it several battle scenes which have been identified as portraying this battle at Courtrai. In all these illustrations the chief weapon in the hands of the Flemings is a great club about 5 ft. long, reinforced on its head with bands of iron and furnished with a long spike. With some stretching of the imagination these could be made to fit Guiart's description: great sticks or clubs with "their iron pointed in front". However, this description would do equally well for the early form of the halberd, the weapon which the Swiss used for the first time at Morgarten thirteen years later, with apparently the same effect on the Austrian knights as the Godendac had on the French. Most of the accounts of Courtrai make it clear that the Godendac was a cutting weapon like an axe as well as having a forward-pointing spike like a spear; in that respect the weapons on the New College chest fail to equate with the descriptions. The Godendac was not a sort of secret weapon that caused the defeat of the French; this was almost entirely due to the idiotic chivalric gallantry of the French noblemen and the complete lack of tactical sense of their commander, Robert d'Artois. The English suffered a similar defeat at the hands of the Scots at Bannockburn twelve years later; and Morgarten was one year after that. Then in 1346 the chivalry of France went down in ruin on the downs of Ponthieu, at Crécy; they exactly repeated their performance of 1302, charging with the utmost gallantry and foolishness upon a disciplined force of infantry holding a strong position; this time they were shot down by English arrows, not hacked to pieces by Flemish Godendacs.

Courtrai and Bannockburn, Morgarten and Crécy as well as many lesser engagements all pointed to the same thing: the supremacy of the mounted heavily armoured horseman was at an end. He still had two glamorous centuries and more ahead of him, but not as the unrivalled dominator of the battlefield. At the time when these threats to his power were first assailing it, the knight's armour was in the main very little changed from what his ancestors had worn in the ninth century; indeed it was basically the same as had been worn by the Gauls in the first two centuries B.C.—helmet, shield and a shirt of mail. Since the end of the eleventh century each of these had been developed and modified in various ways. The helmet which we have seen on Trajan's Column, in the graves of Frankish warriors, in the Bayeux Tapestry, continued in use far into the thirteenth century. At some time, perhaps during the eleventh century, certainly early in the twelfth, the smiths began to make it from one piece of metal instead of several *Spangen* or plates riveted together, but its conical form remained. For some reason— for a conical headpiece is the most practical defence, offering a deflecting surface to any downward blow—during the twelfth century a new shape made its appearance; this was like a saucepan with a flat top, and must have been less effective in use though probably far easier to make and so much less expensive. The brimmed iron hat ("Kettle-hat") was still very much used. In the Saga of King Sverrer for instance, written down late in the twelfth century by the abbot of Thingore in Iceland from the King's own narrative, we read:

> Sverrer himself was dressed in a good byrnie, above it a strong gambeson and over all a red surcoat. With these he had a wide steel hat (*Vida Stalhufu*) similar to those worn by the Germans. . . .

Similar, too, very likely, to the one worn by the man of "very

Viking-like appearance" of whom Helgi Hardbeinsson was warned by the herdsman two centuries before. In more southerly parts of Europe it seems to have been more favoured by the common soldiery in this period. However, by about 1250 we find it among the equipment of great nobles. We read, for instance, in Joinville's "Vie de St. Louis" how on one occasion he persuaded King Louis to remove his helm, lending him his own kettle-hat so that the King could get some fresh air (*avoir le vent*).

In the Maciejowski Bible kettle-hats are often shown, mostly

Fig. 128. Goliath, from the Maciejowski Bible (1250).

upon the heads of common soldiers or Philistines, though occasionally gentlemen of coat-armour in the *Meinie* of Saul or David wear them. The splendid figure of Goliath from this manuscript gives a good example. I have chosen this (fig. 128) to illustrate thirteenth century armament because it is in its own right an admirable work of art. If only this one figure had survived out of all the quite remarkably good illustrations in the manuscript, it would be enough to show that the unknown artist who produced it ranked high among the great illustrators.

The great helm, so notable a feature of knightly equipment in the thirteenth century, seems first to have been used in the first decade of it. The two knights in fig. 95, of about 1200, show two different styles of helm. The victorious one on the left has a helm almost completely enclosing his head, but the vanquished one on the right has a lighter headpiece consisting of a flat-topped "saucepan" helmet furnished with a visor, reminiscent of the Vendel and Sutton Hoo helmets. The visor covers the face, but the back of the head and the neck are protected only by the mail coif. Similar visored helmets are clearly illustrated in some reliefs on the side of a silver shrine of Charlemagne in Aachen Cathedral (it was made between 1200 and 1207), and there is another on the seal of Gerard de St. Aubert (1199). There is also an illustration of a similar helmet shown from the front in the Apocalypse of St. Beato de Liebana, a twelfth-century manuscript in the Archaeological Museum at Madrid. A feature these visors share with the earlier ones from Vendel is that the "sights" are formed of two semi-circular openings, not rectangular slits.

The helm Richard I wears on his second Great Seal has always been taken for a more advanced type, for it looks as if it completely encloses the head back and front; but if several original impressions of this seal are closely examined, it will be found that what is shown is in fact one of these helms with a face-guard.

There are some good illustrations of early helms in a German manuscript of about 1210–20, the "Eneit" of Heinrich von Veldecke. All these helms are of the same form as the one worn by the left-hand figure in fig. 95, but their greatest interest lies in the heraldic crests which adorn them. Here are crests of exactly the same sort as we find upon the helms of fourteenth-century knights —the heads of various beasts, a star, a pair of small rectangular banners on little poles stuck into the top of the helm, a hand, a dragon, a pair of stag's antlers, a bird's wings, a large blue bow and so on.

Though there are plenty of heraldic charges on shields in the Maciejowski Bible, none of the helms bears a crest. These helms are very clearly drawn and show how they were made; they have flat tops and are more or less cylindrical, but apart from that resemble in construction the few thirteenth-century helms which survive. None of these is as early as 1250, but there is in the Castel Sant Angelo in Rome a fine helm dating from about 1280–1310. It was found in a tower at Bozen and is so well preserved that it is very suitable to demonstrate the usual method of construction (fig. 129).

It is made from five plates of good iron held together with heavy

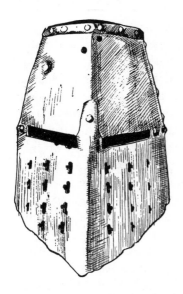
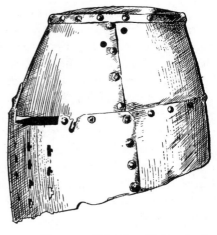

Fig. 129. Helm from Bozen, in the Castel St. Angelo at Rome, c. 1300.

iron rivets with heads of a flattened conical shape. The lower front plate is bent backward in the centre at an acute angle, and overlaps the lower rear plate at each side; the front of its upper edge, which is cut away to lower it by about half an inch, forms the lower rim of the two long slots which form the "sights" or "occularia". A tongue projecting upward from the centre of the plate forms the division between these two eye-slits. The rear plate is bent round in an even curve. The front upper plate is bent back in the same way as the lower one, forming a sharp ridge in front, and in the same way it overlaps the rear upper plate. Its lower front edge is cut away to form the upper edge of the sights, and it inclines backwards at an angle. The two upper plates form together a blunt truncated cone which is capped by another flat elliptical plate whose turned down rim fits over the side plates like a lid and is riveted all round. The upper plates are pierced near the top by four sets of circular holes set diagonally at front, sides and rear; these were to take the laces by which the crest would be secured. Each side of the lower front plate is pierced by eleven T-shaped holes for breathing. On the right upper front plate is a dent caused by a powerful blow, and there is a furrow caused by a cutting weapon or a lance-point on the left.

As you can see, this helm is very much wider from front to back

264

than from side to side; it is no longer nearly cylindrical like the helms of the Maciejowski Bible and of the royal and baronial seals of the thirteenth century (plate 11). The front would be some way away from the face, and it seems likely that the extra weight caused by its larger size would be offset by the better circulation of fresh air inside it. This particular example weighs a little over 5 lb. in its present condition; with its lining and fittings it would probably have weighed originally about 6 lb. One of the earliest of the surviving helms has applied strips of metal cross-wise over the front, and another of rather later date has a cross with floriated ends painted or applied in gold leaf.

These helms may appear in paintings to rest upon the shoulders, but actually the weight was borne entirely by the head; the lower edge nearly touched the shoulders, but cleared them sufficiently for the helm to be turned with the head. Its weight was supported by a fitted lining, made by fixing a deep leather band, cut into a series of triangular gussets and pulled together with a cord at the top, to a strap fixed horizontally round the inside of the helm by the rivets joining the upper and lower plates. Illustration of this method of lining helms is given by many tomb effigies, and in the helm of the Black Prince in Canterbury Cathedral fragments of the original lining still remain.

The head itself had several reinforcing defences below the helm. Primarily there was the warrior's hair—no negligible factor during the thirteenth century, when it was worn long. It was bunched up under a little linen cap, sometimes padded, which fitted closely to the head with two lappets covering the ears and lacing under the chin. This was known as an "arming cap". Sometimes a small, tight-fitting skull-cap of steel was worn over this, and over all went the coif of mail. Occasionally a sort of padded roll of material, worn like a Zulu's head-ring, was fitted over the coif to support the helm and keep it away from the head. Many men preferred to rely only on these defences, and fought without helms—like Sire Everard, who lost his nose at Mansourah because of it.

The heads of many knights on monumental brasses and effigies look unnaturally large and globular; this appearance is given them by the padded arming-caps below their coifs, but mostly it is the masses of bunched-up hair which makes them seem so swollen.

Some are shown with their coifs thrown back on their shoulders, like Sir Robert de Septvans on his brass in the church at Chartham in Kent; here the luxuriant, carefully arranged curls of the knightly hair-do are clearly shown, leaving no doubt as to the appearance the same head would present if the coif were pulled up over it.

Iceland (curiously enough when we consider the far better-known chronicles of England and France) gives us a very complete description of a knight's armour of the mid-thirteenth century. This is in an Icelandic chronicle called the "Speculum Regale" (The King's Mirror) in which the author instructs his son in his military duties. When fighting on foot he is to wear a byrnie or a thick panzar (a garment which in the more southerly parts of Europe was called a *gambeson* or *wambasium*, a long tunic shaped like a byrnie but made of stout padded and quilted material), a strong shield or a buckler—that is a small, circular shield like the old Viking ones, only smaller than they were—and a heavy sword. For sea-fights he says that the best weapons are long spears, and for defence long panzars, good helmets or what he obscurely calls *hangandi stalhufur*, hanging steel-hats; perhaps we may take it that he means a type of helmet with pendant cheek and neck guards like the old Vendel ones, maybe in their more fashionable form of the small helmet with a simple visor such as we discussed on p. 263. With these he recommends a broad shield, not specifying its shape, though for sea-fighting a round one may be presumed.

His directions for a horseman's equipment are more minute: "Let the horseman wear this dress," he says. "First, hose made of soft and well prepared linen cloth, which should reach to the breeches-belt. Then above them good mail hose of such a height that they may be fastened by a double string (i.e., by suspenders from the belt). Next let him put on a good pair of breeches made of strong linen, on which must be fastened knee-caps made of stout iron and fastened with strong rivets. The upper part of the body should be clothed first in a soft linen panzar which should reach to mid-thigh, and over this a good breast defence of iron extending from the bosom (?) to the waist belt; above that a good byrnie and over all a good panzar of the same length as the tunic (that is, the soft linen panzar which went on first) but without sleeves.

"Let him have two swords—one girt round him, the other hung

at his saddle bow, and a good dagger. He
must have a good helm made of tried steel,
provided with all defence for the face, and
a good thick shield suspended from his
neck, especially furnished with a strong
handle. Lastly, let him have a good and
sharp spear of tried steel, with a long shaft."
All this is abundantly illustrated in
thirteenth-century manuscripts and monuments. In the all-providing Maciejowski
Bible there are several pictures in which
we see armour being put on or off,

Fig. 130. Leg armour from
the Trinity College Apocalypse (c. 1230), showing
poleyn and laced mail.

clearly showing the garments detailed in the "Speculum Regale".
There is a difference in one thing—in the manuscript are no linen
breeches furnished with knee caps, only a sort of padded tubular
stocking used to protect the thigh.

These eminently practical knee-caps were in use, though it would
seem infrequently, at as early a date as about 1230, for we see them
in the Trinity College Apocalypse in Cambridge, though here they
are worn without the padded breeches, being fixed directly over the

mail hose—which in some cases are not
complete hose, but broad strips of mail
covering the front of the leg, held on by
being laced up behind it (fig. 130). The
knee-cap ("poleyn" was the contemporary
name for it in English, which I shall use
from now on) fixed to padded breeches
(known as "gamboised cuishes") is clearly
shown in some of the earlier English
brasses, perhaps the best example being
that of Sir Robert de Bures in Acton
Church, Suffolk (1302). His cuishes are very
richly decorated, and the attachment of the
poleyns is clearly visible (fig. 131).

Fig. 131. From the brass of
Sir Robert de Bures, showing
poleyn attached to gamboised
cuish.

In the past there has been controversy
among students of armour as to whether
these early poleyns were made of iron or
of leather; many seem to have been

267

Fig. 132. The effigy of Sir Robert de Shurland,
Minster, Isle of Sheppey, c. 1330.

convinced for some reason that they must have been of leather or "cuir bouilli" (a very tough substance of leather prepared by boiling in wax[1] before being worked), on the grounds that it would be beyond the capacity of a thirteenth-century armourer to make them of iron. Knowing that these same armourers had been beating out first-class conical helmets from single sheets of metal for more than a century, this seems an unnecessary slur on their capabilities.

The panzar (gambeson) recommended as an alternative to the byrnie for fighting on foot was the garment generally worn as a reinforcement with it. However, in manuscript pictures up to the later part of the thirteenth century (the inevitable Maciejowski Bible in particular) no such undergarment is shown; nothing but the soft shirt which may

1 ... *et que les dit bouteilles de cuyr soient boulues de cire neufve ...* (1560: Stat: des gainiers de Paris, Arch. Reg. des Bannieres.) This note applies to the making of bottles of Cuir bouilli, and specifies the fresh wax the leather is to be boiled in.

perhaps be identified with a garment often referred to as an Aketon, though an attempt to identify these garments is probably futile since their names appear to have been interchangeable in contemporary usage, and we find the words aketon and gambeson applied to the same thing. The shirts shown so clearly in the Maciejowski Bible are probably just shirts (Chaucer, for instance, mentions "a breke and eke a sherte" as the essential underwear for a man in armour).

In monuments dating after about 1270 the lower edge of the gambeson (or aketon) shows below the bottom of the byrnie or hauberk; one monument (to Sir Robert de Shurland, in the church at Minster, Sheppey, which I referred to in connection with daggers) provides a perfect illustration of it, for he wears one embroidered with arms (not his own, but those of his liege lord Sir William de Leyburne, under whose banner he fought in Scotland) instead of a surcoat *over* his hauberk. We can be grateful for the oddity of Sir Robert or his executors who caused an effigy to be made unlike any other, so that it shows so clearly the form and construction of the gambeson (fig. 132).

There is abundant literary and pictorial evidence that the gambeson or aketon was worn often as the sole body-defence, particularly when fighting light, on foot. In the Maciejowski Bible, though no knights wear it under their hauberks, most foot-soldiers wear one, sometimes with short sleeves and sometimes long ones to the wrist, and a deeply-dagged knee-length skirt, as their sole body defence.

It is not possible to be certain whether the "good breast defence of iron" was a single plate, or a defence consisting of a number of small plates riveted to the inside of a textile covering; there are several early references to solid iron breast-plates; for instance Guillaume le Breton gives an account of a fight between Richard Count of Poitou (later Richard I of England) and Guillaume des Barres in which each of them wears beneath his hauberk a plate of worked iron (*fera fabricata patena recocto*). This tells of an event in about 1185; an even earlier reference to iron armour is in the account given by Giraldus Cambrensis of the attack by the Danes upon Dublin in 1171. They are described as being clad either in long shirts ("loricis" is the word used) of mail, or an armour of iron plates: *laminis ferreis arte consortis*. During the later part of the thirteenth century such armour was called "Plates", which is precisely what it was, small rectangular plates of iron set in rows vertically and riveted to the inside of the surcoat. There are many clear illustrations of such coats in contemporary art.

Another kind of solid breast-armour in use from the late twelfth century was the *Cuirie*. The term first appears in texts of the third quarter of the twelfth century and occurs frequently until about 1350. It is almost certainly synonymous with *Cuirace* or *Quiret*, a term which remained in use as long as armour did. It is impossible to say exactly how the thing was made since it was always worn under the surcoat and so is never visible in pictures or monuments. From various sources, however, we do know that it was worn over the hauberk but under the surcoat; that it was always made of leather (hence its name), and that it was rigid enough for the guard-chains of sword and helmet (items which will be discussed later) to be fastened to it—a fact which implies the use of cuir bouilli rather than ordinary leather in its making. Sometimes we are told that it was reinforced with metal plates, and on occasions it had additional defences of leather or cloth (presumably quilted) for the arms, and sometimes it was lined with a textile fabric. Nor was it always a defence for the breast alone; there is evidence that it comprised a breast and back plate in combination. In an inventory of the effects of Eudes, Compte de Nevers, made after his death in 1266 is an entry: "Paires de cuiraces", and in two English effigies of about the same period the armholes of the surcoat are wide enough to show beneath it what are apparently single-piece breast and back plates joined by straps at the sides. One of these is in Pershore Church, Worcestershire, and the other used to be in the Temple Church in London. Later, during the fifteenth century, the term cuirass was applied to the combined breast and back plates of metal and as such it survives to the present day.

The Surcoat is a colourful addition to the warrior's gear which, though introduced before the end of the twelfth century, was not universally adopted until about 1210. Its purpose is obscure; many authorities have asserted that it was brought into the west by crusaders who had taken to it while in the Holy Land to mitigate the effect of the burning sun upon their mail; here indeed is a practical theory, but it assumes that the surcoat was unknown in the west, or not thought of, before 1200; after all, crusaders had been coming back from the Middle East since 1099, a century before. Why was it not introduced then? There is also the theory that its main object was to display the arms of its wearer; this indeed seems highly probable, since it began to be universally fashionable at the same time as heraldry did. The oft-quoted passage from a fourteenth-century metrical romance, the "Avowynge of King Arthur", should not be taken too literally as evidence that the surcoat was a kind of mackintosh:

> Then sex or atte on assente
> Hase armut hom and furthe went...
>
> with scharpe weppyn and schene
> gay gownus of grene
> to hold ther armur clene
> and were hitte fro the wette.

More than for any one particular reason, I believe that the surcoat was introduced at the demand of Fashion; practical use it certainly had, for it did keep the sun and some of the wet from the greater part of the iron mesh of the mail, and it provided an excellent field for the display of arms; for purposes of identifying the dead after a battle an armorial coat was invaluable, for the shield might easily be parted from the body and features were likely to be marred and disfigured. But whatever its practical uses might be, it was gay and colourful, and its wearing would have transformed the grim and sombre-looking warrior in his dark brownish-grey hauberk into a gallant and glamorous figure—a transformation entirely in keeping with the way in which the *Gai Saber* had developed by the end of the twelfth century.

The cut of it varied, not so much by period as by preference, for we find very long ones as well as short ones, with sleeves or without, in use throughout the thirteenth century. The illustration on p. 198 (fig. 85) from a manuscript of the early fourteenth century shows two knights fighting on foot in long surcoats which they have tucked up under their sword-belts in order to shorten them. This method of holding a long surcoat up out of the way when fighting is often shown. It was a simple garment, tailored like a night-shirt, sleeveless and slit from the hem nearly to the waist at front and back so that the skirts would set properly when the wearer was mounted. Though nine out of ten were without sleeves, occasionally one is shown with them, sometimes to the elbow and sometimes to the wrist. It was not unusual for them to be made of very rich material (we read in inventories of surcoats of velvet or samite) with the heraldic charges lavishly embroidered.

During the last forty years or so of the period we are dealing with (*c.* 1280–1320) further fashionable ornaments were added to knightly equipment. These were little flat label-like objects worn vertically on the shoulders like small wings—they were aptly named "ailettes"—and no satisfactory single explanation can be given for their popularity. They had no defensive value, for their construction was flimsy (buckram or leather), and they could not have been securely enough fastened to check a blow. Sometimes we see them in paintings bearing the wearer's arms—in the inventory of the effects of Humphrey de Bohun in 1322 we find *iii peire de ailettes des armes le Counte de Hereford*—but quite often they are plain. In sculptured effigies they are shown as if they were worn flat on the back, facing forward, but this is simply because they could not be carved standing free on the points of the shoulders, upright in a fore-and-aft axis as they were were in fact worn. They had an infinite variety of shapes, too. I think that they were probably nothing more than a fashionable bedizenment, gay little bits of nonsense to enhance the appearance of the warrior. Such indeed seems to be the only explanation for the immortal ailettes of Piers Gaveston; in the inventory of his effects made in 1313 we have *Item, autres divers garnementz des armes le dit Pieres, ovek les ailettes garniz et frettes de perles.*

While we trace the development of warlike gear and consider its practical uses, we must not lose sight of the fantasy which played an ever increasing part in the theory and practice of chivalry as the time of its decline drew nearer. The first half of the fourteenth century was a period during which the fashionable knight appears cluttered up with all sorts of colourful gear (and his horse too), not, perhaps, because he fought better for it, or because it protected him in battle, but because it was fashionable.

Perhaps the most cumbersome items in the clutter of fourteenth-century armament were the stout chains whereby sword, dagger and helm were attached to the person. These had indeed a most practical purpose—to prevent these essentials from being completely lost if they were knocked out of the hand or off the head of a warrior in fight. We see them on monuments and in pictures from the late thirteenth century almost to the end of the fourteenth, particularly in Germany where they seem to have been most popular. We may think it almost inconceivable that a man could fight encumbered by a 4-ft. chain joining his sword-hilt to his breast-plate; surely it would wrap itself round his sword-arm or catch round the head of his opponent's horse, or get tangled up with other people's weapons? and if he did lose his sword in the violent and continually shifting movement of a melée on horseback, would it not get mixed up with the spurs and feet of anyone who came near? It seems that there must have been a risk of this sort of thing happening, yet the chain would not need to be longer than the distance from the fist to the right ribs with the arm fully extended, a length of 3 to 4 ft. If it fell and hung down from the chest, the end of the chain itself would reach to a little below the knee, with the sword's point 3 ft. or so below that—well clear of the ground. It must have been practical in use, or it would not have been popular for so long.

William Wenemaer (1325) (fig. 103) has these chains on the brass in the Byloke Museum at Ghent. This shows very clearly how they were fixed to the sword and dagger by rings running freely around the grips. A point of interest in this figure is that the surcoat has two openings through which the chains pass to their fastening over the breast; it is plain to see that they are fixed to the mail of the hauberk not to a solid breastplate or coat of plates; this weakens the theory that where breast chains appear, a solid foundation to secure them is implied.

To fasten the helm, there was a toggle on the end of the helm-chain which engaged into a T-shaped slot near the lower edge of the helm on the right-hand side in front. Among the pieces of equipment still preserved in Canterbury Cathedral (all that is left of the "achievements" of the Black Prince) there is a short length of iron chain whose only justification among such relics is that it must have originally been one of these chains. There is in the helm the

T-shaped slot to take the toggle. The beautiful mounted figure of Can Grande della Scala (Dante's patron) over his tomb at Verona (plate 12) shows the helm slung on the back and fastened by this chain, but this is due to incorrect restoration.

The large kite-shaped shield of the kind used by the Normans was still popular in the second half of the twelfth century. In Scandinavia during this period its form remained unchanged, but further south it tended to be modified by having its upper edge made straight. Here again it is better not to lay down hard and fast rules of development, for personal preference must be considered in the shape of shields as in all else; however, the evidence of innumerable documents shows that after 1150 a type of large triangular shield with a straight upper edge predominated. Some still had central bosses, some not. This feature is occasionally seen as late as the mid-thirteenth century, for instance on the monument of Wilhelm von Groitsch (c. 1240) (fig. 120). From the early years of the thirteenth century the shield was a good deal shorter—about 30 in. from base to apex—and considerably wider, often strongly curved to enclose the body in the manner of the old Roman shields. Towards the century's end a type of very small, flat shield seems to have been popular as an alternative to the big one. We find them on many English brasses and monuments dating between 1280 and 1325. They appear to be rather similar in purpose to the little flat fist-bucklers which were often used for fighting on foot, but they were of the flat-iron shape associated with the horseman's shield instead of circular like the buckler. Incidentally, some of these small round bucklers are still preserved in Scandinavia, many of them in almost perfect condition.

The effigy of Sir Robert de Shurland, thanks to the peculiarities of its design, shows very clearly the arrangement of the various straps by which the shield was held. These are quite complex, and are as it were in two sets, each complementary to the other in handling and managing the shield. First there is the long strap by which it was hung round the neck, called the "guige". This consists of one long strap fixed by a rivet to the inside of the shield near the top on the right-hand side and a shorter one furnished with a buckle similarly placed and fixed on the left. By using two straps buckled together in this manner the length of the guige could be adjusted. The second group of straps are the "enarmes", a system of loops through which the left forearm could be thrust. This method of holding the shield is, of course, similar to what was used by Greeks, Celts, Saxons and Vikings, except that the rigid bar by which the left hand gripped the shield was replaced by a couple of straps. Basically the enarmes consist of three straps; one to the left of the shield, one nearer to the right and a third, considerably smaller than the other two, almost at the right edge.

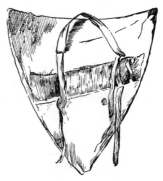

Fig. 133. The "Sitten" shield, showing guige strap and enarmes, late thirteenth century (Tyroler Landesmuseum, Innsbruck).

The forearm passed through the first two; No. 1 on the left held the arm near the elbow, No. 2 held the wrist and No. 3 could be grasped by the fingers if they were disengaged, though the pressure of No. 2 across the wrist was enough to hold the shield if the fingers were needed to hold the reins. The Shurland monument shows one arrangement of these straps (fig. 132), and an existing shield of the same date in the Tyrolean Museum in Innsbruck shows another (fig. 133). The enarmes are more widely spaced and quite separate, not crossed over and very close to each other as in the Shurland shield; one cannot help feeling that in this case all the grips are too far over to the right for such a big shield. However, personal preference may have something to do with this apparent oddity, though we cannot rule out the possibility that here the preference may have been that of the sculptor who made the effigy, striving to show all the enarmes and so not spacing them correctly.

There are some well-preserved shields dating about 1190 and 1320 which show clearly how they were made. One is in the Landesmuseum at Zurich; it was found late in the nineteenth century in a disused cupboard in the church at Seedorf, on Lake Lucerne; it bears the arms (azure, a lion Rampant argent) of Arnold von Brienz, who founded the church and monastery of Seedorf in 1179. The church was later dedicated to the Order of the Knights of St. Lazarus. The shield is somewhat damaged, the lower few inches of

275

the point end being broken away and all the straps having perished, though apart from that it is well preserved. It is made of lime-wood covered inside and out with leather, the silver lion being moulded in low relief in *Gesso Duro*. Much of the silver colouring and the blue of the ground survives.

At Marburg (where also there are extremely fine effigies of some of the Counts of Hesse) are more than twenty well-preserved shields; one of them bears the arms of Konrad von Thuringen and Hesse, Grand Master from 1220 to 1241 of the Teutonic Order of the Knights of Prussia; these arms are applied in tooled leather to the front of the shield while the inside is gilded and painted with a knight and a lady. In the Armeria Real at Madrid is an even better pre-served shield of the late thirteenth century (D. 59) which came from the monastery of San Salvador de Oña at Burgos; this is made of a wood rather like cedar, and is covered on each side with parchment, thicker on the front than on the back. The inside was painted black with a broad band of red running diagonally across it. (This feature is repeated on the back of the shield in the Tyrolean Museum at Innsbruck.) The enarmes are made of strong dressed buckskin lined with purple velvet; part of the guige remains. On the outside are traces of arms; on a red field numerous stripes, some gilded and incised, others of various colours, run from the centre to the outer edges in the manner of an Escarbuncle.

The spur had been used from the time of classical Greece, and the original form changed very little in Europe before the end of the thirteenth century. In classical times it was formed of a short, conical spike set upon two very short arms. These ended in buttons on to which a strap was fitted to hold the spur round the boot. This type was used until the Viking Age; examples were found in the Danish bog deposits which retain the characteristics of the classical spur. During the Viking age the arms were lengthened so that they embraced the heel, while the ends—which were pierced with slots for the strap-end fittings—came a little forward of the ankle-bones. The body of the spur had straight arms and a short and very narrow neck ending in a small spike which was often only about $\frac{1}{4}$ in. long and $\frac{1}{8}$ in. in diameter (fig. 134).

Fig. 134. Spur, c. 1000, found in Walbrook, London (coll. author).

A variation was common outside Scandinavia, where a small bulb
was interposed between the spike and the neck. A most splendid
pair of such spurs survive; they were found in the last century
during repairs to the church of St. Andrews at Chardstock in Dorset,
in a stone coffin containing part of a man's skeleton. Upon the
leg bones were the remains of leather boots, with these spurs
upon their heels.[1] They are of gilded iron, with the neck and
bulb decorated with little spots of gold. The arms are very
slightly curved, and the whole effect is extremely elegant. They
are very well preserved too; much of the gilding on the arms
remains and nearly all the gold spots. There are many pictures in
manuscripts of the ninth to the eleventh centuries showing similar
spurs.

The straight-armed spur seems to have been the only type in
favour until the very end of the twelfth century, when the arms
began to assume a graceful curve which was to be universally
favoured, though often varied, until the early sixteenth century. A
magnificent pair of spurs was found in the coffin of Sancho IV of
Castile and Leon, whose sword was described in Chapter 14. These
are illustrated on plate 10; they are of the same basic type as fig. 135,
but being preserved as they have been, they show how the strap
was fitted. It is a single strap of leather covered with fabric fastened
to the ring on the outside arm-end, passing under the foot, through
the slot at the end of the inner arm, and so over the foot to the
buckle which is fastened to the top of the ring on the outer arm.
The ends of these spur-straps are mounted with little gold animal-
heads, reminiscent of those on the ends of the cross-guard of the
twelfth-century GICELIN sword described on p. 214.

The rowel came into use in the thirteenth century, but until the
second quarter of the fourteenth it was less popular than the old
prick spur. In its earliest form it was quite small, usually with six
points, but during the 1320s a much larger form came in (it seems to
have been very popular in England) which was made of 24 or more
points, each point often in the shape of a
petal, so that the complete rowel looked
like a daisy. These two types of early rowel

Fig. 135. Spur, thirteenth
century: found in London
(London Museum).

[1] These spurs were acquired recently by the
Armouries of the Tower of London.

277

Fig. 136. Spur of gilt bronze, c.
1290: found in London (coll.
author).

Fig. 137. Iron spur, c. 1340:
found in London (coll. author).

spur are illustrated in figs. 136 and 137. The first is an early one of bronze gilt and was found in London. The second, also from London, is a good example of the type of "daisy" spur of the second quarter of the fourteenth century. Much of the gilding and the buckle remains on 136, while 137 retains one of the disc-shaped hooks to which the straps were attached and a certain amount of its original tinning. A few examples of such a spur type are to be seen on English monuments dating between about 1320 and 1360; particularly good ones are the brass of Sir John de Creke (*c.* 1325) at Westley Waterless, Cambridgeshire, and the effigy of Sir Roger de Kerdeston (1337) at Reepham, Norfolk.

Although the spur had its place in the symbolism of chivalry, its use was neither confined to the knightly classes, nor was it purely military. In his prologue to the Canterbury Tales, Chaucer's only mention of spurs is in his description of the Wife of Bath:

> Upon her amblere easily shee satte,
> A foot mantel upon hyr hippes wide
> And on hyr fete a pere of spores scharpe.

The mention of her steed is interesting, too. The valuable warhorse was ridden only in battle; for the ordinary purposes of getting from place to place the man-at-arms (as well as any other member of the mediaeval travelling public) would ride a horse like a hack, variously called a palfrey or a jennet or an ambler or ambling horse.

This was a name descriptive of its gait, which, as far as we can tell with the evidence available, was rather similar to the swift, smooth running gait of the horses ridden by cattlemen in America and Australia. Mediaeval horses were not trained to trot; indeed, a "Great Horse" trotting with a heavily armoured man on its back would be a terrible thing.

There were three kinds of war horse in use during the later Middle Ages. First there was the extremely valuable "Great Horse" (Dextrarius or Destrier) which in the thirteenth century cost anything from 60 to 120 marks. This was a powerful animal heavier than a modern hunter but not so heavy as a shire-horse, capable of carrying a great weight and very highly trained. Then there was the less valuable "Equus", called simply a horse without any qualification, worth from 20 to 40 marks. This probably differed from the destrier only in the matter of breeding, for it seems to have been a comparable weight-carrier. Finally there was the common "Runcinus" or Rounsey of the ordinary trooper, worth between 5 to 8 marks.

The qualification which from the late thirteenth century separated the man-at-arms from the light horseman (after about 1300 he was called a "Hobilar" in England) was that they should ride "Equi cooperti", covered horses. If a man-at-arms with such a horse was a Banneret, his pay from the time of Henry III to that of Henry V was 4s. a day; if a knight, 2s. a day; and if he was a squire or a "Serjeant" ("Serviens"—a trooper of non-noble blood) his pay was the standard 1s. a day. When the horse was not covered (and many men-at-arms could afford no more than the lighter rounsey), the pay rate fell to 6d. or 8d. a day.

So whatever a warrior's own personal equipment may have been, it was the value of his horse and its "couverture" which determined his status, at least as far as pay was concerned. What then was the all-important "covering"? There are a few references as early as the later twelfth century to horses covered with mail, but it was not until the middle of the thirteenth that this became regular. From about 1220 onwards most horses are shown with "bards" of fabric corresponding to the knightly surcoat—the horse on the seal-impression of Roger Fitz-Walter (plate 11c) is an example. We may infer that these sometimes covered trappers of mail or of quilted material like the gambeson. An excellent illustration of a barded horse is provided by the monument over the tomb of Can Grande Della Scala (who died in 1329) at Verona (plate 12).

Matthew Paris (c. 1250) tells that at the battle of Nuova Croce in 1237, between the Imperialists and the Milanese, "a credible Italian asserted that Milan with its dependencies raised a force of 6,000 men-at-arms with iron-clad horses". An ordinance of Philip the Fair in 1303 provides that every holder of an estate of 500 livres rental shall furnish for the defence of the realm *un gentilhomme bien armé et monté à cheval de cinquante livres tournois et couverte de couvertures de mailles ou couvertures de pourpointerie.*

Late in the thirteenth century we first hear of a defence for the horse's head like the later chamfron. In the roll of the Provision for the Windsor Tournament of 1278 is an early mention of these "Copita" of leather, made in the likeness of a horse's head:

D. Miloñ le cuireur, xxxviiij copita cōr de similitud capīt equos pc̄ pec ijs.

They appear again in 1301, under the name of Testerae, in an indenture of the delivery of Montgomery Castle to Sir William de Leyburne:

Item, Liberavit eidem iij par coopertorum ferri et ij testeras et v loricas cum capite et v sine capite . . .

The principal—indeed the only—function of the great war-horse was to provide a platform, mobile, highly trained and supremely sensitive to the slightest movement of its rider, from which to fight. The prime importance of stirrups to this function has been discussed in an earlier chapter; as armour became heavier, the saddle tended to be made with a higher ridge above the horse's withers, so that the rider's legs would not need to be spread at so wide an angle —in short, his "seat" upon his saddle would be more like the sort of stance he would take if he were fighting on his feet.

The saddles which are to be seen in manuscript pictures from

Fig. 138. Figure of St. George, Castle Square, Prague (c. 1370).

the tenth century to the thirteenth vary little in essentials; it is not until plate armour was worn that the ridge of the saddle becomes higher. An admirable example of this which shows the build of the saddle itself and the way the rider sat in it in action is a statue of St. George in the Castle Square in Prague. This was made shortly after 1370, and so should really be included in the next chapter, but it so well illustrates the mediaeval fighting seat that I include it here (fig. 138).

Chapter Sixteen

ARMOUR AND THE LONGBOW IN THE FOURTEENTH AND FIFTEENTH CENTURIES

THE PERIOD BETWEEN 1300 and 1500 saw the slow transition from the mediaeval to the modern world; a transition affecting the art of war as well as everything else. Perhaps the most significant single factor which brought down all the old traditions of mediaeval fighting techniques was the development of the longbow in the hands of Welsh and English peasants directed by brilliant and far-seeing leaders. The longbow was a Welsh national weapon; its potentialities were brought to the notice of Edward I by some of the extremely able soldiers who had fought on both sides during the civil wars in the 1260s. Edward, being the man he was, wholeheartedly encouraged this weapon and saw for himself how effective it could be if properly handled. The traditional enmity between England and the Scots provided arrow-fodder for the Welsh bow in the experimenting hands of English archers. At Falkirk in 1298 the battle was won by Edward's masterly use of a combined force of Welsh bowmen and mounted men-at-arms. A quarter of a century later, at the slaughterous battles of Dupplin (1332) and Halidon Hill (1333), the archers who so successfully mowed down the Scots were all Englishmen, and the century of the longbow's dominance was about to begin. In spite of the Auld Alliance, these battles in the north seem to have made no impression upon those responsible for military affairs in France, for when the now well-tried technique was used in a battle near Morlaix in Brittany in 1346 it seems to have taken the French completely by surprise; it did so again a few months later on the fatal field of Crecy. But the longbow's supremacy lasted only a bare century because

France in the mid-fifteenth century found an answer to it by developing cannon with as much mastery as the English had developed the longbow.

During the fifteenth century war and destruction seemed to be everywhere, and men's minds became obsessed with the thought of death. And the arts of death flourished as never before. After about 1425, the craft of the armourer and the weapon-smith reached its highest pitch. Not only was the armour they made light and easily wearable and of an admirable simplicity, it was beautiful in form. The style of armour known to-day as "Gothic", which was developed by the German armourers during the second half of the century, has been described aptly as "sculpture in steel". Almost every piece of armour made during the fifteenth century has something of the quality and the austere beauty of Chinese pottery of the Sung dynasty. The same applies to weapons, particularly to swords. Not since the Bronze Age had such lovely swords been produced as were made between 1420 and 1480.

Much scholarly and very detailed work has been published during the last twenty-five years concerning the armour of the fourteenth and fifteenth centuries, and much of the actual stuff of it survives. It forms in itself a separate study within the framework of the archaeology of war, and it is best dealt with (as it has been) by specialists. The best and most up-to-date work on the subject which is available at the time of writing is *European Armour*, by Claude Blair (Batsford, 1958). Earnestly recommending this book to the reader who seeks more knowledge, I shall deal very briefly with armour and concentrate on such items as swords and daggers which are my own speciality and which have been very much neglected. However, for the sake of maintaining continuity I shall (very summarily) make some mention of the armour's transition from mail to plate.

This transition took place within a very short span of time; in forty years the change-over was complete. In the middle of the thirteenth century the well-equipped warrior's armour was basically the same as that which his ancestors had worn in the first Crusade, and very little different from the armament of the Gauls in the first two centuries B.C. During the 1320s most men-at-arms still wore that sort of armour plus a coat of plates, yet in the middle '50s every

283

well-equipped warrior had a complete harness of plate except in those lands where the influence of the French war was little felt. Whatever else the reason for this rapid change may have been, it was not that the armourers had suddenly discovered how to shape thin plates of iron to the human frame. The skill was there, and it rose to the occasion when in the middle of the fourteenth century every knight between Edinburgh and Bordeaux and from Exeter to Vienna must have demanded an armour which would keep out English arrows or mitigate the fearful effects of weapons like the Swiss halberd. Between 1302 and 1346 the knight, clad in his reinforced mail, had been made mincemeat of by the despised foot-soldier from one end of Europe to the other; demand created the supply, and it may have been this sudden imperative need for plate-armour which caused a pattern which can almost be called standard to have been adopted simultaneously all over Europe. We get the impression of an armour designed for simplicity and effectiveness being produced by a master-hand and his pattern copied everywhere.

Swift as this transition seems, it was not immediate; there was a steady progression of development from about 1300 in the form of experimental reinforcing pieces being superimposed upon the traditional harness of mail. The brass of William Wenemaer (1325) at Ghent (fig. 103) shows a harness of this kind; greaves and poleyns are worn over the mail chausses, and the arms are reinforced by small roundels on the outside of the elbows; the gambeson has long sleeves, which can be seen under the loose sleeves of the hauberk.

Before the 20s of the fourteenth century the only visible reinforcements were poleyns and occasionally greaves. These had been practically standard equipment for the hoplite of ancient Greece and the cavalryman of Rome and his Gothic adversary, and had continued in common use until the ninth century. After that they do not appear again until the second quarter of the thirteenth century (unless they may have been worn under the mail chausses). Greaves are clearly shown in the Trinity College Apocalypse, which can be dated perhaps as early as about 1230, and twenty years or so later Matthew Paris showed them in his *Lives of the Two Offas*. The Maciejowski Bible shows only one pair—Goliath's—and that only because the text of the Book of Samuel demanded it. Their otherwise complete absence in any of these illustrations suggests that they were uncommon.

All these greaves are of the type known then as Demi-greaves, protecting only the shin. Early in the fourteenth century, many illustrations on monuments and small ivory carvings were made showing "closed greaves" which enclose the entire leg, being made of two plates joined on the outside by hinges and fastening with buckles and straps on the inside. We have little pictorial evidence which can be dated reliably before 1320 of the existence of greaves like this, but there is an item in an inventory I have quoted before, of the arms and effects of Raoul de Nesle, which shows that they were in fact in use before 1302: "Item, ii furbished legharnesses, with closed greaves" (*ii harnas de gaumbes fourbis, de coi les greves sont closes*). The fact that the legharness is described as furbished has been taken to indicate that it was made of metal, not leather, but it is equally likely to imply that all straps, hinges and fittings were complete and in place. One illustration which almost certainly can be dated in the late thirteenth century is the seal of the Guild of St. George at Ferrara. This seal still exists (in the British Museum) and an impression made from it is shown in plate 11b. The Saint is shown wearing closed greaves and a very clearly visible coat of plates; his helm, in contrast to his very up-to-date armour, is of the fashion of the 1250s, and he wears a cloak on his shoulders, a garment very rarely seen in mediaeval military pictures, instead of a surcoat.

During the 1320s, when we may suppose that this sort of leg-harness became popular, we find that similar plates were being worn upon the arms as well. Most of these arm-defences consisted of Couters, small convex plates covering the points of the elbows, and a sort of gutter-shaped plate covering the outside of each forearm and upper arm, while upon the shoulders were plates similar to the couters but larger. At first the plates for the forearm were called Vambraces (*avant bras*) and those for the upper arm Rerebraces (*arrière bras*), but very soon we find the whole harness for the arm is being called a vambrace. The defence for the shoulder was called Espaulier, which the English turned to Spaudler. The monument of Can Grande provides a good illustration of closed greaves, but he wears loose sleeves of mail instead of vambraces.

We have seen how extra defences for the body were in use as

285

early as the twelfth century. During the fourteenth, the coat of plates developed into a more effective defence as a separate garment worn under the surcoat. Our detailed knowledge of the construction of this defence is derived largely from the exhumation of the remains of some 2,000 warriors who fell in a battle fought on July 27, 1361, outside the walls of Visby in Gotland. The bodies were buried in great pits, and to our advantage they were put in with their armour on. This was a very unusual thing to happen, for armour was valuable and was invariably stripped carefully from the dead. It has been suggested, however, that in this case the battle was fought in very hot weather; the victorious army (of Danes, led by Waldemar IV Atterdag), pursuing the defeated Gotlanders had no wish to stop and cope with the dead, while the Gotlanders had not the opportunity. For various reasons nothing was done about clearing the battlefield for three days, by which time the hot sun had done its work for archaeology and the bodies were in a condition which made stripping impossible. Twenty-four more or less complete coats of plates were found in these burial pits, together with much other material. Many skulls were found with the mail coifs still upon them, for instance, and the appearance of some of them brings home in an unforgettable way the horrific aspect of war.

All of these twenty-four coats of plates consist of overlapping iron plates once riveted to the inside of a textile covering. Only traces of this remain on the heavily rusted surfaces of the metal but it has been possible to produce accurate reconstructions of all of them in their original form. Blair describes this construction thus:

Eighteen of the coats of plates had the same basic construction although there are differences in the arrangement of the plates. Each consisted of an oblong, poncho-like garment put on by inserting the head through a hole in the middle. The front part was lined with an arrangement of plates shaped slightly to the base of the neck and the armpits and at the bottom curving down from the hips to just below the fork. Extending from this round the back was a deep girdle, also lined with plates, which fitted over the back flap of the "poncho" and was jointed by a strap and buckle in the centre of the back. In addition the upper edge of the girdle was attached by rings to one or two laces in the centre of the back flap. On all the coats of plates the girdle and the defence for the upper chest are formed of vertical plates, the latter usually of three plates but sometimes of two or more than three. The defence for the lower chest and abdomen varies, consisting either of horizontal hoops or one or more rows of vertical plates. On one armour a shield-shaped plate was attached to the fabric over the top of each shoulder.

The various plate defences were all worn as reinforcing pieces over the traditional armour of mail, and from this seemingly clumsy hotch-potch developed the neat, all-enveloping harness of plate, closely fitting to the body and simple in construction as well as elegant in form. The parish churches of England contain very many effigies made between 1350 and 1410 which show this beautiful armour. Perhaps the best of these effigies, certainly the best-known, is the splendid figure of Edward Prince of Wales—The Black Prince —on his tomb in Canterbury Cathedral, but there are many others carved in stone of almost equal merit. I have chosen the effigy of Reginald Lord Cobham in Lingfield Church, Surrey, to illustrate this armour. Lord Cobham was one of the most famous captains of the English during the first part of the Hundred Years War (fig. 139).

There are three very striking features in this style of armour: the tall, acutely pointed helmet (of a type called "Bascinet") with its deep "aventail" of mail covering the throat, the short, tight-fitting "coat of arms" called by modern students the jupon because of its close resemblance to the civilian garment known as the jupon or gipoun, and the splendid sword-belt of goldsmiths' work round the hips.

The bascinet helmet developed during the first half of the fourteenth century from the small iron skull cap of the thirteenth. This, you will remember, was worn generally under the mail coif and below the helm. In the early fourteenth century it grew more conical in shape like the old Norman helmet. The crown of the great helm became taller as well, to accommodate the cap beneath

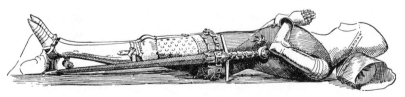

Fig. 139. Effigy of Reginald, 1st Lord Cobham (1361), Lingfield, Surrey.

287

it, though quite early in the century the helm seems to have been relegated to the tilt-yard, seldom being used in war. Thus the bascinet became the sole defence for the head; the sides and back were increased in depth, and instead of the coif being worn below it, a heavy curtain of very fine-linked mail—the aventail—was fastened to the lower rim, covering the chin and throat and falling over the shoulders and upper chest, to which it was sometimes tied with laces. At the same time a movable visor was fitted to the face opening. This took many forms; in Italy and Germany, for instance, a metal nose-piece shaped (like the nose on the Sutton Hoo helmet) to fit over that organ was fastened to the aventail and could be brought up over the face and fastened to the brow of the helmet by a staple. This appears to be an unsatisfactory defence but it was nevertheless very popular. In Germany (it seems) a better arrangement was devised. A complete visor drawn out in front to an acutely pointed snout, with two slots for vision and one below the snout like a mouth (which gave the whole thing the look of a grotesque face), was fastened on a hinge to the brow of the bascinet; it is generally known to-day as a klappvisier. Sometimes this fitting, together with the visor, was made in such a way that it could be removed altogether and carried separately, only being put on again when fighting was imminent.

At about the same time an even more satisfactory form was evolved. The visor itself was shaped like the one just described, only the sides were carried farther back, overlapping the front edges of the bascinet; at the top they swept back farther still to engage by a hinge and pin fastening to a pivot on either side of the head. A perfect example, about 1380, may be seen in the Tower of London. This has its original aventail, and the decorated borders of latten are still in place. Plate 14a shows a similar one in the Wallace Collection.

The gipoun or jupon was the descendant of the loose surcoat, which during the transitional period of the first half of the fourteenth century had become shorter. After about 1355 it had shrunk to the very neat pattern of the civilian tunic, its only variations being that in some cases the lower hem was straight, in others more or less elaborately vandyked or dagged; and that sometimes it had long loose sleeves to the wrist, sometimes short ones ending above the elbow. It was, however, more often made sleeveless. It was usually fastened down the side, though some were buttoned down the front; and some laced down the back or down the front. The jupon which used to hang above the Black Prince's tomb in Canterbury Cathedral is fastened in this way; this lacing may be clearly seen in the newly-made replica of this garment which now hangs in its place.

The hip-belt was an elaborate and splendid piece of jewellery, generally fashioned from a series of brooch-like plaques (usually square in shape), each fastened to its neighbour by a hinge at the sides. In the centre of each plaque a raised boss, either square or circular, contained a shield of arms or a crest or a decorative motif in enamel or engraved silver-gilt. In most cases the central bosses were supported at each corner by a leaf-shaped or trefoil mount. These belts were fastened by a buckle or a hook fixed at the back of a larger plaque or by an ordinary buckle with the free end of the belt looped over and hanging down in front. The sword was suspended either from small straps fitted behind the plaques over the left hip, fastening to a fitting at the back of the locket at the top of the scabbard, or by a large hook engaging into a ring similarly placed. Until recently I had one such fitting in my possession (plate 13a). The hook is fitted to a pair of plaques, identical with the main belt plaques but diminishing in size, which hang vertically. This particular one is of copper gilt; the photograph clearly shows the hook and the method of construction, with the hinges which fastened the main (upper) plaque to its neighbours on either side. What it does not show is the wear in the curve of the hook caused by the friction of the ring on the scabbard mount.

This type of belt continued in use until well on into the fifteenth century, though as a rule after about 1410 the sword hangs from a separate belt worn diagonally over the hips, the great jewelled belt being worn for ornament. The hanger described is of a distinctively fourteenth-century pattern, yet the silver-gilt insets in the central bosses are fifteenth-century replacements. These are of a style very popular as ornament on dagger-hilts (particularly those of a type called "Cinquedea" which will be described later) taking the form of minute roundels, copies of "Gothic" architectural tracery.

The dagger was suspended by a lace looped over the belt in the manner used in the early part of the century, as seen in an effigy at Ash-by-Sandwich, and clearly shown in the effigy of Lord Cobham and countless others.

From the simple "international" style of plate armour all the subsequent forms and fashions developed. Early in the fifteenth century the jupon was discarded, and the warrior appeared in an "all-white" harness of shining metal. In this connection it should be noted that during the fourteenth century it was not uncommon for the legharness and vambraces to be covered in fabric, and occasionally these and the bascinet were painted black, but after about 1410 the "alwyte" armour appears to have been fashionable. Elaboration of the armour began to be noticeable after the 1420s when the small fan-shaped extensions on the outer sides of poleyns and couters were enlarged. After about 1420 the old international pattern diverged into two distinct styles, one German in origin and the other Italian. The German armourers began to decorate their products with radiating patterns of ridges embossed on the surface, though at the first this was confined to breast and backplates. A curious characteristic of this German armour of the second quarter of the century was the "Kastenbrust", a breastplate with its lower part distorted into the shape of a rectangular box. After about 1450 the characteristically long, slender lines of the so-called "Gothic" style emerged, and the patterns of radiating lines extended to the cuishes, vambraces and spaudlers.

In Italy rounded forms were favoured all through the century; these armours retained something of the fourteenth century style, never having any of the over-elaboration of so many of the German Gothic armours. Only the very large fan-plates of poleyns and couters, and the large "pauldrons" which superseded the smaller spaudlers, encroached upon the simplicity of an outline almost as austere as the earlier international pattern. Various reinforcements were added, an extra plate on the lower part of the breastplate (called a Plackart) and very large plates which could be attached to the left couter and the left pauldron. Early in the sixteenth century the Italian and German styles merged, when the flutings of the German fashion were added to the robust rounded forms of the Italian. The resulting style has become known as "Maximilian" armour.

After about 1420 the pointed bascinet gave place to several types of helmet. One of its successors was a very neat, close-fitting helmet known to-day as an Armet, which seems to have evolved in Italy. It completely covered head and face with plates, and when one is seen closed up it is hard to see how it was put on. The dia-

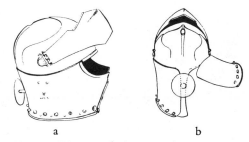

Fig. 140. Diagram of Armet: Milanese, c. 1440. a. showing visor and right aperture; b. from the rear, showing one cheek-plate raised.

gram in fig. 140 shows how this was done; the two cheek-pieces, each extending from the middle of the chin across the cheeks to the nape of the neck are hinged horizontally above the ears. After the helmet was put on, the plates were closed up and fastened by a pin in front of the chin; the short visor, shaped like the beak of a bull-finch and hinged at the sides like the old snouted visor, covered the small aperture left in front of the nose and eyes.

Another development of the bascinet is now known as the Barbuta. The term was in use in the fifteenth century, but there is no evidence that it was applied to this particular type of helmet. There is no visor, the sides of the helmet being brought right round in front of the face, leaving a T-shaped opening like ancient Greek helmets of the Corinthian pattern. Many of these Italian *barbute* had face openings of a shape exactly similar to these ancient exemplars, and though modern students are reluctant to see any connection between the development in the 1440s of this form of helmet, and the great interest which was beginning to be taken at the same time in the newly discovered vase-painting and statuary of Greece, I believe there must be a link (cf. fig. 23 with plate 14c).

The Sallet was a distinctive helmet which was used throughout Europe. It was probably a modification of the old kettle-hat (which was still very much in use) and an elegant head-piece it was, with its graceful lines sweeping out to its tail (plate 14d). It could be worn simply as a hat, the brim coming down low enough to protect the face, but it was more commonly worn with a separate Bevor to cover the chin and throat. The German sallet developed an extremely long tail, sometimes made flexible by the interposition

Fig. 141. Sallet, Italian style.

of three or four narrow lames riveted at the sides like the articulations in a lobster between the skull and the end of the tail. The Italian form was rounder, with a shorter tail and the face opening cut well up and back (fig. 141). This form is not unlike some of the Gaulish helmets of the La Tène period which were found in Italy. In England and the Dukedom of Burgundy another distinctive style was in use, with a crown considerably taller than either the German or Italian styles, often drawn out to a little stalk at the top. A particularly good example is preserved in St. Mary's Hall in Coventry, where it has probably been since the late fifteenth century (fig. 142).

These sallets were often covered with fabric or leather, and some were painted with heraldic devices. A well-known drawing by Albrecht Dürer (dated 1498) shows a man-at-arms wearing a long-tailed visored sallet covered with pale brown leather upon which are the initials W.A.; the visor is uncovered. There are several Italian sallets with their fabric covering (generally velvet) still in place, though many of these coverings are later replacements. Examples painted with arms are in the Wallace Collection in London and the Kunsthistorisches Museum in Vienna. These helmets were fitted to the head in the same manner as the old kettle-hat and the modern tin hat, by a chinstrap fastened to the lining. The head was still protected by the bunched-up hair worn under a padded arming cap; sometimes an additional padding was added to protect the chin from chafing by the bevor. These paddings are shown on many effigies in Germany; to the uninitiated beholder they give the impression that the deceased must have suffered from chronic toothache.

The fashion of wearing the armour completely uncovered lasted only for a short time, for a new form of coat armour was becoming popular, particularly in Italy, during the 1420s. Like the

Fig. 142. Sallet, c. 1460, English or Burgundian style (St. Mary's Hall, Coventry).

292

iupon, it was a very short garment made like a poncho, generally worn hanging loosely over the shoulders, though sometimes its front half was fastened by a waist-belt while the back hung free. This was the Tabard, and has given its name to the only piece of knightly war-harness surviving to-day in an almost unchanged form. Sometimes it was a simple garment with the lower hemlines cut straight, though often the sides and lower hems of both front and back were most elaborately dagged and vandyked. A good example of the former pattern can be seen in Pisanello's painting of St. George and St. Anthony in the National Gallery in London, and of the latter in the great battle pieces by Paolo Ucello, one in the National Gallery in London and the other two in the Louvre and the Ufizzi Gallery in Florence respectively.

The English longbow, which probably hastened the development of plate armour, was no new weapon when it played havoc with the Scots, nor was it in its origins English. The kind of bow which had been used for instance at Senlac had been known from prehistoric times, and as we have seen, some of the bows found in the Danish bogs had staves nearly 6 ft. long. These, however, were not true longbows unless they were drawn to the ear and not to the breast. In England, as all over the Continent, the "short" bow was thought to be of little account; in the Assize of Arms of Henry II in 1181 it was not mentioned at all. The missile weapon *par excellence* of the twelfth and thirteenth centuries was the crossbow, a portable form of the old Roman Balista, just as the hand gun, and later the arquebus and musket, were portable versions of cannon. Richard I was a great admirer of this weapon, and John maintained great numbers of crossbowmen, both horse and foot, among the mercenaries who were such a curse to England. Their unhappy memory is perpetuated in a clause in Magna Carta: "Alien soldiers, arbalestiers ('Balistarios') and Sergeants, who come with horse and arms to the detriment of the realm." Faukes de Bréauté, the captain of John's crossbowmen, is one of the most prominent figures in the civil war of 1215–17.

It is impossible to trace the actual origin of the longbow, but there is good evidence to show that it was much in use in South Wales during the second half of the twelfth century. Giraldus Cambrensis speaks repeatedly of the men of Gwent and Morganwg as excelling all others in the practice of archery; he gives evidence, too, of the effects of their shooting. At the siege of Abergavenny in 1182 the Welsh arrows penetrated an oak door four inches thick. They were allowed to remain there as a curiosity, and Gerald himself saw them six years later in 1188 when he passed the castle, with the iron points just showing on the inner side of the door. A knight of William de Braose was hit by one which went through the skirt of his hauberk, his mail hose, his thigh, and then through the leather and wood of his saddle into his horse; when he swerved round, another arrow pinned him the same way by the other leg. "What more could a bolt from a balista have done?" asks Gerald. Describing the bows of Gwent he says: "They are made neither of horn, ash nor yew, but of elm; ugly, unfinished-looking weapons, but astonishingly stiff, large and strong, and equally capable of use for long or short shooting."

These were the bows, in the hands of South Welsh bowmen, which were used in the Norman invasion of Ireland in 1171. Gerald tells how the first contingent, under Robert Fitz Stephen, sailed for Ireland with ninety mailed men-at-arms and 300 foot archers "of the flower of the young men of Wales". In the last detachment to go over under Richard de Clare ("Strongbow") were 200 horsemen and 1,000 foot who were recruited as he marched along the coast road from Chepstow. This combination of mounted men-at-arms and archers was irresistible. Gerald noted its effectiveness; so, too, a century later, did Edward I in his Welsh wars—for twice the spearmen of Snowdonia went down before archers (from Gwent) laced with horse, at Orewin Bridge and near Conway, just as the Scottish spearmen fell before a similar combination at Falkirk in 1298. Edward III's captains perfected the technique by dismounting the men-at-arms, and using the mixed force entirely as infantry holding well-chosen positions in the triumphant Scottish campaigns of 1332–33, at Dupplin and Halidon Hill.

But before all this happened, a landmark in the history of archery was reached in Henry III's Assize of Arms of 1251. After ordering that the richer yeomanry who own a hundred shillings in land should come to the host with steel cap, gambeson, lance and sword, that document commands that "all who own more than forty or less than 100 shillings in land come bearing a sword and a bow with arrows and a dagger". Similarly citizens with chattels worth more than nine marks and less than twenty are to be armed with bow, arrows and sword. There is a special clause at the end of the paragraph providing that even poor men with less than forty shillings in land and nine marks in chattels should bring bow and arrows if they have them instead of the "*falces, gisarmas et alia arma minuta*" which are spoken of as their usual weapons.

In spite of this, during the Barons' War of 1264–65 we find the crossbow still predominates. The only mention of archery is in a description [1] of an attack made on King Henry's marching columns in the Weald by De Montfort's Welsh auxiliaries, but there is a case (not mentioned by any chronicler) showing that archers could be raised in good numbers and at short notice in a region remote from the Welsh border.

After the Royalist victory at Evesham in 1265, scattered relics of the Barons' party made headway against the King in some places. Among these trouble-spots was Essex and the region of the Cinque Ports; the king sent out an expedition against them under Roger de Leyburn. A writ issued in May 1266 orders Leyburn to raise 500 archers in the Weald to add to other troops assigned to him. In this writ from the Exchequer Accounts, these archers are called *Wallenses, Waldenses et alii* (Welsh, foresters and others), which strengthens the rather obvious theory that all woodland regions were particularly proficient in bowmanship.

More evidence of this is to be found in another Exchequer Account of 1266–67; at Nottingham Castle Reginald de Grey commanded a mixed force of two knights with their attendant troopers, twenty mounted crossbowmen and a captain, ten foot crossbowmen and twenty archers; the knights served for 263 days, the other for 436, *ad debelland inimicos domini regis*, which enemy could be no other than more of the outlawed Baronial party, who were being hunted down in the forest. There were two considerable engagements, one in the heart of Sherwood itself. One of the more sober accounts of Robin Hood makes him a Montfortian, and it is interesting to find a force serving for a very long time and including some royal archers

[1] Wykes of Osney, 1264, §5.

based on Nottingham and operating in his own territory—and suffering losses at the hands of the outlaws too.

Sixty years later we find another landmark in the history of the longbow, for poachers and outlaws in Sherwood were offered a pardon on condition that they served in the king's army as archers. This was not simply a general or meaningless pardon either; the offence for which each man was pardoned is specified, clear indication of the value put upon them. These criminals (like their descendants in Wellington's armies in the Peninsular War) amply vindicated England's fighting capacity by gaining a notable victory at Halidon Hill.

It fell to Edward III to reap the full harvest of English bowmanship, but his grandfather planted and fostered the seed. Even before his first Welsh war of 1277 we find him taking an interest in the Welsh bow; in 1277 a special force of 100 picked men of Macclesfield, in the king's own lands, were purely archers unmixed with spearmen, and they served from the first day of the war to the last, whereas the other infantry came up only for short periods, and they earned the then extraordinary wage of 3*d.* a day. The only other purely bow-armed corps of this war came from Gwent and Crickhowell, and that, too, served for a longer time than usual.

Such were the beginnings of the rise of the English infantry to be a power in war. It remained for Edward I in his later campaigns and for his grandson Edward III to get the English to become expert in the use of the longbow by practice, and to learn to act as disciplined corps; yet even after Dupplin and Halidon Hill, the English had no military reputation whatever. Jehan le Bel is quite explicit in showing that their triumph at Crecy came as a complete surprise to the whole of continental Europe.

The weapon itself was simple, eminently suitable for use by a peasant militia, for it had no complications of mechanism (like the crossbow) and no professional drill was needed. The English archer of the fourteenth century probably had about as little drill—apart from practice at the butts—as the Boer farmer had in 1899, but he took as kindly to his weapon as the Boer did to his rifle.

The whole power of the bow depended upon its being a true longbow, drawn to the ear. The bowman stands sideways to his enemy, and the act of loading and the act of aiming are practically one motion. A maximum of energy is obtained when, standing sideways and bringing hand and eye into play, he makes his maximum reach from outstretched left hand to right hand below right ear. Back, shoulders and arms are used, and weight as well as strength are put into the bow.

Its effectiveness was based upon length of range, accuracy of aim, rapidity of discharge, power of penetration—and of course, the disciplined action of trained men shooting together. As for its range, we may remember how Shakespeare's Old Double, upon whom John of Gaunt betted much money, could shoot an aimed arrow 240 yards and a flight arrow 280 or 290, but a good professional archer of Edward III's time would have been able to beat that up to the traditional 400 yards, for Shakespeare's facts were taken from contemporary practice when the art of archery was in decline. It is well known that Henry VIII would allow no practice range to be less than 220 yards. As for rapidity of discharge, the longbow may be compared as a modern rifle to a flint-lock musket; a longbowman could shoot five aimed shafts a minute while the crossbowman was shooting one. We have already seen something of its penetrating power in a period long before its full development.

The arrows used during its great period were tipped with little steel "piles" no broader than the shafts upon which they were set, small heads about 1 in. long, of a section about $\frac{3}{8}$ in. square at its largest part, fitted to the shaft by a short socket. Against this tiny head and the enormous "muzzle velocity" behind it, mail, for obvious reasons, was no protection. Plate armour, on the other hand, was; hence very probably a good reason for its rapid universal development, after Crécy had at last convinced Europe that the English bowman was a new power to be reckoned with. Plenty of evidence is found in the chronicles of the French wars that if men armed completely in plate advanced against English bowmen without their too-vulnerable horses, they would stand at least some chance of coming to handstrokes. If we imagine a body of knights armoured in the manner of Lord Cobham's effigy, plodding with bent heads into the storm of arrows, it is easy to see that however powerfully the arrows struck the hard, smooth curved surfaces of the armour they would glance off unless they found lodgement where plate overlapped plate; there were no exposed joints except for the weak spots at the shoulders where the spaudlers met the armholes of the breastplate.

However, if the arrows did not penetrate the armour their effect was much as if they did, for the presence of archers in the field compelled their enemies to advance on foot. Though plate armour is not much heavier than mail, and is most flexibly jointed, it is not meant for walking in. The necessity of having to trudge a mile or more, often uphill over ploughed land (as at Agincourt in 1415) or through long grass and scrub (as at Mauron in 1352 and Poitiers in 1356) and to fight at the end of it, was nearly as devastating to the French armies as having their horses shot down under them. It is noticeable that in all the English victories during the Hundred Years War it was always the French who attacked, and trudged up hills in their armour; the English quietly stood about waiting in strong positions and were perfectly fresh when the exhausted Frenchmen came to grips with them.

In addition to these disadvantages, whoever had to face the shafts of the English had to suffer the extremely bewildering and nerve-racking effect of the deadly things hissing and humming past them, smacking on their armour and ricochetting off it. Few soldiers have had to face arrows and musket-balls at the same time, but the evidence of those who have (in India)[1] is conclusive that the arrows were far more demoralizing than the balls.

While the longbow is about the simplest piece of mechanism imaginable, consisting only of a bowstave and a string, the crossbow was in itself far more elaborate and demanded many complexities to draw the string. It is a small and portable version of the Balista which the Romans used rather in the manner of a light field gun; there is the bow itself, made of horn, many thin strips of which were glued together, or, in its later forms in the fifteenth century, of steel. The string was a thick multiple cord made of many strands of twine twisted or plaited together; the bow was fitted to the end of a stock made usually of wood, and when drawn back the string was caught and held by a cylindrical winder-pin with a notch to take the string. This winder-pin revolved in a slot in the stock, and to release the string a trigger caused the pin to revolve, releasing the tensed string from the notch (fig. 143). The early crossbows were

[1] *Sepoy to Subadar*, edit. Col. Norgate.

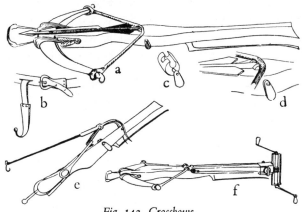

Fig. 143. Crossbows.

a. *Charged and ready to shoot.*
b. *Belt-hook, late fourteenth century.*
c. *Winder-pin.*
d. *Detail of cord held in winder-pin.*
e. *Goats-foot lever, French, c. 1480.*
f. *Windlass, German, c. 1450.*

"charged" either by the arbalestier holding the string in both hands and putting his foot in the stirrup-like loop of iron set in the end of the stock and drawing the bow down (fig. 144), or by doing the same thing with the string held by a strong hook fastened to the front of the belt. The later bows, which were generally heavier and had a more powerful bow, needed actual mechanism to draw them. One device was worked on a ratchet principle, wound up with a long handle; another was worked like a windlass, with two cranked handles pulling a double hook which engaged in the bow-string fastened to cords working on pulleys. A simpler device was a lever-and-fulcrum called a "goats-foot" which performed the same function as the ratchet or the windlass in a quicker and easier way, but which was probably not suitable for use with such powerful bows.

With all this paraphernalia to fit on to the weapon and then wind up before

Fig. 144. *A simple way of charging a light crossbow. From the fifteenth-century MS. of Georgi de Topusko, Cathedral Treasury of Zagreb, No. 354, p. lxxxxvi.*

each shot, it is easy to see why the longbowman could get five shots off with ease while the arbalestier was firing one; it is clear enough, too, that to be really effective, bodies of arbalestiers had to be well trained in the essential drill which such complicated methods of loading would demand.

Chapter Seventeen

SWORDS AND DAGGERS IN THE FOURTEENTH AND FIFTEENTH CENTURIES

WHEN ARMOUR CHANGED from mail to plate, developments in the purpose and shape of sword-blades had to be devised to match it. Against a rigid and smooth surface of armour the old style of light, flat cutting blade must have been practically useless, for its heaviest blows would glance off, while a thrust would just cause it to bend and slide away without penetrating. So at about the middle of the fourteenth century the fashion of sword-blades changed as radically as the fashion in armour.

During the latter part of the thirteenth century a type of blade whose chief purpose was to thrust had come into use. It was acutely pointed, and being made with a strong central rib and a four-sided section (like the swords of the middle Bronze Age and the Roman cavalry swords of the type found in the Nydam bog) was very stiff and rigid. Several swords of this kind exist which by their form could belong to the period 1250–1300, but unfortunately they could equally well be of the period 1350–1400 (fig. 145). There is evidence enough that such swords were used in the thirteenth century; there are many in manuscript illustrations, and one of our well-known English effigies shows one of them clearly. This is the figure of William Longespée the younger, the son of the famous Earl of Salisbury who was the half-brother of Richard I and John. He was killed in the battle at Mansourah during St. Louis' fatal

Fig. 145. Wallace Collection No. 4, c. 1270–1350.

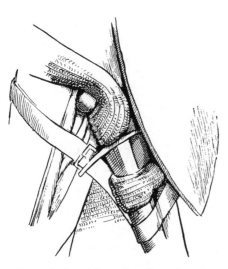

Fig. 146. Sword from the effigy of William Longespée the Younger (died 1250), (Salisbury Cathedral).

crusade in Egypt in 1250, and his monument lies in the north aisle of the Nave of Salisbury Cathedral; he is in the act of sheathing his sword; a couple of inches of its blade protrude from the scabbard mouth, clearly showing its four-sided centrally ridged section (fig. 146). An episode related by the Sieur de Joinville which happened to him during this battle at Mansourah gives an instance of a sword whose function was to thrust. During the battle he got cut off from his companions in the street fighting; a Saracen charged at him with a lance from the side, and struck him in the back, "and hunched me over the neck of my horse, and held me so squeezed up that I could not draw my sword, which I had at my belt; so I contrived to draw the sword which was on my horse, and when he saw that I had my sword drawn he pulled away his lance and released me." Then de Joinville turned his horse and rode against the Saracen, "using my sword in the manner of a lance" and killed him.

There are illustrations contemporary with the period when these memoirs were written (in 1309, in de Joinville's old age) showing knights charging with their swords held like lances, with the pommel tucked up against the shoulder.

During the transitional period between 1320–50, when more and more pieces of reinforcing plate were being added to the old harness of mail, blades of a transitional type were developed too, though the old blunt-ended cutting blades were still popular. These transitional forms combine the acute, rigid points capable of effective thrusting with the wide, flat, fullered section in the old manner. The style is well demonstrated by two identical swords, one in the Danish National Museum in Copenhagen (plate 16a), and the other in the

302

Historisches Museum in Berne. After 1350, when the complete harness of plate was universal, blades became instruments designed almost entirely for thrusting; they were quite slender, but their points were even more acute and their section was stiffer, more like heavy and sharp-pointed bars of steel capable (as Froissart relates in at least two instances) of piercing right through plate armour.

During the second quarter of the fifteenth century swords seem to have reverted to the dual function of cut and thrust. A type of blade which appears early in this century gives an admirable all-purpose sword, much lighter than the massive late fourteenth-century thrusting swords (about $2\frac{1}{2}$ to 3 lb. as against 4 to 5 lb.) with very sharp points but of sufficient breadth at the centre of percussion, and a flat enough section, to provide perfect cutting edges. This blade, with minor variations of breadth and taper, was used extensively throughout the fifteenth century and remained popular until the eighteenth.

During the middle years of the fifteenth century blades akin to the old cutting styles came into fashion again—indeed, we find them in Italy and Spain on the one hand and Scotland, Scandinavia and Hungary on the other throughout the fourteenth century as well. In Germany after about 1450 the broad blades of the thirteenth-century Type XIII came back into favour. Many swords of the second half of the century are in fact old blades of this type re-mounted in fashionable hilts.

One may ask why a type of blade which was inherently ineffective against rigid armour came back into use at the very time when plate armour had come to its highest perfection. There are two possible answers. One is that perhaps this very perfection caused fewer and fewer ordinary men-at-arms to wear complete harness, for as it became finer, it became more and more expensive, and so beyond the reach of all but the wealthiest. The other is that in Spain and Italy, perhaps on account of the climate, complete plate armour was far less generally worn than elsewhere, and in Scotland it was used by comparatively few noblemen; the average Scot could not afford it and would probably have scorned to wear it anyway. The same argument perhaps applies to the Scandinavian countries and to Hungary. Even in England, France and Germany the tendency was more and more to use comparatively lightly-armoured troops whose defences consisted simply of a sallet or a kettle-hat, a mail coif, a garment like the old coat of plates but now called a Brigandine (or in England a Jack) or a mail shirt, mail sleeves and sometimes legharness, either complete or consisting only of poleyns with large lames above and below to afford a little extra protection for the front of thigh and calf. A cutting sword would be effective against such troops, particularly if they were dismounted and the sword was wielded by a mounted man-at-arms.

So during the last two mediaeval centuries there were really only four basic sword-types, though the great variety of swords shown in illustrations gives the impression that there were many more; this is perhaps because there were some new pommel and cross-guard styles, and many decorative variations were added to these and to the old ones. During the fifteenth century sword hilts began to be furnished with extra guards; in its last quarter many swords from Spain and Italy (where the additions were most popular) had hilts which foreshadowed the complexities of guard and counter-guard so typical of late sixteenth-century swords. These developments will be treated apart from the four sword-types and their complementary pommel and cross styles.

Before going on to discuss these, there are two complete and splendid swords of the early fourteenth century which must be described. The first is in the Cathedral Treasury at Toledo (plate 17a); the arms on its pommel (Leon quartering an unidentified coat) suggest a royal origin.[1] It is a sword of Type XII, with a pommel of Type I and a cross of Style 2. Both pommel and cross are of silver-gilt, and the grip is bound with a twisted strand of silver wire. Its principal interest, however, is in its well-preserved scabbard. This is unlike those of Sancho IV of Castile and Fernando de la Cerda, for it is covered with red velvet and has a totally different mode of suspension. There are silver-gilt lockets placed at intervals along the length of the scabbard as well as the chape at its point. Each locket bears an enamelled shield with the owner's arms, and the second one from the mouth of the scabbard (slightly larger than the others) has a ring on either side, one a little higher than the other. To one of

[1] The same arms are on the seal of a son of Alfonso X, Don Juan of Tasifa, killed in battle in 1319; the sword may be his.

these rings are attached two small metal tabs to which the remains of straps are fixed.[1] This method of suspension came in during the second decade of the fourteenth century; it seems to have been rare in N.W. Europe until the 1320s, although one of the early English brasses (Sir Robert de Septvans, at Chartham in Kent, 1307) shows an early transitional form. This is particularly interesting, for the buckle-flap of the belt is fastened directly to the upper locket, if it is not made in one with it, but the belt proper is

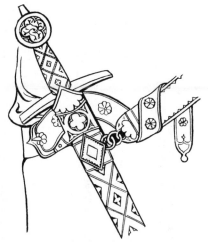

Fig. 147. Sword from the brass of Sir Robert de Septvans (1306) showing transitional belt-fitting.

fixed to a lower separate locket by three interlocking rings (fig. 147: compare this with the almost contemporary brass to Sir Robert de Bures, fig. 94). The effigy of Maurice, Lord Berkeley (about 1310) in St. Mary's Church, Bristol, gives another example. Italian paintings (far too numerous to mention individually) of the period 1310–40 give us many more.

The arms on this sword in Toledo and the silver-mark on the scabbard mounts are interesting but hard to place. The arms are: quarterly, argent a lion rampant purpure: argent, an eagle displayed gules. The dark purple lion on the white ground is the coat of Leon, as used before the fifteenth century, when the colours were changed to black and gold, while the red eagle on the white ground may have a connection with Ferdinand III of Castile's abortive claim to the Empire in the middle of the thirteenth century. The Empire's arms were, of course, of different colours (black on gold), but the arms were sometimes used in different colours by those who considered they had a claim to a kinship with the Empire.

The silver-mark of two crossed keys surmounting a star has a strong Papal flavour; Gregory XII used the same mark, only

---

[1] These straps have been wrongly replaced; there should be one on each side-ring of the locket, not two together on one ring.

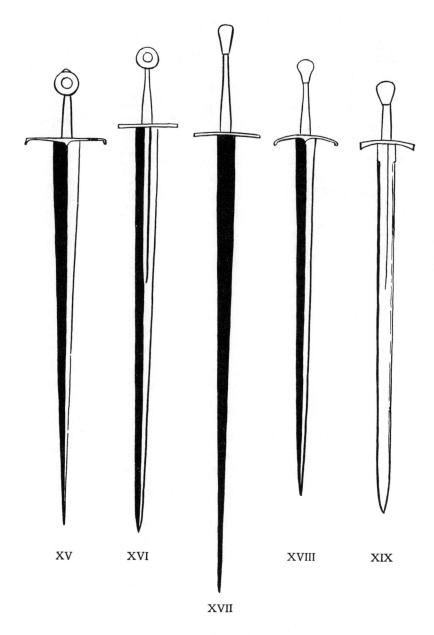

XV   XVI   XVIII   XIX

XVII

Fig. 148. Sword types, 1300–1500.

with the star above the keys, on his coinage early in the fifteenth century.

The second of the actual swords with this kind of scabbard-mounting gives us an exact date. It was found in the coffin of Can Grande della Scala when his tomb in Verona was opened in 1921 and may be seen in the Archaeological Museum in that city (plate 17b). Can Grande died in 1329, so the sword which was put into his coffin must date before that. It has a hilt of plain iron and a grip bound with plain silver wire over which is a cord of yellow silk running criss-cross up the grip; a small knot secures each crossing. This diaper-pattern binding has disappeared in the middle part of the grip where the hand of Della Scala rested. The scabbard is covered with red velvet; it has three mounts of silvered copper—a chape with a little decorative button on the end and a shield-shaped opening in each side, an an upper and lower locket. These lockets are engraved with floral designs; the upper one has a ring on either side, one higher up than the other, and the lower has one ring only on the edge of the scabbard which would be uppermost when being worn. To each of these rings is fastened a loose ring holding a disc-shaped terminal for the narrow straps which attached the scabbard to the sword-belt. This belt, of leather, is wound round the scabbard, and there are two small strap-ends with silver mounts.

Five sword-types of the fourteenth and fifteenth centuries follow directly on from those of the twelfth and thirteenth (fig. 148). Type XV seems first to have appeared in the second half of the thirteenth century. There are a few surviving specimens which may be of this period (No. 4 in the Wallace Collection, fig. 145, is a case in point), though on internal evidence alone it is quite impossible to date them accurately to any time between about 1250 and almost 1400. There is, however, a very similar example (also in London) which by an accident of preservation can be dated with some certainty between about 1310 and 1340; it was found in the Thames when the foundations were being prepared in 1739 for Westminster Bridge, and is now preserved in the London Museum. Evidently it fell into the river in its scabbard, which was of the same kind as Can Grande's, so that when it was fetched out the three silver mounts were still upon its blade. These are of exactly the same type as on the sword of Della Scala and that on the Berkeley effigy at

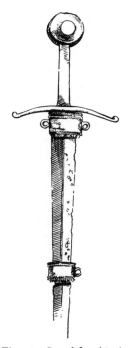

Fig. 149. Sword found in the Thames at Westminster, with identical marks on blade and pommel, c. 1325 (London Museum).

Bristol. The upper locket of this sword is engraved with a scroll bearing the cryptic words "Wilr I, Wilr I" and a heraldic crest—a stag's head. This sword is so similar to No. 4 in the Wallace Collection that it is reasonable to date that also early in the fourteenth century or before (fig. 149).

Many swords of this type have long grips, like the war-swords of Type XIII. After about 1350 nine swords out of ten seem to have such grips, and are to-day variously referred to as "Hand-and-a-half" or "Bastard" swords. The latter term was used in the fifteenth century, but it is not certain that it was applied to this particular kind of weapon. "Hand-and-a-half", though modern, is a name far more apt for it; these swords were single-handed weapons, but by being furnished with long grips, could at need be wielded easily in both.

It is tempting to pigeon-hole the short-gripped swords of this type into the earlier part of the period and the hand-and-a-half ones into the later, but it will not do, for at least one sword in ten up to 1400 had a short grip.

There is a group of swords representing the type in its middle period; they were found in various parts of Europe and all look exactly alike. One from the Thames is in London,[1] another from northern France is also in London in a private collection; one from Lake Constance in Italy used to be in the famous collection of Sir Edward Barry[2]; there is another from France in the Musée de l'Armée in Paris, and another used to be in a celebrated German collection, and finally in the magnificent collection of Mr. C. O. von Kienbusch in New York is one originally from Italy; it bears

[1] In the collection of the Society of Antiquaries.
[2] Illustrated in Laking, Vol. I, fig. 172, and in other publications.

on its blade an Arabic inscription stating that it is a trophy deposited in the Hall of Victories at the Arsenal of Alexandria in the early fifteenth century.

All these are hand-and-a-half swords, with grips about 7 in. long, sharply tapering blades of four-sided section about 32 in. long, straight crosses tapering towards the tips, which are abruptly turned downwards and large pommels of Type J. There are, however, swords like this which are smaller, single-handed weapons with grips of no more than 5 in. One, in the Boissonas collection in Geneva, except for its shorter blade and grip is identical with the big one in Paris; and in the Victoria and Albert Museum in London is one found in Yorkshire which is a smaller counterpart of the one from the Thames.

On English effigies of the second half of the fourteenth century are many such swords; the best (and the best known) is at the Black Prince's side on his tomb at Canterbury; one almost identical is on the effigy of Lord Cobham (fig. 139). In these effigies the cross is nearly always shown as a straight or slightly curved bar of square section, possibly because to portray the rather delicate down-turned tips would be difficult and over-fragile in stone.

The type seems to have gone out of favour for a time in the early fifteenth century, but after about 1440 it became extremely popular again in its earliest form, particularly in Italy. In paintings dating between about 1440 and 1510 swords of this type are frequently shown, all characterized by having short grips and short blades very broad at the hilt and tapering evenly to an acute point, with a well-marked central ridge; their blade section differs from the early examples by being either stouter, with a very strong ridge flanked by very deeply hollowed faces, or by a ridge rising abruptly from nearly flat faces (fig. 150).

Type XVI is really a compromise between Types XIV and XV, for the upper half of the blade retains the old flat fullered section while the lower half (the business end of the sword) is four-sided and acutely-pointed. The sword in Copenhagen (plate 16a) which

Fig. 150. Blade sections of swords of Types XV and XVIII.

I mentioned earlier is an excellent example of this blade form. This particular sword (and its counterpart in Berne) is generally dated in the second half of the fourteenth century, but I believe both rightly belong in its first half. The blade of the Copenhagen sword bears an inscription consisting of five widely-spaced letters (+NnDIC+) which by its style is unlikely to be later than 1350. There is no doubt that these transitional swords are extremely difficult to date, for some of their blades are closely akin to the thirteenth-century Types XII and XIII, though as a rule they are more slender and their fullers are narrower and shorter. Occasionally their points are thickened and reinforced (like the points of many Indian Tulwars and Katahs) to make them more effective in thrusting, and nearly always their hilts are long, like the Black Prince's. One of the best of these transitional swords is illustrated in plate 16b. This is in the British Museum (it was found in London), but unhappily it is now almost unrecognizable since it was a victim to one of the German incendiary bombs which fell on the Museum in 1940. The photograph was taken when it was still in first-class condition; even now one can see how well the London soil preserved it, for its fiery experience only twisted it into an S shape; its almost unrusted surface remains as it was, its smooth black patina changed to a harsh raw red by the flames. It is akin to a group of Scandinavian swords of the same type[1]; these all have "bow tie" crosses of Style 5, but the London one's cross has clubbed ends similar to those on two well-known English effigies of the early fourteenth century, Prince John of Eltham (died 1334) in Westminster Abbey and Sir John de Ifield (c. 1330) in the church at Ifield, Sussex. There is another fine sword of this type in Copenhagen with a short straight cross (Style 2) whose ends are shaped as little beasts' heads very similar to those of the Gicelin sword described in Chapter Fourteen.

Illustrations of these slender transitional swords are to be seen in very many Italian paintings of the early fourteenth century, particularly those of Lippo Memmi and Barna di Siena. There is one very clearly and accurately drawn in a "maesta" by Lippo Memmi (in the Town Hall at San Gemigniano), which was painted in 1317

[1] One of these retains its original leather-covered grip and its "chappe" of tooled leather; this and one other are in the Danish National Museum, while a third is in Oslo.

Fig. 151. St. Paul's sword, from a "maesta" by Lippo Memmi (1317).

(fig. 151). This is held, unsheathed, by St. Paul. An identical sword, found in Switzerland, was in the Boissonas collection at Geneva; were it not for its point-by-point identity with the painted sword dated 1317, one would hesitate to date it earlier than about 1370. There is another which has a blade identical with the Memmi St. Paul's, but a slightly different cross, in Mr. Kienbusch's collection in New York. Another picture by the same artist (also at San Gemigniano) of about the same date shows a sheathed sword of this type with a belt-fitting like the one on the scabbard of the unidentified sword in Toledo Cathedral.

Type XVII (plate 16d) was perhaps the sword most in use during the period 1370–1425. Its section is usually hexagonal and very solid with sometimes a very shallow fuller in its upper half. Many survive; perhaps the finest of them all is one which was found in the River Cam, preserved now in the Fitzwilliam Museum in Cambridge (plate 16c). Swords of this type all have the same blade-form, but considerably varied hilts, and examples have been found all over Europe. One which comes second only to the Cambridge example, with a similar blade but a totally different hilt (both of these hilts will be more fully described when I deal with pommel types and cross-guard styles), is in a famous and very choice private collection in Denmark.[1] This is one which was put in the Hall of Victories at Alexandria, presumably as a trophy.

There are many such trophies, swords of Italian fashion and of fourteenth-century types, with Arabic inscriptions applied to their blades after being deposited in this Arsenal by the Mamluk Sultans of Egypt. Some were probably acquired as gifts from merchants or embassies from Genoa, Pisa or Venice, but others are undoubtedly the spoils of war, captured from Christian forces based on Cyprus. In 1365 one such force (under Peter of Lusignan, titular King of Jerusalem) made an attack upon Cairo. It was beaten off, and several swords bear witness to Peter's

[1] That of Mr. E. A. Christensen of Copenhagen.

defeat. Mr. Kienbusch has one, and Mr. Christensen another; these swords are identical twins; both have very broad Type XIII blades, "bow tie" crosses of Style 5, and pommels made of latten in an unusual form of Type K, with the central bosses very narrow and upstanding like nipples. Both are dated 1368–69, clearly spoil from the defeated Italian force of 1365—and equally clearly they were old swords, being of a type not likely to have been made later than about 1310—an example of the old flat cutting blade being popular in Southern Europe all through the fourteenth century.

In 1426 the Mamluk Sultan Malik el Asraf Barsabay in his turn raided Cyprus, carrying off a number of swords which were duly inscribed, often more than ten years after their capture. Most of the surviving swords are from this time, being dated in the 1430s. Occasionally an actual date (in one instance A.H. 836 = A.D. 1432) was stamped upon them, but more often they bear simply a statement that they are the inalienable property of the Arsenal of Alexandria together with the name of the Emir in charge of it at the time. As these persons held the office only for very brief spells, it is usually possible to date the inscriptions quite accurately by the name.

The sword I was speaking of, belonging to Mr. Christensen in Copenhagen, is one of those later ones, loot from the 1426 raid on Cyprus. Giving a normal life-span of half a century, this dates the sword between 1380–1425. Another very similar sword in the same collection (plate 16d) has the same sort of pommel but a cross of Style 6, identical with the cross of the late twelfth-century "Sword of St. Maurice" in Turin (plate 9b). A noticeable feature of these swords is their great weight and clumsiness. The proportions of this one, which was in my possession for many years, are admirable; one would expect to find that it was easy to handle, but it was always something of a shock to pick it up and feel the blade so heavy in relation to the hilt; there was no feeling of balance. Of course, no mediaeval sword was balanced like a foil, a certain amount of "blade-heaviness" was essential to its function; but in these Type XVII weapons this seems excessive; as I said, they are like solid, sharp-pointed bars of steel.

The best dating-point for the type is the sword found in the tomb (in the Abbey of Konigsfeld in Switzerland) of Fredericks von Tarant, an Austrian knight who fell in the battle of Sempach in 1386.

Type XVIII is a general all-purpose sword which varies a good deal in the shape of its blade's outline as well as in its hilt styles. A typical example is the sword preserved in the Muniment Room at Westminster Abbey, a weapon which may with good reason be connected with the "warlike gear" of Henry V (plate 16e). Its blade is quite light and very flat, but though it has excellent edges and plenty of width at its centre of percussion it has a stiff mid-rib and an acute point, the extreme tip of which is reinforced; in fact the lower part of this blade is shaped like those of the cut-and-thrust swords of the Bronze Age (compare plate 16e with fig. 16 for instance) and perfectly expresses its efficacy for the same dual purpose.

This type of blade was used extensively all through the fifteenth century, some being broad like Henry V's[1] and others much narrower. Most of them had a four-sided section showing a definite mid-rib and slightly concave faces to each of the four sides, but after about 1450 many of them had sharply defined ribs and flat faces, similar to the later blades of Type XV (see fig. 150).

Many of them have built-up shoulders like those of some fourth- and fifth-century blades (see fig. 39), a fact which causes confusion in dating them, since similar blades were made, always with shoulders, in the seventeenth century, whereas in the fifteenth shoulders were rather unusual. It is sometimes hard, too, to distinguish blades of this type from those of Type XV, for the exigencies of wear tend to narrow the taper of the broader, curving edges of Type XVIII into a straight line in the style of Type XV. A sword (No. 8) in the Wallace Collection is a case in point; it may be of Type XV, as its blade shape suggests, but it is more probable that it is an XVIII which has been subjected to a great deal of sharpening.

Swords of Type XIX are rare. Its characteristics are edges which taper very slightly to a rounded point, a thick, flat section with strongly bevelled edges making six sides to it, a short narrow fuller and, in a few cases, a feature which in the late sixteenth century came

[1] A very fine one of great breadth bears an Alexandrian inscription and the date 1419. This is in the Metropolitan Museum in New York.

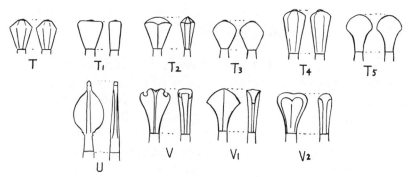

Fig. 152. Pommel types, 1350–1500.

to be called a *ricasso*, a term which has been used ever since to describe a thickened portion of a blade immediately below the hilt. Examples of the type are found as early as 1360 (one of the Alexandrian swords dated 1368–69 is of this type, with a ricasso), but most mediaeval ones come within the fifteenth century. As a type it is far more typical of the sixteenth and seventeenth centuries, and were it not for the conclusive evidence of the Arabic inscriptions on two of them, it would be inevitable that a sword having a mediaeval hilt allied to a Type XIX blade would be judged to be either a dud or an unholy marriage of an old genuine hilt to a much later blade. One of the finest of them is now in the Tower of London; its blade is clearly dated A.H. 836 = A.D. 1432, and its inscription tells that it is part of Sultan Barsabay's loot from his Cyprus expedition of 1426 (plate 20a).

Many of the pommels in use between 1350–1500 are variations of the old disc forms (Types G to K), but a few of them are so distinctive that they should be classified as separate styles in the following brief comment upon the pommels of this period. Late in the fourteenth century three totally new types emerged, and with these and the variations on the old ones, we shall close this sketched survey of mediaeval sword types.

Fig. 152 shows the three new types.

Type T. Sometimes referred to as "fig-shaped" but more aptly it has been called "the scent-stopper" style. First appearing on monuments and in illustrations in about 1360, early forms of it are found on swords dating before 1350—for example that sword in

Copenhagen illustrated in plate 16a and described on p. 310, its double in Berne and a sword in the Wallace Collection (No. 10) of Type XVII. There are several variants: T.1 is its earliest form; T.2 a development most used after about 1360, though there is a much earlier example of it in a picture of St. Francis taking leave of the army which was painted by Simone Martini in about 1340. The effigy of Gunther von Schwarzburg (1368) in the Liebfrauenkirche at Arnstadt gives a very clear example (fig. 153). The pommel of that exceedingly lovely sword at Cambridge (see p. 311) is identical and the pommels of the Sempach knights Frederiks von

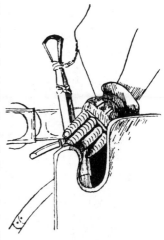

Fig. 153. Effigy of Gunther von Schwarzburg, Arnstadt (1368), with pommel of Type T.2.

Tarant and Freiderich von Griffenstein (1386) are similar.

T.3 is a form to be seen on many English brasses dating between about 1390 and 1420 (it seems to have been much used in Italy as well) and T.4 is an elongated version of it also appearing often on English

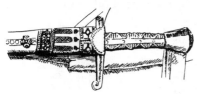

Fig. 154. Effigy of Sir John Wyard, Meriden, Warwickshire (1411), pommel of Type T.4.

monuments (fig. 154). There are some French examples (fig. 155) and some in Germany, but it does not seem to have found much favour in Italy. There is a fine sword (from the Thames near London Bridge), now in the Tower of London, of Type XVII with one of these pommels. Its blade, incidentally, has a ricasso about 6 in. long, the purpose of which seems to have been to allow the left hand of the man wielding it to be brought forward to grasp the blade below the hilt so that the

Fig. 155. Sword of Pierre de Navarre, Count of Evreux, from a window in Evreux Cathedral, c. 1390, with pommel of Type T.4.

315

sword can be "shortened" in close fighting on foot. Similar flattened lengths, with squared-off edges, are to be seen on some other fifteenth-century blades.

T.5 is a pear-shaped pommel, a style very popular in Germany and Spain and, judging by its frequent appearance on English brasses, in this country as well (fig. 156). It remained popular in Germany up to the middle of the sixteenth century.

Type U. This is shaped a little like a key, and the few specimens surviving and its none-too-frequent appearance on monuments suggest that it was a style fashionable in south Germany and perhaps Burgundy.

Fig. 156. From the brass of John Peyrent (1415), Digswell, Herts., with pommel of Type T.5.

There are two beautiful swords in the Swiss National Museum in Zurich (fig. 157) which are preserved in a complete and unblemished condition, another excavated one in the same collection, a couple of good ones in Munich, and one or two shown on south German monuments dating between perhaps 1470 and 1490. One of the best illustrations of such a pommel is in a picture by Hugo van der Goes, at present loaned by Her Majesty the Queen to the National Gallery of Scotland (fig. 158). It is part of a diptych painted probably in 1478–79 for the altar in Trinity College church, and depicts the Queen of Scotland (Margaret of Denmark, wife of James III) and her patron saint, generally believed to be St. Knut, who stands behind her in full armour of mid-fifteenth century Milanese fashion.

Type V. Generally described as "fish-tailed", this pommel is more often seen in illustration than upon

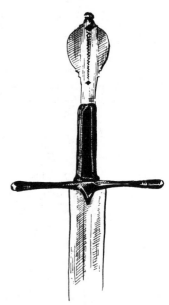

Fig. 157. Sword, S. German, with pommel of Type U (Landesmuseum, Zurich).

actual swords. Three particularly good English effigies in alabaster show it: Reginald, 3rd Lord Cobham (died 1446), in the church at Lingfield in Surrey; an unidentified knight at Porlock in Somerset (about 1440) and a monument to William Phillipp, Lord Berdolf, who died in 1441, in Dennington Church, Suffolk. The drawing of Richard Beauchamp, Earl of Warwick ("The King-Maker") in one copy of the celebrated Warwick Roll about 1480

Fig. 158. Sword hilt from the figure of St. Knut (from the right wing of the Trinity College Altarpiece: collection of Her Majesty the Queen).

shows one (fig. 159) and there is another in a picture by Hans Memling in the National Gallery in London, "The Virgin and St. George", painted about 1470. Yet another is on the effigy of Ulrich von Hohenrechburg (ob. 1458) at Donzdorf, Wurttemberg.

I know of only five actual examples; the best of these—indeed one of the loveliest swords surviving from this period of beautiful weapons—is in the Wallace Collection (No. 36, fig. 160). Its graceful pommel grows like a flower out of the grip of black horn which is shaped to blend with it; the cross is short and straight with knobbed ends, and both it and the pommel are of bronze gilded. The blade, a slender variant of Type XVIII, is as fresh and clean as when it was in use—altogether a most glorious sword. A similar one is in the

Fig. 159. Sword of the Earl of Warwick, from the "Warwick Roll", c. 1480. Pommel of Type V.

317

Fig. 160. Sword. Flemish, about 1450, pommel of Type V (Wallace Collection, No. 36).

Musée de Cluny in Paris, a fine, well-preserved weapon but of proportions inferior to the Wallace Collection example, though both share the same unusual form of shaped grip of horn. Another is in the Ameria Real at Madrid attributed to the ownership of Charles V, though it seems to be of a type earlier than that monarch's time. It is unlike the Wallace Collection one in every respect save its similar pommel; it has a long hand-and-a-half grip, long slender cross and a flat, fullered blade of Type XIII. A sword of similar proportions is in the National Museum in Zurich. The fifth example, a splendid specimen in a very well-preserved state, with a long stout blade of Type XVIII and a beautifully proportioned hilt of gilded iron hangs on the wall beside me as I write. Its provenance is unfortunately not known, though its condition strongly suggests preservation in a church, for though its blade has not suffered more than superficial rusting, it has clearly not been cleaned or cared for as, for example, the similar weapon in the Wallace Collection. Its hilt (plate 19c) is one of the handsomest of the five specimens; the proportions are good and the ends of the cross are shaped to match the graceful curves on the top of the pommel. The original tooled leather (once crimson, now nearly black) of the grip survives.

The Wallace Collection and Cluny swords are always described as being Italian, but I believe the whole group is more likely Flemish or Burgundian. No such pommel form seems to appear in Italian paintings of the fifteenth century—there are a few, by Gentile di Fabriano particularly, which have a superficial resemblance, but are in fact a separate type which I classify as Type V.1 and will describe presently. On the other hand Flemish paintings show several, and there are the English and German examples. During the greater part of the fifteenth century England's ties with Burgundy were very close; we have seen how a distinctive style of sallet seems to have been typical of English and Burgundian fashion; the evidence seems to point to the pommels of Type V being the same.

318

Type V.1 is exemplified by several paintings by Gentile di Fabriano (mostly dating about 1420–35) and a magnificent sword, world famous now for its distinguished record as a collector's gem; this sword made a modest start when the great Bernal collection came under the hammer in 1855, when it was bought for £6 6s. by the Earl of Londesborough. Then in 1921, when it was in the famous Morgan Williams collection, it was bought by Lord Duveen for £3,697 10s. That purchase took it to the United States, where recently it came to rest in one of the most distinguished private collections of our time, that of Mr. C. O. von Kienbusch of New York (plate 19d.). There can be little doubt that it is Italian; its hilt is so similar to those which Fabriano painted, and its fine blade-smith's mark is distinctively Italian, but even more so is the etched decoration on its blade, carried out in a manner reminiscent of the work of Ercole de Fideli of Ferrara. Part of this decoration looks remarkably like a Tudor rose, a fact which has caused much speculation and many hopeful (but I believe quite inappropriate) attempts to attribute it to the ownership of English personages. This sword as a whole is a perfect example of the latest form of Type XV; its date may be anything between 1450 and 1510; its shape alone makes it possible to be as early as 1450, but its etched decoration suggests a time thirty or forty years later. The grip is interesting too; it is always described as being a modern replacement, but (although I have never seen the sword) I believe it may well be contemporary, for it was in place when it was sold in the Bernal Sale as long ago as 1855 [1]; though the business of "improving" old swords or making really clever forgeries had made some progress at this date, most of the convincing fakes date after the 1870s. It seems most unlikely to me that before 1855 anyone would have bothered to make so correct a reproduction of a fifteenth-century grip with its elaborate diaper-pattern cord binding over red velvet.

Another magnificent sword with a pommel of Type V.1, happily still in England, is among the Corporation regalia of the City of Bristol; known as the "pearl" sword, it has a beautiful hilt of silver-gilt, and it is known to have been given to the City by Sir John de

[1] It is described in the catalogue of that sale as: "Lot 2305: A Large Fighting Sword, with broad blade tapering to a point, the grip covered with old velvet and cording, with heavy pommel. The blade is engraved with trophies, etc. Lord Londesborough: £6. 6. 0."

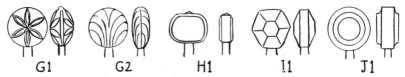
Fig. 161. Disc pommel types, 1350–1500.

Welles in 1431, and so affords a much earlier example of the pommel type than the sword in New York.

There is another variation of Type V, which is known only in a very few examples, but is worth classifying as V.2. The hilt of a sword which once was given by Edward IV to the City of Coventry has one; this sword had a chequered career. Because Coventry sided with the Lancastrian rebels in 1470, Edward took the sword away from the city after his victories at Barnet and Tewkesbury in 1471; it was never seen again until its hilt turned up on a rubbish heap about fifty years ago! The cross and pommel are of latten, once gilt, delicately engraved with the Yorkist motif of roses alternating with Edward IV's personal emblem of the Sun in Splendour. On either face of the pommel is a small circular plaque, one enamelled with the arms of Coventry and the other with those of England. The so-called "Steel" sword of the City of Hereford, made in about 1450, has a similar pommel.

Perhaps the best illustration of the type is from the Beaufort tomb in the chapel of St. Michael in Canterbury Cathedral. Here, one on either side of Margaret Holland (who died in 1439), lie the effigies in alabaster of her two husbands: John Beaufort, Earl of Somerset (died 1410), and Thomas, Duke of Clarence, Henry V's brother, who was slain at the battle of Beaugé (one of the few unsuccessful battles of Henry V's part of the Hundred Years War, when an English force was caught without its proper complement of supporting archers) in 1421. The figures of both men are identical, and their sword pommels are of this rather rare Type V.2, with the tops elaborated, more than the plain V.1s, but not so much as the Vs, so that the pommel is shaped very much like a heart.

The variations on the disc pommel are almost infinite in detail and ornament, but five bye-forms emerge which were not used during earlier periods, so I have arranged these as five separate groups (fig. 161), as follows:

Type G.1. A distinctively Italian variation on the eleventh-century disc form; its faces are rounded and convex, so much so that sometimes it looks more like a rather flattened globe than a blown-out disc. Each face bears an elaborate carved design like a flower with four or six petals made up in a strictly geometrical way by the intersection of arcs. Plate 19 a shows the hilt of a fine sword with a particularly good example of this sort of pommel. It is very similar in shape (the sword as a whole, I mean) to the one I have just described of Type XV in New York, but it is an altogether smaller weapon. As you can see, it is splendidly preserved, obviously never having been allowed to go uncared for since it ceased to be used. Much of the original blueing remains on the iron of the hilt, while the original grip of wood covered with red velvet bound with crossed-over strands of plain steel and twisted silver wire bears upon it the marks of long and hard wear. This, too, I have the happiness of possessing.

The use of this bye-form of the disc pommel seems to have been confined to Italy during the second half of the fifteenth century; another, G.2, is as distinctive and also typically Italian. Here the convex faces of the disc are decorated with radiating flutings, like a cockle-shell (plate 21a).

Type H.1. This first appeared about 1350, and seems to have gone out of favour early in the fifteenth century. It is always very flat, with very shallow chamfered edges, sometimes flat, sometimes deeply hollowed, and is always oval. An effigy over the tomb of another Gunther von Schwarzburg in Frankfurt Cathedral (this one, a predecessor of the Gunther I spoke of earlier, died in 1349) gives an early illustration of this type (fig. 162), while actual specimens are very plentiful. A sword I used to have (plate 15d) has an excellent example of it.

Type I.1. This is really an elaboration of the common "wheel" form, its plain circular shape modified to a hexagonal or an octagonal outline; there are many examples, one of which may be said to provide the earliest certain date of its appearance, for it was found in the Cathedral at Trier, in the tomb of the

Fig. 162. Sword hilt from the effigy of Gunther von Schwarzburg at Frankfurt (1349). Pommel of Type H.1.

Fig. 163. From the effigy of Bishop Johannes von Eglof-stein, in Wurzburg Cathedral (1411). Pommel of Type I.1.

Emperor Albrecht I who died in 1308. We find similar pommels on many German effigies, perhaps the best being in the hand of the figure of a Bishop of Wurzburg, Johannes von Eglofstein who died in 1411, (fig. 163). Many appear on English brasses between about 1360 and 1425; most surviving examples are of either bronze or latten.

Type J.1. The best example of this pommel type is on the sword of Henry V in Westminster Abbey (plate 16e and fig. 164). This is a very large pommel and looks as though it would be excessively heavy, yet it is not. When in 1950 the librarian and Keeper of the Muniments at the abbey allowed me to clean this sword, I found that the deep raised rims or flanges upon each face of the pommel were beaten out of a very thin plate of iron, one brazed to each face of the

solid central disc. This explains the comparative lightness of the pommel and the most excellent "feel" of the sword in one's hand. This pommel (and the cross guard as well) are thickly gilded, and when I was cleaning the gold in the hollows of the pommel's centre, I uncovered a cross painted in red pigment directly upon the gold beneath; there was no trace of any white pigment, so it does not seem to have been a St. George's cross, but simply a symbol. This seems never before to have been noticed.[1]

A similar pommel of solid bronze

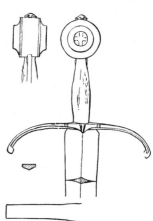

Fig. 164. The hilt of the "Sword of Henry V", West-minster Abbey Library. Pommel of Type J.1, cross of Style 9.

[1] *The Connoisseur*, 1951: "A Royal Sword in Westminster Abbey," R. E. Oakeshott.

is in the University Museum of Archaeology in Cambridge, on a sword of about
1420) found in the River Cam at Southery.
Many English brasses of the period 1410–
1430 show pommels identical with these
examples, and illustrations of it occur in
France and Italy during the first half of the
fifteenth century.

If the pommel types of the fourteenth
and fifteenth centuries are mostly no more
than elaborated versions of the old ones,
the same is even more the case with cross-
guard styles. There is such a bewildering
variety of them after about 1440 that it is
almost impossible to sort out any new basic

*Fig. 165. From the brass of
Richard Fox, 1430 (Arkesden
Church, Essex). Pommel of
Type J.1, cross of Style 9.*

styles into groups. There are, however, three varieties which are set
out in fig. 166; but as you can see there is little real difference
between them and their forerunners.

Style 8. This is a modification of Style 4, a good example of which
in its early form is the GICELIN sword shown on plate 6c. In the
middle of the fourteenth century its section was elaborated and its
central part—known during the sixteenth and subsequent centuries
as the "écusson"—was enlarged and drawn out over the blade in a
small cusped point. The arms of this style taper more sharply than
the earlier ones and their section is rhomboidal as a rule though
sometimes it is circular. The swords of Type XV which I referred
to (p. 308) as a group are fitted with crosses of this style, but apart
from these swords it is rarely found, though crosses of the older
version of the style were popular throughout the fifteenth
century.

Style 9. A modification of Style 7, which, though there are

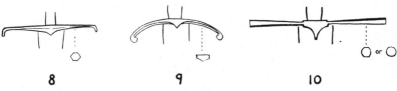

Fig. 166. Cross styles, 1350–1500.

pictured examples in the thirteenth century, seems typical of the fifteenth. The flat, ribbon-like section, with its long axis set at right-angles to the plane of the blade, is sometimes chamfered on its lower side giving it two sloping faces; each end is always turned over in a little roll, and the écusson is built up and cusped. A good example of this style is the Henry V sword. The diagrammatic drawing of its hilt in fig. 164 gives a clear picture of the shape and section of its cross. The drawing of a sword from the Rutland Psalter of about 1250 (fig. 115 on p. 234) shows one like this, even to the cusped écusson which was rarely used at this date, but no actual examples are known dating before the fifteenth century—but then, no example earlier than the fourteenth century of a cross style like the one on the Shaftesbury Gicelin sword was known until 1958, so one cannot be dogmatic about the exact place in archaeology of the Henry V cross style.

Style 10 is characterized by long and slender arms and a prominent cusped écusson. The section is rhomboidal, octagonal or circular; sometimes the tips are knobbed, and the cross can be either straight or curved. A good example is shown on plate 19a. The sword from the Cam at Southery has a similar, though stouter, cross.

The purpose of these large cusped écussons was to fit, when the sword was sheathed, into a similarly shaped recess on either side of the upper scabbard locket (generally made of metal after about 1350) to prevent rain and damp from getting at the blade. The old method of doing this by prolonging the lips of the scabbard mouth upward to enclose the middle portion of the cross was still in use up to about 1440, though it became increasingly rare after 1400.

For the rest of the cross-guard styles in use up to about 1520 we can only refer to the earlier styles of the twelfth century to the fourteenth. Most of them were in use, generally with the addition of a cusped écusson and sometimes with decorated tips. The splendid Italian sword of Mr. Kienbusch's, for instance (plate 19d), has a "bow-tie" cross of Style 5, but the ends are shaped to match the top of the pommel and there is a very deep pointed cusp in the middle; my own Flemish sword with the Type V pommel has a heavier cross of the same style, again with the ends shaped *en suite* with the pommel. The swords on the Beaufort tomb at the sides of the two husbands of Margaret Holland have identical crosses, but the tips are hidden, the upper by the hem of the tabard being draped over it and the lower by the ground it rests upon. This fashion of decorating the cross-ends to match the pommel only became popular durng the fifteenth century, and remained so until the mid-seventeenth.

Another decorative feature sometimes added to the crosses of Styles 5 and 6 during the fifteenth century was a thick rib running longways from tip to tip, interrupted by the écusson; it was either left plain or decorated with some kind of simple pattern; a good example is the sword of St. Knut in the diptych of Van der Goes (fig. 158). A form of decoration very common in the first half of the fifteenth century was a series of three or more radiating lines cut upon the écusson, sometimes supported by similar lines cut on the arms of the cross.

The fashion of inlaying elaborate inscriptions upon sword-blades died out late in the thirteenth century or early in the fourteenth. Inscriptions there were during the first half of the fourteenth, but they had become simpler, mostly consisting of a few widely spaced letters—the Type XVI sword in Copenhagen (plate 16a) is a case in point where five letters are inlaid on either side. While inscriptions died out, inlaid smiths' marks in the manner of the Roman Iron Age came in again and remained the chief decoration, if they can be called such, on the blades of swords, until late in the fifteenth century elaborately etched pictorial designs were introduced.

Many of these smiths' marks are similar to those of the fourth and fifth centuries A.D. and even of the period La Tène II and III. Most of them were made with a punch, being filled in with copper or latten, but some have obviously been made with a chisel. Early in the fourteenth century we find these punched marks applied to the tang inside the hilt in the old Roman manner; an excavated sword of the 1340s which came into my possession several years ago has a very fine mark stamped deeply into the root of the tang just inside the cross; it is of particular interest because it is a mark—the "Wodewose" or Wild Man of folk-lore—which was quite common two or three centuries later. Not that this is anything unusual; many of the Iron Age marks of the La Tène and Roman periods are the same as those in use up to the sixteenth century.

Blades made during the later fourteenth century, if marked at all, often bore several signs, both on the visible part of the blade and on the hidden tang; for instance, the Type XVII sword in the Fitzwilliam Museum in Cambridge has one mark—a sword or dagger—inlaid in latten a few inches below the hilt and another—a large Gothic B—punched into the tang.

Occasionally bladesmiths put their marks on the pommels of swords, which suggests that in the Middle Ages, unlike the period from 1500 or so onwards, the swordsmith made the whole job. Not always, we know, for blades were exported packed in crates and barrels just as they were later, but sometimes we find the marks of bladesmiths stamped into pommels. The sword found in the Thames during the building of Westminster Bridge (fig. 149) proves this; the blade has a smith's mark punched on it about 7 in. below the hilt; and on the pommel, in the flat central portion on one side, is the same mark made by the same punch. There are several late thirteenth- and fourteenth-century swords with marks on their pommels which are duplicated on other blades, and during the second quarter of the fifteenth it seems to have been a custom (particularly in Italy) to stamp pommels with several different marks. Some of these are deeply-punched shield-shaped impressions with nothing in them; they were stamped like this by the smiths, blank, so that customers could have their own arms inset into the space in enamel or painted glass.[1] A mid-fourteenth-century example of a similar tiny shield stamped upon a pommel is in a sword found in the River Gué in France, but this has a charge in it.

Most of the pommels marked thus in the fifteenth century, either with shields alone or combinations of marks, have been of those forms of the "scent-stopper" types of pommel most favoured in Italy. A good example with a blank shield which is an exception is a sword in the Wallace Collection in London which I have already referred to (p. 235). This has a pommel of the pear-shaped variety, Type T.5, which seems to have been most popular in Germany.

This business of marked pommels is made very confusing by

[1] At Monza is the sword of a Visconti, killed while besieging that city in the 1430s. In its pommel (T.5) is a stamped recess containing a silver plate with his arms.

the fact that there are innumerable pommels, mostly of sixteenth-and seventeenth-century types but with many fifteenth-century ones among them, which are stamped all over with marks which have nothing at all to do with swordsmithing. They have been used as weights on shopkeepers' balances between the mid-sixteenth and late eighteenth centuries, and the marks are those of the butchers and bakers and candlestick makers who adapted them for their own use. To make matters worse, many such pommels have been fitted with guards and blades and made into swords again in recent times, swords of which all the parts may be genuine, but which are not particularly desirable all the same. The few existing fifteenth-century swords with these marked pommels, which have never been taken apart and are entirely genuine, have to pass unusually severe tests before they can be accepted as original and un-tampered with. One such is a sword (plate 20b) in my own collection which will be described later, for the matter I should be dealing with has been side-tracked: smiths' marks and blade inscriptions.

During the middle years of the fifteenth century, it seems that the use of invocative phrases inlaid in blades came into fashion again, though far fewer swords bore them in comparison with the numbers made in the twelfth and thirteenth centuries. A favourite phrase seldom used before was *O Mater Dei Memento Mei*. A very fine sword, of Spanish or Italian origin, which was sold in London in 1929 out of the last collection of the Baron de Cosson has an inscription in Gothic letters; on one side *Ave Maria Gracia Plena Domini* and on the other *Autem transiens per medium illum*. Added to the blade of this sword was the mark of the Arsenal at Constantinople, showing that it was taken by the Turks, perhaps at the time of the fall of Constantinople in 1453.

One of the swords captured by the Mamluks during Malik al Asraf Barsabay's raid on Cyrpus in 1426 has a small ring growing from the underside of one arm of its cross, and its blade has a ricasso (plate 20a). It is time to say something more about this feature and about the additional guards with which many swords were furnished during the fifteenth century.

We have seen how in the Bronze Age men gripped their swords with the forefinger over the swelling "shoulders" where hilt and blade meet. Swords have been gripped thus ever since, except in the

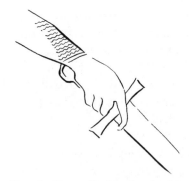

few cases where the shape of hilt or blade makes it impossible to get the forefinger over the cross with its first joint tucked into the angle where the cross and blade-edge meet. The chief purpose of the ricasso was to provide a flat and thickened edge for the finger to press upon.

In the British Museum there is a silver bowl made in Persia during the Sassanian period (about A.D. 600) showing a monarch on horseback hunting lions with a sword. This sword, incidentally, is perfectly straight—all early oriental swords were straight; the curved "scimitar" is based on the eastern European sabres, such as those found in Hungary like the Charlemagne sword in Vienna, and we cannot be sure that it was used in the Middle East until the eleventh of twelfth century and in India until the fourteenth or fifteenth. This Sassanian monarch, with his straight, knightly-looking sword with a "bow-tie" cross of Style 5, is going after his lion with his forefinger over the cross (fig. 167) in a manner similar to that of the ninth-century Frankish warrior in the manuscript of St. Gall who I have illustrated in fig. 77. All through the Middle Ages swords are

Fig. 167. From a Persian silver bowl in the British Museum, Sassanian, fifth century A.D.

shown being held thus, unless the wielder is wearing fingerless mail "mufflers" which were the usual form of armoured glove until late in the thirteenth century. Actual examples of very early swords with ricassos exist, though they are rare; a very good one is a Type XII sword of about 1200 in the collection of Mr. Harold L. Peterson in Arlington, Virginia, U.S.A. (fig. 168). This has a prominent and well-shaped ricasso, and there can be no doubt of the sword's genuineness (it was excavated) and early date.

So we return to the little ring below the

Fig. 168. Early thirteenth-century sword with ricasso (coll. Mr. H. Peterson, Arlington, Virginia).

cross, clearly a logical development of a protection for the forefinger. This particular sword, you will remember, is dated 1436, spoil of Barsabay's raid of ten years before. It is the earliest example to survive (as far as we know) of such a guard, though they appear with increasing frequency in pictures after about 1435—there is a clear example, for instance, in a St. Martin, painted by the Marti de Torres master in 1443, in the Valencia Museum.

Later in the century the ring is duplicated and we get the feature generally known today as the "Pas d'Ane", a term whose origin is as obscure as its meaning. The Portuguese painter Nuno Gonçalves shows many swords so fitted in several paintings dated in the 1460s, and in Italian paintings after 1470 they are innumerable.

Fig. 169. a. Sword from a Spanish MS. (1422–33); b. Sword from Konrad Kyeser's "Bellefortis" MS. (1402–05), Göttingen State University Library.

A number of actual swords survive identical with those painted by Gonçalves. Two particularly fine ones are in the Armeria Real at Madrid, one which belonged to "The Great Captain" Gonsalvo de Cordoba (1453–1515), and another to Ferdinand the Catholic, King of Aragon, who also died in 1515.

At the same time as the single finger-ring appeared early in the fifteenth century a larger arc-shaped guard was sometimes fitted to the side of the cross as a protection for the back of the hand. Examples can be seen in some early fifteenth-century manuscript pictures, though in only a few cases can we be sure that this guard is what the artist really meant to show, for its position on the side of the sword makes it difficult to depict in two dimensions. A good example (dated ambiguously at either 1422 or 1433) is in a drawing from a Spanish manuscript[1] (fig. 169a) and another is from a Bohemian Bible of about 1405 (fig. 169b). There are swords in much earlier manuscripts, for example "The Romance of Alexander" in the Bodleian Library at Oxford (c. 1330) where something remarkably like an angular side-guard is shown; it seems unlikely that

[1] The Casa de Alba of Rabi More Arraguel de Guadalajara.

the artist meant it for a leather "chappe" for the blade is visible between the extra guard and the cross proper. Again, in a "Romance of Lancelot du Lac" (early fourteenth century), we see the same thing in a picture I have reproduced in fig. 85 on p. 198. In an even earlier Spanish manuscript, the "Cantigas" of Alfonso the Wise (about 1275), there is a sword where a thickening of the middle portion of its cross covers part of the back of its wielder's hand—here is a case where it is so hard to tell whether this is indeed a side-ring or a slip of the artist's brush. In this case I believe it is no slip; for one thing the standard of the drawing is high, and the better mediaeval artists were no more prone than their modern successors to do slipshod work—often indeed far less so—and for another, strong shadows are painted at either end of the thickened piece and it has a high-light in the middle. There are literary references, too, which indicate the use of this sort of guard from the fourteenth century onwards.

Actual examples are rare, but I have one. This is the sword referred to on page 327 (plate 20b). The sword is of Type XVIII with a comparatively slender blade; the pommel is of Type T.3 and the cross a curved form of Style 10. The écusson of this cross is not cusped, but is chamfered instead with a slope on each side toward the blade, clearly to allow it to fit between the upward-pointing triangular lips at the mouth of the scabbard. The grip is of a bottle-like shape characteristic of the period 1410–40 as shown on many English brasses of that period (fig. 170 a and b) and in Italian paintings—the St. George of Gentile di Fabriano mentioned earlier, and Pisanello's "St. George and St. Anthony" in the National Gallery in London, for instance. This grip (like the whole sword) is in remarkably good condition. The wooden core is bound with fine twine over which is a tight covering of thin leather, doeskin or some-

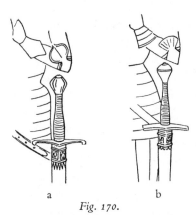

Fig. 170.

a. *from the brass of Sir W. Echyngham, Etchingham, Essex;* b. *from the brass of M. Swetenham, Blakesey, Northants.*

thing similar, which is dyed green. Where the surface has been rubbed in use by the hand of its owner, this colour is worn away. On the back of the grip just above the cross is a shallow depression caused by the constant hard pressure of his second finger as he gripped it. The forefinger was passed over the arm of the cross— the wear upon the underside of this and the shoulder of the blade below it would prove that it was held so, even if it were not obvious that with this sword it is the most satisfactory way of grasping it. And always the finger would have rubbed on only one arm of the cross and the blade below, for it would always have to be held the same way with the side-ring on the outside, the knuckle side, of the hand. On the inside of this grip the marks of the owner's finger-tips can be seen plainly, for the leather of his glove, probably dampened by the sweat of his hand—and he may, of course, have had to fight in the rain on occasions—has discoloured the green leather where his fingers pressed it.

I have described these indications of wear and usage at length because such clues are important. For ten years after I got this sword (it once belonged to Edmund Sullivan, the black-and-white artist) I believed its grip to be a restoration as it was in such good condition. It was only when, one day about fifteen years ago, I was idly waving it about that I noticed the wear on its surface at exactly the points touched by my hand. Then I saw that not only the colour was worn, but the actual surface of the leather, for the small tooled circles (which can be seen in the illustration), in spite of their being quite deeply punched into the leather, were worn away too. This led me to notice the depression below my second finger (when you hold a sword as I have described, with the forefinger over the cross, it is the second finger which presses hardest on the grip) and so to the discoloured finger marks. All this evidence of wear, such as could not possibly have been got in sixty years or so simply by the casual handling of collectors, as well as the material and form of the grip, is convincing proof of its authenticity. Similar signs of wear are on the grip of the Italian sword shown on plate 19a, though here the velvet has worn right through, and the wood below is greased and polished with wear. Similarly the grip of the Flemish sword on plate 19c is worn in the same places.

I have examined many swords with their grips in place, some old and some not. The old ones are always distinguished by these signs of wear, which cannot convincingly be added synthetically to a restoration, as well as by a quality in the leather which covers them and which is not found in recent restorations (i.e., those made in the past 100 or so years). It is extremely hard, and when polished has a translucent look, whereas restorations either look very new, or are too soft, and have often begun to crumble like the backs of old bound volumes of *Punch*.

During the second quarter of the fifteenth century the arms of cross-guards were sometimes curved horizontally in the form of an S; this practice became common later in the century. An early example is in a picture from a manuscript which until recently was in the Dyson Perrins collection, "The Hours of Elizabeth the Queene", dated 1431, and in the Cambridge University Museum of Archaeology there is a sword (from the River Cam) of Type XIX with a ricasso like the two Alexandrian ones, a tall, "scent-stopper" pommel of Type T.4, and a cross of Style 5 modified by a large, built-up écusson and slender arms bent into a graceful S. This dates from about 1430.

At the century's end these crosses were sometimes carried right round until they formed a figure 8. There is a little-known group of hand-and-a-half swords in Denmark with crosses (if we can call them such) of this figure of 8 form, but their most common use was upon the short stabbing swords used as a secondary arm by the German mercenary pikemen of the late fifteenth and early sixteenth centuries who (for some reason not apparent) called themselves Landsknechts. Plate 20d shows a good example of one of these, and a similar one is in the London Museum; this was found on the site of Scotland Yard and may be a relic of the force of Landsknechts which accompanied Charles V when he visited London in 1521—a theory strengthened by the shield of arms displaying the Imperial Eagle embossed on the grip, and by the fact that some of the Emperor's Landsknechts were quartered in that part of Westminster. It is to one of these hilts that the eighth-century pattern-welded blade is fitted, which I mentioned in Chapter 8.

About the middle of the fifteenth century it became customary to fit falchion hilts with a guard curving back over the knuckles; later, during the last quarter of the century, many swords were fitted with these guards in Italy and Spain, always in conjunction with side-rings and a "pas d'âne". A picture of St. Michael by Pinturiccio (now in Leipzig) painted between 1473 and 1481 shows a hilt with all of these guards (fig. 171), which may perhaps be regarded as the earliest representation of a hilt form which was still fashionable in the seventeenth century.

Fig. 171. From a St. Michael painted between 1473 and 1481 by Pinturiccio (Leipzig).

In Italian paintings of the late fifteenth century there are so many hilts like this, some with knuckle guards and some without, that it would be impossible to mention all of them. One illustration worth noting, however, comes not from Italy but—originally—from Portugal. It is datable from within a few years of 1475 and is in one of the great series of tapestries made to commemorate the victory of King Alfonso V of Portugal over the town of Arzila in 1471. In one of these the king wields a sword with a "pas d'âne" and two side rings, one on the cross and another smaller one joining the lower ends of the "pas d'âne". This is a very early date for such an elaborate hilt. A Spanish sword (c. 1480) with a single ring at the ends of the "pas d'âne" is shown on plate 20c.

Before leaving the swords of the fifteenth century there are odd types, regional and rare, which have to be mentioned. Until the sixteenth century and after, the Scots do not seem to have used the *Claidheamh mòr* or Great Sword, but they did have a most distinctive type of single-handed sword. One of these is shown on an engraved tomb-slab, in the deserted church of Kinkell, to Gilbert de Greenlaw, a Scottish knight killed at the battle of Harlaw in 1411 (fig. 172 and plate 18a). The pommel is of Type J, with an elongated rivet-block, and the cross is neither straight nor curved, but has its arms set at an angle of about 120 degrees downwards, the tips being expanded and flattened into a sort of spear-shape. An identical sword (plate 18b) is in the collection of Mr. Kienbusch in

Fig. 172. Engraved slab in Kinkell churchyard to Gilbert de Greenlaw, 1411.

New York. Crosses of this shape, but with the flattened ends elaborated into pierced quatrefoils, were fitted to the big "Claymores" of the next century, and in Ireland several single-handed swords with this type of cross have been found, dating from about the middle of the sixteenth century.

In the Danish National Museum at Copenhagen are several swords all of Danish provenance, which seem to constitute a definite local type. Most of them date from the middle of the fifteenth century; they are large weapons with long, rather slender blades, often with very long ricassos, acutely-arched crosses of Style 6, and excessively long grips divided into sections by a series of ridges (fig. 173) and very small pommels of the "Pear" form, Type T.5.

Fig. 173. Danish sword, mid-fifteenth century (National Museum, Copenhagen).

Another group of swords which also is almost a separate type is Italian, and numbers among its survivors some of the loveliest swords ever to be seen. Characteristic is a broad, flat blade, sometimes of Type XVIII with a mid-ribbed four-sided section, but often of a more elaborate form with two very wide and shallow fullers running the whole length with a short portion of the central rib formed by their junction flattened off just below the hilt. This always has a short, strongly-arched cross, a short, somewhat barrel-shaped grip and one of the later variants of the disc pommel. Some were big weapons but some were quite short, for ever since the early fourteenth century small stabbing or cut-and-thrust swords had been quite common. A picture painted in about 1450 by the French artist Jean Fouquet ("The Battle of Cannae") shows two such swords; the Roman leader wears one with a

Fig. 174. Figures from Jean Fouquet's " The Battle of Cannae", c. 1450.

gilded hilt and a crimson scabbard, while a spearman at his side has another with plain iron hilt in a black scabbard (fig. 174). I have one of these small ones (plate 21a) which is characteristic of the group; note how a notch is cut in the blade below the cross to accommodate the forefinger. A full size example is on the effigy of Sir Robert Harcourt, K.G. (who died in 1471), in the church at Stanton Harcourt, Oxfordshire (fig. 175).

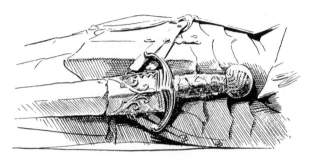

Fig. 175. Effigy of Sir Robert Harcourt (1471), Stanton Harcourt, Oxfordshire.

The finest of all of them was made for that splendidly notorious character Cesare Borgia, Duke of Romagna and Valentino, and it survives in all its splendour in the possession of the Duke of Sermoneta. Its form is purely mediaeval, austere, simple and lovely, but its decoration is as purely of the Renaissance. The hilt is decorated in delicate cloisonné enamel in translucent colours on a copper-gilt ground, set in cloisons of a filigree pattern in a kind of Venetian Gothic style. The blade is etched and gilt in the style which has come to be associated with the work of Ercole de Fideli of Ferrara. In this case the blade is actually signed OPUS HERC. The decoration consists of a pattern formed out of Cesare's monogram and four abbreviations, *Ceas. Borg. Car. Valen*, and the words *"Jacta est Alea. Cum Nomine Cesaris Omen. Fides Prevalet Armis. Bene Merent"*.

Borgia was made Cardinal Valentino in 1493, but in 1498 he was released by his father, Pope Alexander VI, from all ecclesiastical obligations so that he could the better pursue his ambitious political aims, so the sword must have been made at some time between those two dates.

The magnificent but unfinished scabbard of this sword is in the

335

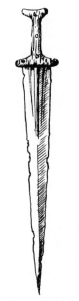

Victoria and Albert Museum. It is of leather most elaborately tooled with classical figures in high relief, but only the upper part is complete; the lower part has the design sketched upon it, but no more, and there are no metal mounts or belt attachments.

From the time of the adoption of the "international" style of armour in the third quarter of the fourteenth century the dagger became an indispensable and visible part of the man-at-arm's equipment. Every military monument shows a dagger of one sort or another (or the remains of one) at the right hip. Many civilian figures, too, are shown wearing daggers, generally of the "Basilard" type. In fourteenth-century

Fig. 176. Basilard, c. 1350 (coll. author).

Italy it seems to have been almost the only kind in use; hardly a picture painted between about 1300 and 1420 is without one visible somewhere. A popular song from Sloane MS. 2593 of Henry V's reign contains a jingle:

> Ther is no man worthe a leke,
> Bee he sturdy, be he meeke
> But hee bere a Basilard.

The weapon itself is a stout, broad-bladed and sharply tapering dagger usually between 8 and 12 in. long, though a few shown on civilian effigies are longer. The hilt, generally of wood or horn, is shaped simply like a handle (fig. 176). When in civil dress it was customary to wear the dagger at the belt in front, hanging behind a large pouch in the manner of a sporran.[1]

The Ballock dagger (plate 21b) was as popular as the basilard, also seeming to have been more favoured for wear with civil dress though there are many instances of it being worn with armour. A good example of the former is the brass of a civilian in Kings

[1] *Cultellos, quos Daggerios vulgariter dicunt, in powchiis impositis,* Knighton, under the year 1348.

Somborne Church, Hampshire, while the splendid Beaufort tomb in St. Michael's Chapel in Canterbury Cathedral, where each of the twin effigies of Margaret Holland's two husbands has one, is representative of the latter. There are many surviving examples, some of which (like a particularly handsome one in the Wallace Collection in London, No. 113) retain their scabbards, in small compartments on the outside of which one or two small auxiliary instruments (a knife if single, and a knife and an awl or pricker if double) are carried.

A dagger which was very much used in England during the second half of the fourteenth century has a short blade, generally two-edged and of flattened four-sided section, and a hilt like a little sword. Most of their pommels are of either Type I or Type J, and the majority have grips very long in proportion to the blade and very short, thick crosses. There is a very well

Fig. 177. Rondel dagger, early fifteenth century, from Thames St. (London Museum).

preserved one in Mr. Christensen's collection in Copenhagen which is different in that it has a long, slender and curved cross of Style 7 and a short grip which retains its original covering; this is ridged for the fingers in the manner of the Roman sword.

Cross-hilted daggers were used, though not so widely, all through the fifteenth century. A large and splendid example dating from about 1460 was found in Thames Street in London and is now in the London Museum. This has a curious and very distinctive pommel like a tall pointed hat and a long stout blade of four-sided section,[1] the whole weapon being reminiscent of one of the swords of Type XVIII.

During the first half of the fifteenth century the military dagger *par excellence* seems to have been the "Rondel" dagger, so called because its guard and pommel are both formed of discs set horizontally one at either end of the hilt (fig. 177).

[1] London Museum Mediaeval Catalogue, Plate VII, I. No. 33 296/1.

A type of which perhaps more examples have been found than any other is a short single-edged knife with a cross of Style 5 curved horizontally into an S and a rectangular pommel, usually with a sort of lug projecting from one side. A few examples are quite nicely made, but most are coarse and common and look just what they are—ordinary mediaeval sheath-knives.

These are the basic types of dagger used in the period 1350–1500, but there was infinite scope for individual taste. Many daggers survive, in fact and illustration, which seem to be almost unique. The hilt of one such, a lovely work of art in carved ivory, is in the Victoria and Albert Museum, and a complete one which, though its design is slightly different, is clearly from the same source, if not the same hand, is (or used to be) in the Hermitage at Leningrad. Here the scabbard and its straps for attachment to the belt survive (fig. 178).

Fig. 178. Dagger with hilt of carved ivory, Paris school, late fourteenth century (Hermitage, Leningrad).

A weapon which is always classed as a dagger, yet which has many of the attributes of a sword, stands so much on its own that it must be treated separately. Before about 1460 or 1470 it seems to have been unknown, and there are no specimens which can be said with certainty to have been made after about 1520 and it is exclusively Italian. It is always known now as the "Cinquedea" by reason of its extremely broad blade, five fingers' width at the hilt. It is sometimes called the ox-tongue dagger, "Langue de Bœuf". Its hilt was of a style previously unknown, clearly based upon ancient models in the fashion of the hilts of Greece and Mycenae; its only difference being a short and very sharply curved cross (plate 22). A distinctive feature in nearly every example is the insetting of three small, beautifully-made roundels of openwork tracery, like those in the fourteenth century belt-fitting shown in plate 13a.

Some of these weapons were quite tiny, with blades only about 6 in. long; others are a little larger (about 9 in. long), but the majority are big things, with great blades from 15 to 20 in. long and about 3½ to 4 in. wide at the hilt. A few of these very distinctive hilts were fitted to sword blades, too. One such used to be in my possession and is illustrated in plate 19b, which shows only the hilt and not the magnificent blade. A similar long sword in a Cinquedea hilt is in the Tower of London.

The blades of most of the true Cinquedeas were elaborately blued, etched and gilded; the etching upon many of them has been attributed to Ercole de Fideli of Ferrara, but there is a group which seems to have been the work of another Ferrarese artist, Ercole Grandi. Most of this group are medium-sized cinquedeas, two of which are in the Wallace Collection, and one of the best-preserved of them is now in the collection of Mr. Kienbusch in New York (plate 22a). In 1951 this weapon was unknown; it came up for sale in London and I got it for a ridiculous price—it looked too good to be genuine. However, my own opinion that it was a good one was well supported; a few years later I parted with it to a friend who gave me two very fine swords (those shown on plates 19 a and b) in exchange.

As the photograph shows, the quality of the etching is superb, and its condition is nearly perfect; the effect of the rich dark blue, tinged with purple, of the background with the gleam of the gold is very striking. The design on one side, the most important, showing a coat of arms of Colonna impaled with Malvezzi of Mantua, is a little more masterly than the other, which shows just the arms and crest of Malvezzi—a fact which leads one to suppose that though the Master did the work upon the most important face, a lesser craftsman was entrusted with the work on the other.

A feature of this cinquedea and the two similar ones in the Wallace Collection is that instead of having the typical cinquedea hilt they are furnished with ordinary sword-hilts in the same style as some of the swords in the Borgia group.

Until documentary evidence appears, it will be impossible to say for certain what quirk of fashion brought this short-lived weapon into being late in the fifteenth century; it is quite unrelated to the main stream of development of its mediaeval predecessors, and it left no trace of its passing in any of its successors. We are drawn inevitably to the conclusion that its true origin must be sought in

the rebirth of classical culture, for its hilt form is akin to no weapons other than the Greek and Etruscan swords, examples of which were being found and studied along with sculpture and vase-painting during the fifteenth century in Italy. The only other weapon like it was popular in southern Europe during the La Tène period, the last few centuries B.C. and it is very like a Cinquedea; there is one in the British Museum (fig. 179) which shows how close the kinship is between the Ancient and the late mediaeval weapon.

Fig. 179. Dagger, third century B.C., from Italy (British Museum).

In the foregoing chapters I have sketched some aspects and items of the Archaeology of Weapons, but in spite of some 130,000 words and 241 illustrations, it is still no more than a sketch. A great deal has gone into it, but far more has been left out. I have made no mention at all of the early use of cannon or the development of hand firearms in the fifteenth century, for instance, nor of fortification and siegecraft. My apology must be that the scope of archaeology is limitless, but the scope of this book or its reader's patience is not.

Any work of this kind has to be in the nature of an interim report; in a few years new discoveries will have added to our knowledge and may reverse, or at least radically alter, some of our conclusions. In producing this report I have, like anyone in a similar position, climbed upon the shoulders of many scholars in my efforts to see a little more clearly what, in the framework of history, is what. I hope that others may find stimulus in my work and will in their turn stand upon it with the telescope of fresh discovery to their eye, peering ever deeper into the distances of the past.

APPENDIX
Four Date-Charts

THE PREHISTORIC PERIOD

Date	Egypt	Biblical History	Mediterranean Countries and Asia	Western Europe
B.C. 2000	Middle Kingdom	The Age of the Patriarchs	Middle Minoan period in Crete	Late Stone Age (Neolithic) culture
	Occupation by the Hyksos invaders	Joseph in Egypt	Aryans overthrow civilization of the Indus	
1500	XVIIIth Dynasty		Empire of the Hittites	Early Bronze Age
	Period of Empire	The Exodus	Golden Age of Mycenean culture	
	XIXth Dynasty	Conquest of Canaan		
	XXth Dynasty			Stonehenge probably built
1200	Ramses III defeats invasion by "Peoples of the Sea" (Philistines)		Trojan War	Middle Bronze Age
1000	Decline of the Empire	Saul Reigns of David and Solomon		Late Bronze Age
			Start of Assyrian domination	Early Iron Age
750	Domination of Ethiopians	Conquest of Israel and Judah by Assyria	Beginning of "classical" period of Greece	"Hallstatt" culture
	Conquest by Assyria			
600			Assyria destroyed by Medes	Celtic domination of whole area

B.C.	Egypt	Judea	World Events	Archaeological Period
500	XXVIth Dynasty Revival	Captivity in Babylon	Rise to power of Babylonians / Rome becomes powerful / Persia absorbs Medes and subdues Babylonian power	Period of "La Tène I"
400			Period of Athenian dominance in Greece / Peloponessian War	The Gauls sack Rome, 390 B.C.
300	Alexander conquers Egypt		Macedonian domination under Alexander / Punic Wars between Rome and Carthage	Period of "La Tène II"
200	Dynasty of Ptolemy	Wars of the Maccabees		
100	Egypt becomes a Roman province			Period of "La Tène III" / Caesar's conquest of Gaul
1				

THE HEROIC AGE

Date	Britain	The Roman Empire	Scandinavia
0	Roman invasion begun, A.D. 47 Completed by Agricola, 78–84		
100		Conquest of Dacia by Trajan, A.D. 106 Hadrian; greatest extent of Empire Franks and Alemanni break frontiers on Rhine, 236 Goths set up revived Persian power under the Sassanids, 251	The bog-deposits of Thorsbjerg and Vimose laid down
250	Carausias declares himself Emperor, 286		
		Constantine the Great, 324–37 Goths cross Danube and settle in Moesia, 375 Battle of Adrianople, 378	The bog-deposits of Nydam laid down
400	Revolt of the Roman army, 406 Legions finally withdrawn, 410	The Vandals cross the Rhine and sweep through Gaul Alaric and his Goths sack Rome, 410	
	Increasing raids and settlements by Angles and Jutes	Vandals secure domination of North Africa, 435 Attila's invasion of Gaul; battle of Chalons, 451 Vandals sack Rome, 455	The bog-deposits of Kragehul laid down
	Period of "King Arthur" Saxons settle in Hampshire under Cerdic, 495	Clovis becomes King of Salian Franks, 476 Theodoric the Ostrogoth becomes ruler of Rome, 493	
500	Saxons defeated at battle of Mount Badon, 520	Justinian Emperor of East Roman Empire, 527	

Ida founds Saxon Kingdom of Bernicia, 547	Belisarius defeats the Vandals in North Africa, 533	
St. Augustine begins conversion of Kent, 597	Gothic War in Italy, 535–51; Italy is recovered for the Empire, 553	
	The Lombards overrun northern Italy, 560	Period of the Saga of Hrolf Kraki
	Mohammed born at Mecca, 569	
600 Reign of Edwin of Northumbria, 617–33		
700 Ida, King of Wessex, lays down first Code of Anglo-Saxon law, 688–726	The Mohammedan Saracens make conquests throughout Asia Minor and the Mediterranean and settle in Spain, 635–711	

THE VIKING PERIOD

Date	England	France	Germany and Italy	Scandinavia
750	Supremacy of Mercian Kingdom under Offa, 758–96 First Viking attack on England recorded, 787	Charlemagne becomes King of the Franks, 771	Charlemagne defeats the Lombards and is crowned King at Pavia, 774	
800	Egbert of Wessex defeats the Mercians at Ellandun, 825		Charlemagne crowned Emperor of Rome, 800 Death of Charlemagne, 814 Battle of Fontenay; the Empire is divided between the grandsons of Charlemagne, 841	Period of the Sagas of Ragnar Lodbrok (Hairy Breeks), and Ragnar Lodbrok's sons
850	The Northmen winter in the Isle of Sheppey, 855 The Danes conquer Northumbria, 867, and invade Wessex, 871 Accession of Alfred, 871	The Vikings plunder Rouen and Paris, 841–45 Great siege of Paris, 865–66		Harold Haarfagr (Fairhair) King of Norway 860–930
900	Death of Alfred, 901	The French make the Treaty of Clair-sur-Epte with the Northmen, giving them the whole Duchy of Normandy, 911	Henry the Fowler King of the Germans, 919; defeats Hungarians, 933, and Danes, 934, and unites Germany	Period of the Saga of Egil Skallagrimsson Gorm the Old, King of Denmark, 900–40
950	Athelstan defeats Scots and Northmen at Battle of Brunanburgh, 937 Reign of Edgar the Peaceful, 958–75		Otto I (the Great) becomes King, 936, and is crowned Emperor in Rome, 962	Period of Kormak's Saga

Date	England	France	Germany / Empire	Scandinavia and the North
	Accession of Ethelred II (the Redeless), 979 English defeated by Norwegian Vikings at Maldon, 991	Hugh Capet elected King of France, 987	Reign of Otto III, 983–1002	Harold Bluetooth, King of Denmark, 940
1000	Conquest of England by Danish King Sweyn, 1013 Knut the Great, King of England, 1014–35		Otto III's son, Henry II, crowned Emperor, 1014	Period of Gretti's Saga Knut the Great, 1014–35
	Accession of Edward the Confessor, 1040	Robert the Devil, Duke of Normandy, 1028–35 William becomes Duke, 1036		Eric the Red sails from Greenland and discovers America
1050	Death of Edward, accession of Harold and Conquest by Normans, 1066	The "Truce of God" is proclaimed by the Clergy throughout Europe, forbidding all fighting between Thursday evening and Monday morning		

THE AGE OF CHIVALRY

Date	England	France	Germany and Italy	Spain and the Mediterranean
1100	The Norman Kings, William I to Stephen, 1066–1154	The First Crusade, 1099–1100; capture of Jerusalem and foundation of Latin kingdom		Ruy Diaz de Bivar (The Cid) captures Valencia from the Moors, 1094
1150	The Angevins, Henry II, to John, 1154–1217 Richard I goes on Crusade	with Philippe II (Augustus)	Frederic I (Barbarossa) Emperor, 1152–90	Saladin defeats Latin kingdom at Hattin, 1187, and recaptures Jerusalem Siege of Acre, 1192
1200	John's war with the Barons Second battle of Lincoln, 1216 Accession of Henry III, 1217	John loses Normandy and other possessions in France, 1204	Frederic II ("Stupor Mundi"), 1215–50	The combined Kings of Castile, Aragon and Navarre defeat the Moors at Las Navas de Tolosa, 1212
1250	The Barons' War (Simon de Montfort) Battles of Lewes, 1264, and Evesham, 1265 Accession of Edward I, 1272 Conquest of Wales, 1277–84 War with Scotland begins, 1296	Accession of Louis IX (St. Louis), 1226 His Crusade in Egypt and defeat and capture by the Saracens at Mansourah, 1250 His death on his second Crusade in Tunis, 1270		Accession of (St.) Ferdinand III of Castile, followed by Alfonso X (the Wise), 1252–84 Sancho IV (the Brave), 1284-95 End of Latin Kingdom in Palestine, 1291
1300	Death of Edward I, 1307 Defeat of English at Bannockburn, 1314 Accession of Edward III, 1327	Revolt of Flemings, 1302; battle of Courtrai	Swiss begin the struggle for independence; defeat of Austria at Morgarten, 1315	

	England and France	Central Europe	Eastern Europe and Spain
	Beginning of war for French crown, 1337; battles of Crecy, 1346; and Poitiers, 1356; Treaty of Bretigny, 1360		The Ottoman Turks defeat a crusading force in Eastern Europe at Nicopolis, 1396
	Death of Black Prince, 1376, and of Edward III, 1377		
	Richard II; period of truce between England and France		
	Peasants' Revolt, 1386		
	Usurpation of Lancaster, 1399		
1400	Henry V, 1413; renewal of French War; Agincourt, 1415	Martyrdom of John Huss in Bohemia; start of Hussite War against the Emperor, 1415-36	First siege of Constantinople by Ottoman Turks under Murad I, 1422
	Death of Henry V, 1422		
	Jeanne d'Arc, 1428-31		
	The English lose ground in France		
1450	End of Hundred Years War, 1453		Capture of Constantinople by Mahomed II, 1453
	Louis XI (1471-81) restores France to power		
	Wars with Charles the Rash, Duke of Burgundy	Maximilian, later Emperor, becomes Duke of Burgundy, 1475	
	Start of Wars of the Roses, 1459		
	Plantagenet Dynasty ends at Bosworth, 1485; accession of Henry Tudor		Ferdinand and Isabella of Spain capture Granada, 1492 Columbus sails to America

SHORT BIBLIOGRAPHY

BEHMER, ELIS. *Das Zweischneidige Schwert der Germanischen Völkerwanderungszeit.* Stockholm, 1939.

BORENIUS, T., and TRISTRAM, E. *English Medieval Painting.* Florence and Paris, 1927.

BRØNSTED, J. *Danmarks Oldtid,* I–III. 1938–40.

BRUHN HOFFMEYER, ADA. *Middelalderes Tvaeeggede Svaerd.* Copenhagen, 1954.

BURNE, LT.-COL. A. H. *The Crécy War.* London, 1955.

—— *The Agincourt War.* London, 1957.

CODEX MANESSE MS., facsimile. Leipzig, 1925–27.

CROSSLEY, A. H. *English Church Monuments,* 1150–1550. 1921.

DEHIO, G., and BEZOLD, G. V. *Die Denkmäler der deutschen Bildhauerkunst,* vols. I–III. Berlin, 1905.

DECHELETTE, JOSEPH. *Manuel D'Archéologie,* 1912–15.

DU CHAILLU, PAUL B. *The Viking Age.* London, 1889.

EVANS, JOAN. *Medieval Art in France, 987–1498.* London, 1948.

FETT, PER. *Arms in Norway Between 400 and 600 A.D.* Bergen Museums Aarboge, 1938–39.

FOX, SIR CYRIL. *A Find of the Early Iron Age at Llyn Cerrig Bach in Anglesey.* National Museum of Wales, 1946.

FREYHAN, F. *Die Illustrationen zum Casseler Willehalms Codex.* Marburg, 1928.

FRYER, A. C. *Wooden Monumental Effigies.* 1924.

GARDNER, A. *Alabaster Tombs.* Cambridge, 1940.

—— *Medieval Sculpture in France.* 1931.

GAY, VICTOR. *Glossaire Archéologique.* Paris, 1887.

GOLDSCHMIDT, A. *Die Skupturen von Freiburg und Wechselburg.* 1924. *German Illumination:* I. *Carolingian Period;* II. *Ottonian Period.* Florence and Paris, 1928.

HAMANN, R. *Die Elizabeths Kirche zu Marburg.* 2 vols. Marburg, 1929.

HARMAND, ADRIEN. *Jeanne D'Arc: Ses Coutumes, Son Armure. Essai de Reconstruction.* Paris, 1929.

HEWITT, JOHN. *Ancient Armour and Weapons in Europe.* 3 vols. London and Oxford, 1860.

JAMES, M. R. *The Romance of Alexander*. A Collotype Facsimile of MS. Bodley 264. Oxford, 1933.

KUEAS, H. *Die Naumburger Werkstatt*. 1937.

LAKING, SIR G. F. *A Record of European Armour and Arms through Seven Ages*. London, 1920.

LANORD, A. FRANCE. *La Fabrication des Epées Damassées aux Époques Merovingiennes et Carolingiennes*. Nancy, 1949.

LONDON MUSEUM CATALOGUES No. 7 (Medieval Catalogue). 1927.

LORANGE, A. *Den Yngre Jernalders Svaerd*. 1889.

LOT, FERDINAND. *L'Art Militaire et les Armées du Moyen Age*. Paris, 1946.

MADRID: Catologo Historico Descriptivo de la Real Armeria de Madrid el Conde de Valencie de Don Juan. Madrid, 1898.

MANN, SIR JAMES G. "The Sanctuary of the Madonna delle Grazie, with notes on the Evolution of Italian Armour during the Fifteenth Century," *Archaeologia*, LXXX, 1930.

—— "A Further Account of the Armour Preserved in the Sanctuary of the Madonna delle Grazie." *Ibid.*, LXXXVII, 1938.

—— "Notes on the Armour Worn in Spain from the Tenth to the Fifteenth Centuries." *Ibid.*, LXXXIII, 1933.

—— "Notes on the Evolution of Plate Armour in Germany in the Fourteenth and Fifteenth Centuries." *Ibid.*, LXXXIV, 1935.

MERTON, A. *Die Buchmalerei in St. Gallen vom IX bis XI Jahrhunderts*. 1923.

MORRIS, J. E. *The Welsh Wars of Edward the First*. Oxford, 1901.

OMAN, SIR CHARLES. *A History of the Art of War in the Middle Ages*. London, 1924.

PETERSEN, JAN. *De Norske Vikingesverd*. 1919.

PIGGOTT, STUART. *Prehistoric India*. 1950.

—— "Swords and Scabbards of the Early British Iron Ages", *Proc. Prehistoric Society*, 1950.

PRIOR, E. S., and GARDNER, A. *An Account of Medieval Figure Sculpture in England*. Cambridge, 1921.

SHETELIG, HAAKON. *Scandinavian Archaeology*. London, 1937.

—— *Viking Antiquities in Great Britain and Ireland*. 1940.

THORDEMANN, BENGT. *Armour from the Battle of Visby*. Stockholm, 1939.

—— In the series "Nordisk Kultur", no. XIIB. *Vapen*. 1948.

TRAPP, GRAF OSWALD, and MANN, SIR J. G. *The Armoury of the Castle of Churburg*. London, 1929.

SZENDREI, J. *Ungarisch Kriegsgeschichtliche Denkmäler*. Budapest, 1896.

VAN MARLE, RAIMOND. *The Italian Schools of Painting*. 14 vols. The Hague, 1931.

WHEELER, SIR R. MORTIMER. *London and the Vikings*. 1927.

INDEX

References to illustrations are in brackets

A CATALOG OF SELECTED
DOVER BOOKS
IN ALL FIELDS OF INTEREST

A CATALOG OF SELECTED DOVER
BOOKS IN ALL FIELDS OF INTEREST

CONCERNING THE SPIRITUAL IN ART, Wassily Kandinsky. Pioneering work by father of abstract art. Thoughts on color theory, nature of art. Analysis of earlier masters. 12 illustrations. 80pp. of text. 5⅜ x 8½. 23411-8

ANIMALS: 1,419 Copyright-Free Illustrations of Mammals, Birds, Fish, Insects, etc., Jim Harter (ed.). Clear wood engravings present, in extremely lifelike poses, over 1,000 species of animals. One of the most extensive pictorial sourcebooks of its kind. Captions. Index. 284pp. 9 x 12. 23766-4

CELTIC ART: The Methods of Construction, George Bain. Simple geometric techniques for making Celtic interlacements, spirals, Kells-type initials, animals, humans, etc. Over 500 illustrations. 160pp. 9 x 12. (Available in U.S. only.) 22923-8

AN ATLAS OF ANATOMY FOR ARTISTS, Fritz Schider. Most thorough reference work on art anatomy in the world. Hundreds of illustrations, including selections from works by Vesalius, Leonardo, Goya, Ingres, Michelangelo, others. 593 illustrations. 192pp. 7⅛ x 10¼. 20241-0

CELTIC HAND STROKE-BY-STROKE (Irish Half-Uncial from "The Book of Kells"): An Arthur Baker Calligraphy Manual, Arthur Baker. Complete guide to creating each letter of the alphabet in distinctive Celtic manner. Covers hand position, strokes, pens, inks, paper, more. Illustrated. 48pp. 8½ x 11. 24336-2

EASY ORIGAMI, John Montroll. Charming collection of 32 projects (hat, cup, pelican, piano, swan, many more) specially designed for the novice origami hobbyist. Clearly illustrated easy-to-follow instructions insure that even beginning papercrafters will achieve successful results. 48pp. 8¼ x 11. 27298-2

THE COMPLETE BOOK OF BIRDHOUSE CONSTRUCTION FOR WOODWORKERS, Scott D. Campbell. Detailed instructions, illustrations, tables. Also data on bird habitat and instinct patterns. Bibliography. 3 tables. 63 illustrations in 15 figures. 48pp. 5¼ x 8½. 24407-5

BLOOMINGDALE'S ILLUSTRATED 1886 CATALOG: Fashions, Dry Goods and Housewares, Bloomingdale Brothers. Famed merchants' extremely rare catalog depicting about 1,700 products: clothing, housewares, firearms, dry goods, jewelry, more. Invaluable for dating, identifying vintage items. Also, copyright-free graphics for artists, designers. Co-published with Henry Ford Museum & Greenfield Village. 160pp. 8¼ x 11. 25780-0

HISTORIC COSTUME IN PICTURES, Braun & Schneider. Over 1,450 costumed figures in clearly detailed engravings–from dawn of civilization to end of 19th century. Captions. Many folk costumes. 256pp. 8⅜ x 11¾. 23150-X

CATALOG OF DOVER BOOKS

STICKLEY CRAFTSMAN FURNITURE CATALOGS, Gustav Stickley and L. & J. G. Stickley. Beautiful, functional furniture in two authentic catalogs from 1910. 594 illustrations, including 277 photos, show settles, rockers, armchairs, reclining chairs, bookcases, desks, tables. 183pp. 6½ x 9¼. 23838-5

AMERICAN LOCOMOTIVES IN HISTORIC PHOTOGRAPHS: 1858 to 1949, Ron Ziel (ed.). A rare collection of 126 meticulously detailed official photographs, called "builder portraits," of American locomotives that majestically chronicle the rise of steam locomotive power in America. Introduction. Detailed captions. xi+129pp. 9 x 12. 27393-8

AMERICA'S LIGHTHOUSES: An Illustrated History, Francis Ross Holland, Jr. Delightfully written, profusely illustrated fact-filled survey of over 200 American lighthouses since 1716. History, anecdotes, technological advances, more. 240pp. 8 x 10¾. 25576-X

TOWARDS A NEW ARCHITECTURE, Le Corbusier. Pioneering manifesto by founder of "International School." Technical and aesthetic theories, views of industry, economics, relation of form to function, "mass-production split" and much more. Profusely illustrated. 320pp. 6⅛ x 9¼. (Available in U.S. only.) 25023-7

HOW THE OTHER HALF LIVES, Jacob Riis. Famous journalistic record, exposing poverty and degradation of New York slums around 1900, by major social reformer. 100 striking and influential photographs. 233pp. 10 x 7⅞. 22012-5

FRUIT KEY AND TWIG KEY TO TREES AND SHRUBS, William M. Harlow. One of the handiest and most widely used identification aids. Fruit key covers 120 deciduous and evergreen species; twig key 160 deciduous species. Easily used. Over 300 photographs. 126pp. 5⅜ x 8½. 20511-8

COMMON BIRD SONGS, Dr. Donald J. Borror. Songs of 60 most common U.S. birds: robins, sparrows, cardinals, bluejays, finches, more—arranged in order of increasing complexity. Up to 9 variations of songs of each species. Cassette and manual 99911-4

ORCHIDS AS HOUSE PLANTS, Rebecca Tyson Northen. Grow cattleyas and many other kinds of orchids—in a window, in a case, or under artificial light. 63 illustrations. 148pp. 5⅜ x 8½. 23261-1

MONSTER MAZES, Dave Phillips. Masterful mazes at four levels of difficulty. Avoid deadly perils and evil creatures to find magical treasures. Solutions for all 32 exciting illustrated puzzles. 48pp. 8¼ x 11. 26005-4

MOZART'S DON GIOVANNI (DOVER OPERA LIBRETTO SERIES), Wolfgang Amadeus Mozart. Introduced and translated by Ellen H. Bleiler. Standard Italian libretto, with complete English translation. Convenient and thoroughly portable—an ideal companion for reading along with a recording or the performance itself. Introduction. List of characters. Plot summary. 121pp. 5¼ x 8½. 24944-1

TECHNICAL MANUAL AND DICTIONARY OF CLASSICAL BALLET, Gail Grant. Defines, explains, comments on steps, movements, poses and concepts. 15-page pictorial section. Basic book for student, viewer. 127pp. 5⅜ x 8½. 21843-0

THE CLARINET AND CLARINET PLAYING, David Pino. Lively, comprehensive work features suggestions about technique, musicianship, and musical interpretation, as well as guidelines for teaching, making your own reeds, and preparing for public performance. Includes an intriguing look at clarinet history. "A godsend," *The Clarinet,* Journal of the International Clarinet Society. Appendixes. 7 illus. 320pp. 5⅜ x 8½. 40270-3

HOLLYWOOD GLAMOR PORTRAITS, John Kobal (ed.). 145 photos from 1926-49. Harlow, Gable, Bogart, Bacall; 94 stars in all. Full background on photographers, technical aspects. 160pp. 8⅜ x 11¼. 23352-9

THE ANNOTATED CASEY AT THE BAT: A Collection of Ballads about the Mighty Casey/Third, Revised Edition, Martin Gardner (ed.). Amusing sequels and parodies of one of America's best-loved poems: Casey's Revenge, Why Casey Whiffed, Casey's Sister at the Bat, others. 256pp. 5⅜ x 8½. 28598-7

THE RAVEN AND OTHER FAVORITE POEMS, Edgar Allan Poe. Over 40 of the author's most memorable poems: "The Bells," "Ulalume," "Israfel," "To Helen," "The Conqueror Worm," "Eldorado," "Annabel Lee," many more. Alphabetic lists of titles and first lines. 64pp. 5$\frac{3}{16}$ x 8¼. 26685-0

PERSONAL MEMOIRS OF U. S. GRANT, Ulysses Simpson Grant. Intelligent, deeply moving firsthand account of Civil War campaigns, considered by many the finest military memoirs ever written. Includes letters, historic photographs, maps and more. 528pp. 6⅛ x 9¼. 28587-1

ANCIENT EGYPTIAN MATERIALS AND INDUSTRIES, A. Lucas and J. Harris. Fascinating, comprehensive, thoroughly documented text describes this ancient civilization's vast resources and the processes that incorporated them in daily life, including the use of animal products, building materials, cosmetics, perfumes and incense, fibers, glazed ware, glass and its manufacture, materials used in the mummification process, and much more. 544pp. 6⅛ x 9¼. (Available in U.S. only.) 40446-3

RUSSIAN STORIES/RUSSKIE RASSKAZY: A Dual-Language Book, edited by Gleb Struve. Twelve tales by such masters as Chekhov, Tolstoy, Dostoevsky, Pushkin, others. Excellent word-for-word English translations on facing pages, plus teaching and study aids, Russian/English vocabulary, biographical/critical introductions, more. 416pp. 5⅜ x 8½. 26244-8

PHILADELPHIA THEN AND NOW: 60 Sites Photographed in the Past and Present, Kenneth Finkel and Susan Oyama. Rare photographs of City Hall, Logan Square, Independence Hall, Betsy Ross House, other landmarks juxtaposed with contemporary views. Captures changing face of historic city. Introduction. Captions. 128pp. 8¼ x 11. 25790-8

AIA ARCHITECTURAL GUIDE TO NASSAU AND SUFFOLK COUNTIES, LONG ISLAND, The American Institute of Architects, Long Island Chapter, and the Society for the Preservation of Long Island Antiquities. Comprehensive, well-researched and generously illustrated volume brings to life over three centuries of Long Island's great architectural heritage. More than 240 photographs with authoritative, extensively detailed captions. 176pp. 8¼ x 11. 26946-9

NORTH AMERICAN INDIAN LIFE: Customs and Traditions of 23 Tribes, Elsie Clews Parsons (ed.). 27 fictionalized essays by noted anthropologists examine religion, customs, government, additional facets of life among the Winnebago, Crow, Zuni, Eskimo, other tribes. 480pp. 6⅛ x 9¼. 27377-6

FRANK LLOYD WRIGHT'S DANA HOUSE, Donald Hoffmann. Pictorial essay of residential masterpiece with over 160 interior and exterior photos, plans, elevations, sketches and studies. 128pp. 9¼ x 10¾. 29120-0

THE MALE AND FEMALE FIGURE IN MOTION: 60 Classic Photographic Sequences, Eadweard Muybridge. 60 true-action photographs of men and women walking, running, climbing, bending, turning, etc., reproduced from rare 19th-century masterpiece. vi + 121pp. 9 x 12. 24745-7

1001 QUESTIONS ANSWERED ABOUT THE SEASHORE, N. J. Berrill and Jacquelyn Berrill. Queries answered about dolphins, sea snails, sponges, starfish, fishes, shore birds, many others. Covers appearance, breeding, growth, feeding, much more. 305pp. 5¼ x 8¼. 23366-9

ATTRACTING BIRDS TO YOUR YARD, William J. Weber. Easy-to-follow guide offers advice on how to attract the greatest diversity of birds: birdhouses, feeders, water and waterers, much more. 96pp. 5³⁄₁₆ x 8¼. 28927-3

MEDICINAL AND OTHER USES OF NORTH AMERICAN PLANTS: A Historical Survey with Special Reference to the Eastern Indian Tribes, Charlotte Erichsen-Brown. Chronological historical citations document 500 years of usage of plants, trees, shrubs native to eastern Canada, northeastern U.S. Also complete identifying information. 343 illustrations. 544pp. 6½ x 9¼. 25951-X

STORYBOOK MAZES, Dave Phillips. 23 stories and mazes on two-page spreads: Wizard of Oz, Treasure Island, Robin Hood, etc. Solutions. 64pp. 8¼ x 11. 23628-5

AMERICAN NEGRO SONGS: 230 Folk Songs and Spirituals, Religious and Secular, John W. Work. This authoritative study traces the African influences of songs sung and played by black Americans at work, in church, and as entertainment. The author discusses the lyric significance of such songs as "Swing Low, Sweet Chariot," "John Henry," and others and offers the words and music for 230 songs. Bibliography. Index of Song Titles. 272pp. 6½ x 9¼. 40271-1

MOVIE-STAR PORTRAITS OF THE FORTIES, John Kobal (ed.). 163 glamor, studio photos of 106 stars of the 1940s: Rita Hayworth, Ava Gardner, Marlon Brando, Clark Gable, many more. 176pp. 8⅜ x 11¼. 23546-7

BENCHLEY LOST AND FOUND, Robert Benchley. Finest humor from early 30s, about pet peeves, child psychologists, post office and others. Mostly unavailable elsewhere. 73 illustrations by Peter Arno and others. 183pp. 5⅜ x 8½. 22410-4

YEKL and THE IMPORTED BRIDEGROOM AND OTHER STORIES OF YIDDISH NEW YORK, Abraham Cahan. Film Hester Street based on *Yekl* (1896). Novel, other stories among first about Jewish immigrants on N.Y.'s East Side. 240pp. 5⅜ x 8½. 22427-9

SELECTED POEMS, Walt Whitman. Generous sampling from *Leaves of Grass*. Twenty-four poems include "I Hear America Singing," "Song of the Open Road," "I Sing the Body Electric," "When Lilacs Last in the Dooryard Bloom'd," "O Captain! My Captain!"–all reprinted from an authoritative edition. Lists of titles and first lines. 128pp. 5³⁄₁₆ x 8¼. 26878-0

CATALOG OF DOVER BOOKS

THE BEST TALES OF HOFFMANN, E. T. A. Hoffmann. 10 of Hoffmann's most important stories: "Nutcracker and the King of Mice," "The Golden Flowerpot," etc. 458pp. 5⅜ x 8½. 21793-0

FROM FETISH TO GOD IN ANCIENT EGYPT, E. A. Wallis Budge. Rich detailed survey of Egyptian conception of "God" and gods, magic, cult of animals, Osiris, more. Also, superb English translations of hymns and legends. 240 illustrations. 545pp. 5⅜ x 8½. 25803-3

FRENCH STORIES/CONTES FRANÇAIS: A Dual-Language Book, Wallace Fowlie. Ten stories by French masters, Voltaire to Camus: "Micromegas" by Voltaire; "The Atheist's Mass" by Balzac; "Minuet" by de Maupassant; "The Guest" by Camus, six more. Excellent English translations on facing pages. Also French-English vocabulary list, exercises, more. 352pp. 5⅜ x 8½. 26443-2

CHICAGO AT THE TURN OF THE CENTURY IN PHOTOGRAPHS: 122 Historic Views from the Collections of the Chicago Historical Society, Larry A. Viskochil. Rare large-format prints offer detailed views of City Hall, State Street, the Loop, Hull House, Union Station, many other landmarks, circa 1904-1913. Introduction. Captions. Maps. 144pp. 9⅜ x 12¼. 24656-6

OLD BROOKLYN IN EARLY PHOTOGRAPHS, 1865-1929, William Lee Younger. Luna Park, Gravesend race track, construction of Grand Army Plaza, moving of Hotel Brighton, etc. 157 previously unpublished photographs. 165pp. 8⅞ x 11¾. 23587-4

THE MYTHS OF THE NORTH AMERICAN INDIANS, Lewis Spence. Rich anthology of the myths and legends of the Algonquins, Iroquois, Pawnees and Sioux, prefaced by an extensive historical and ethnological commentary. 36 illustrations. 480pp. 5⅜ x 8½. 25967-6

AN ENCYCLOPEDIA OF BATTLES: Accounts of Over 1,560 Battles from 1479 B.C. to the Present, David Eggenberger. Essential details of every major battle in recorded history from the first battle of Megiddo in 1479 B.C. to Grenada in 1984. List of Battle Maps. New Appendix covering the years 1967-1984. Index. 99 illustrations. 544pp. 6½ x 9¼. 24913-1

SAILING ALONE AROUND THE WORLD, Captain Joshua Slocum. First man to sail around the world, alone, in small boat. One of great feats of seamanship told in delightful manner. 67 illustrations. 294pp. 5⅜ x 8½. 20326-3

ANARCHISM AND OTHER ESSAYS, Emma Goldman. Powerful, penetrating, prophetic essays on direct action, role of minorities, prison reform, puritan hypocrisy, violence, etc. 271pp. 5⅜ x 8½. 22484-8

MYTHS OF THE HINDUS AND BUDDHISTS, Ananda K. Coomaraswamy and Sister Nivedita. Great stories of the epics; deeds of Krishna, Shiva, taken from puranas, Vedas, folk tales; etc. 32 illustrations. 400pp. 5⅜ x 8½. 21759-0

THE TRAUMA OF BIRTH, Otto Rank. Rank's controversial thesis that anxiety neurosis is caused by profound psychological trauma which occurs at birth. 256pp. 5⅜ x 8½. 27974-X

A THEOLOGICO-POLITICAL TREATISE, Benedict Spinoza. Also contains unfinished Political Treatise. Great classic on religious liberty, theory of government on common consent. R. Elwes translation. Total of 421pp. 5⅜ x 8½. 20249-6

CATALOG OF DOVER BOOKS

MY BONDAGE AND MY FREEDOM, Frederick Douglass. Born a slave, Douglass became outspoken force in antislavery movement. The best of Douglass' autobiographies. Graphic description of slave life. 464pp. 5⅜ x 8½. 22457-0

FOLLOWING THE EQUATOR: A Journey Around the World, Mark Twain. Fascinating humorous account of 1897 voyage to Hawaii, Australia, India, New Zealand, etc. Ironic, bemused reports on peoples, customs, climate, flora and fauna, politics, much more. 197 illustrations. 720pp. 5⅜ x 8½. 26113-1

THE PEOPLE CALLED SHAKERS, Edward D. Andrews. Definitive study of Shakers: origins, beliefs, practices, dances, social organization, furniture and crafts, etc. 33 illustrations. 351pp. 5⅜ x 8½. 21081-2

THE MYTHS OF GREECE AND ROME, H. A. Guerber. A classic of mythology, generously illustrated, long prized for its simple, graphic, accurate retelling of the principal myths of Greece and Rome, and for its commentary on their origins and significance. With 64 illustrations by Michelangelo, Raphael, Titian, Rubens, Canova, Bernini and others. 480pp. 5⅜ x 8½. 27584-1

PSYCHOLOGY OF MUSIC, Carl E. Seashore. Classic work discusses music as a medium from psychological viewpoint. Clear treatment of physical acoustics, auditory apparatus, sound perception, development of musical skills, nature of musical feeling, host of other topics. 88 figures. 408pp. 5⅜ x 8½. 21851-1

THE PHILOSOPHY OF HISTORY, Georg W. Hegel. Great classic of Western thought develops concept that history is not chance but rational process, the evolution of freedom. 457pp. 5⅜ x 8½. 20112-0

THE BOOK OF TEA, Kakuzo Okakura. Minor classic of the Orient: entertaining, charming explanation, interpretation of traditional Japanese culture in terms of tea ceremony. 94pp. 5⅜ x 8½. 20070-1

LIFE IN ANCIENT EGYPT, Adolf Erman. Fullest, most thorough, detailed older account with much not in more recent books, domestic life, religion, magic, medicine, commerce, much more. Many illustrations reproduce tomb paintings, carvings, hieroglyphs, etc. 597pp. 5⅜ x 8½. 22632-8

SUNDIALS, Their Theory and Construction, Albert Waugh. Far and away the best, most thorough coverage of ideas, mathematics concerned, types, construction, adjusting anywhere. Simple, nontechnical treatment allows even children to build several of these dials. Over 100 illustrations. 230pp. 5⅜ x 8½. 22947-5

THEORETICAL HYDRODYNAMICS, L. M. Milne-Thomson. Classic exposition of the mathematical theory of fluid motion, applicable to both hydrodynamics and aerodynamics. Over 600 exercises. 768pp. 6⅛ x 9¼. 68970-0

SONGS OF EXPERIENCE: Facsimile Reproduction with 26 Plates in Full Color, William Blake. 26 full-color plates from a rare 1826 edition. Includes "The Tyger," "London," "Holy Thursday," and other poems. Printed text of poems. 48pp. 5¼ x 7. 24636-1

OLD-TIME VIGNETTES IN FULL COLOR, Carol Belanger Grafton (ed.). Over 390 charming, often sentimental illustrations, selected from archives of Victorian graphics—pretty women posing, children playing, food, flowers, kittens and puppies, smiling cherubs, birds and butterflies, much more. All copyright-free. 48pp. 9¼ x 12¼. 27269-9

PERSPECTIVE FOR ARTISTS, Rex Vicat Cole. Depth, perspective of sky and sea, shadows, much more, not usually covered. 391 diagrams, 81 reproductions of drawings and paintings. 279pp. 5⅜ x 8½. 22487-2

DRAWING THE LIVING FIGURE, Joseph Sheppard. Innovative approach to artistic anatomy focuses on specifics of surface anatomy, rather than muscles and bones. Over 170 drawings of live models in front, back and side views, and in widely varying poses. Accompanying diagrams. 177 illustrations. Introduction. Index. 144pp. 8⅜ x11¼. 26723-7

GOTHIC AND OLD ENGLISH ALPHABETS: 100 Complete Fonts, Dan X. Solo. Add power, elegance to posters, signs, other graphics with 100 stunning copyright-free alphabets: Blackstone, Dolbey, Germania, 97 more—including many lower-case, numerals, punctuation marks. 104pp. 8⅛ x 11. 24695-7

HOW TO DO BEADWORK, Mary White. Fundamental book on craft from simple projects to five-bead chains and woven works. 106 illustrations. 142pp. 5⅜ x 8. 20697-1

THE BOOK OF WOOD CARVING, Charles Marshall Sayers. Finest book for beginners discusses fundamentals and offers 34 designs. "Absolutely first rate . . . well thought out and well executed."–E. J. Tangerman. 118pp. 7¾ x 10⅝. 23654-4

ILLUSTRATED CATALOG OF CIVIL WAR MILITARY GOODS: Union Army Weapons, Insignia, Uniform Accessories, and Other Equipment, Schuyler, Hartley, and Graham. Rare, profusely illustrated 1846 catalog includes Union Army uniform and dress regulations, arms and ammunition, coats, insignia, flags, swords, rifles, etc. 226 illustrations. 160pp. 9 x 12. 24939-5

WOMEN'S FASHIONS OF THE EARLY 1900s: An Unabridged Republication of "New York Fashions, 1909," National Cloak & Suit Co. Rare catalog of mail-order fashions documents women's and children's clothing styles shortly after the turn of the century. Captions offer full descriptions, prices. Invaluable resource for fashion, costume historians. Approximately 725 illustrations. 128pp. 8⅜ x 11¼. 27276-1

THE 1912 AND 1915 GUSTAV STICKLEY FURNITURE CATALOGS, Gustav Stickley. With over 200 detailed illustrations and descriptions, these two catalogs are essential reading and reference materials and identification guides for Stickley furniture. Captions cite materials, dimensions and prices. 112pp. 6½ x 9¼. 26676-1

EARLY AMERICAN LOCOMOTIVES, John H. White, Jr. Finest locomotive engravings from early 19th century: historical (1804–74), main-line (after 1870), special, foreign, etc. 147 plates. 142pp. 11⅜ x 8¼. 22772-3

THE TALL SHIPS OF TODAY IN PHOTOGRAPHS, Frank O. Braynard. Lavishly illustrated tribute to nearly 100 majestic contemporary sailing vessels: Amerigo Vespucci, Clearwater, Constitution, Eagle, Mayflower, Sea Cloud, Victory, many more. Authoritative captions provide statistics, background on each ship. 190 black-and-white photographs and illustrations. Introduction. 128pp. 8⅞ x 11¾. 27163-3

LITTLE BOOK OF EARLY AMERICAN CRAFTS AND TRADES, Peter Stockham (ed.). 1807 children's book explains crafts and trades: baker, hatter, cooper, potter, and many others. 23 copperplate illustrations. 140pp. 4⅝ x 6.   23336-7

VICTORIAN FASHIONS AND COSTUMES FROM HARPER'S BAZAR, 1867–1898, Stella Blum (ed.). Day costumes, evening wear, sports clothes, shoes, hats, other accessories in over 1,000 detailed engravings. 320pp. 9⅜ x 12¼.   22990-4

GUSTAV STICKLEY, THE CRAFTSMAN, Mary Ann Smith. Superb study surveys broad scope of Stickley's achievement, especially in architecture. Design philosophy, rise and fall of the Craftsman empire, descriptions and floor plans for many Craftsman houses, more. 86 black-and-white halftones. 31 line illustrations. Introduction 208pp. 6½ x 9¼.   27210-9

THE LONG ISLAND RAIL ROAD IN EARLY PHOTOGRAPHS, Ron Ziel. Over 220 rare photos, informative text document origin (1844) and development of rail service on Long Island. Vintage views of early trains, locomotives, stations, passengers, crews, much more. Captions. 8⅞ x 11¾.   26301-0

VOYAGE OF THE LIBERDADE, Joshua Slocum. Great 19th-century mariner's thrilling, first-hand account of the wreck of his ship off South America, the 35-foot boat he built from the wreckage, and its remarkable voyage home. 128pp. 5⅜ x 8½.
40022-0

TEN BOOKS ON ARCHITECTURE, Vitruvius. The most important book ever written on architecture. Early Roman aesthetics, technology, classical orders, site selection, all other aspects. Morgan translation. 331pp. 5⅜ x 8½.   20645-9

THE HUMAN FIGURE IN MOTION, Eadweard Muybridge. More than 4,500 stopped-action photos, in action series, showing undraped men, women, children jumping, lying down, throwing, sitting, wrestling, carrying, etc. 390pp. 7⅞ x 10⅝.
20204-6 Clothbd.

TREES OF THE EASTERN AND CENTRAL UNITED STATES AND CANADA, William M. Harlow. Best one-volume guide to 140 trees. Full descriptions, woodlore, range, etc. Over 600 illustrations. Handy size. 288pp. 4½ x 6⅜.   20395-6

SONGS OF WESTERN BIRDS, Dr. Donald J. Borror. Complete song and call repertoire of 60 western species, including flycatchers, juncoes, cactus wrens, many more–includes fully illustrated booklet.   Cassette and manual 99913-0

GROWING AND USING HERBS AND SPICES, Milo Miloradovich. Versatile handbook provides all the information needed for cultivation and use of all the herbs and spices available in North America. 4 illustrations. Index. Glossary. 236pp. 5⅜ x 8½.
25058-X

BIG BOOK OF MAZES AND LABYRINTHS, Walter Shepherd. 50 mazes and labyrinths in all–classical, solid, ripple, and more–in one great volume. Perfect inexpensive puzzler for clever youngsters. Full solutions. 112pp. 8⅛ x 11.   22951-3

PIANO TUNING, J. Cree Fischer. Clearest, best book for beginner, amateur. Simple repairs, raising dropped notes, tuning by easy method of flattened fifths. No previous skills needed. 4 illustrations. 201pp. 5⅜ x 8½.   23267-0

HINTS TO SINGERS, Lillian Nordica. Selecting the right teacher, developing confidence, overcoming stage fright, and many other important skills receive thoughtful discussion in this indispensible guide, written by a world-famous diva of four decades' experience. 96pp. 5⅜ x 8½.   40094-8

THE COMPLETE NONSENSE OF EDWARD LEAR, Edward Lear. All nonsense limericks, zany alphabets, Owl and Pussycat, songs, nonsense botany, etc., illustrated by Lear. Total of 320pp. 5⅜ x 8½. (Available in U.S. only.)   20167-8

VICTORIAN PARLOUR POETRY: An Annotated Anthology, Michael R. Turner. 117 gems by Longfellow, Tennyson, Browning, many lesser-known poets. "The Village Blacksmith," "Curfew Must Not Ring Tonight," "Only a Baby Small," dozens more, often difficult to find elsewhere. Index of poets, titles, first lines. xxiii + 325pp. 5⅜ x 8¼.   27044-0

DUBLINERS, James Joyce. Fifteen stories offer vivid, tightly focused observations of the lives of Dublin's poorer classes. At least one, "The Dead," is considered a masterpiece. Reprinted complete and unabridged from standard edition. 160pp. 5³⁄₁₆ x 8¼.   26870-5

GREAT WEIRD TALES: 14 Stories by Lovecraft, Blackwood, Machen and Others, S. T. Joshi (ed.). 14 spellbinding tales, including "The Sin Eater," by Fiona McLeod, "The Eye Above the Mantel," by Frank Belknap Long, as well as renowned works by R. H. Barlow, Lord Dunsany, Arthur Machen, W. C. Morrow and eight other masters of the genre. 256pp. 5⅜ x 8½. (Available in U.S. only.)   40436-6

THE BOOK OF THE SACRED MAGIC OF ABRAMELIN THE MAGE, translated by S. MacGregor Mathers. Medieval manuscript of ceremonial magic. Basic document in Aleister Crowley, Golden Dawn groups. 268pp. 5⅜ x 8½.   23211-5

NEW RUSSIAN-ENGLISH AND ENGLISH-RUSSIAN DICTIONARY, M. A. O'Brien. This is a remarkably handy Russian dictionary, containing a surprising amount of information, including over 70,000 entries. 366pp. 4½ x 6⅛.   20208-9

HISTORIC HOMES OF THE AMERICAN PRESIDENTS, Second, Revised Edition, Irvin Haas. A traveler's guide to American Presidential homes, most open to the public, depicting and describing homes occupied by every American President from George Washington to George Bush. With visiting hours, admission charges, travel routes. 175 photographs. Index. 160pp. 8¼ x 11.   26751-2

NEW YORK IN THE FORTIES, Andreas Feininger. 162 brilliant photographs by the well-known photographer, formerly with *Life* magazine. Commuters, shoppers, Times Square at night, much else from city at its peak. Captions by John von Hartz. 181pp. 9¼ x 10¾.   23585-8

INDIAN SIGN LANGUAGE, William Tomkins. Over 525 signs developed by Sioux and other tribes. Written instructions and diagrams. Also 290 pictographs. 111pp. 6⅛ x 9¼.   22029-X

CATALOG OF DOVER BOOKS

ANATOMY: A Complete Guide for Artists, Joseph Sheppard. A master of figure drawing shows artists how to render human anatomy convincingly. Over 460 illustrations. 224pp. 8⅜ x 11¼. 27279-6

MEDIEVAL CALLIGRAPHY: Its History and Technique, Marc Drogin. Spirited history, comprehensive instruction manual covers 13 styles (ca. 4th century through 15th). Excellent photographs; directions for duplicating medieval techniques with modern tools. 224pp. 8⅜ x 11¼. 26142-5

DRIED FLOWERS: How to Prepare Them, Sarah Whitlock and Martha Rankin. Complete instructions on how to use silica gel, meal and borax, perlite aggregate, sand and borax, glycerine and water to create attractive permanent flower arrangements. 12 illustrations. 32pp. 5⅜ x 8½. 21802-3

EASY-TO-MAKE BIRD FEEDERS FOR WOODWORKERS, Scott D. Campbell. Detailed, simple-to-use guide for designing, constructing, caring for and using feeders. Text, illustrations for 12 classic and contemporary designs. 96pp. 5⅜ x 8½. 25847-5

SCOTTISH WONDER TALES FROM MYTH AND LEGEND, Donald A. Mackenzie. 16 lively tales tell of giants rumbling down mountainsides, of a magic wand that turns stone pillars into warriors, of gods and goddesses, evil hags, powerful forces and more. 240pp. 5⅜ x 8½. 29677-6

THE HISTORY OF UNDERCLOTHES, C. Willett Cunnington and Phyllis Cunnington. Fascinating, well-documented survey covering six centuries of English undergarments, enhanced with over 100 illustrations: 12th-century laced-up bodice, footed long drawers (1795), 19th-century bustles, 19th-century corsets for men, Victorian "bust improvers," much more. 272pp. 5⅝ x 8¼. 27124-2

ARTS AND CRAFTS FURNITURE: The Complete Brooks Catalog of 1912, Brooks Manufacturing Co. Photos and detailed descriptions of more than 150 now very collectible furniture designs from the Arts and Crafts movement depict davenports, settees, buffets, desks, tables, chairs, bedsteads, dressers and more, all built of solid, quarter-sawed oak. Invaluable for students and enthusiasts of antiques, Americana and the decorative arts. 80pp. 6½ x 9¼. 27471-3

WILBUR AND ORVILLE: A Biography of the Wright Brothers, Fred Howard. Definitive, crisply written study tells the full story of the brothers' lives and work. A vividly written biography, unparalleled in scope and color, that also captures the spirit of an extraordinary era. 560pp. 6⅛ x 9¼. 40297-5

THE ARTS OF THE SAILOR: Knotting, Splicing and Ropework, Hervey Garrett Smith. Indispensable shipboard reference covers tools, basic knots and useful hitches; handsewing and canvas work, more. Over 100 illustrations. Delightful reading for sea lovers. 256pp. 5⅜ x 8½. 26440-8

FRANK LLOYD WRIGHT'S FALLINGWATER: The House and Its History, Second, Revised Edition, Donald Hoffmann. A total revision–both in text and illustrations–of the standard document on Fallingwater, the boldest, most personal architectural statement of Wright's mature years, updated with valuable new material from the recently opened Frank Lloyd Wright Archives. "Fascinating"–*The New York Times*. 116 illustrations. 128pp. 9¼ x 10¾. 27430-6

PHOTOGRAPHIC SKETCHBOOK OF THE CIVIL WAR, Alexander Gardner. 100 photos taken on field during the Civil War. Famous shots of Manassas Harper's Ferry, Lincoln, Richmond, slave pens, etc. 244pp. 10⅝ x 8¼. 22731-6

FIVE ACRES AND INDEPENDENCE, Maurice G. Kains. Great back-to-the-land classic explains basics of self-sufficient farming. The one book to get. 95 illustrations. 397pp. 5⅜ x 8½. 20974-1

SONGS OF EASTERN BIRDS, Dr. Donald J. Borror. Songs and calls of 60 species most common to eastern U.S.: warblers, woodpeckers, flycatchers, thrushes, larks, many more in high-quality recording. Cassette and manual 99912-2

A MODERN HERBAL, Margaret Grieve. Much the fullest, most exact, most useful compilation of herbal material. Gigantic alphabetical encyclopedia, from aconite to zedoary, gives botanical information, medical properties, folklore, economic uses, much else. Indispensable to serious reader. 161 illustrations. 888pp. 6½ x 9¼. 2-vol. set. (Available in U.S. only.) Vol. I: 22798-7
Vol. II: 22799-5

HIDDEN TREASURE MAZE BOOK, Dave Phillips. Solve 34 challenging mazes accompanied by heroic tales of adventure. Evil dragons, people-eating plants, blood-thirsty giants, many more dangerous adversaries lurk at every twist and turn. 34 mazes, stories, solutions. 48pp. 8¼ x 11. 24566-7

LETTERS OF W. A. MOZART, Wolfgang A. Mozart. Remarkable letters show bawdy wit, humor, imagination, musical insights, contemporary musical world; includes some letters from Leopold Mozart. 276pp. 5⅜ x 8½. 22859-2

BASIC PRINCIPLES OF CLASSICAL BALLET, Agrippina Vaganova. Great Russian theoretician, teacher explains methods for teaching classical ballet. 118 illustrations. 175pp. 5⅜ x 8½. 22036-2

THE JUMPING FROG, Mark Twain. Revenge edition. The original story of The Celebrated Jumping Frog of Calaveras County, a hapless French translation, and Twain's hilarious "retranslation" from the French. 12 illustrations. 66pp. 5⅜ x 8½. 22686-7

BEST REMEMBERED POEMS, Martin Gardner (ed.). The 126 poems in this superb collection of 19th- and 20th-century British and American verse range from Shelley's "To a Skylark" to the impassioned "Renascence" of Edna St. Vincent Millay and to Edward Lear's whimsical "The Owl and the Pussycat." 224pp. 5⅜ x 8½. 27165-X

COMPLETE SONNETS, William Shakespeare. Over 150 exquisite poems deal with love, friendship, the tyranny of time, beauty's evanescence, death and other themes in language of remarkable power, precision and beauty. Glossary of archaic terms. 80pp. 5³⁄₁₆ x 8¼. 26686-9

THE BATTLES THAT CHANGED HISTORY, Fletcher Pratt. Eminent historian profiles 16 crucial conflicts, ancient to modern, that changed the course of civilization. 352pp. 5⅜ x 8½. 41129-X

THE WIT AND HUMOR OF OSCAR WILDE, Alvin Redman (ed.). More than 1,000 ripostes, paradoxes, wisecracks: Work is the curse of the drinking classes; I can resist everything except temptation; etc. 258pp. 5⅜ x 8½. 20602-5

SHAKESPEARE LEXICON AND QUOTATION DICTIONARY, Alexander Schmidt. Full definitions, locations, shades of meaning in every word in plays and poems. More than 50,000 exact quotations. 1,485pp. 6½ x 9¼. 2-vol. set.
Vol. 1: 22726-X
Vol. 2: 22727-8

SELECTED POEMS, Emily Dickinson. Over 100 best-known, best-loved poems by one of America's foremost poets, reprinted from authoritative early editions. No comparable edition at this price. Index of first lines. 64pp. 5³⁄₁₆ x 8¼. 26466-1

THE INSIDIOUS DR. FU-MANCHU, Sax Rohmer. The first of the popular mystery series introduces a pair of English detectives to their archnemesis, the diabolical Dr. Fu-Manchu. Flavorful atmosphere, fast-paced action, and colorful characters enliven this classic of the genre. 208pp. 5³⁄₁₆ x 8¼. 29898-1

THE MALLEUS MALEFICARUM OF KRAMER AND SPRENGER, translated by Montague Summers. Full text of most important witchhunter's "bible," used by both Catholics and Protestants. 278pp. 6⅝ x 10. 22802-9

SPANISH STORIES/CUENTOS ESPAÑOLES: A Dual-Language Book, Angel Flores (ed.). Unique format offers 13 great stories in Spanish by Cervantes, Borges, others. Faithful English translations on facing pages. 352pp. 5⅜ x 8½. 25399-6

GARDEN CITY, LONG ISLAND, IN EARLY PHOTOGRAPHS, 1869–1919, Mildred H. Smith. Handsome treasury of 118 vintage pictures, accompanied by carefully researched captions, document the Garden City Hotel fire (1899), the Vanderbilt Cup Race (1908), the first airmail flight departing from the Nassau Boulevard Aerodrome (1911), and much more. 96pp. 8⅞ x 11¾. 40669-5

OLD QUEENS, N.Y., IN EARLY PHOTOGRAPHS, Vincent F. Seyfried and William Asadorian. Over 160 rare photographs of Maspeth, Jamaica, Jackson Heights, and other areas. Vintage views of DeWitt Clinton mansion, 1939 World's Fair and more. Captions. 192pp. 8⅞ x 11. 26358-4

CAPTURED BY THE INDIANS: 15 Firsthand Accounts, 1750-1870, Frederick Drimmer. Astounding true historical accounts of grisly torture, bloody conflicts, relentless pursuits, miraculous escapes and more, by people who lived to tell the tale. 384pp. 5⅜ x 8½. 24901-8

THE WORLD'S GREAT SPEECHES (Fourth Enlarged Edition), Lewis Copeland, Lawrence W. Lamm, and Stephen J. McKenna. Nearly 300 speeches provide public speakers with a wealth of updated quotes and inspiration—from Pericles' funeral oration and William Jennings Bryan's "Cross of Gold Speech" to Malcolm X's powerful words on the Black Revolution and Earl of Spenser's tribute to his sister, Diana, Princess of Wales. 944pp. 5⅜ x 8⅜. 40903-1

THE BOOK OF THE SWORD, Sir Richard F. Burton. Great Victorian scholar/adventurer's eloquent, erudite history of the "queen of weapons"—from prehistory to early Roman Empire. Evolution and development of early swords, variations (sabre, broadsword, cutlass, scimitar, etc.), much more. 336pp. 6⅛ x 9¼. 25434-8

AUTOBIOGRAPHY: The Story of My Experiments with Truth, Mohandas K. Gandhi. Boyhood, legal studies, purification, the growth of the Satyagraha (nonviolent protest) movement. Critical, inspiring work of the man responsible for the freedom of India. 480pp. 5⅜ x 8½. (Available in U.S. only.) 24593-4

CELTIC MYTHS AND LEGENDS, T. W. Rolleston. Masterful retelling of Irish and Welsh stories and tales. Cuchulain, King Arthur, Deirdre, the Grail, many more. First paperback edition. 58 full-page illustrations. 512pp. 5⅜ x 8½. 26507-2

THE PRINCIPLES OF PSYCHOLOGY, William James. Famous long course complete, unabridged. Stream of thought, time perception, memory, experimental methods; great work decades ahead of its time. 94 figures. 1,391pp. 5⅜ x 8½. 2-vol. set.
Vol. I: 20381-6 Vol. II: 20382-4

THE WORLD AS WILL AND REPRESENTATION, Arthur Schopenhauer. Definitive English translation of Schopenhauer's life work, correcting more than 1,000 errors, omissions in earlier translations. Translated by E. F. J. Payne. Total of 1,269pp. 5⅜ x 8½. 2-vol. set. Vol. 1: 21761-2 Vol. 2: 21762-0

MAGIC AND MYSTERY IN TIBET, Madame Alexandra David-Neel. Experiences among lamas, magicians, sages, sorcerers, Bonpa wizards. A true psychic discovery. 32 illustrations. 321pp. 5⅜ x 8½. (Available in U.S. only.) 22682-4

THE EGYPTIAN BOOK OF THE DEAD, E. A. Wallis Budge. Complete reproduction of Ani's papyrus, finest ever found. Full hieroglyphic text, interlinear transliteration, word-for-word translation, smooth translation. 533pp. 6½ x 9¼. 21866-X

MATHEMATICS FOR THE NONMATHEMATICIAN, Morris Kline. Detailed, college-level treatment of mathematics in cultural and historical context, with numerous exercises. Recommended Reading Lists. Tables. Numerous figures. 641pp. 5⅜ x 8½.
24823-2

PROBABILISTIC METHODS IN THE THEORY OF STRUCTURES, Isaac Elishakoff. Well-written introduction covers the elements of the theory of probability from two or more random variables, the reliability of such multivariable structures, the theory of random function, Monte Carlo methods of treating problems incapable of exact solution, and more. Examples. 502pp. 5⅜ x 8½. 40691-1

THE RIME OF THE ANCIENT MARINER, Gustave Doré, S. T. Coleridge. Doré's finest work; 34 plates capture moods, subtleties of poem. Flawless full-size reproductions printed on facing pages with authoritative text of poem. "Beautiful. Simply beautiful."–*Publisher's Weekly.* 77pp. 9¼ x 12. 22305-1

NORTH AMERICAN INDIAN DESIGNS FOR ARTISTS AND CRAFTSPEOPLE, Eva Wilson. Over 360 authentic copyright-free designs adapted from Navajo blankets, Hopi pottery, Sioux buffalo hides, more. Geometrics, symbolic figures, plant and animal motifs, etc. 128pp. 8⅜ x 11. (Not for sale in the United Kingdom.) 25341-4

SCULPTURE: Principles and Practice, Louis Slobodkin. Step-by-step approach to clay, plaster, metals, stone; classical and modern. 253 drawings, photos. 255pp. 8⅛ x 11.
22960-2

THE INFLUENCE OF SEA POWER UPON HISTORY, 1660–1783, A. T. Mahan. Influential classic of naval history and tactics still used as text in war colleges. First paperback edition. 4 maps. 24 battle plans. 640pp. 5⅜ x 8½. 25509-3

CATALOG OF DOVER BOOKS

THE STORY OF THE TITANIC AS TOLD BY ITS SURVIVORS, Jack Winocour (ed.). What it was really like. Panic, despair, shocking inefficiency, and a little heroism. More thrilling than any fictional account. 26 illustrations. 320pp. 5⅜ x 8½. 20610-6

FAIRY AND FOLK TALES OF THE IRISH PEASANTRY, William Butler Yeats (ed.). Treasury of 64 tales from the twilight world of Celtic myth and legend: "The Soul Cages," "The Kildare Pooka," "King O'Toole and his Goose," many more. Introduction and Notes by W. B. Yeats. 352pp. 5⅜ x 8½. 26941-8

BUDDHIST MAHAYANA TEXTS, E. B. Cowell and others (eds.). Superb, accurate translations of basic documents in Mahayana Buddhism, highly important in history of religions. The Buddha-karita of Asvaghosha, Larger Sukhavativyuha, more. 448pp. 5⅜ x 8½. 25552-2

ONE TWO THREE . . . INFINITY: Facts and Speculations of Science, George Gamow. Great physicist's fascinating, readable overview of contemporary science: number theory, relativity, fourth dimension, entropy, genes, atomic structure, much more. 128 illustrations. Index. 352pp. 5⅜ x 8½. 25664-2

EXPERIMENTATION AND MEASUREMENT, W. J. Youden. Introductory manual explains laws of measurement in simple terms and offers tips for achieving accuracy and minimizing errors. Mathematics of measurement, use of instruments, experimenting with machines. 1994 edition. Foreword. Preface. Introduction. Epilogue. Selected Readings. Glossary. Index. Tables and figures. 128pp. 5⅜ x 8½. 40451-X

DALÍ ON MODERN ART: The Cuckolds of Antiquated Modern Art, Salvador Dalí. Influential painter skewers modern art and its practitioners. Outrageous evaluations of Picasso, Cézanne, Turner, more. 15 renderings of paintings discussed. 44 calligraphic decorations by Dalí. 96pp. 5⅜ x 8½. (Available in U.S. only.) 29220-7

ANTIQUE PLAYING CARDS: A Pictorial History, Henry René D'Allemagne. Over 900 elaborate, decorative images from rare playing cards (14th–20th centuries): Bacchus, death, dancing dogs, hunting scenes, royal coats of arms, players cheating, much more. 96pp. 9¼ x 12¼. 29265-7

MAKING FURNITURE MASTERPIECES: 30 Projects with Measured Drawings, Franklin H. Gottshall. Step-by-step instructions, illustrations for constructing handsome, useful pieces, among them a Sheraton desk, Chippendale chair, Spanish desk, Queen Anne table and a William and Mary dressing mirror. 224pp. 8⅛ x 11¼. 29338-6

THE FOSSIL BOOK: A Record of Prehistoric Life, Patricia V. Rich et al. Profusely illustrated definitive guide covers everything from single-celled organisms and dinosaurs to birds and mammals and the interplay between climate and man. Over 1,500 illustrations. 760pp. 7½ x 10⅛. 29371-8

Paperbound unless otherwise indicated. Available at your book dealer, online at **www.doverpublications.com**, or by writing to Dept. GI, Dover Publications, Inc., 31 East 2nd Street, Mineola, NY 11501. For current price information or for free catalogues (please indicate field of interest), write to Dover Publications or log on to **www.doverpublications.com** and see every Dover book in print. Dover publishes more than 500 books each year on science, elementary and advanced mathematics, biology, music, art, literary history, social sciences, and other areas.